THE CULTURE OF

| POLITICS AND CULTURE IN THE
TWENTIETH-CENTURY SOUTH |

Series Editors

Bryant Simon, Temple University
Jane Dailey, University of Chicago

Advisory Board

Lisa Dorr, University of Alabama
Grace Elizabeth Hale, University of Virginia
Randal Jelks, University of Kansas
Kevin Kruse, Princeton University
Robert Norrell, University of Tennessee
Bruce Schulman, Boston University
Marjorie Spruill, University of South Carolina
J. Mills Thornton, University of Michigan
Allen Tullos, Emory University
Brian Ward, University of Manchester

THE CULTURE OF PROPERTY

RACE, CLASS, AND HOUSING LANDSCAPES IN ATLANTA, 1880–1950

LEEANN LANDS

THE UNIVERSITY OF GEORGIA PRESS | ATHENS AND LONDON

© 2009 by the University of Georgia Press
Athens, Georgia 30602
www.ugapress.org
All rights reserved
Set in Minion and Frutiger by Graphic Composition, Inc.,
 Bogart, Georgia

Printed digitally in the United States of America

Library of Congress Cataloging-in-Publication Data

Lands, LeeAnn, 1967–
 The culture of property : race, class, and housing landscapes in Atlanta, 1880–1950 / LeeAnn Lands.
   p. cm. — (Politics and culture in the twentieth-century South)
 Includes bibliographical references and index.
 ISBN-13: 978-0-8203-2979-6 (hardcover : alk. paper)
 ISBN-10: 0-8203-2979-7 (hardcover : alk. paper)
 ISBN-13: 978-0-8203-3392-2 (pbk. : alk. paper)
 ISBN-10: 0-8203-3392-1 (pbk. : alk. paper)
 1. Housing—Georgia—Atlanta—History.
 2. Home ownership—Social aspects—Georgia—Atlanta—History.
 3. Homeowners—Georgia—Atlanta—Social conditions.
 4. Social classes—Georgia—Atlanta—History.
 5. Segregation—Georgia—Atlanta—History.
 6. Discrimination in housing—Georgia—Atlanta—History.
 7. Whites—Housing—Georgia—Atlanta—History.
 8. African Americans—Housing—Georgia—Atlanta—History.
 9. Atlanta (Ga.)—Race relations—History.
 I. Title.
 HD7304.A7L36 2009
 307.3'360975823109041—dc22   2009009181

British Library Cataloging-in-Publication Data available

Portions of chapter 1 previously appeared in the *Journal of Urban History* 28 (July 2002): 546–72. Reprinted with the permission of SAGE Publications.

Portions of chapter 3 previously appeared in the *Journal of Planning History* 3 (May 2004): 83–115. Reprinted with the permission of SAGE Publications.

Portions of chapter 4 previously appeared in the *Journal of Social History* 41 (Summer 2008): 943–65. Reprinted with the permission of the *Journal of Social History*.

to my family

CONTENTS

Acknowledgments / ix

Introduction / 1

One. Housing the City, 1865 to 1910 / 13

Two. Atlanta, Park-Neighborhoods, and the New Urban Aesthetic, 1880 to 1917 / 41

Three. A City Divided, 1910 to 1917 / 71

Four. Homeownership and Park-Neighborhood Ideology, 1910 to 1933 / 107

Five. Exclusion and Park-Neighborhood Building, 1922 to 1929 / 135

Six. Park-Neighborhoods, Federal Policy, and Housing Geographies, 1933 to 1950 / 158

Seven. White Property and Homeowner Privilege / 199

Appendix / 219
Notes / 229
Selected Bibliography / 267
Index / 281

ACKNOWLEDGMENTS

I have many people to thank for their time, support, advice, and knowledge. At Georgia Tech, Ronald Bayor, Douglas Flamming, Larry Keating, Robert McMath, and Steven Usselman provided important feedback on how to think about class and racial segregation historically. All gave generously of their time. Anonymous reviewers for *Journal of Urban History, Journal of Planning History,* and *Journal of Social History* helped me hone some of my first ideas about segregation in Atlanta, and I am grateful for their comments. The reviewers for the University of Georgia Press prompted me to think harder (and write more carefully) about some of the phenomena I discuss in the book. I appreciate the substantial time and effort they put toward this manuscript.

It was my earlier MA work with Ray Mohl and Mark Rose that attracted me to urban history. Ray and Mark have continued to encourage my scholarly and professional development. They and the other members of the Urban History Association have created a supportive environment for young scholars, for which I am thankful.

At Kennesaw State University, Sarah Robbins, Ulf Zimmerman, and Tim Hedeen commented on various essays, chapters, and proposals related to this project. Nancy Hill, Gayle Wheeler, Rhonda Nemeth, Janet Medearis, Janie Mardis, Caitlin McCannon, and Jessica Killcreas all contributed to this work in various ways over the last eight years. The College of Humanities and Social Sciences, the dean of the Graduate College, and the Center for Excellence in Teaching and Learning at Kennesaw State University financially supported portions of the work investigating the intersection of homeownership and housing landscapes. Finally, my department chair, Howard Shealy, ensured that I had time and money to pursue this and many other projects.

The book relied heavily on the services of libraries and archives. I am particularly grateful to the Interlibrary Loan and other library staff at Kennesaw State University.

At the Kenan Research Center at the Atlanta History Center, Michael Brubaker, Helen Matthews, and several other staff members provided immeasurable assistance. Mary Daniels at the Frances Loeb Library at Harvard University helped dredge up the Robert Whitten materials on Atlanta. I am also grateful to the librarians and archivists at Archives and Special Collections,

Robert W. Woodruff Library at Atlanta University Center; the Manuscript, Archives, and Rare Book Library at Emory University, Atlanta; the National Archives and Records Administration, College Park, Maryland; the National Archives and Records Administration, Southeast Division, Atlanta; Library of Congress (Manuscripts Division), Washington, D.C.; the Auburn Avenue Research Library on African American Culture and History, Atlanta; and the National Association of Realtors Archives, Chicago.

My friends and family have waited patiently for this first book. My mother, father, and brother provided steady support and cheerleading when necessary. My husband, Ben, served as a sounding board for the arguments scattered through this book and supplied much love and laughter throughout the process.

THE CULTURE OF PROPERTY

INTRODUCTION

At the turn of the twenty-first century, Atlanta's metropolitan statistical area sprawled across twenty counties. If you were born that year to a family in the Summerhill neighborhood, in the shadows of Turner Field in Atlanta's central city, you most likely went home to one of the city's most concentrated centers of poverty, where blacks experienced a high degree of isolation and where most families paid rent in excess of the federal guidelines. You may well have lived in one of the many homes in the area cited for building-code violations that year. One in five children in your neighborhood had a parent in state prison. More than one in ten of your neighbors suffered unemployment. More likely than not, your family lived below the federal poverty line. As you grew up, you might have heard about how your older neighbors took to the streets to demand increased city services or to protest police brutality in the 1960s. At the time of your birth, your neighbors were still recovering from a failed neighborhood redevelopment plan that had left many in the area bitter and distrustful of city government.[1]

If you were born to a family living in Alpharetta—about twenty-five miles north of downtown Atlanta—you were born into a city with an average household income of over $70,000 and an average home value of $225,000, and you were slated to attend north Fulton County's highest-performing public schools. It was unlikely that any of your neighbors suffered any sustained unemployment. Your neighborhood was likely entirely white, and its less-than-ten-year-old single-family homes were owner occupied and served by private amenities such as tennis courts and pools. Your family may have participated in the public meetings about a controversial zoning variance allowing multifamily housing.[2]

Atlanta was not always a city spatially divided by race and class. One hundred years earlier, Atlanta was diverse even on a microscale. Real-estate dealers capitalized on high in-migration in the 1880s and 1890s, and small-scale investors, speculative builders, and larger developers built rental housing throughout the city. Operating in a culture not yet concerned about housing segregation, a city mixed in class and race resulted. One-room tenement shacks were tucked behind bungalows and Queen Annes. Homes abutted businesses. Office clerks passed their railroad worker neighbors as they made their way to the streetcar line, and lawyers would have seen laborers readying for the day if they glanced down an alley. Social practices and understandings may have separated classes and races, but housing location did not. Only in the city's few industrial suburbs, where capitalists took advantage of tax-free land by building industrial towns, textile mill villages, and scattered start-up subdivisions catering to Atlanta's small group of civic elite, did neighborhoods exhibit much racial and class homogeneity.[3]

This book is about this transition from a city unconcerned with residential segregation, neighborhood aesthetics, and property control to one marked by extreme concentrations of poverty and racial and class exclusion. Specifically, it examines how and why, from the 1880s to 1950, ideologies of residential property and space changed, how those ideas became normalized, and how they were made public policy. The study does not investigate every variable that led to a city organized by race and class. Rather, the work analyzes how particular cultures of property were produced, cultivated, and disseminated and how they reflected and constituted race, class, and power relations. It traces how the iconic status of the American single-family home came to encompass the neighborhood and how this particular landscape became a site of privilege. It details how the park-neighborhood evolved to signal whiteness and how public and private interests reasserted homeownership as a desired status marker in the years immediately following World War I. Finally, it exposes how *homeownership* as an American institution was discursively constructed and deployed as part of a larger negotiation over power, locally and nationally. By examining the ideologies that informed and then emanated from residential landscapes, this study elucidates everyday enactments of power. It exposes how white, propertied power responded to changing circumstances and challenges in the early 1900s in order to divide the city by race and class, naturalize housing segregation, imbue the white park-neighborhood landscape with status, and privilege the residents of that landscape.[4]

◈

The Culture of Property draws on and contributes to the growing body of work on twentieth-century housing geographies. This literature is now rich and diverse and includes Olivier Zunz's detailed studies of the change from ethnic enclaves to class-based geographies during the rise of industrial capitalism, Sam Bass Warner Jr.'s work on the emergence of streetcar suburbs, and Kevin Kruse's and Matthew Lassiter's examinations of white flight and "community" formation in the 1970s.[5] Some of the most extensive housing studies have probed the local, regional, and national trends that produced an array of segregation patterns and histories. Nearly two decades ago, city planning historian Christopher Silver applied Jack Temple Kirby's analysis of race and the South's Progressive

Era ideology to segregation, contending that racial-segregation ordinances in the second decade of the twentieth century were part of the South's reform movement that, among other things, sought to control blacks.[6] Garrett Power, George Wright, and other historians have revealed how black migration and the sudden arrival of blacks in formerly white neighborhoods in the Northeast and the Midwest influenced the rise of housing segregation by law.[7] Other scholars have unmasked how local real-estate agents managed and constructed the housing landscape. Margaret Garb, for example, has described how Chicago real-estate interests used racism and black desires for homeownership to sell property, a process that resulted in the racializing of various neighborhoods.[8]

In the now voluminous literature on federal housing policy and race, historian Arnold Hirsch's work is foundational, exposing how New Deal agencies and structures reinforced and extended racially discriminatory practices.[9] Historians Kenneth Jackson, Amy Hillier, and David Freund have investigated the role played (or not played) by the Home Owners' Loan Corporation (HOLC), the Federal Housing Administration (FHA), and the Federal Home Loan Bank Board (FHLBB) of the 1930s in launching white flight to city suburbs. Scholarly indictment of the federal role in dividing American cities has grown, even if popular understanding of the state's influence over spatial segregation has not.[10]

Recently, scholars have examined the intersections of policy, race, class, economy, urban space, and culture. Andrew Wiese's *Places of Their Own*, for example, demonstrates that blacks' suburbanization patterns differed from whites' in both intent and outcome, and Kevin Kruse has revealed how tensions over housing and school desegregation in Atlanta exposed white class divisions and ultimately gave rise to a larger conservative political movement.[11]

The Culture of Property is in conversation with many of these studies, but it is primarily concerned with the culture of residential property and residential landscapes. Like historians Becky Nicolaides and David Freund, I am concerned with tracing how neighborhoods, housing, and urban space came to constitute race and class identity, and how this constellation of relationships manifested itself in different places and changed over time.[12] To examine and interpret certain patterns and phenomena, this study draws on works and approaches culled from cultural geography and sociology. Using approaches and frameworks culled from David Roediger's and Eduardo Bonilla-Silva's studies of white discourse practices and Nancy Duncan and James Duncan's analysis of landscape aesthetics, *The Culture of Property* demonstrates how whiteness became discursively and spatially attached to cultural constructions such as homeownership and material landscapes such as park-neighborhoods.[13] I contend that Atlanta's white property owners, real-estate professionals, and federal officials actively managed cultural understandings of housing landscapes as part of a larger movement that extended white propertied power within the American political economy. This study exposes how this culture of property benefited whites and property owners and how it solidified, expanded, and protected white homeowner entitlement as "color-blind racism" came to the fore.[14] It illustrates that property ideologies require, in geographer Nicholas Blomley's words, "a continual doing."[15] That is, faced with a variety of challenges, white propertied power remained agile, able to reconstitute, justify, and defend structures that enabled and secured white privilege.

Throughout this study, I emphasize how particular residential landscape ideas circulated within public culture. The diffusion of new property ideologies occurred on two separate but related levels. First, debates and discussions about the organization of housing in an urban context took place in academic, professional, and bureaucratic circles. City planners, academicians, and housing developers frequently detailed new thinking about city development, neighborhood building, and land economics at workshops and professional conferences and in public agencies and offices. I contend that this exchange of ideas—and the texts produced by these people and within these venues—mattered. They propagated new philosophies of class- and race-based organization among bureaucrats, policy makers, office staff, and housing and financial professionals. Ultimately it was this group and this structure that interacted with and influenced the thinking of civic elites and rank-and-file residents. Civic elites may not have read HOLC reports and the FHA's *Underwriting Manual,* but they adopted (indeed, embraced) the ideologies these agencies and texts promulgated.

As Joe Feagin and others have demonstrated, these discursive practices ultimately formed and buttressed a system of privilege that delivers tangible rewards. This is no accident of history; Feagin, Bonilla-Silva, and George Lipsitz have demonstrated how whites diligently maintain and protect this white privilege. Reflective and constitutive of culture, material landscapes contribute to shared meaning making, as James Duncan, Nancy Duncan, and other human and cultural geographers have shown.[16] To better understand the cultural production of housing landscapes and segregated housing geographies historically, this study investigates Atlanta's evolution from a heterogeneous city in the late nineteenth century to a race- and class-segregated geography at mid-twentieth century.

✧

If Atlantans were unperturbed by their haphazard city in the 1880s and 1890s, the city's civic elite sought order and a modern city by the 1900s. At the turn to the twentieth century, Atlanta shifted its attention to city building and urban aesthetics, a project manifested in both exclusive park-neighborhoods and City Beautiful proposals typical of other cities throughout the United States. Business leaders in particular spoke confidently about how parks and a new civic plaza were sure to attract business, conventions, and workers. At the same time, civic elites looked to the emerging park-neighborhood—with its designed natural landscapes, distinguished architecture, single-family homes, private parks, and pleasant drives—to display and, in a sense, perform the city's New South status.[17] Though Peters Park and Inman Park failed to live up to this promise in the 1880s and 1890s, Druid Hills and Ansley Park delivered acres of rolling hills, elite white neighbors, and sylvan views. City Beautiful proposals were less successful (most were never realized), largely because the most Atlantans declined to spend public money on such urban primping.

The park-neighborhood and City Beautiful designs that emerged from 1900 to 1915 marked an important change in thinking in a city accustomed to speculative development and functional building. The new park-neighborhood and its associated visual culture combined with the City Beautiful movement's push for linearity, plazas, and parkways to change elite Atlantans' ideas about public and private space. Media hype and real-estate advertisements emphasized the new planned neighborhood aesthetic of wooded lots, winding roads, and natural terrain. New plans for parks, park improvements, and civic centers suggested the aesthetic superiority of big, designed spaces. Images of neatly designed, self-contained neighborhoods and class and racial homogeneity heightened residents' sensitivity to disorder; people and planners alike increasingly saw incongruous land-uses and incongruous *people* where they had seen none before.

Both the City Beautiful and the park-neighborhood movement favored a *landscape way of seeing*, the practice of looking and absorbing (consciously or unconsciously) an extended, wider view of the natural *and* man-made environment and attaching meaning to what one sees.[18] Whereas homeowners had heretofore been concerned only with what was contained within their property boundaries, park-neighborhood and City Beautiful practices encouraged residents to look past their property lines to consider street lengths and the neighborhood. Moreover, these movements encouraged people to consider residents as part of the landscape, as part of the *view*. That is, *who* occupied the property—and their race and class—became part of the park-neighborhood aesthetic.

Often couched in the benign language of beautification and urban improvement, the park-neighborhood fashion relied on class and racial exclusion. Developers of early, designed park-neighborhoods intended them for white elites. Inman Park, Druid Hills, and Ansley Park—all launched between 1880 and

1920—utilized minimum lot sizes and other restrictions to ensure not just a consistent landscape but a narrow range of residents, a practice that continued into the 1920s building boom. Indeed, park-neighborhood developers and agents selling and leasing those properties flagrantly sold social status and exclusion. Ads promised "Atlanta's best people" as neighbors, "restrictions," and proximity to "the great Peachtree thoroughfare." Ansley Park, initiated in 1904, specifically excluded residents "of African descent" in its restrictive covenants, a practice that become more common after World War I. Indeed, park-neighborhoods not only relied on exclusion, they made it fashionable, associating it with the park-neighborhood landscape itself as well as social status. Not surprisingly, such expectations spread.

Shortly after developers introduced exclusive park-neighborhood living to Atlanta's suburbs, residents of established Atlanta neighborhoods launched a sustained movement to impose racial residential segregation in other parts of the city. In 1910, elite white residents of Atlanta's Jackson Hill neighborhood, just east of downtown, declared their neighborhood "whites only" and demanded that agents quit selling and renting homes in the area to blacks. When that failed, whites attempted to move historically black Morris Brown College from the east to the west side of town. When that effort also failed, Jackson Hill residents led various drives for local ordinances that implemented segregation across the entire city. In 1922, Atlanta introduced racial classifications into its comprehensive land-use zoning plan. Thus, while whites initially concerned themselves with "protecting" their own neighborhood from "undesirables," they eventually moved to formally sort the entire city.

The rising cultural significance of homeownership in the second decade of the twentieth century but particularly in the 1920s intersected with and informed new thinking about Atlanta's residential landscapes. The need to stimulate home building, settle the labor force, and calm political tensions encouraged the National Association of Real Estate Boards and the National Departments of Labor and Commerce to join forces, launch, and manage homeownership drives throughout the country. Emerging as they did in the World War I era and amid a rising interest in 100 percent Americanism, Own Your Own Home campaigns employed appeals to citizenship, domestic ideals, and patriotism. Texts as diverse as posters, films, place mats, model homes, school essay contests, poems, and songs linked homeownership to masculinity, citizenship, democracy, antiradicalism, and family. Agents, agencies, builders, and material suppliers used different combinations of these appeals at different times, implicitly inviting the reader to equate designed neighborhoods of single-family homes with homeownership and its constellation of meanings. Atlanta's real-estate dealers joined the national movement promoting homeownership in 1922, adopted the rhetoric and performances practiced elsewhere, and helped Gate City residents link homeownership, citizenship, and family values. Using an annual home exposition as their signature event, agents, builders, subdivision developers, home decorators, and others implored Atlantans to become homeowners to protect their family, stabilize the nation, support their city, and attain full citizenship.[19]

Post–World War I economic recovery not only revitalized the homeownership movement, it revived interest in planned communities, catalyzing the development of Atlanta's inner and outer suburbs into park-neighborhoods and park-neighborhood-inspired communities. Many of the planned subdivisions birthed in the 1920s adopted the aesthetic language and practices popularized by Ansley Park and Druid Hills. To be sure, few of the post-1920 subdivisions relied on the holistic landscape design or offered the amenities available in most elite park-neighborhoods.[20] Nonetheless, smaller subdivisions and their associated advertisements and rhetoric propagated the park-neighborhood ideology by emphasizing trees, parkways, good neighbors, and the like. The diffusion of the park-neighborhood meant the spread of racial and class exclusion via informal methods or restrictive covenants. Local policy buttressed private enterprise, and civic elites used comprehensive land-use zoning to assign certain land uses—including residential use by different races and classes—to particular areas of the city.

The park-neighborhood fashion and the Own Your Own Home movement overlapped in time and in their strategies and tactics. As a result, the cultural understandings and practices associated with the two trends coalesced, sometimes incidentally and often intentionally. The 1920s homeownership campaigns, for example, adopted the single-family home and park-neighborhood aesthetic in their advertisements and expositions, and thus homeownership and park-neighborhoods became correlated—a set of cultural practices and products linked in popular discourse and understanding, what I refer to here as a "status good set." The materiality of park-neighborhoods that had emerged by 1915 and spread rapidly beginning in the 1920s—which encompassed linearity, designed and natural landscapes, and architectural harmony—signaled residents' citizenship, social and financial stability, patriotism, and whiteness. Thus, in the second and third decades of the twentieth century, a variety of texts encouraged Atlantans to think of "home" and housing in new ways. These texts worked cumulatively, iterating an appreciation for the themes mobilized by both local and national aesthetic movements and reinforcing new ways of seeing and performing whiteness and property.

After the launch of the New Deal in 1933, the HOLC and the FHA mortgage-risk rating texts and the Federal Housing Administration's *Underwriting Manual* codified the relationship between the park-neighborhood aesthetic, homeownership, and whiteness in the 1930s and 1940s and made it public policy. The *Underwriting Manual* required appraisers to assess not just a house or individual property but the neighborhood. It discouraged heterogeneous environments, favored park-neighborhood landscapes, and encouraged the use of restrictive covenants—including racially restrictive covenants. The FHA (and later the Veterans' Administration) awarded whites who adopted and practiced these ideals with generous mortgage terms and the cultural capital associated with homeownership. Blacks, whom the FHA systematically excluded from its Title II home mortgage program until the 1950s, did not enjoy such benefits.

A growing economy and federal largesse spurred park-neighborhood and park-neighborhood-inspired housing production in the late 1930s and the 1940s, pulling whites further into Atlanta's suburbs while new public housing programs concentrated black families within the city's three-mile radius. Many builders and developers embraced FHA standards, focused their attention on home building for whites, and planned and executed larger planned communities. Subdivision production prevailed over the early twentieth-century practice of building one to five homes on lots often purchased individually or in small bundles. In this manner, subdivisions resulted in ever larger suburban spaces that developers assigned specifically to whites. Thus, when Eugene Haynes subdivided Haynes Manor in 1939, he produced eight contiguous blocks—about 125 homes—restricted only to whites. And the four-square-block addition to Morningside in 1939 meant not just four more blocks of whites but the expansion of an earlier, larger plat intended for white occupation. Local policies buttressed federal and private building in the 1930s and 1940s. When Georgia permitted counties to zone beginning in 1937, Fulton County immediately approved white residents' requests to "protect" their Buckhead estates. In 1946, the city's zoning plan (developed in partnership with Fulton County) reserved the outer suburbs for single-family homes and for families able to afford lots of nine thousand square feet to two acres. The suburbs, at mid-twentieth century, had been reserved for the white and well-off. Black families, on the other hand, were largely ignored by the FHA until after 1950. Instead, federal and local officials used new public housing programs to sharpen racial divisions. Public housing programs followed "local culture" and allowed officials to assign projects to a specific race. Local officials then sited projects in areas that further concentrated black families within the city's three-mile radius. Local officials also continued their campaign to racially segregate housing by using local slum-clearance programs to eliminate mixed-race neighborhoods as well as the few remaining black neighborhoods on Atlanta's north side. Consequently, federal policies, local modes of implementation, and resulting private building practices helped enlarge monoracial spaces in the city and harden boundaries between blacks and whites.

Black subdivision building patterns, particularly in the late 1940s, reinforced this geography. Though smaller in total project size when compared to the elite park-neighborhoods being installed in the outer suburbs, black subdivisions enlarged the space dominated by single races in Atlanta. Walter Aiken, for example, originally subdivided Dixie Hills into about six square blocks of homes for blacks, but later expanded the community. And the Atlanta Urban League's work to open up new housing for blacks in the 1940s and 1950s facilitated the building of new subdivisions or apartment complexes for black families, particularly on the city's west side but also to the south. Thus, constrained by racially biased local and federal policies, Atlanta developers and home builders planned and implemented subdivisions and park-neighborhoods in the 1920s through the 1940s that reinforced local and federal policies segregating white and black housing and neighborhoods.

The human geography, cultural texts, and material environment generated by the park-neighborhood movement, homeownership campaigns, and federal and local policies from the 1880s to 1950 had a lasting impact on white homeowner landscape expectations as well as white understanding of residential geography. Housing advertisements, segregation ordinances, zoning plans, news stories, homeownership campaign materials, and the park-neighborhood landscape itself taught Atlantans to look at and value housing and residential landscapes in new ways. Through these public exchanges and negotiations, new cultural understandings about race, class, space, and landscape aesthetics developed, spread, and became naturalized. They buttressed—and protected—a city divided by race and class.

The study concludes with 1950, before local civic elites launched Forward Atlanta and a new chapter of slum clearance and urban renewal, and before school desegregation battles prompted whites to, as Kevin Kruse details, fashion a "freedom of association" defense to stave off what they saw as threats to their schools and neighborhoods.[21]

Although *The Culture of Property* examines one city, it offers insight into how the interests of white homeowners nationwide became institutionalized, culturally embedded, and eventually hegemonic. Land agents, builders, and federal officials alike cultivated a new discourse of neighborhood and homeownership in the early twentieth century as white elites attempted to assert control over neighborhood aesthetics and residential geography. By examining how Atlanta's land dealers were enticed into active participation in the homeownership ideology and elevation of park-neighborhood living, we can better understand how, throughout the United States, the terms *homeowner* and *homeownership* became charged with particular meanings, and how these ideas underlay the aesthetic and segregationist values spread by park-neighborhoods in cities around the country.

Sociologist Pierre Bourdieu's concept of *habitus* is useful to this discussion of evolving ideas about homeownership and changing understandings of housing landscapes and residential geography. *Habitus* is the internalized structure(s) that individuals bring to any situation, the disposition or way of thinking that people develop over time through socialization. *Habitus* includes the possibility of individual agency, but it orients people. What we see when we look closely at the transition in residential geography in early twentieth-century Atlanta is a change in *habitus*—a new framework by which white citizens viewed and performed property. During these years, white property owners mobilized particular discourses that influenced and altered popular understanding of space, race, and cultural hierarchies to correspond to a white elite worldview.[22] By the mid-1930s, these discourses and the white privilege they relied on prevailed, and they influenced how Americans viewed, valued, and approached residential landscapes for the balance of the century.[23]

By imbuing homeownership with values associated with citizenship, nationalism, and frugality, white property owners secured policies that benefited their race and class economically as well as culturally. Moreover, by freighting homeownership with symbolic capital, public and private land interests were able to make assuming substantial mortgage debt attractive to Americans.[24] Even without direct participation by purchasing or mortgaging, Americans were enticed into supporting or passively accepting the new culture of homeownership. Indeed, even those who did not own a home outright but were in the process of purchasing a home through mortgage were extended the privilege and benefits of the title "homeowner."

By weaving class and racial interests into different layers of American culture and society, white property owners reshaped Atlantans' *habitus* regarding residential geographies. That is, they reoriented majority perceptions about neighborhoods and urban design and produced new ways of thinking about how different groups of people "fit" into particular residential landscapes. These perceptions and dispositions served to reproduce group privilege, in this case the privilege of white homeowners.[25] Whites acted to spatially and materially construct whiteness, and they positioned these constructions within a political, economic, and social network that both secured and favored those landscape sensibilities.

These points are critical to understanding the persistence of class and race segregation in housing in the twentieth-century United States. Thousands of new investors purchased homes with an understanding that to secure their investment or to grow their wealth they needed to maintain the particular cultural practices in operation at the time of the home's purchase. That is, home buyers who bought property at least in part because it was situated in a parklike community of families valued for its conservative architecture, well-maintained lawns, and white residents worked overtime to maintain that same collection of attributes. To the buyer, these particular attributes were not merely features incidental to an evolving set of cultural practices. Rather, the buyer considered these features *necessary* to the maintenance of the property value. That is, neighborhoods forged in the mold of whiteness resisted change not only because of the espoused prejudices of individual owners but also because owners were convinced that those practices were not racial at all.[26] In this case, the purchasers became active participants in a system of white homeowner privilege, or what Nancy Duncan and James Duncan describe as "aversive" racism. Here racist practices are real, with real effects, but racism itself has become invisible.[27] Racism was built into a system in network with other cultural meanings and practices, such as class segregation. Over time, as openly racist rhetoric became taboo, homeowners mobilized this other collection of cultural meanings and practices to maintain the system of white homeowner privilege.

Finally, class was particularly useful to the construction of white propertied power. After 1925, class segregation was widely accepted and rarely questioned. Thus, when the Georgia Supreme Court ruled the racial components of Atlanta's 1922 zoning plan unenforceable, whites could still safely mobilize class to maintain their privilege. White elites thereby created a collection of cultural constructions around property that effectively stood in for one another. When racial zoning was overturned, class zoning served the same end. When racist rhetoric became taboo, language and assertions regarding tenants and rental property could substitute. Moreover, the planning of neighborhoods by structures that effectively organized by class became normalized. To white homeowners and to those conversant with the new culture of property, the division of neighborhoods into clusters based on narrow price ranges and lot or home sizes—practices that only emerged in Atlanta in the second and third decades of the twentieth century—seemed rational, and the property-values argument used to explain them was widely accepted.

※

To trace how thinking about residential landscapes and the landscape itself evolved in the early twentieth century, the book begins by surveying Atlanta's growth from 1880 to about 1910. In these years, Atlanta developed without central public planning and with little concern about residential racial and class divisions. Speculative home building in a city without land regulation resulted in a heterogeneous residential geography. Chapter 2 describes the birth of the park-neighborhood movement in Atlanta, including its reliance on exclusion. Chapter 3 traces and interprets white demands for residential segregation ordinances in the second decade of the century and discusses the relationship between those demands and changing neighborhood expectations. Chapter 4 introduces Atlanta's 1922 homeownership campaign and explains how it intersected with segregation trends and park-neighborhood sensibilities. Chapter 5 demonstrates how, in the 1920s, park-neighborhood building accelerated, embedding and disseminating new understandings about the material, residential landscape. In the same period, comprehensive land-use zoning infused local policy with white elites' park-neighborhood expectations. Chapter 6 examines federal practices and programs, analyzing how they helped circulate elite park-neighborhood expectations and encourage their adoption. Chapter 7 explores how housing landscape ideologies birthed prior to 1950 played out over the balance of the twentieth century and connects the patterns and practices discussed in chapters 1 through 6 to Atlanta's class and racial segregation patterns today. New cultural constructions of property both encouraged residential segregation patterns and masked their cultural history. Even when Americans became aware of how housing landscape practices and understandings had emerged as part of a raced, classed production, they had become so attached to the resulting array of American cultural and economic capital delivered by planned suburban communities that most were reluctant to disinvest.

CHAPTER ONE

Housing the City, 1865 to 1910

In 1864, General William Tecumseh Sherman's Union troops plundered and burned Atlanta as they marched to the sea. Citizens returned to find bent rails, solitary chimneys, and scattered cannonballs in what had once been a thriving trading center at the nexus of the Western and Atlantic, Georgia, Atlanta and West Point, and Macon and Western railroads. Thousands of Atlanta homes had been destroyed that summer, leaving only a few hundred to shelter returning residents and refugees. Visitors painted a dismal scene. In 1865, journalist J. T. Trowbridge wrote that hundreds lived in "wretched hovels" covered with "ragged fragments of tin roofing from the burnt government and railroad buildings." Others had constructed makeshift homes of "irregular blackened patches, and partly of old boards, with roofs of huge, warped, slouching shreds of tin."[1] But quickly rebuilt roads and rail lines and the subsequent business revival lured job seekers and entrepreneurs. In 1866, Whitelaw Reid reported that Atlanta's streets were "blockaded with drays and wagons" as workers and artisans, merchants and city boosters, fashioned a new city.[2] The flurry of home and business building combined with lack of regulation and the spirit of short-term gain to produce a muddled and haphazard town. Journalist Sidney Andrews, touring the region in 1865, commented that, with the exception of Boston, Atlanta was "the most irregularly laid out city [he] ever saw."[3] Newly designated streets were "narrow, crooked, and badly constructed," and they began "nowhere and end[ed] nowhere."[4]

Amid the jumble, builders and factory owners built worker housing among the factories, distributors, and service providers that flanked the rail lines trisecting the city. Operating decades before whites proposed residential segregation ordinances and prior to the widespread selling of planned neighborhoods and subdivisions, hundreds of builders and investors scattered homes throughout the city. As a result, the homes of Atlanta's workers, nascent middle class, and business elite were intermixed with one another and distributed among warehouses, fashionable hotels, factories, and smaller businesses. The South's social rules dictated black-white interaction, precluding any perception of need for residential segregation by law. Some neighborhoods housed a range of blue-collar and white-collar workers; some were mixed by race; some

13

by both occupational class and race. By 1900, though, whites' discomfort with this housing geography—and race relations more generally—was evident, and white elites in particular sought new ways to remake neighborhoods and housing landscapes.[5]

Rebuilding the City, 1865 to 1890

City boosters were determined to fashion Atlanta into not just the state's but the South's leading city. Prior to the Civil War, Atlanta had been a weak competitor to Savannah, the state's major port. But the Gate City's comparatively high altitude cut some of the lower South's humidity, making it a good storage place for sensitive crops like tobacco, and less subject to the yellow fever and cholera epidemics that plagued many southern towns in the late 1800s. Business recovered quickly after the war. "New stores are opening every week," recounted Octavia Hammond in 1865.[6] But these were no stalwart business houses; traders threw together temporary shacks in an effort simply to get business up and running. The former president of the Board of Trade secured the basement under the only standing building on Alabama Street to reopen his grocery and produce trade. The *Daily Intelligencer* explained that the new buildings were "neither large nor elegant"; the structures would, however, as the report observed, "answer the purposes of our people until more prosperous days will on us dawn."[7]

The steady flight from the rural South to Atlanta and the frequent blusters of New South rhetoric masked the Gate City's halting industrial development in the two decades after the Civil War. Much has been made of *Atlanta Constitution* editor Henry Grady's petitions for industrial and agricultural diversification, but the editor's bold prescriptions effectively hid the region's—and Atlanta's—struggles with business development. To be sure, many local leaders promoted investment in manufacturing in order to stabilize the city's economy. Indeed, much of the South actively pursued industrial expansion after the Civil War. Historian Constantine Belissary notes, for example, that "no sooner were the guns stacked than the Nashville press began a vigorous campaign for more factories."[8] But antebellum Atlanta had been little more than an agricultural trade town, and many Atlantans were content with such a locally important though not regionally significant status. Certainly, the town, like the region, was preoccupied with Reconstruction and "Yankee-rule." But more importantly, money was scarce, and governments were only beginning to expand their role in commercial and industrial development. Thus, in practice, industrial and urban expansion was riddled with setbacks and constrained by volatile business cycles, making urban growth a complex project.[9]

In Atlanta, businessmen organized among themselves to spur commercial activity. As retailers and wholesalers rebuilt their facilities, business owners started commercial associations. In early 1866, the Board of Trade, which had been inactive during the war, re-formed at George Jack's confectionery on Whitehall Street "for the purpose of establishing uniformity of action in the promotion of its mercantile interests."[10] The members formally adopted a constitution at the April 1866 meeting. In 1871, the group reorganized as the city's chamber of commerce.[11]

Leaders were hopeful, and boosterism marked the 1870s and 1880s. According to Mayor John Thomas Glenn, the city's Committee on Manufacturing and Statistics could not keep up with all the inquiries from those wishing to establish their businesses in Atlanta. Promotional materials asserted that Atlanta was the only southern city that had all the factors required for profitable manufacturing: a good supply of cheap labor, affordable insurance, low taxes, cheap water, good banks with liberal interest rates, a ready market for products, and raw materials at "first cost."[12] The Committee on Manufacturing and Statistics assured, "Mechanics and laborers will come here in preference to any other city in the South, and [he added hopefully] even work for less wages here rather than higher wages elsewhere."[13] Despite the city's posturing and promises, the city council gave only limited financial support to promotional campaigns. In 1890, the Committee on Manufacturing and Statistics report explained that the committee had been unable "to carry out any plan for advertising the city as an excellent point for the location of manufacturing industries." Advertising was critical to Atlanta's growth, the committee asserted. Birmingham, Chattanooga, Nashville, Decatur, Anniston, Fort Payne—cities with "fewer advantages" than the Gate City—were "made" by advertising. The committee blamed the city council for failing to deliver the low-cost services they contended Atlanta possessed. They implored city leaders to "offer cheap taxes, cheap water and low freight fates," arguing, "The future prosperity depends a great deal on the manufacturers that are located here and those that are to come.... The very life blood of the City depends on her manufacturing industries."[14]

Despite the limited financial support, city promoters were able to get Atlanta's name and advantages circulated regionally, and later nationally. The city distributed *Guide to Atlanta* at expositions and to those inquiring about the city by mail or otherwise. The chamber of commerce published a number of promotional materials throughout the era, including *Handbook of the City of Atlanta: A Comprehensive Review of the City's Commercial, Industrial and Residential Conditions* (1891); *Atlanta, a Twentieth Century City* (1903); and *Souvenir*

Album, Atlanta, Georgia (1907). The city forwarded materials to fifteen thousand inquirers in 1903.[15]

By 1900, though, it is clear that some promoters envisioned Atlanta moving within a larger national urban network. Committee leaders chose the likes of Chattanooga and Fort Payne to mark Atlanta's progress, suggesting that boosters sought only regional prominence in the years immediately following the war. The city competed against Georgia's, Alabama's, and Tennessee's manufacturing centers—not Pittsburgh's or Cleveland's—for business and for workers. Still, the city advertised itself nationwide. The Greater Georgia Association, started by Atlanta's chamber in 1903, advertised in journals nationwide, promoting the city to craftsmen, investors, and industrialists. That year Atlanta spent $500 on ads in *Harper's Weekly* and $272 on the *Saturday Evening Post*, two of the most widely circulated publications in the United States. The Committee on Manufactures, Freight Rates and Statistics reported, "Answers to these advertisements are pouring in, and the indications are that the tide of immigration will soon turn southward."[16]

Industrial and business growth finally came to the city, drawn perhaps by sales tactics but more likely by the convergence of the four railroads that linked Atlanta to ports and inland markets. The Western and Atlantic connected Atlanta to cities in the Midwest. The Central of Georgia tied Atlanta to eastern towns. The Atlanta and West Point, Macon and Western, and Georgia Railroads provided the important links to all the South's agricultural lands and port cities. The railroad network meant strong wholesale relationships with Cincinnati, Louisville, and St. Louis and access to foodstuffs from the West.[17]

Given the high demand for market access and absent regulation limiting industrial location, by the mid-1880s factories, businesses, railroad depots, and roundhouses stretched about one-half mile along the Georgia Railroad, the Western and Atlantic, and the East Tennessee, Virginia, and Georgia lines. Southern Agricultural Works and the Atlanta Bridge Works located a few blocks north of the rail convergence, on the Western and Atlantic. Atlanta Cotton Compress and Warehouse opened a few blocks south on the East Tennessee, Virginia, and Georgia. Commercial houses, banks, hotels, and the like were sprinkled amid the factories and warehouses. About twenty square blocks from Broad Street to Spring Street and Marietta Street to James Street had a high concentration of stores and offices. Within one-half mile of one another in the city's center lay the governor's mansion, the city's major churches, and the opera house—a blend of interests and people.[18]

Many of these factories and processors remained in the central city for decades, but by 1880 city boosters had come to view manufacturers, railroad shops, and the like as urban pests. In 1882 the city council responded to the industrial "nuisances" by asking the city attorney to investigate potential controls on businesses that used coal or wood to produce steam power, as the smoke and soot was "a great nuisance" and brought "serious complaints."[19] The next year a councilman complained about the powder magazine and its "dangerous proximity" to area homes. A special committee recommended it be moved near the waterworks, about six miles from the city on the banks of the Chattahoochee River, "where it [would] not damage or interfere with [Atlanta's] citizens."[20] Livestock-trading facilities and processors were likewise removed to the city's outskirts. In 1884, the city prohibited the building of stockyards and stock pens within two hundred yards of any dwelling. That same year the city ordered Union Stock Yards to erect a retaining wall to protect the watershed and reservoir. In 1891, residents filed complaints after a city-limit change inadvertently brought several slaughterhouses into the city. Slaughterhouse operators and factory owners likely viewed constantly changing regulations as "nuisances," but the exclusion of some industries from the city opened more job opportunities at Atlanta's perimeter.[21]

Atlanta's manufacturing, retail, and service geography meant that jobs were available throughout the city as well as just outside the city limits. Manufacturers lined the three major railways that trisected Atlanta, providing low-skilled, semiskilled, and skilled positions to all sections. And while heavier industries pulled workers toward the city's periphery, hotel and passenger rail positions drew other workers toward the center.

Migration

Atlanta's job opportunities offered hope to many who endured a slow postwar reconstruction. North Georgia farms recovered slowly from war damage, and a drought from 1865 to 1867 sent farmers into further distress. Crop liens kept sharecroppers and tenant farmers at the mercy of plantation owners for decades. Dissatisfied with agreements or with final settlements, croppers often changed farm employers yearly, ever searching for a better deal. Increasingly these rural wage earners struck out for the cities, and Atlanta's population increased for decades. A U.S. Department of Labor bulletin explained that in Covington, Georgia, for example, "large numbers of country people [were] being constantly tempted to leave their farms and move to town."[22] Leola Young and her parents moved to Atlanta after years of sharecropping, explaining, "If we farmed the next year it would have been necessary to go in debt for everything we would need to make a crop with. By selling our mule and cows we

Table 1.1. Atlanta Population, 1870–1950

Year	Population	Percent change	African American population	Percent African American population
1870	21,789		9,929	45.6%
1880	37,409	71.7%	16,330	43.7%
1890	65,533	75.2%	28,117	42.9%
1900	89,872	37.1%	35,727	39.8%
1910	154,839	72.3%	51,902	33.5%
1920	200,616	29.6%	62,796	31.3%
1930	270,366	34.8%	90,075	33.3%
1940	302,288	11.8%	104,533	34.6%
1950	331,314	9.6%	121,416	36.6%

Source: U.S. Census.

could pay our debt."[23] Leola, thirteen, and her eleven-year-old brother turned bags at the Fulton Bag Factory after moving to the Gate City. To many African Americans, a move to Atlanta meant the hope of regular and better wages and represented the final severing of ties to plantation life. As historian Georgina Hickey observes, the city was particularly attractive for single black women who found sharecropping and tenant farming difficult without a male partner or other family member. Rural influx quadrupled Atlanta's population, raising it to nearly ninety thousand by 1900 (see table 1.1).[24]

Former farmers and other migrants filled positions at Atlanta's rail shops, factories, slaughterhouses, hotels, and other businesses. Fresh from the farm, most with few industrial or commercial skills, new arrivals dominated unskilled positions. However, carpenters, plasterers, brick masons, and stonecutters likewise arrived to rebuild the city. The National Hotel and the Kimball House (built in 1866 and 1870 respectively) provided jobs in food and domestic services. African American women took many of the laundry positions at the hotels, but they also worked independently as laundresses, picking up and delivering laundry for other Atlanta families. The Atlanta Cotton Factory employed upward of 200 unskilled white women and girls. Generally speaking, women could be found in most garment-, candy-, and box-making outfits. The Atlanta Rolling Mill rebuilt in 1866 along Marietta street and furnished at least 250 skilled and unskilled positions. The Georgia Railroad shops provided employment for 48 workers that same year, and the Western and Atlantic shops

177. By 1869, the Western and Atlantic utilized over 700 workers, mostly skilled and semiskilled. John Smith and David McBride's carriage factory employed 23 workers by 1875. The smaller operations of craft artisans remained interspersed among these larger employers. In 1871, 19 boot and shoe shops operated. Marion Gaines's shops employed only 4 adult males in 1880, and W. E. Guthright employed 6. W. R. Hanleiter Bookbindery employed 8 to 10 men in 1871. Staffing businesses large and small or working independently as draymen and laundrywomen, Atlanta's workforce moved from 17,000 employees in 1880 to almost 30,000 by 1890.[25]

The business-minded people who launched these shops and factories formed a new class in the urban South. While a few entrepreneurs had roots in business prior to the Civil War, most of Atlanta's economic elite, like Jacob Elsas of the Fulton Cotton Mills, honed their moneymaking skills after the war. Some of the city's economic elite started in white-collar professions, but a few came from humbler beginnings. Frank P. Rice worked as a machinist before owning a lumberyard, and Anthony Murphy as a newsboy before operating a planing mill and lumber business. Hotel magnate and city booster Hannibal Ingalls Kimball, a northerner, started out as a carriage maker. Most of the new entrepreneurs hailed from the South, many beginning their careers in small towns before setting out for the Gate City, and most were assisted financially by friends, colleagues, or family members. Philip and Thomas Dodd, for example, became successful wholesale grocers with the assistance of their father, a wealthy planter.[26]

The business elite tended to wield power through the chamber of commerce rather than seeking elected positions, though they worked closely with the city's politicians. Real-estate leader George W. Adair and railroad and land developer Richard Peters, for example, worked with mayors, councilmen, and aldermen to help the city operate in a business-friendly manner, which included providing such things as municipal aid to railroads, tax concessions to businesses and factories, or contracts for streetcar lines. Such leaders, like *Atlanta Constitution* editor Henry Grady, were concerned with presenting a good face to potential investors and immigrants so that Atlanta emerged the winner in the urban competitions of the late 1800s.[27]

Workers and the business elite both sought to renew Atlanta, but the two groups' visions of modernization and individual success frequently collided in the late 1800s. Factory and business owners and managers controlled workers through layoffs and wage cuts. Class tensions manifested themselves in politics and on the shop floor. In the 1890s, for example, Fulton Mills introduced employee contracts that protected the employer from liability due to accidents and allowed mill management to lay off workers without notice. What is more, the contracts did not specify wage rates. Managers and owners effectively dehumanized workers by suggesting that, like out-of-date technology or aging machinery, they could and would be discarded at will.[28]

Workers sought fairer treatment and greater control of the workplace by articulating demands, staging strikes, and forming unions. Knights of Labor assemblies strengthened in this period of unrest and eventually represented over four thousand Atlanta workers. Other workers formed such organizations as the Atlanta Federation of Trades in 1890, found solidarity with the Socialist Labor Party, or organized other collectives representing specific industries or trades. Many workers struck to achieve their demands, whether represented by a union or not. In the 1890s local tinners struck, and workers in the building trades held work stoppages periodically throughout the 1880s and 1890s. When the Fulton Mill's white weavers struck for higher wages, they went so far as to break machinery to assert their voice.[29]

White and black workers had uneasy alliances from the 1870s through the 1890s, sometimes joining forces to achieve common aims but mostly working through separate unions and by different methods. By century's end, white workers sought a better deal for themselves by playing the race card and ousting black workers from many workplaces and positions. In 1889, for example, whites walked out when a black postal clerk was hired. In 1897, white workers at Fulton Bag demanded that recently hired black workers be immediately let go. As historian Gregory Mixon explains, white workers were unhappy with black attempts to control and change the workplace. Black protest through absenteeism and "loafing" was viewed as laziness by white workers, and whites deployed this stereotype when they seized shop-floor power. The South's racial climate in the 1890s—which had already adopted imagery of black disease and indolence—encouraged such thinking and facilitated the use of divisive racial strategies by white workers.[30]

Atlanta's white civic elite established and maintained a more insidious power over workers through selective allocation of city services. As historian James Michael Russell has demonstrated, elites ensured that their neighborhoods were some of the first to receive municipal water and sewer service and later electric lights. The greatest concentration of these resources outside the central business district lay along the northern section of Peachtree Street, where many of Atlanta's wealthy and powerful families built large, distinctive homes. Besides the convenience these services offered, they delivered a more healthful environment for elite white families, which in turn supported social and educational success and other outcomes that further solidified white power. This healthful environment contrasted starkly with the neighborhoods of Atlanta's workers, where sewage was dumped into nearby lots and into water supplies, and where yellow fever and other diseases stifled the development of individuals and generations of families.[31]

Atlanta's Land Industry

Speculators quickly offered their services to new arrivals and workers seeking housing, adding low-cost homes to the landscape of makeshift business buildings and hovels thrown together by the poor and recovering. Many stood to profit from the urban migration, and price-gouging was widespread. As journalist J. T. Trowbridge related in 1866, "One man had crowded into his back yard five of these little tenements, which rented for fifteen dollars a month each, and a very small brick house that let for thirty dollars."[32] Other speculators offered their own land on which families could build homes—homes that were occupied rent free by the builders for one year, after which they reverted to the speculator. But even in these initial stages of rebuilding, many anticipated the sprawling merchant center that Atlanta was to become. Whitelaw Reid, touring the city in 1865, explained, "The soil of the country, for many miles in all directions, is poor. . . . [but] the people were infected with the mania of city building; and landholders gravely explained to you how well their plantations, miles distant, would cut up into corner lots."[33] But such speculative subdividing and backyard tenement building failed to deliver sufficient housing affordable to the city's ever-growing workforce.

In the 1870s and 1880s, the housing shortage plagued manufacturers, and factory owners built homes to ensure a steady workforce. In 1880 the *Atlanta Constitution* explained that rents near the Atlanta Cotton Factory were so high that operatives were unable to take available positions. Mill managers, the editor concluded, "will find it not only convenient but profitable to provide cheap, neat and comfortable accommodations" for their workers.[34] As was common with rural and small-town textile factories, Atlanta's yarn and weaving mills built housing to attract (but also to control) workers. So, too, did Randall Brothers lumber company and Chattahoochee Brick Company. In contrast to textile mill villages, where whole neighborhoods were established, some manufacturers merely squeezed shanties and more substantial homes between their various production and storage facilities.[35]

From 1865 to the 1880s, then, land speculation and small-scale home building by employers, speculators, contractors, and residents largely shaped Atlanta's residential geography. But rapid population growth attracted more people into home building, real-estate sales, and even larger feats of speculation. Although real-estate dealers went out of business frequently, subdividers, contractors, and agents established a long-term presence in the city, influencing land-use practices and the residential landscape itself.

By the 1890s, Atlanta's real-estate industry had taken form. As in other cities, land dealers organized professional associations, rationalized land subdivision, and standardized sales practices, while home builders fashioned both niche specialties and mass production techniques. The southern land market had its peculiarities, though. The need to follow job markets meant that few southerners had an interest in purchasing homes, and, in any case, the region's cash-poor economy meant few residents had the means to do so. Thus, the South's owner-occupied housing market lagged behind that of the Northeast and the Midwest. In Atlanta a real-estate industry emerged that focused on investment in and production and management of rental properties for the city's exploding population of blue-collar workers.[36]

Producing Rental Housing

The production of rental property involved subdividers, agents, builders, investors, tenants, and at times property managers. Agents selling subdivisions, lots, and improved properties either operated independently, working for the growing number of land dealers, or established one of the dozens of firms that came and went in the South's Gate City. By 1867, Atlanta's city directory listed six real-estate offices, and no doubt other individuals acted to facilitate exchange without formally advertising. Three years later, seven real-estate agents advertised in the directory. Significantly, four offices listed in 1867 were no longer included, and five new firms had taken their place, suggesting the unstable and speculative nature of the young industry. Indicative of the expanding role of real estate into land management, the category "renting agents" had been added. The list included seven firms, though it did not include major agents such as G. W. Adair and H. M. Scott. The larger land-management companies may have preferred to maintain a single, primary listing under "real estate," a broader and more inclusive category. By 1890, thirty-eight companies claimed real estate as their practice, and one year later this number had increased to fifty-five. At this point, land agents, builders, and neighborhood developers locally, regionally, and nationally began formalizing their profession.[37]

The real-estate sales profession had its roots in the South in these postwar rebuilding years. The first national organization of real-estate agents, the National Real Estate Association, formed in Birmingham, Alabama, in 1891; the group held its second national meeting in Nashville the following year. Atlanta agent Samuel Goode served as the vice president for Georgia in 1892, and that same year Atlanta's land dealers, along with agents from Chicago, Toledo, and Duluth, pervaded the membership rolls. The organization's goals were—not surprisingly, given the trading fervor of the period—to discourage fictitious booms and wild speculation and to make homeownership simpler and safer. To control fly-by-night agents, association members sought licensing and other ways to create a divide between "professionals" and "curbstoners."[38]

Atlanta's land sellers officially organized at an 1891 banquet. In keeping with the city's booster spirit, banquet planners opted not to invite dealers from other towns because, in the words of the *Atlanta Constitution* editor, "To invite real estate men here to blow up their own towns at the expense of Atlanta would be a foolish thing to do."[39] Here Atlanta's dealers modeled their practices after those of other cities. Like New York City's agents, the Atlanta Board of Realtors formalized its property-sales practices, establishing offices where any member could list property. The agent who listed the property and the agent who sold it divided the commission equally. The Atlanta board also called for the establishment of a Georgia Board of Realtors and invited agents throughout the state to a convention on the topic in May 1892.[40]

Atlanta's real-estate dealers encouraged locals with investment interests to consider putting their money in rental housing for the city's workers, homes that would shelter "good renters" at a "nice profit." Agents targeted investors by highlighting the proximity of factories and other employers, purchase price and current rent, and potential profit. Samuel Goode's advertisement for the Clarawood subdivision was typical:

> INVESTORS, buy these lots, build cottages, receive good interest and sell at a profit on easy terms to home-builders. CAPITALISTS, your money will be safe here and it will pay you well. SALARIED PEOPLE, this is the place for your surplus money. These lots are convenient to the Exposition Mills, Collins' Brick Co., Van Winkle & Boyd's Foundry, Boyd & Baxter's Furniture Factory, the Stove Works, and many other manufactories are close enough for the men and women working in them to step home to a hot dinner at noon.[41]

Frierson and Leak likewise described some of their available property as "very fine and desirable lots for suburban homes, renting houses, speculations, or investments." Details of the property's location indicate that the agents saw railroad and textile workers as likely future tenants; the lots were "just the right distance from the cotton factory and the Air-Line [railroad shops] . . . for homes for the operatives."[42] Similarly, the Adair brothers advertised the sale of "Seven beautiful Unimproved lots. . . . Very convenient to all the Work Shops on the State Road and Marietta street."[43] Another Frierson and Leak ad described a cluster of homes as "near the cotton factory."[44] Samuel Goode explained, "Parties wishing lots on which to build houses for rent will find all this property admirably adapted for the purpose. The enlargement of the cotton factory will increase the demand for houses in that locality."[45] Ads outlining sale price and current asking rent allowed potential investors to easily calculate profit. For example, in 1885 L. M. Ives advertised property by noting, "$350—property renting for $12. $650—property renting for $16."[46] Land agents and investors alike profited from city boosterism as workers migrated to fill Atlanta's expanding service and manufacturing basis.

In addition to selling properties, many realty companies managed properties for investors. As early as 1868, George Adair advertised that he was "prepared to take charge of a rent or lease and make collections for the same, on residences, stores, or other property in this city or county. Especial attention [would] be given to property of non-residents."[47] In another ad, he advised property owners, "[The Adair company will] rent your property if placed with us."[48] According to his son, Adair formed one of the earliest comprehensive real-estate firms in the nation, acting as agent "not solely of estates, but of living owners of property, where the agent takes practically entire charge, leases property, collects rents, pays taxes and insurance, and does everything that would relieve the owner of the responsibility and trouble of handling property."[49] By 1890, Adair touted a "rent department"; he assured potential clients, "Messrs. Harwell and Mahone show houses and collect rents promptly, and Mr. Howard, my cashier, will render statements regularly."[50]

Other Atlanta agents followed suit. By 1900, listings for properties managed by real-estate firms could be found throughout Atlanta's classified ad pages. Agents Robson and Rivers advertised that they provided "personal attention with years of experience given to renting property, collecting rents and seeing to repairs."[51] In addition to collecting rent, George Adair's office paid water bills, cleaned (presumably between tenants), whitewashed, and repaired scores of floors, windows, and roofs.[52] Agents passed repair and upkeep charges on to property owners and otherwise kept them up to date regarding their properties. T. J. Cheshire of the B. M. Grant–A. S. Adams agency reported to Mrs. M. R. Benning of Athens, Georgia, that he was "working on the Greenwood Avenue lots" and expected "to dispose of them soon."[53] The agency notified A. M. Benning that his unit on Whiteford had been vacated and subsequently posted as available. The agency hoped "to be able to tenant it again" in a few days.[54]

Rental-housing investors usually hailed from the upper and middle classes and included doctors, lawyers, grocers, and small business owners. Grocer Lane

Mitchell, for example, purchased three one-story frame dwellings on Simpson Street in 1904. Lawyer R. H. Sullivan likewise invested in multiple homes on Simpson. In 1909, pharmacist Frank Edmondson contracted for the building of four one-story frame houses on Ashby Street at a cost of $1,200 each. And tailor T. C. Wesley purchased two small apartment houses on Capitol Avenue. In Atlanta, enterprising families used rental-housing investments to supplement professional incomes or provide an additional source of income to families operating seasonal businesses.[55]

Speculators and investors responsible for building Atlanta's rental properties did not tend to build in the park-neighborhood form that was slowly growing in popularity throughout the nation in the late nineteenth century. Rather than developing a few hundred homes on lots set back a standard distance from curvilinear streets in single-class neighborhoods, most of Atlanta's contractors working in this period built just two or three houses, a block of homes, or some other small stretch of housing. Building on this small scale made construction and investment more affordable to builders and investors of limited capital. Two or three empty lots or even an entire block length were much easier to locate, buy, and build on than the large plots of land that the later suburban-community builders sought. For example, in 1905 black contractors Alexander Hamilton and Son built four one-story frame homes on Rawson Street for white investor Bertram Maier at a total cost of two thousand dollars. (Hamilton also built investment housing for well-known black entrepreneur Alonzo Herndon.) White contractor Green Howell built two one-story frame homes on Hayden Street for attorney Albert Boylston.[56]

Builders, agents, and suppliers understood the potential of this market and improved lots at their own expense, holding or later selling the improved lots. White builders J. J. and J. W. Harvil, for example, erected many rental homes on the west side of Atlanta for other owners, but they also bought and built homes at their own risk. On Elm Street in 1908, the Harvils built two three-room dwellings for C. W. McClure at the cost of $400 each. On the next block of Elm, from 1907 to 1911, they erected one two-room dwelling and two three-room dwellings at their own risk for sale as rental property. Builder Alexander Hamilton had $4,150 worth of property investments in 1890. Real-estate dealers W. E. Treadwell and Company, Edwin Ansley, and Saunders and Johnson all arranged for the building of rental housing at their own risk. Similarly, lumber companies did not just supply the major materials used for home building; many also produced housing themselves. The Chamlee Lumber Company, for example, built four rental homes on Simpson Street in 1908 at a cost of $2,000 each.[57]

This infill approach to home building, which erected homes a handful at a time, left its mark on the architectural landscape of the city. Homes varied in appearance and size, and not more than a half dozen of uniform construction were usually seen in a row. That said, builders did follow basic construction patterns. Most working-class homes, whether occupied by blacks or whites, had one to four rooms, and the larger rooms often had a porch (or veranda) that provided relief from the city's summer heat. The common freestanding three-room house consisted of two rooms facing the street with an entrance door between them. One larger room faced the back, and usually served as a combination kitchen and living room. This same house form could be made to accommodate four rooms, with the back room divided to form a dining room. In another common building form, the three-room duplex, rooms were arranged three deep, from front to back, with no entranceway or hall. Interior bathrooms were uncommon, regardless of housing type, even in 1910. Several tenants normally shared the sanitary facilities, which were usually grouped in the backyard. Generally speaking, houses occupied by African Americans were smaller (often two to three rooms) and of lower grade than those occupied by whites, even when the residents held similar positions and salaries. Thus, Atlanta's landscape resembled Boston's "weave of small patterns" in that the Gate City's housing size, form, and architecture varied across the city and often within individual blocks.[58]

Two blocks illustrate how the accumulative building process resulted in a variegated built environment in turn-of-the-century Atlanta. The west Atlanta block near Atlanta University bounded by Low (later renamed Electric Avenue), Rhodes Street, Carter Street, and Davis Street (see fig. 1.1) reveals the wide variety of building footprints, setbacks, and house sizes in neighborhoods within the one-mile radius from Atlanta's city center in 1899. The homes on Low show the common cost-saving practice of erecting several homes using the same plan. Built in shotgun style (rooms aligned front to back), the five homes on the block (including the store on the corner of Carter and Low) were identical, as were the duplexes at 41 and 43 Carter. The larger homes on Rhodes and Carter show a variation in style and form, and the houses have irregular setbacks and side yards. Only the homes on Carter (to Low) enjoyed water service. By 1911, the city had installed water service on Rhodes and on Low (Electric Avenue) north of Carter.[59]

The block on the border between the Summerhill and Mechanicsville neighborhoods and defined by Rawson, Martin, Clarke, and Fraser Streets (see fig. 1.2) is another example of housing variation within a single block. The frame, shingle-roof homes from 16 to 36 Rawson were built in pairs of identical design. Each measured about 180 square feet. Front porches ran the length of each unit, with the exception of 24 and 28 Rawson. In the latter two cases, either the

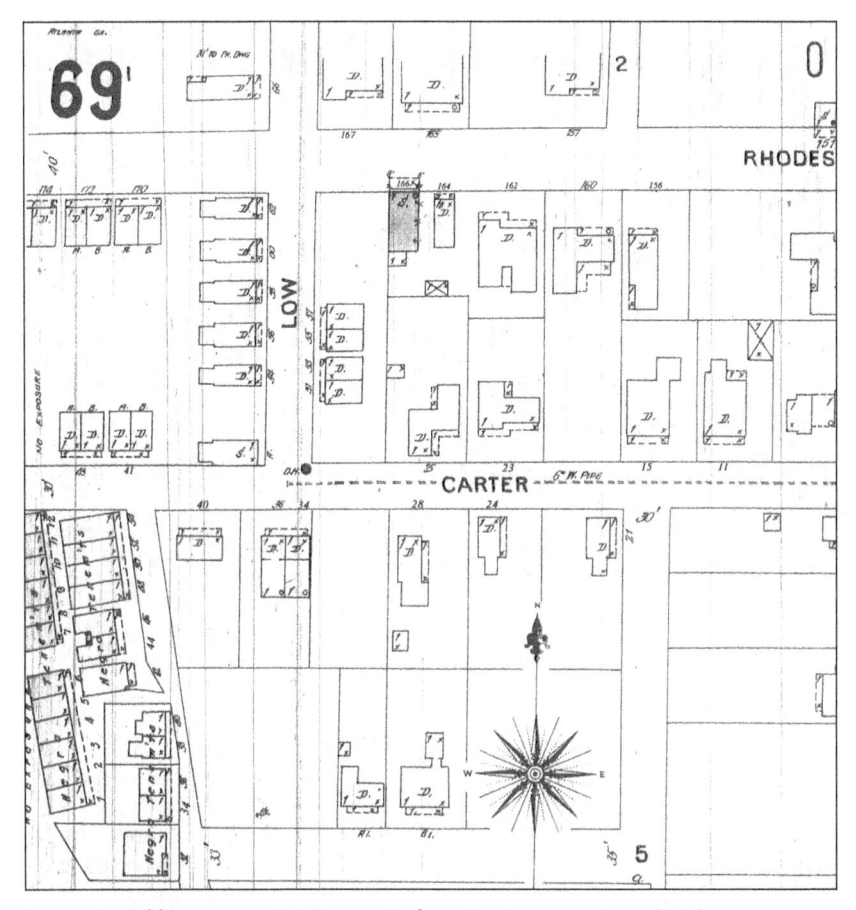

Figure 1.1. Building variety, 1899. Source: Sanborn Fire Insurance Maps (1899).

28 Chapter One

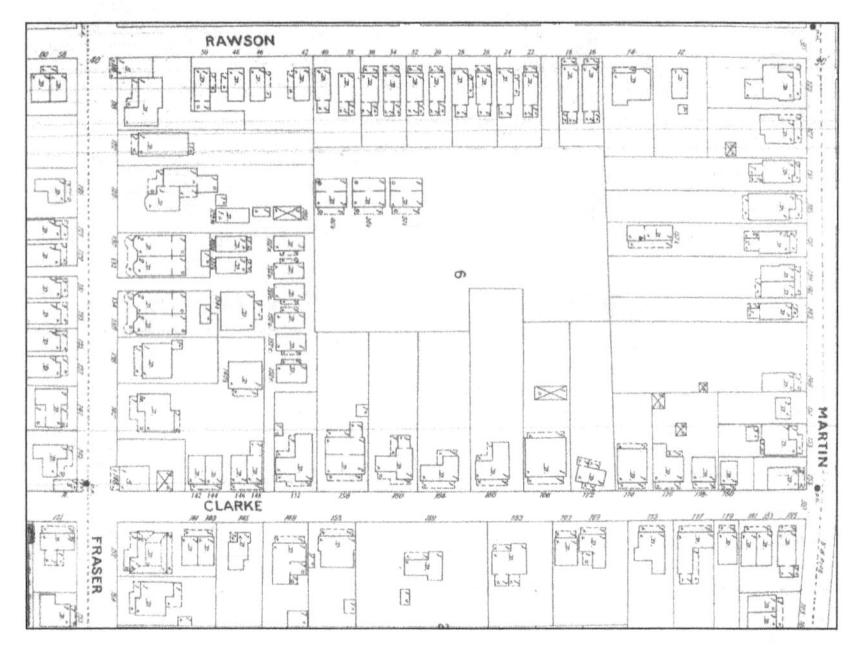

Figure 1.2. Martin, Clarke, Fraser, and Rawson Streets, 1899. Source: Sanborn Fire Insurance Maps (1899).

homes sat perpendicular to the street, or the porches ran along the side of the home. Most houses had ten-foot setbacks, and about eight feet separated each unit. In contrast, the homes along Clarke Street varied in size and design. Two sets of duplexes occupied 142 to 148 Clarke, but the eight units directly east of the duplexes differed in footprint, setback, and size. Sixteen alley units were tucked behind homes on the west end of the block. The alley units varied from 450 to 1,200 square feet, and most had porches. Pairs of alley homes behind 152 Clarke Street faced each other, with about five feet separating each porch front. Tenants likely reached their homes via ten-foot alleys that ran between 148 and 152 Clarke Street and 132 and 134 Fraser Street. Generally speaking, most homes in these two neighborhoods were small and of frame construction, but sizes, form, and setbacks varied. Residences could be found in alleys, and quite a few residents lacked water and sewage service. All were located within one mile of the city center and near a variety of employers.[60]

Though completed more slowly, neighborhoods in Atlanta's inner suburbs (that is, outside the 2-mile radius in 1905) differed little in physical development pattern from core city neighborhoods. Like homes in the central city, most were built as rental investments and for workers in suburban railroad shops and fertilizer plants. The city's edge developments, large and small, maintained the traditional rectilinear structure and lot sizes of the core city, but often adjoined acres of undeveloped property. Located at the city's 2-mile radius, the neighborhood that became known as Pittsburgh, for example, was subdivided well ahead of most of the southwest section, and the neighborhood's rectilinear streets and consistent lot sizes contrasted sharply with the undeveloped plats on the abutting sides. Lakewood Heights, Thomasville, and South Atlanta, all near the city's 2 ½-mile mile radius, developed similarly. South Atlanta was subdivided in the 1880s, and investors and private owners added housing throughout the next three decades.[61]

In sum, in the late 1800s and early 1900s, Atlanta's rental-housing owners and developers paid little mind to "neighborhood character," landscape planning, and other ideas that emerged in the suburban home movement. Instead, they focused on potential gains from smaller building ventures. Large, single-class, single-race neighborhoods were the exception rather than the rule in Atlanta from 1890 to 1905. Indeed, the nature of property development in Atlanta hampered such building. A street length of fifteen houses might be held by nine different investors who had purchased the lots over a period of five or more years. Investors were unlikely to have consulted one another on any element of the property. Instead, owners let the area market dictate the race or class of the person renting. As a result, most neighborhoods within the city limits housed workers and white-collar occupants, blacks and whites, though some variation existed.[62]

A block sample study across Atlanta for the years 1891 and 1899 reveals that blue-collar workers could be found throughout the city in nearly every neighborhood (see figs. 1.3 and 1.4 and table A2). In 1891, thirty-nine of forty blocks housed working-class households, and in 1899, forty-seven of fifty blocks housed workers. With the exception of the Fulton Bag and Cotton Mill employees, who tended to live in company housing near the mill, and Southern Railway employees, who congregated at the southern edge of the city in new housing erected near the shops, most employees of large firms lived throughout the city. Workers, generally speaking, did reside within one mile of their employers. This was not a difficult achievement; in 1899, the city stretched a mere three miles across. In short, workers of any single firm almost never made up whole street lengths or blocks, much less entire districts. Similarly, doctors, large-business directors, and other high white-collar professionals could be found throughout Atlanta, suggesting that perhaps managers, business owners, doctors, and other white-collar professionals chose proximity to work or availability of housing over class identification in this period.[63]

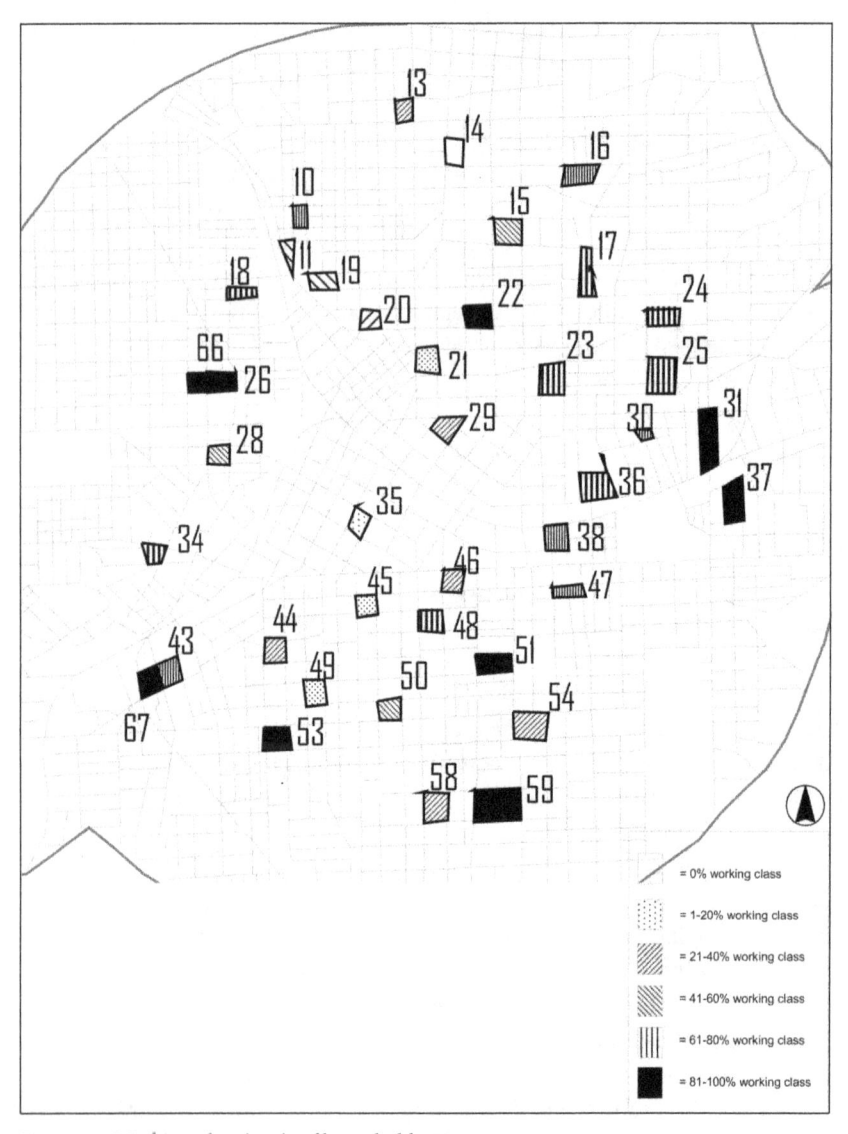

Figure 1.3. Working-class heads of household, 1891.

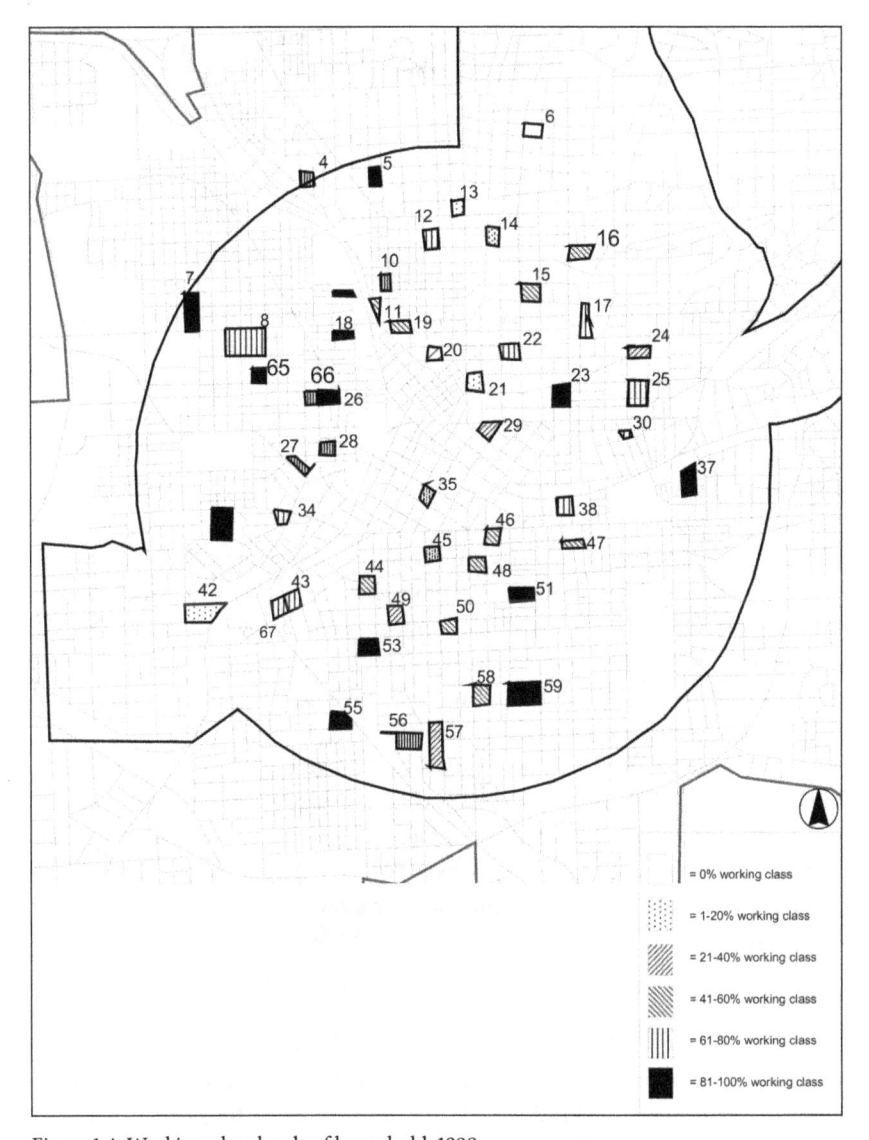

Figure 1.4. Working-class heads of household, 1899.

Indeed, most of Atlanta's workers had occupations that would serve them well in any section of the city, and thus they were not limited to living in a particular part of town. Besides washerwomen, the most common occupations in the 1899 data—laborer, carpenter, and cook—were jobs available from many different types of employers and in every section of the city. Given the tight housing market that followed the depression in the 1890s, it is possible that workers found employment and housing where available and simply suffered the resulting commute. Despite its proximity to the Atlanta Compress and the Southern Spring Bed manufactory, for example, the block between Hill and Yonge Streets, Hunter Street, and the Georgia Railroad tracks housed few workers claiming those companies as employers. Rather, about 40 percent of that block's heads of household worked at Georgia Railroad and Southern Railway. Other block residents worked as building contractors, policemen, postal carriers, and clerks.[64]

The workers who did tend to congregate clustered by occupation rather than by place of employment—most significantly, washerwomen. In fact, washerwomen, most of whom were black, comprised the largest occupational category for the 1899 block sample. Working as independent contractors, washerwomen gathered the clothes, towels, and linens of various Atlanta families one day a week, washed and dried them in their own homes and yards, and returned the laundry on another established day. Not surprisingly, given that white Atlantans throughout the city used such services, washerwomen lived in most neighborhoods. Washerwomen did cluster together residentially, largely as a result of the city's built environment, rental-housing development patterns, and racialized housing practices. Spans of so-called Negro shanties and Negro tenements could be found on numerous side streets and at the edges of more expensive property in all areas.[65]

Racing the Landscape

Atlanta's housing practices were *raced* more than *classed* in the late 1800s. In practice, owners assigned individual homes to blacks or to whites. That is to say, investors decided whether they would rent their property to blacks or whites. Contemporary advertisements lay bare such racial assignments. E. H. Robert advertised, "For Sale By Owner—Good negro-renting property . . . above are always rented."[66] Property ads and plats illustrate both the racializing of individual properties and the proximity of black- and white-occupied housing. Claude Norris advertised, "I have one double house and three Negro houses on a lot 50 x 190, that is in the best of locations. The double house is rented to white people at $30 per month and the negro houses are rented for $39.60 per month [for all three]."[67] Real-estate developer Edwin Ansley, for example, announced, "We have twelve negro houses, eight of them built less than one year ago . . . on lot 500 x 90, renting for $720 per year, which we can sell for $5000."[68] Similarly, Faver and Black advertised, "$6,500 buys big lot of negro houses on Houston."[69] The *Atlanta Journal* reported in 1911 that "the demand for negro investment property was shown in the sale by A. L. Dallas of fourteen vacant lots and nine four-room houses on Lee, Henry and Culver street. These brought a total of $13,955."[70] The Adair brothers commended, "Here is a nice little investment for some one. No. 53 Kennesaw Alley (rear of 244 W. Fair St.), a 3-room house renting for $4 a month, price $400. . . . The lot is 50x96, located in good negro renting section."[71] George Ware advertised a $2,200 house as "Negro property renting for $30 per month, in the midst of 'negro heaven.'"[72] Edwin Ansley commented that one of his rental properties was "located in the heart of the best negro renting section of Atlanta and [brought] in annual rental of $206."[73]

Transfer of housing between different races also operated under particular constraints. Blacks could move into housing formerly occupied by whites, but it was unusual for whites to move into homes where blacks had lived. A United Kingdom Board of Trade study of working conditions throughout the world reported that Atlanta property owners were reluctant to allow occupancy to change from white to black, as "such a change [was] final and irretrievable, and as a rule [took] place only in the case of property which for some reason or other [was] deteriorating and [could not] continue in the hands of the whites."[74] Thus, once occupied by blacks, homes generally remained occupied by blacks. No explanation could be found for this particular practice, but it is possible that whites viewed housing much as they did clothing and schoolbooks—as highly personal items that came in close contact with the "black body." Once these objects had been handled or worn by blacks, whites considered them "unclean" and potential transmitters of disease. Thus, as a rule, whites stigmatized houses that were or had been occupied by blacks. Consequently, an investor's decision to rent property to blacks was no small matter, as it affected the future use of that property in a way that white occupancy did not.

While phrasings in advertisements and on plat maps such as "negro renting section" and "negro heaven" suggest a preponderance of black-dominated neighborhoods, the U.K. Board of Trade report found that "there [were] no large districts occupied by coloured people" in Atlanta. The report went on to explain, "Portions of certain streets and clusters of houses here and there can be pointed to as accommodating only coloured occupants, but in no case would it be necessary to traverse more than a few yards in order to come again to the dwellings of the other race."[75] City block sampling confirms that blacks found housing throughout the city and in most neighborhoods, and that so-called Negro sections were actually small concentrations of black-occupied housing. In 1891, for example, blacks lived on 36 of the 39 study blocks returning racial data, and 35 of 52 blocks in 1899 (see table A3). Whites occupied 38 of 39 study blocks in 1891 and 49 of 52 blocks in 1899. Thus, whites and blacks could be found in all quadrants of the city in 1891 and 1899 and on the majority of blocks (see figs. 1.5 and 1.6). That being said, racial segregation at the block level was emerging by 1899. In 1891, only 1 study block was 100 percent black, and only 6 of the 39 blocks were disproportionately (that is, greater than 65 percent) black. By 1899, however, 10 of 52 study blocks were disproportionately black. From 1891 to 1899, the percentage of blocks that were disproportionately white rose from 38 percent to 52 percent—and of the 52 study blocks, 17 were 100 percent white.[76] By 1899, then, whites had begun to isolate themselves from black families, moving into blocks occupied only by other whites. Viewed another way, black families occupied homes on 35 of 52 study blocks in 1899—67 percent of the study blocks.[77]

In the late 1800s and early 1900s, then, prior to segregation ordinances and absent restrictive covenants, multiblock neighborhoods or even single blocks were rarely *wholly* assigned to blacks; 19 percent of the 1899 study blocks are disproportionately black, and only three were 100 percent black. Rather, individual houses and apartments were racialized at the discretion of the owners, and that practice dictated the city's racial geography. This practice produced concentrations or enclaves of blacks and whites, and over time many of these spaces came to be known popularly as "black neighborhoods" or "white neighborhoods." To be sure, investors considered the proximity of other races when deciding where to invest, but there were apparently no hard-and-fast rules about "appropriate" distances between white and black housing. This practice of individual property allocation resulted in the close proximity of whites and blacks throughout the city, a phenomenon that was perceived more negatively by whites as particular neighborhoods became more developed and populated.

Housing proximity did not equate to housing equality. Whites relegated most blacks to small homes, often on property lacking water and sewer service and many times "in the rear" of other properties along with the outhouses. To some degree, the dearth of services reflects African Americans' low pay and inability to pay the market rents for safe and healthy facilities. Absent building codes, white landlords could and often did exploit blacks for higher profit without fear of repercussion. At the same time, whites accused blacks of poor housing

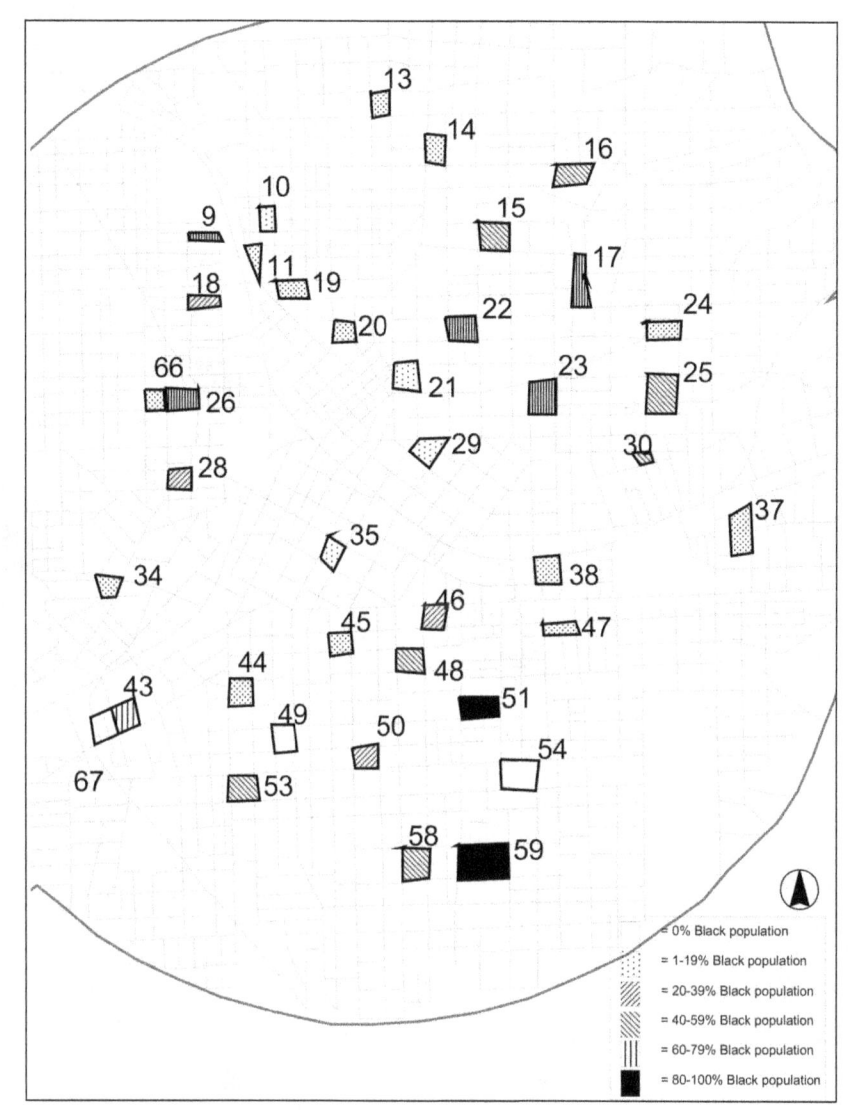

Figure 1.5. Black heads of household, 1891.

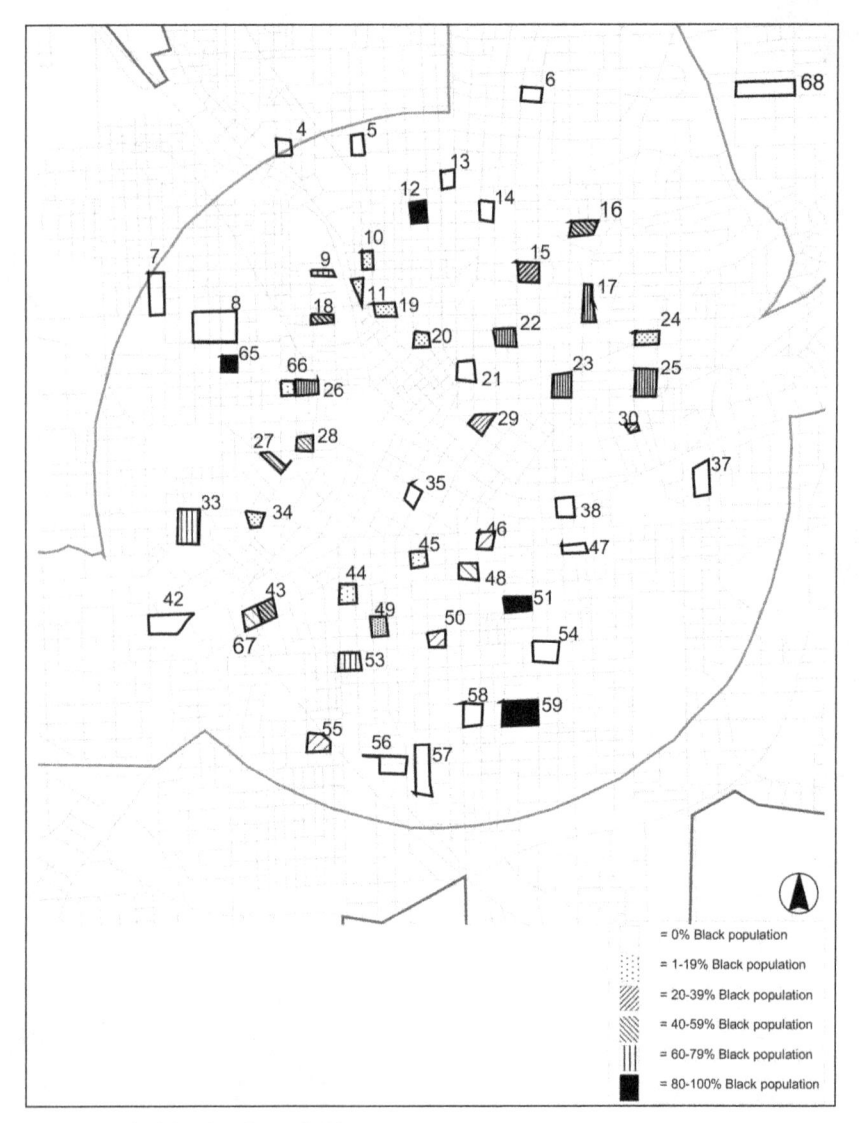

Figure 1.6. Black heads of household, 1899.

practices while withholding services or paying wages sufficient to live in a manner consistent with "white" housing expectations.

The Summerhill neighborhood block defined by Richardson, Fulton, Martin, and Connolly Streets reveals the fabric of one of the 1899 study's all-black blocks (see fig. 1.7). The footprint of the homes varied across the block, as did setbacks, suggesting that homes had accumulated in the area over time and likely had been erected by different builders. Generally speaking, the houses were small; one of the duplex units at 413 Richardson measured 256 square feet. The street's largest home, 427 Richardson, measured about 1,300 square feet. Richardson and Martin Streets both had water service. Although the neighborhood homes varied in size and form, they were uniformly small. Overall, the positioning of the small homes toward the block fronts opened up backyard space into what could have served as space for washing, children's games, or storage. Residents consisted mostly of washerwomen, including Mary Oglesby, who paid a mortgage on her home at 415 Richardson. Oglesby had two other couples boarding with her, washerwomen and laborers. Jerry Davis, who owned 429 Richardson, worked as a laborer and supported his family of four. A family of three, supported by washerwoman Hallie Baxter, boarded with Davis. Annie Hardaway, who lived next door at 417 Richardson, also paid a mortgage on her home with a washerwoman's salary and supported her school-age son. Washerwomen also owned the homes at 437 and 440 Richardson. Plasterers and draymen also occupied homes along Richardson. Many families had children in school, likely at the Summerhill School at the corner of Richardson and Martin. Overall, most residents rented their homes, which were primarily frame, one-story structures with deep backyards. Little differentiated tenants from owners; occupations and family sizes were similar. Families ranged in size from two to six, and some families with mortgages took in boarders, but others did not. Generally speaking, most of the block's residents held low-wage jobs, though clearly some families were able to initially finance and then meet mortgage obligations, and most adults were currently employed.[78]

The southwest Atlanta block described earlier (see fig. 1.1) illustrates how race, class, and material environment varied over a small, multiblock area. In 1899, the most substantial homes shown, those on Carter and Rhodes Streets, were occupied by a diverse group—low-white-collar, skilled, semiskilled, and unskilled workers. A white widow, Mrs. E. H. Watts, lived at 11 Carter, and Louis Barber, a white car inspector for Central of Georgia Railway, occupied both 15 and 23 Carter. Barber may have lived in one house and rented out the other. James Harris, a white watchman for the Western and Atlantic, occupied the last home on the block. Immediately across the street, in smaller homes, lived two

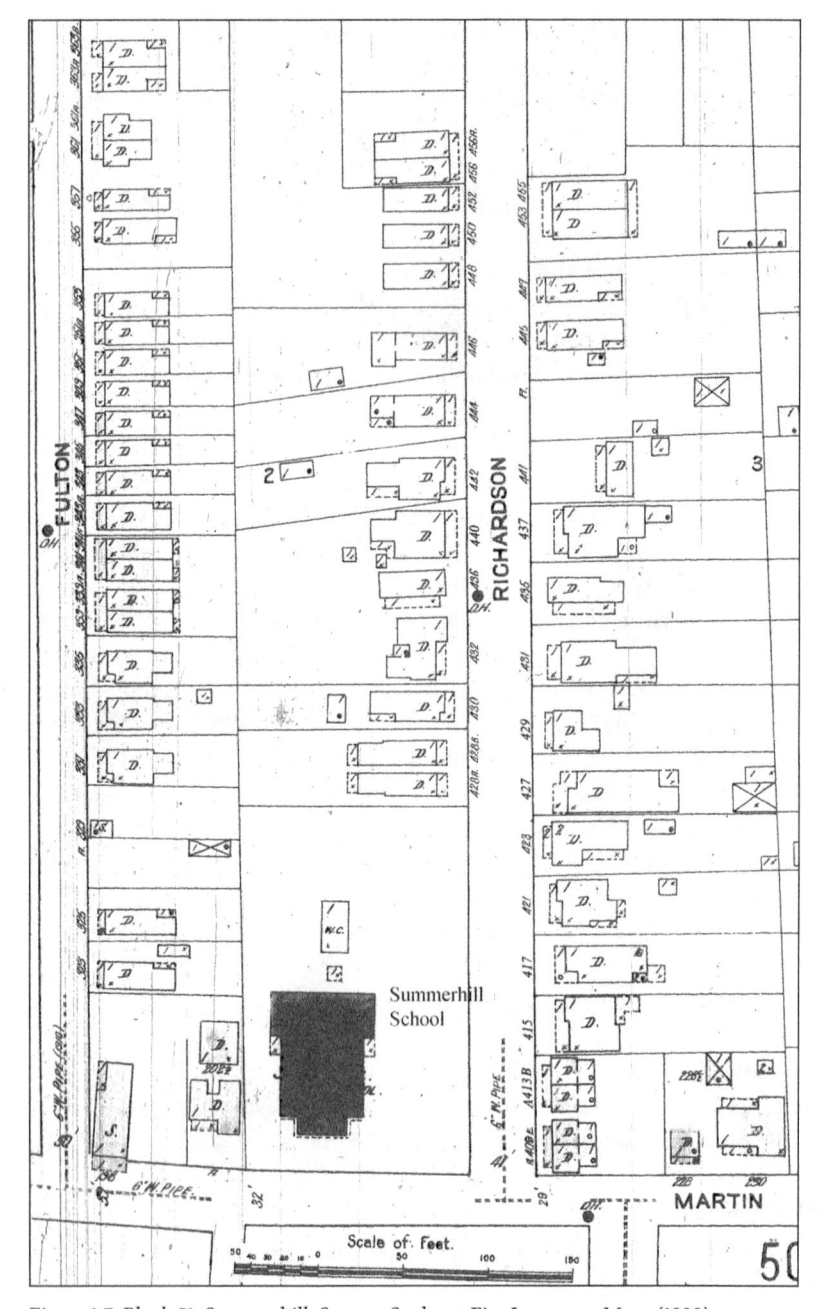

Figure 1.7. Block 51, Summerhill. Source: Sanborn Fire Insurance Maps (1899).

black skilled workers. Leroy Tonsell, a carpenter, lived at 24 Carter, and Cosby Jones, who worked at Central of Georgia, occupied 28 Carter. Gilbert Lewis, an unskilled black worker, and black whitewasher George Eason lived in the duplex at 34 and 40 Carter. Around the corner, on Low, unskilled black workers (including washerwomen, laborers, and a mill worker) dominated the shotgun houses and duplexes. Laundress Laurie Stalworth lived in 44 Low, and laundress Anna Dougherty and her five children lived at 34 Low. Rhodes Street, in contrast to Carter Street, was all white. Charles Errick, of Costan and Errick, occupied 156 Rhodes, and his neighbor William Ray worked as a brakeman for Western and Atlantic. Shoemaker Lee Hannah resided in and may have worked from 164 Rhodes. Carpenter Fred Patrick lived there as well, and may have been boarding with his employer, shoemaker Hannah. Across the street lived John Hodo, a commissioner, and O. C. Fisher, a postal carrier. Next door to Hodo, at 167 Rhodes, resided Pinkney Smith, who worked for Winship Manufacturing. The block's residents may have shopped at Sam Sullivan's grocery, located nearby at 166 Rhodes. Sullivan had a short walk back to his home at 162 Rhodes. The so-called Negro tenements on Low, shown to the southwest, were dominated by black washerwomen and unskilled laborers. Thus, Atlanta proved heterogeneous not only when viewed citywide but often even at the block and neighborhood level.[79]

What explains Atlanta's seeming racial heterogeneity at a time of spreading jim crow laws and visceral, racist political rhetoric? To some degree, social protocols governed interactions between whites and blacks, imposing social distance that made physical distance unnecessary. Whites expected blacks to actively remove themselves from spaces that whites occupied, be they sidewalks or store counters. In other cases, blacks were assigned place or service use on particular days and times so that whites could control physical and social distances. For example, whites often assigned blacks particular trade days in southern towns; on other days blacks were prevented from converging on county seats. Though practices varied from place to place, whites often relegated blacks to particular sections of mixed-race churches (one side, the back, or the balcony), movie theaters, and restaurants. In doing so, whites consistently enacted their power by controlling access to particular places. White acts of power were capricious and therefore more terrifying; almost none of these spaces had firm demarcations, and therefore rules could be imposed or changed at individual (white) will. Thus, the proper physical (and social) distances were constructed and reconstructed continually.

Atlanta entered the twentieth century with few established residential patterns, a product of an industrializing southern city with little regulation and much speculation. Because development was dominated by a shifting rental-housing market targeting a working-class city, homes often lacked services and amenities and were more functional than elegant. The haphazard residential patterns operated to whites' satisfaction for some time. In the late 1800s, however, the status quo faced challenges—not just by the disorder that accompanied rapid urban growth and industrialization, but by generations of upwardly mobile blacks unwilling to accept artificial political and economic ceilings imposed by white tradition and "culture." White residents and city leaders were forced to confront the racial tensions that marked the South of this period while simultaneously boosting their city regionally and nationally. These regional and national forces would combine to alter Atlanta's residential landscape—and its *thinking* about residential landscapes—in the second and third decades of the twentieth century.

CHAPTER TWO

Atlanta, Park-Neighborhoods, and the New Urban Aesthetic, 1880 to 1917

"The improvement of cities is a matter of vital concern," Walter G. Cooper, the secretary to Atlanta's chamber of commerce wrote in *South Atlantic Quarterly* in 1908.[1] Cooper went on to trace the origins of the aesthetic movements that were redrawing and reshaping cities throughout the world. He described the impact of Daniel Burnham's White City at the 1893 World's Columbian Exposition in Chicago and explained the international origins of contemporary city plans. He was knowledgeable regarding building-height restrictions, a practice only just gaining a following within the United States, and restrictive covenants, limits on property use that were spreading through the newest and most fashionable neighborhoods. Cooper's rhetoric celebrated balance, order, and thoughtful composition of public *and* private space. He concluded, "The old principle of law that a man has no right to do that which will injure his neighbor, in its modern application, is carried into the realm of aesthetics, and anything that grates upon the ear or offends the eye or the nose is held to be an injury."[2] Turning to Atlanta, Cooper highlighted the city's plans for parkways and parks, use of deed restrictions, and adoption of radial and gridiron street layouts, implicitly arguing that the South's Gate City could hold its own in this new movement. As if confirming this assertion, three years later Harvey Johnson explained to readers of *American City* that, after a series of infrastructure expansions, city leaders were mounting plans for parks and a civic center.[3]

These and other articles demonstrate Atlanta leaders' awareness of and support for urban trends taking hold throughout the United States and world. Indeed, the articles reveal how common city boosterism—situated in an era of urban competition and communication expansion—helped transmit aesthetic knowledge, taste cultures, and city planning know-how. In the early 1900s, Atlanta's white civic elite assessed how their city compared with not just the region's Annistons and Augustas but with the nation's Cincinnatis and Chicagos. What they found was a haphazard array of business and industry, houses, alleys, and vacant lots.

To Johnson, Cooper, and other elites, the modern American city possessed a particular aesthetic and form, and this ideal encompassed public and private space, city centers and neighborhoods. To civic elites, the modern city should emanate from a city center—a monument, a neatly organized square, or a pleasant, manicured park. The city's different functions would be organized to run smoothly together—industrial sections with transportation networks, business centers with factories. Transportation networks would connect workers with their factory jobs, businessmen with their offices and suburban homes. Thus, Atlanta's civic elites insisted on remaking the city. From the late 1800s to 1917, at various times they proposed a chain of parks, a "driveway" featuring the area's historic battlefields, and a civic plaza that would hide the city's railroad gulch.

The park-neighborhood movement overlapped Atlanta's quest for the modern city and echoed many of its themes, including artful design, planning, rational organization, and status. Enamored with the new housing fashion featuring wholly designed communities, natural landscapes, aesthetic control, and like-minded neighbors, some civic elites simply relocated to the city's new exclusive subdivisions. Others sought to bring park-neighborhood sensibilities into older, established sections of the city. In the process of refining their ideas about the proper city and the respectable neighborhood, elites negotiated new taste cultures, cultivated a new urban vocabulary, and disseminated practices that would divide spaces and people in the name of harmony and refinement.[4] But privatized park-neighborhoods were more than an ideal environment for the cultivation of self and family as posited by some mid-nineteenth-century promoters; they were a commodity to be sold, a status marker to be enacted, and an instrument to effect power.

Private Interests and the Park-Neighborhood Aesthetic

As historian Mary Corbin Sies has observed, between 1877 and 1917, developers and residents of elite suburban enclaves across the United States honed and articulated a particular residential landscape ideal. That landscape—single-family homes situated in spacious yards, amid homes and families of similar status and outlook—captured the popular imagination in cities across the United States. Designers intended planned suburban communities both to deliver a sense of place and to disseminate a domestic ideal—a space that promoted cultivation of self and family by allowing for private reflection, pleasant social engagement, or vigorous recreational activity.[5]

The elite park-neighborhood aesthetic that became associated with the suburban experience was built on ideals popularized in the United States by

Andrew Jackson Downing and others after the 1840s. Downing's house-pattern books, such as *The Architecture of Country Houses,* offered readers a complete ideal of home, which included house, decoration, and landscaping. As housing historian Gwendolyn Wright explains, the Hudson River landscape designer "foresaw a far-reaching, pastoral landscape, dotted with pleasant houses, varied but always orderly, each one set on its own extensive, well-tended garden."[6] Downing asserted that picturesque scenes expressed morality and domesticity. That is, a specific landscape could embody a particular set of values and practices. Downing's pattern books and essays were widely disseminated in the mid-nineteenth century, and his ideas resonated with an elite populace that sought a unifying American narrative as well as a material expression of financial success and status.[7]

Lawns and gardens were essential to this imagery. As historian Virginia Scott Jenkins notes, beginning in the mid-1800s, the nascent middle class "deliberately reshaped the landscape" by buffering single-family homes with yards. Golf clubs and park green space further cultivated an appreciation for grasses and lawns. Garden clubs simultaneously gave women of means and leisure time a place to socialize, share particular taste cultures, and develop new domestic knowledge and skills. Thus, a combination of influences moved elite housing preferences from a narrow focus on the single-family home to a tableau encompassing a single-family home with a pristine yard, a managed landscape, and defined boundaries.[8]

Several planned residential developments gave shape to these principles in the mid-nineteenth century. Alexander Jackson Davis's Llewellyn Park, New Jersey, combined the picturesque landscape with domestic ideals and emphasized curvilinear streets, topographically conscious lot design, periodic green spaces, and dramatic views. Like the domestic environment idealized by Downing and others, such neighborhoods incorporated public and private spaces so as to promote reflection and cultivation of self. Similarly, Frederick Law Olmsted's Riverside subdivision, launched in Illinois in 1868, intended to provide "tasteful" residences with the benefit of natural landscapes without compromising access to the city. What Riverside lacked in natural environment, Olmsted provided, planting over 35,000 trees and 45,000 shrubs on the 1,600-acre tract. Here, Olmsted attempted to produce a park landscape by ensuring that lawns ran continuously without walls. As Olmsted himself described it, Riverside was intended as a place of "pleasant openings and outlooks, with suggestions of refined domestic life." Not surprisingly, such trappings came at a cost, and Llewellyn, Riverside, and other highly landscaped, private park-neighborhoods housed few beyond the wealthy.[9]

After the Civil War, Atlanta's elites, too, built distinguished homes situated in neat and tended landscapes along Peachtree Street north, as well as along Jackson Hill just east of downtown. While Peachtree Street became identified locally with the city's commercial-civic elites and eventually enjoyed easy access to downtown by carriage or streetcar, the area lacked the deliberate planning that marked exclusive park-neighborhood communities. But even if Atlantans did not actively participate in the earliest phases of elite subdivision building (and few cities did), Atlanta's elite made careful observations of park-neighborhood building around the country, and they carried on extensive conversations with subdivision designers as the city recovered from war in the 1870s and 1880s.

New South Neighborhoods

Inspired by elite suburban developments elsewhere, a handful of local professionals envisioned new park-neighborhoods for Atlanta, often coupled with their transportation networks and companies. Real-estate innovator George Adair, entrepreneur and city booster Hannibal Kimball, and engineer and investor Richard Peters partnered to establish Peters Park just northwest of downtown in the early 1880s. George Adair explained that he had been inspired by "his visits north" and impressed by the "enormous profits" yielded by suburbs in western cities. Kimball identified Chicago's planned Pullman community as his inspiration when the three assembled just over 180 acres near Peachtree Street and North Avenue in 1884. Adair's description of the project revealed his knowledge of neighborhood-planning trends throughout the country. He explained that they would build Peters Park into a "beautiful suburb," by which he meant "a large tract of land improved by one company, under one control, so that every lick struck, and every clod of dirt moved, and every shrub planted, has its relation to the whole."[10] In Adair's view, and as many subdivision developers believed, a neighborhood should be planned in totality. As to a city, comprehensive planning could be applied to a neighborhood.[11]

The Peters Park Improvement Company imagined a 180-acre subdivision directed at the city's elite that would work directly with a streetcar line owned by two of the three partners. Peters and Adair had spent the previous few years building the Atlanta Street Railway Company, which supplied easy transportation to the pair's real-estate investments. The Peachtree Street line already helped pull elites north, and that or the Marietta line could be used by residents of the new Peters Park. In reality, however, the lines were not as convenient to the neighborhood as the Peachtree line was to Peachtree Street homes, or as other lines were to well-established (if less formally designed) neighborhoods.

Consequently, Atlanta's elite declined to purchase many lots, despite the attractive plans for winding roads, a lake, and a planted boulevard.[12]

A few years later, civil engineer Joel Hurt also drew inspiration from planned communities in the Northeast and the Midwest when he planned Inman Park, an exclusive community just east of downtown. Having traveled frequently to cities with active suburban development and consulted leading architects such as Daniel Burnham and John Wellborn Root (Root later prepared the plans for Atlanta's Equitable Building), Hurt set out to build a park-neighborhood intended exclusively for Atlanta's white elite.[13]

Hurt's admiration for Frederick Law Olmsted's concepts, and his adaptation of them, is evident in the developer's 1889 plans for Inman Park. Following Olmsted's suburban-design principals, Hurt incorporated winding streets, open spaces, pleasant outlooks, parks, and playgrounds. To Olmsted, such features reflected a "refined domestic life."[14] Well-designed suburban communities, Olmsted asserted, provided relief from the city, fostered family life, and encouraged private reflection. Hurt may have admired Olmsted's suburban products, but Hurt's changes to Inman Park's original design suggest that the investor was more interested in profit than in Olmsted's environmental idealism.

Designing the community with local landscaper Joseph Forsyth Johnson, Hurt laid out curvilinear, tree-lined streets and incorporated green spaces and terraces that set the development apart from the light industrial landscape and street grids just west of the neighborhood's entrance. A man-made lake situated within a five-acre park was home to goldfish, and other planned green spaces such as Springvale Park added variety to the landscape. Hurt's initial plan included rows of homes within a narrow price range, consistent house setbacks, uniform grading, consistently spaced trees, and lot sizes starting at one-half acre.[15]

Easy access to the city was critical to the subdivision's success, and Hurt used his ties to bankers, financiers, and politicians to secure needed infrastructure improvements. Hurt's East Atlanta Land Company agreed to purchase the land needed to widen and extend Foster Street and build a bridge necessary to traverse the Richmond and Danville Railroad. The company agreed to cover any expenses over twenty thousand dollars that the city spent completing the road linking Inman Park to downtown. The city, in turn, condemned thirty properties and demolished ninety-four buildings, including many workers' homes, to install a streetcar line to the property. When finished, residents and visitors took the electrified cars to the new suburb for five cents.[16]

Hurt intended Inman Park for Atlanta's privileged whites, and ads for the development often pointed to the social status of new residents. Pitched to elites who sought to live among neighbors of similar position, these ads referred to future residents as "gentlemen" and asserted that "first-class neighbors of culture, refinement, and means [were] a certainty."[17] Ads referencing residents' social standing appeared early in the life cycle of Atlanta's exclusive suburban development and suggest that Hurt and the other investors may have identified an unmet demand for such enclaves. That is, civic elites previously had lived in pockets throughout the city, never far from skilled workers, clerks, and manual laborers. In building for and appealing to "gentlemen" and people of "culture" and "refinement," the East Atlanta Land Company may have been responding to Hurt's impression that a market existed for larger communities home only to members of the city's privileged class. On the other hand, Hurt may have hoped to create demand for the kind of homogeneous, elite-oriented neighborhoods that were emerging in other cities.

Whether a market for elite-concentrated living preceded or followed the building of Inman Park, the movement of many of Atlanta's civic professionals into Inman Park indicates that many of that group did opt to reside together in an exclusive park-neighborhood once the opportunity became available. Although many would quickly move on to other, even more prestigious areas, Inman Park initially housed two former state governors, the president of Emory University, Coca-Cola founder Asa Candler, and owners of many large business houses. By 1905, 16 percent of the subdivision's residents were listed in Atlanta's *Social Register*, indicating residents' high status in local society.[18]

Despite its elite presence, streetcar access, and fashionable amenities, Hurt's property paled in comparison to Olmsted's Riverside. The deed-protected Chicago suburb, after all, encompassed 1,600 acres, straddled a river, and incorporated 134 acres of parks. In contrast, Inman Park counted a mere 189 acres, with parks and green space making up less than 4 acres. Moreover, Inman Park's roads may have "gently curved," but they failed to wind and lose the resident in the natural landscape the way larger developments could. Historian Rick Beard concludes that Inman Park's landscaping, "while not unattractive, lacked any real imagination," and that only the hundreds of trees that Hurt planted relieved Inman Park from its "rather flat, uninteresting arrangement of residential lots."[19] The subdivision faced more challenges in the 1890s that distanced it further from elite suburban practices. To offset slow sales, the land company sold the Mesa green space for development in 1896. Other open space continued to be subdivided, and speculative home builders altered the landscape by introducing smaller homes of similar design. Such changes to the original design philosophy may have hampered sales as well.[20]

Even if Inman Park did not match Olmsted's Riverside or Davis's Llewellyn Park, the planned suburb stood in stark contrast to Atlanta's central-city

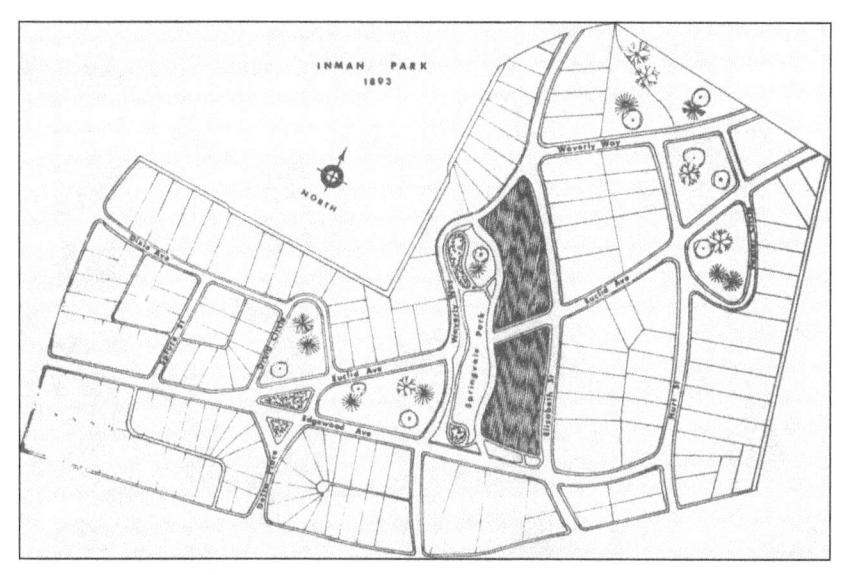

Figure 2.1. Inman Park, 1893. Source: Rick Beard, "Hurt's Deserted Village: Atlanta's Inman Park, 1885–1911," in *Olmsted South: Old South Critic/New South Planner*, edited by Dana F. White and Victor A. Kramer (Westport, Conn.: Greenwood Press, 1979), 187. Copyright © 1979 by Dana F. White and Victor A. Kramer. Reproduced with permission of Greenwood Publishing Group, Inc., Westport, Conn.

neighborhoods, with their collections of "Negro tenements," alley housing, and pockets of working-class homes (see fig. 2.1). The neighborhoods just west of Inman Park, for example, reflected the layout of the bulk of the city (see fig. 2.2). House lots typically measured 4,000 square feet and lined grids of streets. Housing ranged from one-room duplexes and alley dwellings to more substantial bungalows of about 1,200 square feet. House setbacks varied throughout the area, and homes consumed a significant portion of their lots. Alley dwellings filled some rear yards, creating a crowded environment. No green spaces, ravines, playgrounds, or reflective spaces offered respite from "the city" or encouraged residents to cultivate "harmonious associations" as idealized by Olmsted and other suburban designers.[21]

If Inman Park failed to meet Hurt's expectations, and Peters Park was barely realized, early attempts to build these two park-neighborhoods, the movement of some elite families to Inman Park, and the fact that the two projects were risked by a few well-known Atlanta investors suggest that Atlanta elites were beginning to think differently about residential landscapes in the 1880s. To the developers, such projects promised profit from a new or unexploited market.

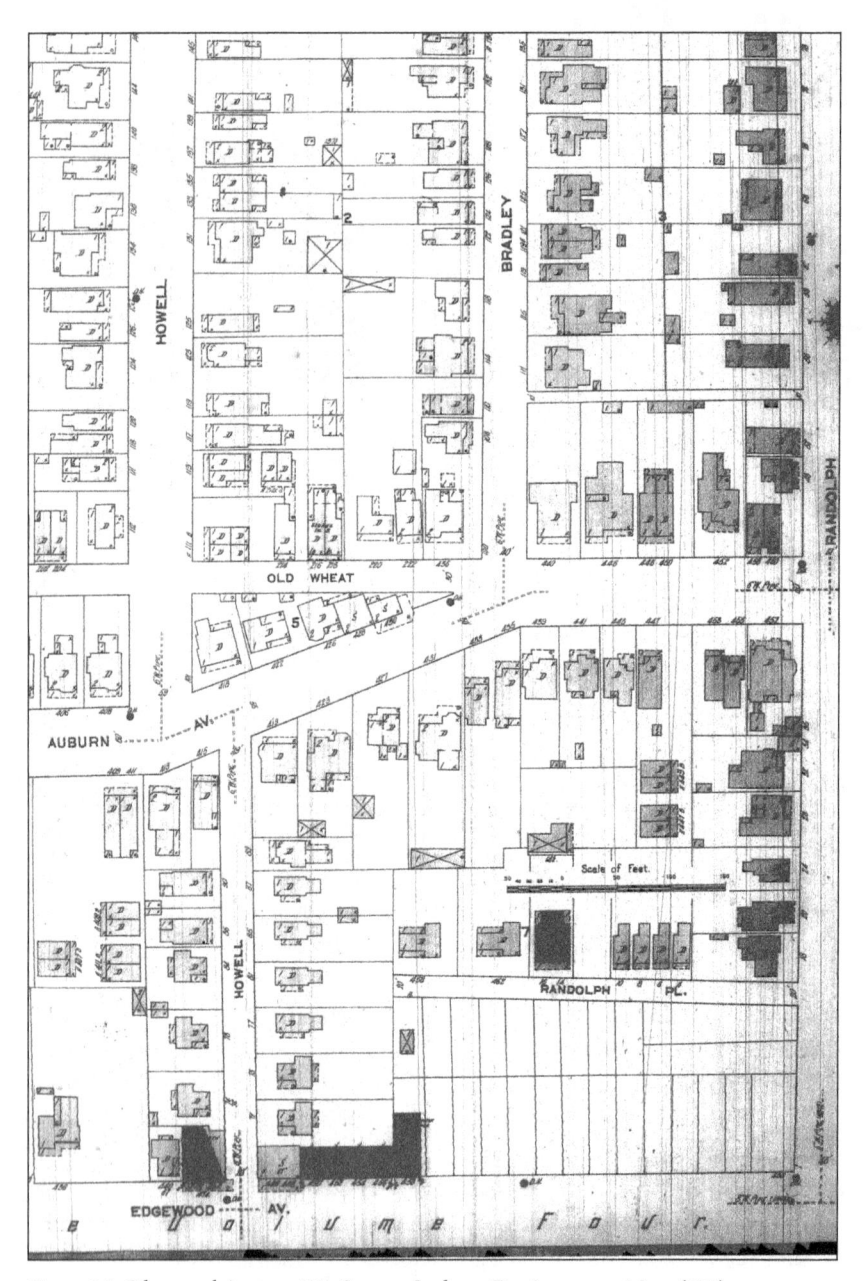

Figure 2.2. Edgewood Avenue, 1911. Source: Sanborn Fire Insurance Maps (1911).

To residents and future residents, they offered more amenities than typically available, a controlled environment, and neighbors much like themselves. At the same time, park-neighborhoods offered a new way of displaying status.

As in other cities, the park-neighborhood landscape reflected the social position of Atlanta's civic elites. By design, exclusive park-neighborhoods limited access to the city's wealthiest citizens. The landscape aesthetic adopted by the park-neighborhood—single-family homes set back within a seemingly natural landscape—thus became associated with the white elite. Literally, the residential landscape became a symbol for a particular group and a way of life.[22]

The visual display of social standing may have felt more urgent to the Gate City's elite in the 1880s. Besides confronting the change wrought by a rapidly industrializing United States, Atlanta's elite faced the formidable task of constructing and performing a New South. As noted in chapter 1, Atlanta's civic professionals simultaneously pushed for industrial and commercial development while they actively touted Atlanta's urban status. Elite residential landscapes imported from the nation's leading cities worked within this framework, allowing elites to communicate and solidify their status locally while also signaling the adoption of urbane cultural practices that situated them in a nationally circulating urban culture.

Phase 2

Despite the shortcomings of Peters Park and Inman Park, exclusive park-neighborhood understandings and practices diffused throughout Atlanta between 1900 and 1917 with the building of Druid Hills and Ansley Park. The two developments focused local attention on elite park-neighborhood aesthetics specifically and suburban subdivision development in general. Other subdivisions that lacked comprehensive planning or the benefits of sophisticated landscape design borrowed the park-neighborhood rhetoric, helping to spread the expectations of park-neighborhood amenities and increase their cultural value.

Encouraged by John Olmsted, Joel Hurt decided to invest in and develop a *more* exclusive development than those currently available in Atlanta. There was more profit in building "highly developed lots or even handsome, thoroughly well built comfortable houses," Olmsted insisted.[23] After various delays, Druid Hills relaunched under the guidance of the Olmsted Brothers firm in 1902, promising all that exclusive northeastern and midwestern suburbs offered—parks, parkways, distinctive architecture, restrictive covenants, and exclusivity.[24]

Olmsted's reference to Hurt's desire for profits highlights the difference in thinking between the Olmsted brothers and their father, and between park-neighborhood developers like Hurt and, for example, Kansas City's J. C. Nichols. Frederick Law Olmsted's writings indicate that he was a firm believer in the significance of the suburban experience to American domestic life. J. C. Nichols, on the other hand, delivered subdivision design that ensured financial stability and profit for investors. He studied which designs and practices resulted in those outcomes and then disseminated his ideas to other planning and real-estate professionals at conferences and in professional journals. The Olmsted brothers viewed city planning as a process and suburban design as a commodity with a market. They, too, worked professionally at subdivision design, studying and corresponding with other professionals on the subject. Compared to their father, however, the Olmsted brothers spent less time espousing the social benefits of park-neighborhood environments. Correspondence between Hurt and the Olmsteds' firm suggests that the Olmsted brothers were always keenly aware of the elite market and the practices that moved property and maintained investment value. Finally, to Hurt, park-neighborhoods were an investment and an investment only. He cared little for their social benefit, changed professional designs at will, and cut corners when he felt it necessary (and sometimes against professional advice). Suburban development may have had some social value, as Olmsted Sr. posited, but to the Olmsted brothers it was a business. To Hurt, it was speculation.[25]

Druid Hills' ample 1,400 acres dwarfed Peters Park and Inman Park and allowed the Olmsteds to incorporate more of the features identified with exclusive subdivisions in other regions, including extensive green spaces, recreational parks, country clubs, and elegant drives. Ponce de Leon Avenue linked Atlanta and the new subdivision on the city's northeast side and served as a dramatic entry point into the new park-neighborhood. Heading east past Moreland Avenue, the road broke into a wide "double parkway," and chains of parks and rolling green space divided the road as it wound through the subdivision. As historian Elizabeth Lyon explains, the Olmsteds designed Druid Hills to be a "natural and uncluttered space," a thoroughly planned landscape intended to hide its very design.[26] But the Olmsteds avoided having the area appear *too* natural, an aesthetic buyers reportedly devalued. In 1902, Olmsted recommended that Hurt and Ruff "radically alter" the parkway approach, as purchasers were unwilling to pay "the highest price for land covered with natural forest." Specifically, Olmsted suggested they "thin out the existing forest trees very radically, leaving only a comparatively few but those of the sorts most suitable for the embellishment of nicely kept lawns."[27] He explained that residents associated naturally forested areas with low values; they apparently sought a landscape that had been labored over.

And labored over it was. In addition to the parkway, parks and green spaces were sprinkled throughout the property. Some parks simply provided visual effect, while others offered children's playgrounds. Olmsted designed Springdale Park for recreation and included a playground, and Shadyside provided open green space for rest and reflection. Trees dominated Deepdene. The *Atlanta Journal* summed up the planners' vision (and its intended market) in 1908 when they told readers that "with its breezes and ozone laden parks, no one would think of leaving such a home for a trip to a summer retreat."[28] Together, the parkway, one-to-ten-acre lots (themselves with designed landscapes), and the mixture of parks offered a respite from the urban environment just beyond.[29]

Though Hurt clearly saw a market for exclusive subdivisions, he and his engineer, Solon Ruff, were willing to cut corners to generate income or to save money. Although Hurt had sought out the nation's leading neighborhood designers for his second park-neighborhood venture, he often deviated from plans, sometimes without explanation. In May 1902, John Olmsted expressed disappointment that Hurt established slopes "uniformly 3 to 1"; Olmsted had sought "to make them steeper in some places to save trees." He suggested some variations in the slopes so as to "produce a more pleasing effect." In his July visit, Olmsted remarked in his report, "No attention was paid to my directions for steeper banks and terraces on deep cuts." Olmsted's reports are punctuated by notes about Hurt deciding to alter entrances and other elements of the subdivision. On one visit, Olmsted reported, "Hurt has had various pines cut that I intended to save," and "Hurt has not agreed to the sanitary sewage system I advised."[30] To Hurt, park-neighborhoods were simply a business, a commodity easily reproduced from city to city or subdivision to subdivision. The details of landscape design or the social influence of park-neighborhood living were of little importance.

Such was the case with Ansley Park, a park-neighborhood launched in 1904 by Edwin Ansley and the Southern Real Estate Improvement Company. Ansley Park encompassed less property than Druid Hills but embraced the same elite suburban aesthetic. The 325-acre subdivision adopted design elements similar to Druid Hills in part because Ansley hired engineer Solon Ruff to implement the project. Focusing on the park-neighborhood aesthetic as the salable element of his new project, Ansley explained to a reporter, "The streets will be laid out . . . according to the topography of the land rather than at right angles." The writer concluded that the proposed seventy-five-foot-wide boulevard was "an adornment that Atlanta ha[d] needed."[31] Another *Atlanta Constitution* story compared the property to Cleveland planner Robert Whitten's restricted and exclusive Euclid Heights. As in Inman Park and Druid Hills, Ansley Park's winding streets broke with the area's established road pattern and set the development apart as its own neighborhood. But Ansley Park offered more than the era's current neighborhood design fashions; it offered *location*. That is, Ansley Park provided not easy access to employment centers or shopping but proximity to status—four blocks of the subdivision lined the celebrated Peachtree Street, home to many Atlanta elites.[32]

Like Hurt, Ansley did not voice any social-improvement goals in realizing Ansley Park; elite subdivision building was a business that relied on fashionable neighborhood practices. Ansley had a keen eye for emerging housing markets and access to the financial resources to exploit them. The real-estate dealer honed and directly benefited from the emerging movement to segregate classes through residential planning and aesthetic design; as he planned and built Ansley Park, Ansley continued to invest in, sell, and manage rental-housing units intended for workers (black and white). As was the case with Druid Hills, Ansley Park was a commodity to be sold to elites seeking status markers and a neighborhood aesthetic that exuded order, harmony, and graceful living.

As with Inman Park, Ansley Park's ads and newspaper coverage helped construct and solidify associations between elites and the park-neighborhood landscape aesthetic by combining pastoral imagery with references to exclusivity or to neighbors with social status. One 1905 *Atlanta Constitution* article detailing that year's land auction pointed to the presence of many society ladies as well as the subdivision's plans for boulevards and beautiful homes for "high class people."[33] Ansley's 1909 ad directed attention to the neighborhood's mountain foothills, flower gardens, and "breathing spaces," as well as its proximity to "the city's most exclusive thoroughfares of culture, wealth, and fashion."[34] Ansley Park had greater success than Inman Park in attracting the city's elite. By the beginning of World War I, over 20 percent of Ansley Park's residents were listed in the city's social register. (By 1925, 29 percent of its residents were listed.)[35]

The financial backers, operators, and new residents of Atlanta's pre–World War I park-neighborhood subdivisions themselves drew from Atlanta's civic-commercial elite, or what historian Mary Corbin Sies describes as the professional-managerial stratum. In the South, as in other regions, this group largely comprised native-born men, usually of northern European descent. This group led the New South as it industrialized. The Kirkwood Land Company, which launched Druid Hills, for example, included well-established Atlanta businessmen and politicians, such as banker James English, *Atlanta Journal* editor and former governor and senator Hoke Smith, and banker Robert J. Lowry, in addition to developer Joel Hurt. The Southern Real Estate Improvement

Company, which launched Ansley Park, included lawyer Walter P. Andrews, Lee Douglas, builder W. F. Winecoff (who built the Winecoff Hotel), and real-estate agent and developer Edwin P. Ansley.[36] As bankers, attorneys, builders, and investors, these professionals also were the New South's foundation, leadership, and voice.

Ansley and Hurt intended to keep their neighborhoods exclusive by adopting deed covenants: legal restrictions that limited or dictated how an individual property could be used.[37] Deed covenants prevented major alterations to the park-neighborhood spectacle and helped to maintain a larger, carefully assembled display—a landscape that ranged between a natural scene and a carefully maintained park. Deed restrictions often established house setbacks, minimum lot sizes, or minimum housing costs. Some covenants dictated the placement of sheds and servants' quarters or the height of fences. Thus, covenants applied only to the individual lot, but their demands worked in concert with the covenants of abutting property. In the park-neighborhood, property may have been owned by an individual, but it was intended to work collectively. The Olmsteds explained to Joel Hurt, for example, that planted property borders should be at least eighty feet from the street line, as it would "be more agreeable to have a continuous, unbroken lawn in front of two or more houses."[38] In this managed landscape, the tableau of a single house surrounded by undulating hills gave way to a scene comprising a length of houses with lawns and greenery that *recalled* the verdant, idealized landscape. Deed restrictions ensured that individual owners would not break that larger effect.[39]

Prior to World War I, the park-neighborhood aesthetic was not universally accepted, as covenant protections implicitly acknowledged. New park-neighborhood residents may have sought this neighborhood form (or at least the cultural associations that accompanied it), but that did not mean they understood its control and maintenance. The unschooled might build their houses too close to the road or out of line with established homes, for example. They might erect sheds in the front yard or line the front yard with the wrong type of trees. With deed restrictions, a buyer could be confident that the landscape in which he or she invested would not be marred by the acts of a neighbor.[40]

Moreover, many developers assumed that park-neighborhood residents needed the "discipline" provided by deed restrictions, at least until they learned and adopted park-neighborhood practices. As J. C. Nichols, developer of Kansas City's famed Country Club District, explained to National Association of Real Estate Boards convention attendees, subdividers needed to actively cultivate a sense of self-reliance among homeowners. He reflected, "I think the quicker you can create a feeling of responsibility in the buyers and homeowners themselves the better it is," as they will then act "to make the subdivision a success."[41] Thus, "property maintenance" in the park-neighborhood context did not simply mean maintaining the structural integrity of the house nor even keeping the property clean and free from vermin; it meant preserving the original designed neighborhood aesthetic. Nichols and others contended that these behaviors must be required of homeowners until they learned to take "interest in" and responsibility for maintaining their properties. Restrictive covenants, the developers hoped, disciplined newcomers until they adopted park-neighborhood expectations and practices.[42]

Atlanta's early park-neighborhood developers kept their covenants to a minimum. Subdivided beginning in 1888, Inman Park's covenant limited land use to single-family homes, set minimum housing costs of $3,000, and established setbacks of thirty feet. Hurt could have borrowed from the practices of subdivision designers in other regions and added far more restrictions on building and landscape practices, such as side yard minimums and limitations on outbuildings and livestock. Hurt apparently did not see the need to establish such rules (and since he tended to alter his original plans in the face of economic downturn, it is likely that Hurt did not want to limit his own development options by imposing overly restrictive deed covenants). Though Olmsted encouraged Hurt to adopt the more-extensive restrictions he had recommended for Druid Hills, Hurt resisted. In requesting that Druid Hills' restrictions be shortened to fifty years, Hurt explained, "There is a natural abhorrence in this democratic region to restrictions, and the longer they appear, the more abhorrent."[43] Olmsted insisted that Hurt lengthen the restrictions to sixty years, explaining that lots in his Brookline, Massachusetts, neighborhood remained unsold up to twenty-five years, a market reality that necessitated longer deed restrictions. Also, Olmsted explained, landowners could vote to change the restrictions if they liked. Olmsted pressured Hurt: "We earnestly hope that you will stiffen up on this subject of length of restrictions."[44]

Although few in number, Druid Hills' deed restrictions did control access to Atlanta's park-neighborhood by limiting development to single-family homes and by establishing minimum lot sizes or building costs. When consulting with Hurt on Druid Hills, John Olmsted explicitly advised the use of large lots to guard against "undesireable occupation of land." And Hurt launched the land sale with one-to-three-acre lots listed between $4,000 and $12,000, prices beyond the reach of all but the wealthiest Atlantans. Such restrictions helped establish and solidify the park-neighborhood as an elite cultural practice reserved for a particular social group. That said, neither Inman Park nor Druid Hills explicitly excluded nonwhites in their deed covenants.[45]

Nothing in the extensive correspondence between Hurt and Olmsted regarding deed restrictions in Druid Hills indicates that the two ever considered imposing restrictions against nonwhites or any other specific ethnic or religious groups in that neighborhood. Olmsted was certainly aware of the use of such restrictions. The landscape designer's own Riverline neighborhood, an exclusive park-neighborhood he referred to often in correspondence with Hurt, explicitly excluded people of African descent. It is possible, though, that Hurt or Olmsted assumed that white elites would not consider selling property in an exclusive neighborhood to nonwhites. Or they may have taken for granted that class-exclusionary elements would preclude the introduction of nonwhites. That is, the developers may have assumed that the $6,000 minimum housing cost would prevent the influx of "the poorer classes," which they assumed included all nonwhites. This explanation is buttressed by Olmsted's correspondence suggesting that the presence of black children was undesirable and perhaps even dangerous. In early letters recommending deed restrictions for Druid Hills, Olmsted suggested that Hurt prohibit "houses for servants employed on the property." He explained, "The raising of negro children, even those of gardeners, coachmen and others often provided for is almost certain to result in disagreeable conditions through the noise which they are apt to create even if not through trespassing, pilfering and other criminal acts."[46] Olmsted assumed black families were not present in the park-neighborhood as residents and discouraged their presence as live-in workers. Black children, he asserted, were likely to be noisy and disturb the environment. What's more, Olmsted implied, black children possessed a natural criminal tendency. To Olmsted, nonwhites had no place in an exclusive park-neighborhood, and he encouraged his clients to think likewise.[47]

Geography may also have informed Hurt and Olmsted's decisions not to explicitly exclude nonwhites through deed covenants. First, Druid Hills and Inman Park were not in the direct path of black residential growth. Areas with higher black populations on the city's near west side were expanding westward. And swaths of undeveloped property separated Ansley Park, Druid Hills, and Inman Park from concentrations of black housing in the lower Fourth Ward on Atlanta's east side. Consequently, Hurt and his partners may not have seen any need to consider overt racial controls. Also, as previously noted, Olmsted and Hurt may have assumed that Druid Hills' minimum building costs would control race by controlling class.

In contrast to the elite park-neighborhoods of Druid Hills and Inman Park, Ansley Park—subdivided slightly later, in 1904—specifically excluded blacks through restrictive covenants. There is no evidence revealing why Ansley opted to be the first elite park-neighborhood in Atlanta to incorporate racial covenants. However, the decision was consistent with Ansley's previous land practices, which included racializing property. While the agent did not *always* identify race in his housing advertisements, he *routinely* used such phrases as "black tenants" or "negro houses" in ads for properties outside his park-neighborhood. In practice, Ansley used race and class to his economic advantage; as Ansley cultivated a market for an all-white, elite, exclusive subdivision north of downtown, he simultaneously marketed and managed a substantial amount of racially sorted rental housing in Atlanta's core. Ansley was ahead of the class- and racial-segregation curve. His park-neighborhood set the precedent for the segregation practices that spread rapidly across the Atlanta landscape in the 1920s.[48]

Park-neighborhood amenities introduced by Edwin Ansley and subsequent park-neighborhood developers reinforced class and racial exclusivity. Parks were particularly key to this project: they contributed to the park-neighborhood aesthetic, offered residents recreational opportunities and spaces for quiet reflection; and limited social exposure to members of the same status group. These luxuries, placed within private neighborhoods with restricted access, augmented the privatizing nature of the suburban home. By introducing particular amenities into privatized subdivisions, park-neighborhoods bolstered the suburban domestic ideal and reserved it exclusively for white elites. Such placement narrowed residents' social opportunities to people like themselves—park-neighborhood residents drawn from similar social strata and who, presumably, appreciated similar residential landscapes and exclusivity.

Shared social spaces such as parks (or clubhouses or golf courses) provided opportunities to cultivate shared elite meaning systems and taste cultures. Advertising emphasizing the exclusive use of parks or other comforts suggests that a market may have existed for privatized amenities, but such rhetoric also reinforced meaning systems that associated high status with parks, property ownership, and exclusive rights to particular places and amenities. One agent, for example, pitched the Spring Lake subdivision as "Atlanta's Finest Home Park" and explained, "You, as a Spring Lake property owner, will have the exclusive use of this park."[49] Ansley emphasized that his subdivision was the only one offering "every facility for automobiling, horseback riding, driving (including the Piedmont Driving Club as a near neighbor) fast tennis courts and a fine golf course."[50] But as exclusionary communities propagated, residents' exposure to and view of larger society narrowed. Thus, while many neighborhood designers (and city planners) contended that people sought out neighbors of a similar class or status group, it is clear that residential infrastructure increasingly dictated those associations rather than simply allowing for them. Thus, exclusive park-neighborhood practices and expectations were self-reinforcing.

Park-neighborhood exclusivity, and the situating of parks *within* neighborhoods with restricted access, indicates a shift away from the philosophy that parks would, in historian David Schuyler's words, "act as agents of moral improvement" by bringing the working classes into contact with the (presumably) genteel influences of the middle and upper classes. Purveyors of the social-improvement thesis such as architect Andrew Jackson Downing argued that through public parks, libraries, museums, and other public cultural spaces, "you would soften and humanize the rude, educate and enlighten the ignorant, and give continual enjoyment to the educated."[51] Frederick Law Olmsted and Calvert Vaux concurred and promoted parks for their positive social outcomes. But after 1910, as historian Peter Baldwin argues, urban thinking moved from a concern for the amelioration of social ills and poor health to the acceptance of particular conditions. This shift encouraged urban elites and bureaucrats to segregate the city, to spatially control rather than to mitigate behaviors labeled undesirable. Atlanta's experience suggests that this change in thinking began earlier in the South and also influenced the evolution of park-neighborhoods. Elites still embraced the power of a positive social environment, but they insisted on reserving some parks for their own families and realized this goal by situating them within privatized residential environments.[52]

From the 1800s to the second decade of the twentieth century, community builders intended to erect profitable elite neighborhoods that delivered a planned, arcadian environment, free from aesthetic disruptions. The park-neighborhood's orderly and controlled environment, natural landscapes, tasteful architecture, and elite white residents offered respite to civic elites disconcerted by an increasingly crowded, unruly Atlanta. This elite neighborhood development, based on new aesthetic ideals, class and race division, and privatization, was mirrored by a larger urban-booster campaign that sought to fashion a city that embodied elite sensibilities and taste cultures. Masked by a push for economic development and southern rejuvenation, southern city building celebrated the modern and monumental. To be sure, Atlanta and other southern towns lacked the capital (and perhaps desire) to introduce Chicago-style city plans or L'Enfant plaza designs, but civic elites nonetheless longed for a city reflective of elite white taste cultures and practices.

An Urban Ethos

As park-neighborhood builders produced a new visual landscape at the city's perimeter, Atlantans feasted on tales of America's industrial and commercial cities, their glories and horrors. Elite Atlantans sorted through myth and legend to find a model for their own city, compiling lists of disorders they hoped to abate or control and identifying markers of sophisticated urban living, such as monuments, civic centers, parks, and parkways. Urban ideals—an urban ethos, as historian Blain Brownell describes it—transferred rapidly in the late 1800s and early 1900s, particularly through journals, travel accounts, and tours featuring city practices.[53]

Newspapers and popular literature helped create, reinforce, and make accessible modern urban practices and taste cultures to the growing mass of city leaders and residents. In the 1890s and early 1900s, More and more people read of and talked about streetcars, sidewalks, and lighting. Middle- and upper-class literati knew which cities had what, which were clean, which were known for vice, and which attracted industry. Periodicals transmitted city development ideas from coast to coast and border to border. One 1911 *American City* article explained that Lynchburg, Virginia's "streets were ill-paved, its main business thoroughfares were congested, the stores rendered hideous by wooden awning frames, while the side streets intersecting the main thoroughfares were narrow, unsightly and further marred by buildings here and there encroaching irregularly on the sidewalk or building lines."[54] Here, urban residents and city leaders learned to avoid awnings and irregularly set-back buildings, lest they be subject to similar nationally broadcast lashings. Boosters grew sensitive to such critiques, and in Atlanta aldermen and councilmen introduced ordinances that required the removal of signage or awnings that they thought spoiled the appearance of the burgeoning commercial center. Mayor Livingston Mims, for example, cringed in the wake of criticism from competitors. He told Atlantans in his annual address in 1901:

> I read with no degree of pleasure the frequent communications in the city papers and even in the papers of other cities all manner of criticisms of the City, and its Government, as to this disgusting condition. Indeed, I see with my own eyes, and as I ride over them, feel the truth of all complaint and criticism. There is nothing by which a city is judged both by its own people and visitors as the streets and sidewalks.[55]

To Mims, paving was not about efficient movement of goods or safety, but about appearance. Cities were "judged" by their sidewalks. They suggested orderliness and cleanliness and signaled that Atlanta's citizens had the resources and desire to maintain a modern city.

Trips to other cities by urban leaders and merchants also helped situate Atlanta in a national culture of urban improvements and reform. Mayors and major business leaders visiting other centers were not left to wander about town but were escorted, with host officials entertaining the esteemed visitors with stories of the city's latest building, sidewalk, depot, or industry. Charleston's mayor and other leaders celebrated the visit of Atlanta's mayor Livingston Mims and various council- and aldermen and trucked the visitors around the city in bannered streetcars. During the two-day trip, Atlantans discussed street railways and reviewed waterworks with Charleston politicians and bureaucrats. Realizing the importance of such urban tourism, Atlanta's mayor appointed five council members to take charge of the entertainment of the 250 delegates of the International League of Press Clubs when they stopped in Atlanta on the way to the Jamestown Exposition in 1907. Invitations to visit were extended from city to city, and in 1898 Nashville's chamber of commerce invited Atlanta's mayor and city authorities to participate in Nashville's July 4 celebration.[56]

State, regional, and national expositions likewise encouraged urban competition and helped to nationalize urban taste cultures. States and cities set up booths and displays in other states' and regions' expositions, eager to encourage labor and business migration to their homelands. At Chicago's Columbian Exposition in 1893, thirty-six nations and forty-six U.S. states exhibited. California secured a booth at Atlanta's Cotton States and International Exposition in 1895. California leaders considered their promotion a great success, asserting, "While one purpose of the Atlanta Exposition was to attract people to the South, I am sure that a fair proportion of those so attracted were ... diverted to California."[57] Atlanta's city council saw a "great and lasting benefit" from exhibiting at the Louisiana Purchase Exposition in 1904. Exposition organizers asked Atlanta to develop a reproduction of the city's new Terminal Station for the Model City exhibit, an endeavor the city estimated to cost ten thousand dollars. But after the city and exposition leaders failed to agree on construction details, Atlanta dropped its proposal and instead agreed to support the funding of the Georgia building. Thirty-six other states showcased themselves similarly. Atlanta furnished a room for itself in Georgia's hall at the Jamestown Exhibition in 1907, and the city council sent the mayor, five council members, the city's drum corps, and the Fifth Regiment of the Georgia Militia to the expo for Georgia Day. As historian William Cronon notes, multistate displays within individual expositions fostered a competitive spirit between cities, states, and regions. In doing so, they facilitated the exchange of taste cultures and cultivated particular urban expectations.[58]

As fairs, news, and travel stoked urban competition and fostered knowledge transfer, the study of other cities' activities became de rigueur when planning new projects. A variety of sources indicate that Atlanta's leaders were well aware of national practices in city governance, planning, business, and infrastructure. Atlanta's building inspector kept up to date on building-material specifications, sanitary and fire limits, and other regulations in force around the country. In 1899, the inspector recommended that the council adopt an ordinance prohibiting builders from blocking streets and sidewalks during construction, "as is done in other large cities, especially in the center of the city."[59] And when Atlantans considered changing from the aldermanic to the commission form of government, "a strong committee from [the chamber of commerce conducted an] investigation of the systems used elsewhere."[60] Atlanta's early participation in this urban exchange laid the groundwork for its formal role in new city-planning associations such as the National Chamber of Commerce and the League of American Municipalities. Through these relationships and others, Atlanta's civic elites could benchmark city plans, civic centers, and urban regulation and see how their city measured up to the competition.

Reflecting the city's ambitions to be a player on the national urban scene, Atlanta's civic elites joined many of the major Progressive Era city-oriented organizations. For example, the League of American Municipalities, formed in 1897, included in its first slate of officers Atlantans C. A. Collier and Mayor W. A. Black. The league's annual meetings included discussions of sewerage, franchises, woman suffrage, taxation, street railways, and municipal ownership of utilities, among many other topics. Atlanta sent four to six delegates to league meetings each year, and sometimes the mayor himself attended. Through these engagements Atlanta's leadership viewed the attractions of Grand Rapids, Toledo, Chicago, and Norfolk while meeting and learning from delegates of cities throughout the United States. Atlantans failed in their attempt to secure the league's annual meeting in 1906, but Atlantans continued to play key roles in the organization's leadership.[61]

In addition to actively participating in the league, Atlanta's civic elites joined and led other national organizations concerned with urban issues, including public health, economic development, and city planning. The National Municipal League elected Judge Ernest Kontz to the executive committee in 1906. And the National Chamber of Commerce invited the Gate City into membership in 1907. That same year, Atlanta sent delegates J. W. Pope, Walter G. Cooper, D. Woodward, and L. A. Ransom to the first meeting of the National Council of Commerce, where they engaged with representatives from over thirty other cities. And at a 1916 National Anti-Tuberculosis Association meeting, Atlanta's representatives discussed the city's nascent housing campaign with the nation's foremost housing activist (and founder of the National Housing Association) Lawrence Veiller. Through these organizations, Atlanta gained political-economic and city planning know-how and acquired knowledge of urban trends and aesthetic fashions. And they brought their new knowledge home.[62]

Aesthetics as Public Policy

Steeped in national urban fashions, Atlanta's civic elite looked to improve its urban landscape by adding parks, parkways, and monuments. But the city's working class saw little value in such spending, in park-neighborhood aesthetics, or in a "modern" city. Nonetheless, to Atlanta's civic elites, urban aesthetics were a matter of economic development and a way of establishing urban status. They argued the financial value of parkways, monuments, balance, linearity—and then used that purported economic value to justify public funding of particular initiatives. From 1900 to 1910, the parks movement, especially, laid the foundation for the integration of aesthetics into public policy in Atlanta, and despite setbacks, elites followed park building proposals with plans for city plazas and other practices associated with the City Beautiful movement.[63]

Hoping to launch a sustained park movement in 1902, park-neighborhood developer and now park commissioner Joel Hurt turned to his favored landscape architect team, the Olmsted brothers, about "a general review of [Atlanta's] whole park system." A year later, the outfit began planning improvements for Grant, Mims, and Springvale parks. By early 1904, the Olmsteds had furnished preliminary plans that included features similar to their housing subdivisions: formal gardens, stone arches, shrubs, lakes, banks and hills, and walks and drives designed to highlight particular views.[64]

Sylvan walks and reflective pools may have been on the agenda of the city's elites, but they did not impress Atlanta's workers. In 1904, soon after his election, working-class mayor James Woodward stymied elite beautification efforts by replacing nearly the entire park commission with members reflecting his spending philosophies, leaving only one veteran member. Former park commissioner Hurt understood the implications of the election and the commission's replacement and explained to the Olmsteds in 1905 that the park plan would likely be dropped.[65]

Hurt's correspondence with the Olmsteds on parks and city planning in this period reveals the civic elites' classist sentiment and concern for order. First, Hurt labeled officials in Woodward's administration corrupt and charged the group with mismanaging the city, particularly poignant criticisms in an era when the civic elites actively positioned themselves as reform minded and as utilizing business methods to run local government. In one letter, for example, Hurt suggested that Woodward ran a political machine.[66] In a follow-up letter, Hurt asserted that John Parks, the newly appointed park superintendent, was a "broken down politician, one of the old gang that were in Council in 1900 when Woodward was mayor last time."[67] Hurt went on to paint the new commission as unruly and in disarray; soon after the election and the replacement of the parks commission, the commission "had a row," fired all but two of the employees, and reduced the salary of the superintendent. Another commissioner accused the board of being "illegally organized." Hurt suggested that the group needed to be disciplined. To bring order back to government (and to parks), the city council considered abolishing the park commission and placing parks under the control of the city council.[68] To Hurt and other civic elites, city governance and city planning were the purview of the city's "best citizens," those who appreciated and practiced order, discipline, and decorum.

Hurt went on to contrast the civic elites with the "unruly" and corrupt. In the same letter that portrayed the new leadership as unmanageable, he enclosed an article that he said conveyed "the sentiment of a large majority of the *best people* of Atlanta" (emphasis added).[69] The contents of the article were not included in Olmsted's records, but Hurt's reference to the city's best people reflects the decades-old elite-propagated philosophy that Atlanta (and all governments) should be led by those vested with cultural capital and an elite outlook. Promoters like Hurt presented reform as the use of business methods that they claimed were fair and neutral. In practice, however, elites tended to stock city offices with members of their own limited social network, a network fostered through membership in particular clubs and residence in particular neighborhoods. Newspapers and other media often signaled membership by labeling someone "one of the best businessmen" or "one of the best men" of the city or labeling behaviors such as "business-like methods" and "conservative conduct."[70]

Language deployed by those outside Atlanta's civic-elite circles reveals widespread recognition of class divisions throughout the post-Reconstruction era up to World War I. In one attack, a candidate on the People's Ticket tried to raise voter ire by describing another candidate as, in the words of historian Eugene Watts, "living in his palatial home, reclining on velvet cushions, drinking fine wine and smoking Havana cigars."[71] Despite the newness of the New South, papers assigned some candidates elite status through their long-term association with the city. As early as 1878 a newspaper noted the deep local roots of one candidate, describing him as "the son of an old and worthy citizen of Atlanta, who has lived among us for a number of years." The *Atlanta Constitution* and other outlets helped situate "the best people" in the social spectrum by describing workers as transients with "a roving disposition." Mill owner Oscar Elsas likewise described his workers as "not interested in their own welfare."[72]

Despite these class tensions and challenges to civic-elite power, Atlanta's white elites persevered in their attempts to beautify Atlanta through parks and green and recreational spaces, and by 1906 they were rekindling ties to Olmsted. This time bypassing not just the Woodward administration but the city government as a whole, park supporters operated through the chamber of commerce and proposed a twenty-five-mile boulevard connecting battlegrounds around the city. Significantly, chamber secretary Walter G. Cooper stated, "Before we can take up this work successfully, we will have to conduct a campaign of education among our own people." That is, the positive attributes of park improvements were not immediately obvious to those outside elite circles or directly involved in city boosterism and urban competition; nonelites would need to be persuaded of the efficacy of park building and city beautification.[73]

Chamber of commerce members tied beautification to economic growth to convince voters of the need for parks and related aesthetic practices. Coca-Cola founder Asa Griggs Candler, in his inaugural presidential address to the chamber of commerce in 1908, announced that Atlanta's rapid growth necessitated "the adoption of some well-considered general plan for the improvement of its streets, parks and public buildings," a plan that might incorporate "the largest possible degree of harmonious beauty." He implored, "This is not simply a matter of sentiment, but is a business proposition, whose soundness has been demonstrated by most of the world's great cities."[74] The chamber recommended the creation of a nonpolitical metropolitan commission that would formulate, adopt, and carry out a comprehensive plan for beautifying the city. As part of the program, the chamber would acquire new parks and "regulate the construction of public buildings along aesthetic lines."[75] Architects would take photographs of "unsightly places" and suggest "how they [might] be beautified."[76]

Political leaders and city bureaucrats echoed the business leaders' call for aesthetic improvements, particularly through the addition and improvement of city parks. In 1908, the same year that chamber of commerce president Candler championed parks in his inaugural address, Mayor Walthall Joyner singled out parks as needing particular attention by the city. Dan Carey, secretary and general manager of the Atlanta Park Commission, explained to *Atlanta Constitution* readers, "All writers on the question of 'City Beautiful' admit that parks are the basis of everything." Carey buttressed his argument by identifying organizations that promoted parks and green spaces in other cities, including Boston's Commons Society, Kansas City's Tree Planters Association, and Buffalo's Forestry Association.[77]

As Carey's list suggests, Atlantans stayed alert to beautification trends practiced elsewhere. In 1907, for example, the *Constitution* detailed Columbia, South Carolina's launch of a civic league and the plans Columbia explicitly defined as "city beautiful." The article outlined the public entities created to implement the proposal, which included trees, grounds, gardens, underground telephone lines, and "embellishment." The Georgia Federation of Women's Clubs likewise discussed "town beautiful" movements throughout Georgia at their 1907 meeting in Tifton. Advocating planning to create the "town beautiful," president Lizzie Wilson Hines explained, "We mean—beautiful school and station grounds, inviting parks and squares, no unsightly vacant lots, well-kept cemeteries, fine trees, no billboards, clean streets—yes and back yards."[78] Thus, Atlanta primped with others, attempting to establish its place among well-groomed modern cities.

Advocates like Hines laid bare the aesthetic sensibilities that white elites sought to impose through public policy. Good architecture and a liberal use of (planned) nature would promote "good taste." Like City Beautiful promoters elsewhere, Georgia's town-beautiful advocates were sure that a carefully planned landscape would "improve" their towns through a subtle introduction of order. But if Hines thought beautification was about social reform or good health, she did not say it. Emphasizing arcadian spaces with terra cotta, lawn vases, and settees, Hines did not seek to ease poverty, improve health, or build safe housing. "Improvement," in civic-elite terms, meant the adoption of a white, middle- and upper-class aesthetic.[79]

Like local town-beautiful movement promoters, park interests mobilized arguments *other* than public health to advance their cause. Although Atlanta certainly had its share of congested alley dwellings, they did not resemble the larger impoverished districts of New York or Chicago. Atlanta lacked the overcrowded conditions that drove many reformers to lobby for parks, green spaces, and other such "breathing spaces" for the masses. Southern cities in general were less dense than northern manufacturing centers, and Atlanta's housing stock tended toward single-family homes and duplexes instead of "tenements" and apartment houses. In fact, in this period, only park professional Dan Carey consistently mobilized public-health rhetoric. Frustrated with the park commission's inability or unwillingness to secure funds for substantive park development and maintenance, Carey pled his case for aggressive fund-raising using a public-health appeal. To park commission president George Eubanks he asserted, "The public park has always been the best aid of the health department in overcoming the unsanitary conditions of crowded streets, and in providing pure and healthy air to lungs that are stifled by the foul air of congested districts." Atlanta was comparatively free of the tenement apartments that marked New York, Pittsburgh, Chicago, and other similar cities, but Carey used rhetoric that had been successful in large cities, contending, "Tall buildings are making it more difficult each year for sunlight and pure air to reach the streets of the city, and flats and apartments are rapidly taking the spaces that were once front yards."[80] Nor did Atlantans call for the use of parks as a social-reform measure, pointing to the need for parks so that the "lower" classes might observe and adopt the refined manners of their betters. Rather, elite Atlantans' reasoning was boosterish and situated within a national atmosphere of urban competition; participation in a national landscape movement indicated and expressed taste cultures and signaled urbanity.[81]

Despite the civic elites' confidence in the efficacy of city beautification, parks continued to be actively debated. When the city council considered the Hancock-Huddleston park system ordinance, which proposed a general superintendent of parks (with an annual salary of three thousand dollars), council members expressed concerns about rising costs. But parks were no luxury to Atlanta's elite; they were necessary markers of urban status, and believers actively pressed the issue. One council member revealed to the *Atlanta Journal* that the council would likely adopt the ordinance, "for those interested in its adoption [were] bringing all possible political pressure to bear on the various members of council."[82] Parks may have been the "basis for everything," but in the second decade of the twentieth century, and consistent with other cities in the Progressive Era, Atlanta's white elite proposed a civic center—a plaza in central Atlanta.

Parks to Plazas

A city plaza promised a larger, more direct statement of order, symmetry, and monumentalism—a symbol of Atlanta's modern status. Architect Haralson Bleckley recommended covering the city's centrally located railroad gulch with an elongated plaza anchored at the western end by a "public comfort building" in "French Renaissance style" (see fig. 2.3). A new skyscraper would include a city hall, a railroad depot, and municipal and public offices. Besides the plaza and building additions, the project would free the city from the soot of the intersecting rail lines it would cover and unite the city geographically. Although the plan ultimately failed, the rhetoric surrounding the project helped spread new spatial and visual cultures and expectations among Atlanta's white middle and upper classes. Certainly, the pavement-heavy plaza was not the "natural" environment adopted by parks and park-neighborhoods, but it mirrored the themes of dignity, linearity, and order.

As was the case with planned green spaces and other urban trends, elites attempted to persuade city leaders and residents to fund a civic center by trucking out the practices of other cities. Frank Hawkins, president of Third National

ARCHITECT'S DREAM OF "CIVIC CENTER"

Figure 2.3. Architect Haralson Bleckley's vision of an Atlanta civic center. Source: *Atlanta Constitution*, August 7, 1909.

Bank, asserted, "[There are] few cities the size of this anywhere in America or Europe that are without a place of this sort."[83] And W. L. Cosgrove, president of Atlanta Gas Light Company, emphasized, "Why even Marietta has an open space in the center of town. Take the other cities of Georgia, Savannah, Augusta, Macon. They all have something of the kind—either a park, a plaza, a broad street, or something similar."[84] Cosgrove's discussion emphasized the new spatial options cities had to choose from—a park, a plaza, a parkway— and suggested that he and others shopped other cities for new aesthetic practices just as they did for governmental forms or pavement types. But Cosgrove and others like him actively limited urban alternatives as well by constantly returning to the same list of options.

In the *Atlanta Constitution*'s "Modern Alice in the Wonderland City," Br'er Rabbit spins a tale of the glory the Bleckley Plan offered the Gate City. Alice is tired, dirty, and cross after enduring "roundabout journeys" through a dirty city and finally descending into the chaos of Union Station. Later Alice steps into "the Atlanta that might be," strolling down a "wide parkway" and enjoying "snow white pavement" and electric lights. The plaza, Br'er explains, would feature a gymnasium for men and a place for women to rest. All things considered, the rabbit concludes, "strangers immediately see Atlanta to be a City Beautiful."[85]

The rhetoric generated in support of a civic plaza was the closest Atlanta's elites came to using social-improvement rhetoric to justify city-planning initiatives. Rather than promoting the plaza as a means to expose the masses to genteel influences by bringing the classes together, promoters asserted that the plaza would literally serve as a bridge to downtown; that is, it would provide access to the city for the heretofore isolated populations. While many of the *Atlanta Journal*'s respondents waxed eloquent about the need for plazas and beautification, others continued to promote "bridging" the city north to south, east to west. In one such letter to the editor, V. O. Rankin explained, "There is no better way of reaching over into the long-neglected west side than by an extension of this very plan by viaduct to Haynes street." Thomas Martin, a consulting engineer, remarked similarly, noting that not only will the plan alleviate Atlanta's "sewer of smoke," but "it would solve still another far-reaching problem, of a social nature—the division of Atlanta into 'south' and 'north' sides. Of course we would all like to forget the existence of any such sentiment, but we can not dispute it, for it is a fact. I think the Bleckley plan would do more to wipe out this sectionalism than anything that could possibly be done."[86] (As Br'er Rabbit explains it, one could not be an Atlantan because one was too concerned about pointing out that he was from the north side.)[87] Likewise, another 1910 *Atlanta Journal* blared, "PRACTICAL PLAN TO BRIDGE ATLANTA'S 'SEWER OF SMOKE,' UNITE FOR ALL TIME THE GREAT 'SOUTH' AND 'NORTH' SIDES" (emphasis in original).[88] Attorney Alex Smith wrote Bleckley:

> The importance of the movement greatly outweighs the physical advantages and improvements which will flow from carrying out your plans, because the dividing line between sections in our beloved city will be wiped out and, thus far, no plan for wiping out this dividing line has ever been suggested. The various viaducts tended toward this very desirable object, but did not and cannot accomplish it.[89]

Harvey Johnson's review of "Atlanta, the Gate City of the South" in *The American City* even mentioned the proposed plaza and the city's trust in its ameliorative power.[90]

The *Atlanta Journal* forwarded copies of the proposal to leaders throughout the state, requested their comments, and then used the comments in appeals to authority. "Civic Center Plan Indorsed by Many Prominent Citizens," read one headline, while others claimed, "Eminently Practical, Says F. J. Paxon," "Government Officer Thinks It Feasible," and "F. J. Cooledge Thinks Scheme Is Great."[91] Although they quoted individual men of note, the newspaper lumped all women together and wrote "Atlanta Women Will All Favor Bleckley's Idea."[92]

Civic-center promoters painted a dim picture of the railroad center they hoped to transform. Drawing on techniques used in the era's popular dime novels, writers forced readers to paint their own mental images of a "blackened gulch" and "chasms." "Uncovered sewer of smoke" and "sewer of smoke" were sprinkled liberally through stories. "Chasm of smoke and din," "blackened gulch," "smoke-blackened chasm," and "black, gaping wound" added even more fodder for the imagination. Photographs of the railroad center were dark and dim in black and white, and railcars appeared to be sinking into the earth. In contrast, pen-and-ink drawings of Atlanta's "future" were majestic—trees and skyscrapers reaching to heaven. Significantly, the language rarely alluded to health issues, though imagery suggested unsightliness and noise.[93]

The plaza debate continued for years, and ultimately Bleckley's plan failed. The final report submitted by the Atlanta-based committee to the state road commission did not persuade the state of the need, and in 1916 the commission rejected the proposal after a year's review. The chamber of commerce revived the plaza proposal in 1923, 1927, and then again in 1930. In each phase, the railroad gulch was a space painted as ugly, unpleasant, and thus something not necessarily to be eliminated, but hidden, an approach white elites used throughout the city in the early 1900s.[94]

The language adopted to promote both civic plazas and parks smacked of the verbiage used to sell elite park-neighborhoods. Articles highlighted large and neatly laid out spaces, labeled them "beautiful," and assigned them "refined" status. In promoting the plaza, W. L. Cosgrove spoke of "beautifying our environment" and "a breathing space," the same phrases adopted by real-estate salesmen hawking park-neighborhoods. In all these venues, activities promoting beautification became virtuous endeavors; proponents equated elite cultural tastes with human progress. In a story about the Bleckley plan, for example, the *Atlanta Journal* reminded readers, "To attain and to conceive the beautiful is the noblest function of man." In another instance, the *Journal* wrote, "As knowledge, culture and refinement advance in a community, so the desire and love for cleanliness, for the beautiful and for the artistic in life keep step among its people."[95] And "beauty," at least to white elites, meant homogeneity, order, and balance. By repeating these urban visions, white elites constantly devalued the mixed, heterogeneous landscape of Atlanta's older neighborhoods. With the exception of the "uncovered sewer of smoke," journalists did not specify which neighborhoods or spaces exhibited squalor or what aesthetic styles were specifically to be avoided, leading the reader to assume that any places without boulevards, stately trees, and "cleanliness" were undesirable. Moreover, the consistent assignment of the terms *artistic, grand,* and *beautiful* to specific architectural styles, building and street types, or landscape design subtly equated those products with those descriptors. Readers knew boulevards were grand because the two words were almost always used in combination.

◈

From 1880 to 1910, Atlantans sought to keep pace nationally in trade and commerce, but elites also thirsted for a genteel and sophisticated city, and they eagerly competed in this arena as well. Urban competition and boosterism fostered the circulation of development plans and innovations between cities and regions. Through this exchange, Atlantans learned about other cities, their residential and industrial forms, planning methods, and services. City proposals, news editorials, and real-estate ads demonstrated Atlantans' heightened awareness of other cities' practices and competitive mind. References to cities with macadamized sidewalks and fire limits could be found throughout city council minutes and were used to persuade leaders to take action on urban matters. Elite desires to shape Atlanta into a particular type of urban environment meant, for example, demonstrating the presence of civic centers in other major cities. Such comparisons helped justify similar expenditures in Atlanta. But most importantly, city leaders could incorporate other cities' practices and ideas into their own city's form. With their counterparts in cities across the country, Atlanta's civic elites attempted to fashion the modern urban aesthetic, at least as it was defined by civic elites.[96]

But for all their aspirations, civic elites did not achieve their goals for a modern city. The city's rank-and-file rejected beautification and other elite expenditures and practices by electing a notorious mayor (James Woodward) and council members and aldermen who questioned some of the "best people's" desires. In other cases, entities blocked plans, as when the railroads and the state halted the Bleckley Plaza plan. Nonetheless, the elite taste cultures remained to be reattempted in other projects. Even in half achievements, City Beautiful ideals and park-neighborhood sensibilities propagated throughout Atlanta, informing established taste cultures and molding new ones.

The City Beautiful movement, with its celebration of parks and monumentalism, combined with the growth of Atlanta's middle and upper classes and the emerging appreciation of park-neighborhoods to change elite Atlantans' concept of urban space, including residential space.[97] To elites, the city violated emerging cultural norms. Housing styles were mixed within neighborhoods, and distinguished houses sat near more-modest homes. The new park-neighborhood and planned spaces did not allow for scattered clusters of shotgun homes, duplexes, and "negro shanties" amid Victorian homes and their manicured lawns. Increasingly, elites sought neighborhoods where homes and lawns worked collectively to create what they perceived as an orderly, tranquil landscape. Individualism had its place, but it was not in the exclusive park-neighborhood. Rather, residential landscapes should be fashioned into stately yet calming and verdant tableaus. Such ideologies collided with older speculative real-estate patterns. Between 1890 and 1910, elites moved their new landscape aesthetic ideals from planned communities to public policy. Other middle-class and elite homeowners attempted to pull this new aesthetic into their aging neighborhoods.

CHAPTER THREE

A City Divided, 1910 to 1917

If the home-owning whites who occupied the distinguished homes lining Jackson Hill, just east of Atlanta's downtown, were uncomfortable with the presence of African Americans in the area, it did not surface publicly until 1910. That year, local whites attempted to remove historically black Morris Brown College to another part of the city. When blacks declined to move, whites drew and announced a boundary line to prevent what they called "Negro encroachment" and "invasion." When black families continued renting and purchasing homes within Jackson Hill, whites pushed through segregation ordinances in 1913 and 1916.

Jackson Hill whites seemed increasingly disconcerted by the growing city. Homes filled in empty lots in the neighborhood. And African American families drew nearer. Worse, in whites' view, black success meant that African American families no longer occupied small rows of "Negro tenements" and alley housing but were renting and purchasing bungalows next door. Black presence on street fronts challenged white notions of the proper place of blacks spatially and in social status.

Moreover, Jackson Hill's whites made their segregation demands as Edwin Ansley, Joel Hurt, and other elite investors established exclusive park-neighborhoods at the city's northern and eastern edges. Arcadian landscapes, distinguished homes, calming tableaus—and a greater-than-average presence of homeowners—lured many civic elites away from the increasingly crowded city. Indeed, Atlanta's boosters celebrated the modern city, but its mixture of backyard tenements, businesses, and homes paled in comparison to the era's acclaimed monumentalism, planned neighborhoods, and civic centers. New neighborhood and city designs—and the promise of white neighbors—likewise attracted Jackson Hill's whites. But rather than moving to Ansley Park or Druid Hills, white elites attempted to bring park-neighborhood practices and controls into their established neighborhood, and demanded that black families move out—or be moved out.

White elites insisted on whitening Jackson Hill. They attempted to move historically black Morris Brown College out of the neighborhood and to the west side of the city. When that action failed, they declared a fourteen-block section of Jackson Hill for whites only. Unsuccessful with that measure, they established segregation ordinances in 1913 and 1916. Beginning in 1917, Jackson Hill whites directed the rehabilitation of the fire-damaged Fourth Ward toward their goals of whiteness. None of these actions proved successful. However, throughout the segregation campaigns of the second decade of the century, whites consistently deployed language that helped residents associate new landscape characteristics with one another; linearity, harmony, setbacks, orderliness, homeownership, and whiteness increasingly became linked and part of a single status good set. In rebuilding proposals, newspaper editorials, ordinances, and declarations, white elites repeated these assumptions and continually fashioned a new set of cultural understandings regarding neighborhood, housing, and human landscapes. What is more, as white civic elites asserted control through ordinances and declarations, they both borrowed from and contributed to park-neighborhood discourses nationally, helping cultivate and disseminate new expectations about neighborhood and housing landscapes across the United States.

Race in Atlanta

In cities throughout the South from the 1890s to the second decade of the twentieth century, whites and blacks engaged race in entirely new ways, challenging older racial sensibilities. Jammed streetcars and commercial streets meant jostling and crowding and made interracial body contact a common occurrence. Decatur Street's juke joints, penny arcades, and bars provided for more-intentional interactions. Whites became acutely aware of blacks. As historian Mark Smith explains, southern whites began to complain of crowds and crowding, indicating their discomfort with seeing, smelling, hearing, and touching blacks. Whites responded by imposing segregation ordinances, initially targeting places of close and frequent physical contact such as streetcars and nightclubs for formal segregation. In 1891, for example, Georgia passed a law allowing local governments to implement segregation ordinances on public transportation. Whites segregated other points of potential interracial engagement as well. Laws legally forbade a range of activities, including the practicing of medicine by blacks on whites, black barbering of white women, and mixed-race education.[1]

Other social codes and jim crow laws controlled indirect contact between blacks and whites and reinforced racial hierarchies. In Atlanta, courts instituted the use of separate Bibles to swear in witnesses so that whites would not have to touch objects blacks had touched, even a bit. White-operated stores frequently forbade blacks from trying on hats, shoes, or clothes. Such practices and laws both iterated and disseminated notions of black immorality, inferiority, and savageness on a daily basis, fortifying white power.[2]

But as scholars have noted, whites were inconsistent in their application of jim crow social rules and laws. Blacks commonly served as nursemaids to white children, worked as cooks in white households and other businesses, and washed white clothing and bedding as laundresses in white homes and hotels. Indeed, in these arenas blacks and whites shared *intimate* contact. But as the group possessing nearly unchecked power in the post-Reconstruction South, whites neither had to explain nor be consistent in their reasoning. Segregation, as Mark Smith asserts, was not a complete system of separation; rather, whites "derived their authority by defining when and where sensory intimacy was permitted."[3] In practice, then, social rules and jim crow laws did not simply control interracial interaction; they instilled ideologies of "white supremacy."

Whites applied these same notions as rationales for controlling and terrorizing blacks in the South of the late 1800s. Black men were brutes and animals, so the reasoning went, and thus a constant threat to white womanhood. African Americans were immoral and demanded Christian guidance. They were childlike and needed discipline. These myths and beliefs combined with elite Atlantans' concerns about a rapidly urbanizing environment and their discomfort with a changing sociopolitical environment.

Whites used terror to suppress growing black power. Lynching incidents remained high in the South through World War I, peaking in 1892, when 156 blacks were lynched. About one-third of the lynchings were carried out for the alleged rape of white women. A particularly horrific display of white power and southern white society's degradation, lynchings signaled a new level of lawlessness and paranoia for the period. Photographers' postcards from the era confirm the widespread acceptance of terrorism and torture by whites. Families are seen enjoying the event. Occasional postcard scribblings indicate that the spectators shared these scenes with others, and that whites accepted such displays at times lightly, at times with glee.[4]

While the new wave of legislation limited black movement and interracial interactions, southern blacks met segregation by forging new community and business institutions and cultivating new political networks that stretched from big cities to small towns across the United States. In Atlanta, for example, blacks moved from unskilled positions into skilled trades and dominated much of the city's metal work. Local black leaders Walter White, W. E. B. Du Bois, John Hope, Alonzo Herndon, and others worked collectively to produce new publications, open banks and businesses, launch fraternal organizations, and otherwise foster institutions that provided a strong foundation for and indication of black success and middle-class formation. But black success, rather than being the desired entrée into political life that many black leaders hoped for, often brought further white backlash. Black achievement challenged white status and highlighted gaps in white thinking by demonstrating that white supremacist rhetoric (and the science of racial eugenics) was simply wrong.[5]

Class complicated race in the South of the late 1800s and early 1900s, and the intersections are readily visible in Atlanta's political workings from the late 1800s to World War I. In local politics, laborers and elites, whites and blacks, formed and re-formed political coalitions that at different times promised economic renewal, equal suffrage for blacks and whites, or more equitable treatment for blacks. After Republicans lost power in the city and the state in the 1870s, Atlanta's white elite launched citywide campaigns in 1871 to entrench white Democratic power in the city. But with the reintroduction of ward-based voting in 1884, a "reform" movement pitted white and black workers against the ruling white elite. The alliance between white and black workers, however, proved weak and dissolved quickly, despite the strong antiprohibition sentiment the two groups shared. In the years that followed, whites in various coalitions occasionally vied for the black vote by promising such things as black schools or jury access. At other times, whites threatened to eliminate black representation or access to the vote itself. Ultimately, white laborers severed opportunities for coalition building with blacks in the 1890s and supported the reintroduction of the white primary, a move that elites already actively promoted. By 1897, the white primary was the central political issue advocated by whites statewide—a new electoral "reform." Blacks were not the only losers in this "reform" effort; taxes kept many white workers from the polls, as did the single polling location within each ward, and the scheduling of voting during working hours.[6]

A larger, visceral movement that encompassed politics and social life brewed as Georgians considered the white primary. Populist Thomas E. Watson and other white politicians used black disfranchisement as a rallying point in the 1890s and launched vigorous, race-baiting campaigns in city, county, and state races. In print, casual conversations, letters, and speeches, Watson and others renewed attacks on black progress and demanded the public assertion of white supremacy. Spewing antiblack rhetoric, Watson took over the Democratic Party in 1896. Atlantan Hoke Smith followed Watson into office, mobilizing race during his gubernatorial campaign in 1906. Once considered a moderate on race questions, Smith and the *Atlanta Journal* called for a "war" against black political and economic power. Smith's opponent, Clark Howell, likewise adopted the increasingly standard rhetoric, at one point calling Smith "a negro lover." Both candidates used scare tactics to rally whites to their ticket and leveraged imagery equating black voting with "negro domination" and "revolution." As noted by historian John Dittmer, after the 1906 election, "Race became the essential issue for Georgia politicians."[7]

The publication of Thomas Dixon's *Clansman* in the *Atlanta Journal* in 1905 only exacerbated the racially charged atmosphere. The novel, printed in two editions of the paper that summer, gives form to various white myths and narratives of the period. It asserts that white northerners persuaded blacks to challenge white southern power and ideals during Reconstruction. At the novel's end, whites "redeem" the South from the scourge of northern influence and rising black power. To many whites, *The Clansman* offered fantasy. To other whites, it offered hope.[8]

Such popular racist fiction combined with the political theater offered by the likes of Watson and Smith to incite a wave of race and class fear that spread throughout the South in the first decade of the twentieth century. White elites attempted to control blacks and workers whom they deemed "unruly" through codes, ordinances, workplace controls, and political machinations, all the while inviting northern investment in cities like Atlanta. Black and white laborers responded loudly and at times violently, challenging hierarchies and disrupting the capital-friendly regional scene peddled by business and civic elites.

On September 22, 1906, these tensions exploded when white gangs launched raids on Atlanta neighborhoods housing blacks and on almost any black person who crossed the mobs' paths. Prompted by rumors of assaults against four white women by black men that spread through word of mouth and newspaper headlines, white mobs pursued blacks through streets and into homes and even the Kimball Hotel. Mayor James Woodward attempted to reign in groups of white men who gathered at Five Points ready to set out against "black brutes," as did other prominent white leaders, but outbursts of violence continued for four days. Blacks actively defended their families and property and attempted to drive white gangs away from their homes and businesses. The state militia arrived on September 23, but confusion reigned. Blacks shot at streetcars in the lower Fourth Ward, and whites became brazen in their gun toting, inviting challenge and often getting it. In the Brownsville neighborhood, blacks and police engaged in at least one gun battle. The riot ended on September 25, but racial tensions remained unsettled.[9]

Besides reinforcing divisions between blacks and whites, the Atlanta race riot revealed and exacerbated class fissures within Atlanta's black and white communities. White and black leaders quickly took control of the event's analysis and established their position within the fray. Black assaults on white women (whether true or not) were attributed to a "lower class" of blacks. White gangs were composed of "the lower element." As historian Gregory Mixon observes, interracial cooperative efforts that emerged after the riot concluded that ongoing racial tensions were best handled through continued and enforced racial separation. Within this framework, white elites expected black leadership to accept a paternalistic relationship and white social and political governance. Black leaders accepted this relationship, at least to some degree, because they sought to distance themselves from lower-class blacks and align themselves with others of high social status.[10]

In spite of increasing animosity between workers and elites, blacks and whites, through the turn of the century, Atlanta's residential landscape remained curiously heterogeneous in terms of race and class. Blacks and whites, business owners and laborers lived in close proximity in the late 1800s, often on the same block. As city block samples in 1891 and 1899 confirm, both blacks and whites, workers and elites found housing throughout the city and in most neighborhoods. Individual blocks often housed people in a range of occupations, from manual laborers to store owners. To be sure, white elites concentrated along Peachtree Street, and some white mill workers lived in housing provided by Fulton Bag and Cotton Mills, but in 1900 most sections of the city remained mixed by race and occupational class.

Nonetheless, ongoing racial and class tensions encouraged white elites to reject the heterogeneous city and lead an increasingly influential movement to establish class and racial segregation in housing. Like the city-planning and park-neighborhood movements, this campaign relied not merely on local concerns but on a national network of city-planning professionals and urban leaders who surveyed, absorbed, and implemented "best practice" in dividing cities. In Atlanta, white home-owning elites in the Jackson Hill neighborhood were among the leaders of this effort. They launched and doggedly pursued housing segregation, first attempting to isolate their own section and, when that failed, pushing to regulate housing throughout the city.

Jackson Hill

Located just east of Atlanta's central business district in the city's lower Fourth Ward, Jackson Hill housed white New South entrepreneurs and an emerging middle and upper class. Most of the larger homes on Jackson Street, Houston

Street, and Boulevard dated to the 1880s, and their building footprints suggest the era's prevalent Queen Anne–style architecture, a style popular among the region's elite (see fig. 3.1). Attorney and Georgia assemblyman Walter McElreath recalled the section as distinguished, if slow to establish itself:

> There were many large, handsome and, for that day, expensive homes on North Boulevard and Jackson Street, and on that part of Houston Street between Jackson Street and North Boulevard. These houses stood far apart, only one or two to the block, with vacant lots between evidencing the fact of arrested development. North of North Avenue and south of Ponce de Leon Ave there was no house east of Jackson Street.[11]

Not simply the home of the city's emerging elite, Jackson Hill housed an "old guard," a distinction McElreath made clear when he explained that "the homes on Houston and Jackson streets and North Boulevard were occupied by some of the most prominent and well-to-do people of the city"; Peachtree Street, McElreath explained, housed "the nouveau riche and social strugglers." Surrounding the grander homes of Houston, Boulevard, and Jackson, "less prominent people and those of smaller means lived on Johnson Avenue, Randolph Street, Highland Avenue . . . East Avenue, Rice Street, Angier Avenue, Morgan Street, and Pine Street, which at that time were very respectable streets."[12] To McElreath, Jackson Hill was well off—and white.

African American resident Millie Jordan remembered an area that elite whites tried to ignore. Jordan recalled Houston Street, which intersected with Jackson, as "one of the very finest black residential streets in what was once called the Old Fourth Ward." She pointed to the many prominent families who once lived on Houston, including Walter White, the executive secretary of the NAACP. Real-estate agent Antoine Graves and builder Alexander Hamilton lived around the corner on Howell. To Jordan, "This ward was the elite section of its day."[13]

McElreath's memoir ignored Jordan's lower Fourth Ward and the growth of black institutions in Jackson Hill. African American Big Bethel Church, built in 1886, held the corner of Butler Street and Auburn Avenue. Historically black Morris Brown College consumed much of the block fronting Boulevard between Houston and Irwin Streets when it was built in the 1880s, and the white congregation of Grace Methodist Church built their new sanctuary directly across the street in 1884. White students attended North Boulevard School one block south. Auburn Avenue, a predominantly African American commercial and entertainment area that served as the principal business district for the city's black community, was a mere two blocks south of the white

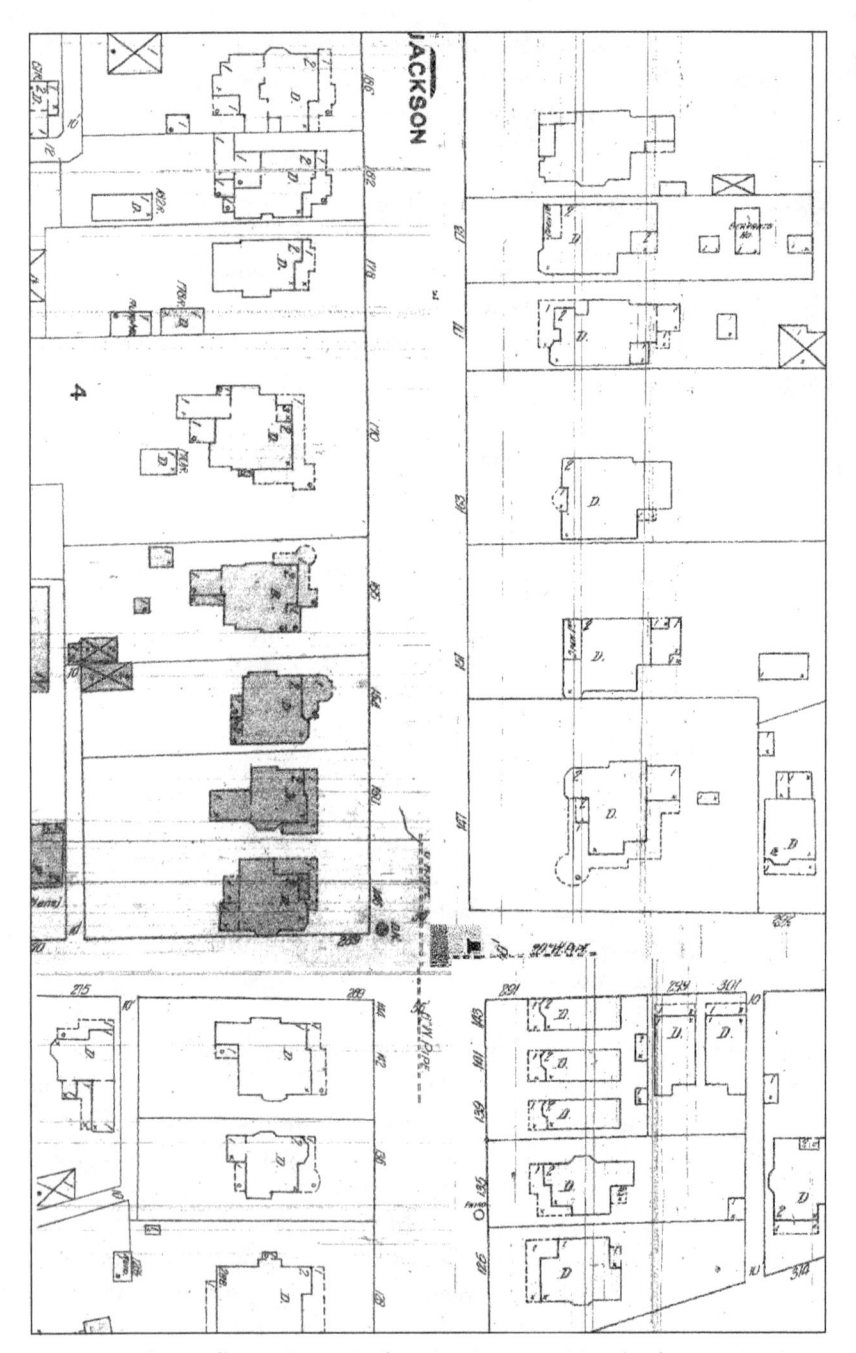

Figure 3.1. Jackson Hill, 1911. Source: Sanborn Fire Insurance Maps (1911).

school. Although the heyday of "Sweet Auburn" would not peak until the 1920s to the 1940s, early (now landmark) African American institutions were established there by 1900, including Wheat Street Baptist Church and Ebenezer Baptist Church.[14]

Homes of blacks and whites were interspersed among the churches, schools, and businesses. Whites occupied most of the length of Howell Street between Edgewood and Auburn Avenues in 1899, but blacks and whites were scattered throughout the block just south of Edgewood. There were only a few homes on Jackson Boulevard between Auburn and Irwin, but whites occupied a smattering of larger homes just north on the hill. Whites and blacks shared the length of Edgewood between Jackson and Boulevard. Indeed, whites and blacks built Jackson Hill together, literally side by side.[15]

Despite its appearance, the neighborhood was hardly socially integrated; racial social codes and local ordinances still shaped day-to-day interactions in the lower Fourth Ward. Indeed, it was the presence of such social rules that allowed blacks and whites to live in close proximity in a period of extreme racial tension. Whites expected blacks to adopt a particular racial etiquette and deference, expectations enforced by violence and local ordinances. As southerners continued migrating to Atlanta, land-use conflict intensified, sparking racial and class conflict.[16]

Jackson Hill developed rapidly after 1900. Walter McElreath explained, "New homes began to be built in the Fourth Ward, and in a very few years practically every vacant lot in the Ward was built upon; and the Jackson Hill community, as the section in which we lived was known, became one of the best and most delightful communities in the city."[17] But its delightfulness was about to end, at least according to the old-guard whites. As McElreath suggested, many lots in the Jackson Hill neighborhood were unimproved before 1900, but by 1904 building in the area had increased substantially. White and blacks, laborers and business owners moved in, filling in the neighborhood's empty lots and back alleys and intensifying integration.

In the building-boom years between 1903 and 1911, home builders and investors paid little mind to the class hierarchy implied by the grander structures that lined Jackson and Boulevard from Irwin north to Highland. Banking on the larger worker-housing market, speculators installed modest bungalows, duplexes, and shotgun homes in the immediate vicinity. The pace and character of new construction on the block defined by Houston, Randolph, Howell, and Irwin (two blocks east of Jackson) was typical (see fig. 3.2). Before 1900, homes of about 1,000 to 1,200 square feet on 5,500-square-foot lots predominated along Houston Street. But around 1906, speculative builders filled in the southwest portion of the block with duplexes, smaller single-family homes, and

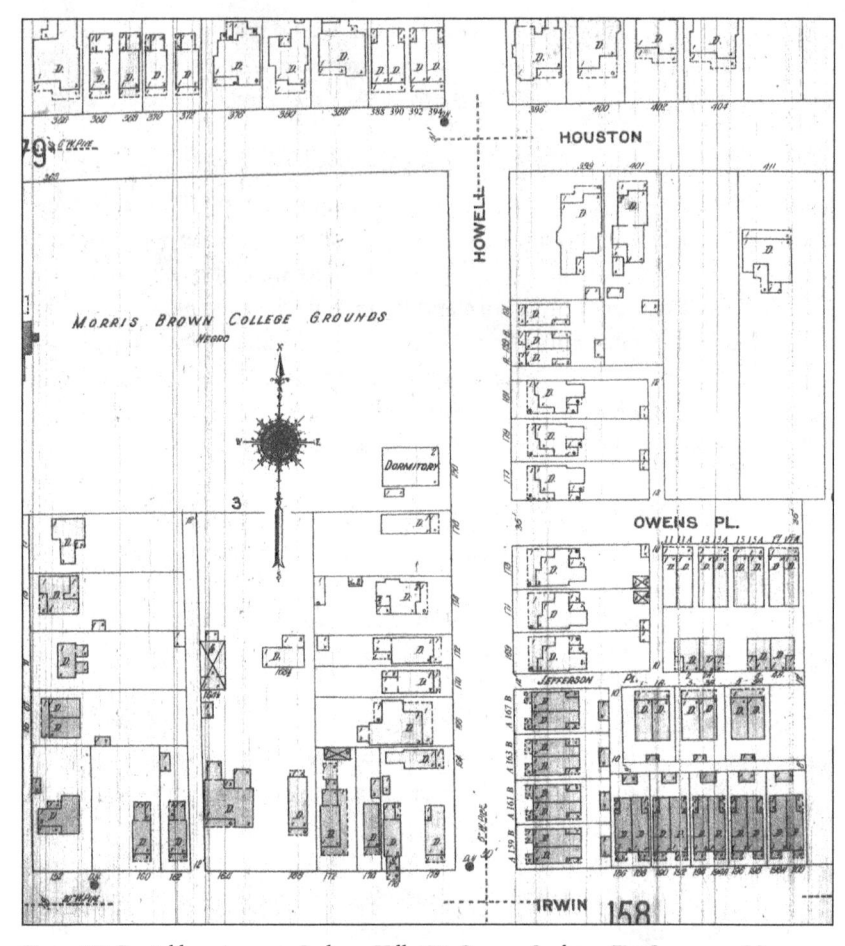

Figure 3.2. Rental housing near Jackson Hill, 1911. Source: Sanborn Fire Insurance Maps (1911).

one-room shacks in rear alleys—all renting immediately to African Americans. A number of similar units nearby housed groups of whites. The new additions were considerably smaller than the neighborhood's original housing; each unit of the duplexes measured 400 square feet, while the single-family homes measured about 900 square feet. Nearby, rental-housing developers packed five small duplex units onto the northwest corner of Houston and Howell, houses that contrasted with the existing structures in the immediate vicinity. These new units rented to whites. Turnover of established homes from whites to blacks occurred as well. By 1906, for example, African Americans lived in over half the units formerly housing whites on Houston Street, occupying both the stately homes and the simpler structures.[18]

Whites dominated this speculative building practice. For example, in 1905, white land developer James R. Black (of Green, Morris and Black) built four frame dwellings at 159, 161, 163, and 167 Howell for about $750 each. In 1909, then with Black and Storry, he built four small frame alley dwellings at 11, 13, 15, and 17 Owens Place at the cost of $600 each (see fig. 3.2). In 1907, the Mutual Investment Company paid white builder R. P. Pool to erect four frame dwellings at 388, 390, 486, and 488 Houston and two frame dwellings at 210 and 212 Howell. In 1909, white contractor D. J. Lee erected four frame dwellings for Mrs. W. A. Gregg, the wife of a clerk, at 125, 127, 129, and 131 Randolph. Thus, while blacks established schools, churches, and businesses in the lower Fourth Ward, housing production remained largely controlled by white investors, builders, and agents.[19]

From 1900 to about 1915, Jackson Hill residents confronted an influx of rental housing that, rather than significantly altering the architectural, class, and racial landscape of the area, intensified the patterns of diversity already there. But as lots filled in, people drew nearer. The infill development distressed some white residents. In response, in 1910 white Jackson Hill elites launched a sustained movement to control black population growth in their neighborhood, initially by relocating a major black institution, later by legally controlling black residential access to the area.

Moving Morris Brown

White elites attempted to control black population growth in the lower Fourth Ward by diverting potential new residents to the west side of the city. Specifically, whites sought to remove historically black Morris Brown College from Jackson Hill to the west side of town, assuming that the institution would attract the growing black population. This white-led plan coincided with black-led initiatives to reformulate Morris Brown's educational mission. Consequently, debates over Morris Brown's location—and black residential geography—were complicated by local black politics as well as black resistance to white control over housing choice.

A fire that damaged Morris Brown College in January 1910 offered an opportunity to blacks and whites who sought to change the institution. Students, faculty, and administrators considered the fire a setback, but home-owning whites viewed it as a chance to control black presence in Jackson Hill. The latter group moved quickly, asked to purchase the property—for the "greater white development" of the lower Fourth Ward—and offered the college acreage to rebuild the school on the city's west side.[20] At the same time, some local black leaders promoted enlarging and refocusing the school's curriculum on industrial education.[21]

Richard Stinson, the African American former vice president of Morris Brown and financial officer at the school, loudly and publicly promoted the remaking of Morris Brown into an industrial education center. Although the school was conceived in the self-help ideology trumpeted by Booker T. Washington and other conservative leaders, Morris Brown offered both liberal education tracks and skills training. The school initially delivered courses in business, domestic science, teaching, printing, and tailoring, and its first college-level programs focused on liberal arts and theology. By 1900, the school had added agricultural arts, dressmaking, bookkeeping, and carpentry. Stinson sought to strengthen the agricultural- and industrial-education components, which he and others argued required more space, a new facility, and thus a new, larger location.[22]

The move to the west side encouraged by whites may have been attractive to some black leaders in that the west side already housed the campuses of prestigious Atlanta University and Spelman College. Many black elites lived near the west side schools, including entrepreneur Alonzo Herndon and the college presidents and teachers. That said, Morris Brown's location near the black businesses of Auburn Avenue, numerous churches, and a sizable black populace meant that it sat squarely within a substantial and established black community.[23]

The city's west side also had its share of challenges. Those wards still trailed the rest of the city in basic infrastructure development, including water service. And some neighborhoods lacked trunk sewers. (One Realtor hawked West End Heights by advertising that "no sewer water drains in this direction.")[24] Also, the west side remained somewhat isolated from the main part of Atlanta, though viaducts had finally bridged some of the rail lines and provided safer access to and from downtown. Finally, the section suffered inadequate fire protection;

the new viaducts provided vehicular access to the west, but the neighborhood lacked a fire station of its own.[25]

Neither Morris Brown's president nor its trustees expressed any interest in moving the school from the lower Fourth Ward, and Richard Stinson's public appeals for an expansion of industrial education drew immediate, irritated response from college leadership. Morris Brown president E. W. Lee and Georgia's AME Bishop C. S. Smith publicly asserted that Stinson did not represent Morris Brown, and that he should not be taken as an authority on the school or its future direction. In a letter distributed immediately after Stinson's call, Lee emphasized, "The mass meeting which is being so largely advertised to take place at the People's Tabernacle next Sunday afternoon has not been sanctioned by the authorities of the college." Stinson retorted publicly that the president and trustees were "against him," but that the majority of the black population was on his side, along with "practically all of the best of that race in Atlanta."[26]

Besides denying that the college had any plans to move, President Lee defended the administration and school against accusations that Morris Brown had turned away from industrial education. He argued that the institution had never had more than four industrial programs, and that those programs were still in operation. Lee also claimed that students' labor was, in fact, constantly in public view, asserting, "What white man living along Boulevard has not seen every young man at Morris Brown with pick, shovel, and wheelbarrow converting that red hill into terraces and a campus of beauty and comeliness under my administration? There is not a day but what I send out from six to a dozen young men to white families to work and all the white people of this community will testify to this."[27] If Lee did not embrace industrial education wholeheartedly, he made sure that he kept the little that existed at Morris Brown in the white public eye.

For his part, Stinson appealed to white elite authority to bolster his campaign for industrial education, acknowledging white residents' desires to rid the area of a major black institution. In one case, he claimed that his plan had "the approval of the white people ... who believe[d] [Morris Brown was] unwisely located."[28] Stinson reinforced these appeals by contending that Smith's actions undermined black-white relations. In one case, Stinson asserted that Smith seemed willing to "disrupt the good feeling of the two races in the community," presumably by keeping Morris Brown in the lower Fourth Ward. And Stinson painted Smith as a "would-be disturber of the peace between nations."[29] On another occasion, Stinson suggested that Morris Brown's leaders lacked the skills necessary to promote interracial understanding when he asked, "What special fitness has [Smith] or Lee to ... encourage friendly relations between the races?"[30] Stinson then appealed to fears of racial disturbances and accused Smith of taking "action to cause trouble between whites and blacks" by filing a building permit to make five thousand dollars in repairs to the school. Only four years after Atlanta's internationally covered race riot, suggestions that black leaders undermined attempts at interracial cooperation weighed heavy.[31]

It is not clear if the white power structure was explicitly against Lee and Smith or their academic vision, but Stinson's play to white leadership brought the city's strongest white financiers to the table. White business leaders James English and Samuel M. Inman were not only expected to attend the meeting on industrial education called by Stinson, but English—president of the Fourth National Bank, noted philanthropist, and real-estate investor—was slated to preside over the discussion. English's position as meeting facilitator should not be overlooked. Although the newspaper did not reveal who might finance or donate land on the west side to Morris Brown, English may well have been the financial power behind the offer.[32]

Moreover, English and Inman both had financial ties to the exclusive park-neighborhoods being erected on the city's north and east side. Both literally banked on the success of the homogeneous, park-neighborhood aesthetic emerging in Atlanta and throughout the South, an aesthetic that relied on notions of harmony, balance, natural surroundings, and whiteness. Although there is no evidence directly exposing Inman's and English's sympathies for the desire of Jackson Hill elites to shunt blacks to the west side, their investment choices suggest that they identified park-neighborhoods and racially homogeneous residential environments as an emerging landscape fashion and white elite expectation. It is not surprising, then, that they lent their assistance to colleagues and fellow elites seeking to introduce park-neighborhood attributes and impose racial controls on Jackson Hill.[33]

Faced with a recalcitrant Morris Brown administration, white Fourth Warders reworked their approach and drew on the power of the state; they pursued the Morris Brown property for use as a public school facility. The Atlanta Chamber of Commerce proposed a meeting with the AME bishops, and the *Atlanta Journal* canvassed white Fourth Ward residents as to whether they were willing to subscribe thousands of dollars toward moving Morris Brown. The paper went on to assert that other money doubtless would come from the city, "since the plan contemplate[d] the use of Morris for purposes of public school education."[34] In the spring of 1910, the city council charged a committee to investigate the relocation, which included city council and aldermanic members as well as local citizens: physician Charles J. Vaughan, physician Samuel D. Warnock, attorney Edgar Pomeroy, Judge John S. Candler, John W. Grant, S. R. Johnston, attorney F. M. Mitchell, future mayor and attorney Courtland S.

Winn, attorney and Fourth Ward resident Walter McElreath, real-estate agent J. C. Baldwin, B. J. Conyers, and W. M. Terry. After study by the committee, the city council approved a motion by Charles Vaughan and Samuel Warnock in support of the relocation plans.[35]

The proposal to purchase Morris Brown for use as a public school changed a formerly private land matter into an issue of public policy, with the power of the "public good" and the weight of the city behind it. In this new schema, white Atlantans would receive a new public school facility, and a private black institution would receive land "better suited" to its new pursuits. Thus, whites transformed their demand to remove a black institution from what elites perceived as a "white area" into a public initiative that appeared to be a fair deal for everyone.

Even so, Morris Brown's leadership refused to yield to these performances of white power. Morris Brown leaders ignored white overtures, improved the school, and denied any plans to move. In a March 18, 1910, letter to Atlanta University president Asa Ware, Morris Brown president E. W. Lee explained that Morris Brown was "not on the market for sale.... We are not seeking any other location."[36] While white Fourth Warders continued their discussions of the move, the president of Morris Brown restored the burned section of the main building and kicked off a campaign to add a second structure to the campus. Whether this move was political posturing by Lee is unclear, but the building renovation was complete by the beginning of May 1910. What is more, Morris Brown's administrators fired Stinson in June, and the school remained in the Fourth Ward until 1932.[37]

White home-owning residents of the Fourth Ward went to considerable lengths to relocate a major African American institution in the hopes that the black populace would follow. They organized meetings between white political leadership and school and AME officials. They offered cash. They offered land. And black Fourth Warders declined each. Faced with effective black resistance, white propertied elites turned again to the state to secure a whites-only neighborhood.

Jackson Hill's white home-owning residents met in October 1910 to delineate a racial boundary line in the neighborhood and, as the *Atlanta Constitution* reported, "put the public and all real estate developers on notice that the sale or renting of property within the white territory [specified] would be considered a reprehensible and unfriendly act."[38] Encompassing fourteen blocks, the boundary was described as

> commencing at the junction of Irwin and Hilliard streets and running east along both sides of Irwin street to Howell street; thence north along Howell street to

Houston street; thence east along both sides of Houston street to the Southern railway; along both sides of Summit avenue to Highland avenue; then along Fort street to south side of Highland avenue; thence along south side of Highland avenue to Hilliard street; thence along both sides of Hilliard street to Irwin street. (See fig. 3.3.)[39]

Boundary line promoters contended that blacks had been "encroaching" on and "rapidly taking possession" of "white residential sections," specifically "Jackson Hill."[40]

As the *Atlanta Constitution* noted, it was the "prominent citizens" of the Jackson Hill area who met in Grace Methodist Church to introduce the boundary proposal, and the list of attendees was remarkably similar to the committee named to study the Morris Brown move. B. Lee Smith, an advertising solicitor for the *Georgian,* led the meeting. Attorney Walter McElreath, attorney Eugene Mitchell, and real-estate dealer J. C. Baldwin all spoke in support of the proposed boundary line.[41]

Attendees debated the causes and potential "remedies" to black movement within the neighborhood. McElreath and Mitchell complained that streetcar access brought African Americans into the area, and they proposed rerouting the car lines. Others blamed Bishop C. S. Smith of Morris Brown College, who they claimed was encouraging blacks to settle in the area "and mix with whites." Lee Smith identified real-estate agents as the culprits for purported racial change. Curiously, no one commented on Atlanta's burgeoning population growth, black and white, though the real-estate agents were acutely aware of the tight housing market. The meeting attendees concluded that, "for the best interests of both the white people and colored people," whites and black housing should be segregated, though they did not state why it was in blacks and whites' "best interest."[42]

It is unclear if Jackson Hill's white residents truly expected Realtors and landlords to turn black-occupied units over to whites after the 1910 boundary line declaration. *Atlanta Independent* editor Benjamin Davis scoffed at the prospect and queried,

The *Independent* would like to know how the race haters . . . are going to dispossess the Negroes of all the homes they own north of Irwin street. . . . Now, Negroes own the property on both sides of Irwin street, east of the Boulevard, and up both sides of Howell street to Houston, down both sides of Houston to the Boulevard, down both sides of Houston street from Hilliard street to Courtland street, on both sides of Cain street, from Fort street to Jackson, and a majority of the property on both sides of Hilliard street, from Houston to Highland.[43]

A City Divided 87

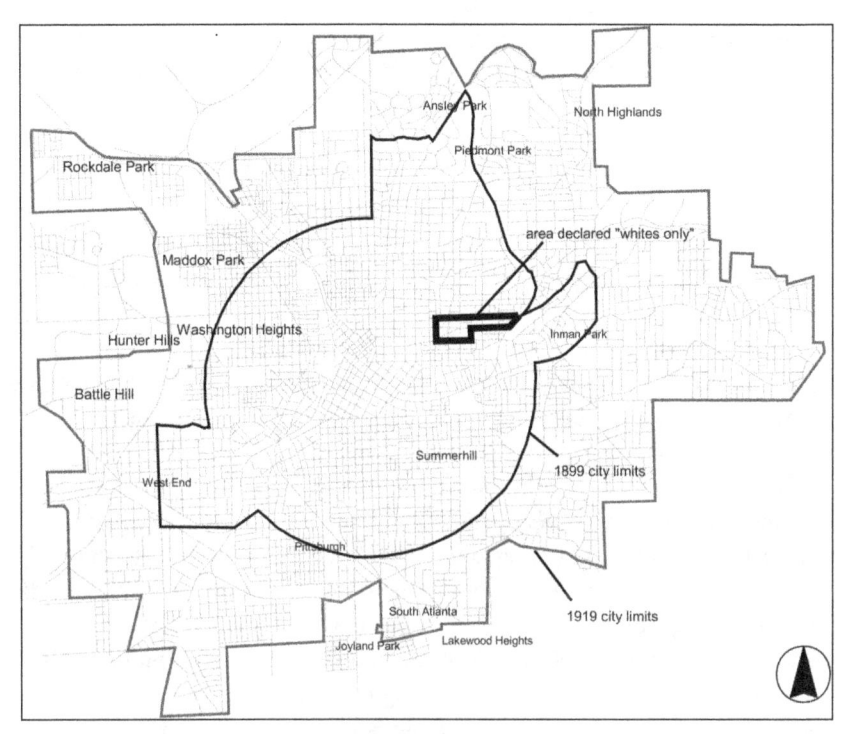

Figure 3.3. "Whites only" area of Fourth Ward, as declared by a 1910 agreement between residents and particular realtors, in context of the entire city.

Indeed, a turnover of black-occupied housing to white occupants would have violated racial norms. While white-occupied homes in Atlanta occasionally passed to blacks, black-occupied housing rarely passed to whites. The question was and is moot, however; black families remained in Jackson Hill, and duplex and single-family homes ranging from about four hundred to one thousand square feet continued to be built, rented, or sold to African Americans in the "whites only" area. Johnson Avenue, for example, between Boulevard and Randolph, turned from 100 percent white to 54 percent black from 1911 to 1912.[44]

If elite whites were concerned about growing black population, it is curious why they waited until 1910 to publicly demand the expulsion of African Americans from what they considered to be a white neighborhood. After all, racial tensions had exploded only four years earlier in a race riot, and residential proximity could have been understood by whites as increasing the likelihood of interactions between black males and white females—a relationship that whites feared. That said, it may not have occurred to whites to demand black residential segregation; after all, social codes and local and state ordinances controlled much of the interaction between whites and blacks already (though obviously these codes could be and were violated).[45] Perhaps the mixed-race, heterogeneous built environment that existed until about 1900 had been acceptable to elite whites when Jackson Hill and the lower Fourth Ward were less dense. When land use grew more intense and black occupancy increased, elite whites became distressed about *more* African American homes, which they equated with urban disorder. From 1899 to 1910, the number of households within the declared whites-only area increased by 50 percent. Or whites may have found the changing status of blacks disorienting. No longer were African American families settling for rows of shanties and back-alley tenements. Rather, they seized housing appropriate to their economic status—on the street fronts and occasionally side by side with whites.[46]

White elites may also have become more acutely aware of land use and urban environments as new models of suburban living filled in the city's perimeter. The neat lawns, well-kept homes, and tranquil scenes identified with the city's park-neighborhoods enticed many former in-town property owners, even if Atlanta's core city did not house the noxious industries that pushed city dwellers to the suburbs of places like Cleveland and Chicago. The *Atlanta Constitution* regularly updated readers on the progress of park-neighborhood buying and building. In one of his regular columns on "Atlanta Dirt," real-estate investor and agent George Adair described his drive through Ansley Park, noting its "beautifully shaded avenues, all well paved," and "artistic" design.[47] For those who remained in town, weekend tours to the new park-neighborhoods reminded well-heeled Atlantans of the freshest ideas in architecture, landscape, and living. One 1910 *Atlanta Journal* article explained that the trolley-car route to Druid Hills was "one of the most attractive trolley rides in the entire system" and would "very likely prove one of the most popular for pleasure rides, as it afford[ed] an opportunity to see the beautiful homes on Peachtree and Ponce de Leon avenue, as well as the handsome new homes now in Druid Hills."[48] Thus, Jackson Hill's home-owning whites experienced change in their neighborhood's built environment and land use at the same time that new landscape aesthetic trends aroused homeowners' senses. But in Jackson Hill in the early twentieth century, white homeowners did not flee the urban core as density increased (at least initially) but demanded a complete alteration of the existing landscape.

In their attempt to halt neighborhood change, Atlanta's whites borrowed new land-use controls introduced in other cities, just as they had followed national trends in adopting city-beautification practices, parks, and green spaces.

In this case, Atlantans looked to Baltimore, which, in December 1910, became the first city in the United States to pass a race-based housing segregation ordinance.[49] Sparked by a black couple's purchase of a home in the heretofore white Baltimore neighborhood of Druid Hill in June, the city passed the West segregation ordinance, which prevented blacks from moving into predominantly white blocks and whites from moving into predominantly black blocks. Although the act was quickly overturned by the courts, a persistent Baltimore city council responded with a second and then a third ordinance that same year. A fourth try was necessary in 1913. Other cities followed. Richmond passed a racial segregation ordinance in April 1911; Norfolk in June 1911; Ashland, Virginia, in September 1911; Greenville, South Carolina, in May 1912; and Winston, North Carolina, in June 1912. Although whites in many cities copied Baltimore's proposal, white leaders in some cities opted to wait and see how the public and courts received segregation ordinances before formulating their own. For example, confronted with demands by a few Louisville citizens that the local real-estate exchange support a proposed segregation ordinance, local exchange president J. D. Wright responded that the public had not settled its opinion on mandated segregation, and that segregation ordinances might bring discrimination against the city as a whole.[50]

After Jackson Hill's 1910 declaration failed to control renter and black movement into the Fourth Ward, whites adopted tactics current throughout the urban South and increasingly utilized in the urban North; in 1913 they proposed a city ordinance outlining racial residential segregation procedures. Claude Ashley, a Fourth Ward resident and city councilman, led the charge. While the proposal would extend segregation to every city block, rhetoric surrounding the plan focused solely on Jackson Hill, suggesting that white concerns about black presence were geographically limited in scope, at least at this time. According to reports in local newspapers, Ashley and his neighbors took action in response to the transfer of homes in Jackson Hill, specifically on Houston, Johnson, and Hilliard Streets.[51]

Ashley and the attorneys he consulted modeled the Atlanta segregation proposal on ordinances used in Baltimore and cities in Virginia. The resulting ordinance forbade blacks from occupying homes on "white" blocks and whites from occupying homes on "black" blocks unless the majority of *owners* agreed that a house was open for occupancy by either whites or blacks. Supporters contended that the ordinance did not illegally segregate blacks and whites since it did not assign blacks to particular sections or blocks.[52]

Word of Atlanta's ordinance spread nationally through black periodicals, including the NAACP's *Crisis*, the *Chicago Defender*, and the *Pittsburgh Courier*.

No doubt this is how Booker T. Washington learned of the Ashley proposal, after which he dashed off a letter to Benjamin Davis, editor of the *Atlanta Independent,* demanding a public response. In his letter to Davis, Washington commented on the act's passage and its likely unconstitutionality and demanded, "What are you all going to do about it?" He continued, "I should be greatly disappointed if the colored people of Atlanta do not begin to fight this unjust act."[53] If Davis responded to Washington, that correspondence has been lost.[54]

Locally, black community members protested the housing segregation onslaught at public meetings, through newspapers, and in lawsuits. Reverend Henry Proctor and former U.S. collector J. T. Rucker led a group of black citizens to the June 12, 1913, council meeting in order to register their dissatisfaction with the proposed ordinance. There, the delegation pointed out that Baltimore's ordinance was likely unconstitutional. (In response, Ashley declared, "I don't care if all the courts in the United States declared the law to be invalid I would still insist that council give the people of the Fourth Ward the relief they are asking for.")[55] In a more effective protest in 1914, African American John Carey sued Atlanta when a white neighbor complained about the presence of Carey's black tenant. In 1915, the Georgia Supreme Court ruled that the Ashley ordinance violated due process clauses in both the state and the federal constitution. Ashley vowed to rewrite the ordinance to exclude the unconstitutional portions.[56]

Although black leadership contested the ordinance, Atlanta's African American community was not united against racial residential segregation. *Atlanta Independent* editor Benjamin Davis promoted separate areas for blacks and whites, but only if blacks gained substantive, sanitary housing in the process. However, it is difficult to say how many black residents agreed with Davis and were willing to accept segregated housing in return for higher-quality shelter.[57]

According to the *Atlanta Independent,* discussions regarding residential segregation resurfaced in 1915 when black families moved into homes on Houston Street formerly occupied by whites. A local white committee led by Fourth Ward councilman Claude Ashley established "dead lines" of Irwin Street and Fort Street, beyond which black families could not reside. Ashley and Councilman A. W. Farlinger continued their Ku Klux Klan–inspired show and proposed that residents attend a "rally" at Grace Methodist Church, where, according to the *Atlanta Constitution,* "the negroes would be given final warning not to exercise . . . their constitutional privileges."[58] In October 1915, black and white Fourth Ward residents met at Westminster Presbyterian Church and developed a public declaration regarding housing segregation. The statement, as reported by the *Atlanta Constitution*, read:

> Be it resolved—(1) That we will use all our moral influence to prevent any colored person from purchasing or renting any property in blocks now predominantly white and, on the other hand, any white person from living in any block now predominantly colored. (2). We will condemn with all means and methods in our power, any person, owners, real estate or other agent, who seeks to sell or rent any place in these blocks to persons of the opposite race.[59]

Local whites reportedly ordered black families currently living within the "dead lines" to move "under penalty of violence."[60] The black families moved out, but Jackson Hill whites would soon launch another campaign to impose racial housing segregation by law.[61]

The 1915 actions differed from previous movements in that blacks appeared to be directly involved in housing segregation discussions with whites; however, the *Atlanta Independent* editor charged that the meeting's black leadership did not truly represent the community affected, a complaint that had surfaced earlier in the negotiations over Morris Brown's location. Davis went on to paint the black representatives as acquiescing sycophants, writing, "But, boss, dem dar niggers want to live side you white folks, and boss, we will not only help you run dem out of de Fourth Ward, but we will help you run dem clean out of town. If you don't do dat, boss, de nigger women will run down and commit rape on your sons."[62] Here, Davis depicted black representatives as Uncle Toms and accused whites of manipulating events and rhetoric to their own advantage. And he charged area black leadership with accepting white terms at the expense of blacks.[63]

White elites quieted opposition when they could, and Benjamin Davis paid for his flippancy. After initially allowing the Odd Fellows' building roof garden to be used for dances, the white-led police committee shut it down by labeling it a "dance hall." Davis, a national leader of the fraternal organization, questioned the decision and found that it had been prompted by his opposition to a housing segregation agreement.[64]

White elites followed the declaration by proposing a second segregation ordinance in April 1916. Prepared by city attorney James L. Mayson and modeled on Louisville's segregation ordinance, the order stated that a majority of property owners on a block would determine if a block was to be considered "white" or "colored," and all building permits would be reviewed and assigned to whites or blacks. Significantly, Atlanta's mayor James Woodward signed the ordinance into law the day after arguments began in the U.S. Supreme Court case *Buchanan v. Warley*, which challenged Louisville's segregation ordinance, knowing that the ruling could affect Atlanta's 1916 law. The Atlanta City Council resolved to send their state senators to the proceedings in support of Louisville's ordinance.[65]

The Heterogeneous City

While segregation ordinances proposed to sort the entire city by race, news reports on and commentary about white concerns about black presence continually pointed to Jackson Hill, Jackson Hill residents, or the Fourth Ward. Indeed, this pattern is consistent with that of other cities imposing segregation ordinances. Baltimore's segregation campaign, for example, started with the movement of blacks into previously all-white Druid Hill. The segregationist narrative implied that Atlanta (or Baltimore) had been neatly divided between blacks and whites until, perhaps through tight housing markets or rapid black in-migration, blacks crossed some informal boundary line and moved into a "white" neighborhood. However, in Atlanta block sampling of the city indicates that racial change had long been at work throughout the city; Jackson Hill's white property owners were the only population consistently *protesting* the changing demographics and housing landscape.

Significantly, although local battles over segregation by law were waged in a small section of Atlanta's lower Fourth Ward, racial heterogeneity and racial flux marked almost the entire city in the first two decades of the twentieth century, as they had at least since 1890. As chapter 1 demonstrates, prior to the introduction of zoning and planned neighborhoods, even the owners of Peachtree Street's grander homes had to walk only a block or two away from the famous street to encounter worker bungalows, duplexes, or spans of one-room shacks housing African American laundresses. Many residents could look in their own backyard for cooks' or other servants' quarters. As noted, Jackson Hill's finer homes were less than two blocks from the race- and class-mixed Auburn Avenue. If the entire city was marked by heterogeneity (even while some neighborhoods moved toward greater homogeneity), what then was unique about Jackson Hill and its residents? What made that neighborhood's whites demand housing segregation when other neighborhoods—other neighborhoods experiencing racial flux and speculative activities—did not?[66]

Jackson Hill was unusual in early twentieth-century Atlanta not in that it was predominantly white (which it was), but rather that it was disproportionately comprised of owner-occupied housing. While about 25 percent of Atlanta homes were owner occupied in 1910, about 33 percent of the white-occupied homes in the declared "whites only" area of Jackson were owner occupied, and over 50 percent of the homes on Jackson Street between Irwin and Highland were owner occupied. Moreover, residents expressed a set of views and actions that can be identified as an emerging "status good set." To Jackson Hill's elites— like Ansley Park's or Druid Hills' civic elites—homeownership, class and racial homogeneity, whiteness, and neighborhoods exhibiting aesthetic balance, harmony, and linearity were intertwined.[67]

By 1910, homeownership, whiteness, increased attention to landscape aesthetics, and concerns about neighborhood effects—the influence of neighborhood factors on an individual's property's value—were evolving into a set of status markers associated with one another. White elites actively managed the cultural meanings of the status good set, positioning it in a cultural hierarchy of urban space and materiality and in a network with a wider set of political and economic resources. Although this status set was associated particularly with park-neighborhoods, the language and actions mobilized by Jackson Hill white elites indicate that this set of cultural understandings and practices had gained traction in at least one unplanned community in Atlanta.

To protect their status good set, whites contended that any changes to it— though particularly black neighbors—threatened property values. In his plea to the Louisville Real Estate Exchange, W. D. Binford alluded to the possibility of lost property-tax revenue were property values to drop. He warned, "There is no problem so grave, nor one so fraught with so much danger to property values as the gradual influx of the negro into blocks or squares where none but whites reside. It is not necessary to inform you that this menace has cost the city many thousands of dollars in taxes, to say nothing of the loss of property owners." Similarly, the *Louisville Times* remarked, "There are many sections of the city where property values have deteriorated almost 50 percent through the influx of colored people."[68] After Baltimore passed its segregation ordinance, the *New York Journal* commented, "It is true that the establishment of homes of colored people in neighborhoods hitherto unfrequented by them causes antagonism and may produce trouble *and disturb real estate values*" (emphasis added).[69]

In reality, it would be difficult to sort out the effects of black neighbors on white property values in the second decade of the twentieth century. Then as now, myriad variables influenced land value: local economic conditions and land markets, inflation, government policies, employment trends, and lending practices. Moreover, the economy fluctuated significantly in this period. When social scientists began investigating racial effects on property values in the 1940s, they found that black entry into white neighborhoods did not lower property values but was more likely to raise sale prices. Economist Luigi Laurenti's study of price behavior of single-family homes in San Francisco demonstrates that prices of formerly white-occupied homes were not only not driven down by nonwhite entry, but that prices became slightly higher. Laurenti concludes that "the over-all picture of comparative market prices should be reassuring to those who fear nonwhite entry will harm prices."[70] Other social scientists attribute any detectable price decline to whites "dumping" property on the market. Herman Long and Charles Johnson, for example, assert that "in brief, the disposition of white owners to sell at any price in fear of a Negro 'invasion' is the most important factor in depressing market values."[71] In the 1960s, when Rose Helper studied real-estate dealers' perceptions of how black neighbors influenced white property values, agents also reported that white responses to black movement (and perception of black movement) into white areas produced a reaction that, in reality, was the cause of value fluctuation. Nonetheless, white agents and residents repeatedly mobilized the claim that blacks depressed property values, across the nation, in the press, and in public declarations.[72]

Atlanta's whites never offered any evidence to support their claims that black encroachment depreciated values of white owner-occupied property. In Atlanta, it was a difficult argument to make given the city's historically mixed-race residential geography. The sudden escalation of this claim along with demands for residential segregation by law suggests that white elites deployed the idea as a scare tactic in order to secure a park-neighborhood-like environment in an older, established area of the city. White elites argued implicitly that they had a right to maintain or increase their property values, but they did not clarify why this was so. Despite the flaws in the justification, arguing that homeowners had an inherent right to increased property values and then following with a claim that black presence lowered (white) property values was a rational way for advocates to secure racial housing segregation. Moreover, in articulating and enforcing these claims, whites continually asserted and secured economic and social power by relegating blacks to sections with lower property values.

The arguments surrounding property values reinforced rhetoric promoting aesthetic balance, harmony, and linearity to produce a white property owners' discourse that favored not just architectural but class and racial homogeneity. Those adopting these practices would be rewarded with stabilized if not increased property values. White *homeowners* in Jackson Hill and the lower Fourth Ward drove the campaign for housing restrictions, and their efforts centered on the areas in which they themselves resided. Their concerns regarding racial mixing of blocks did *not*, for example, reach to areas in which they or others owned rental property. Nor did protest emanate from areas dominated by tenants, areas that were also mixed by race or undergoing racial transition. White homeowners implicitly argued that they had a right to increasing property values and then called upon the state to protect these investments.

◈

Whites may not have been as concerned with proximity to blacks as they were sensitive to neighborhood organization. That is, whites remained distressed about spatial arrangements that suggested equal status between blacks and whites. The 1913 segregation ordinance, for example, allowed blacks to live in servants' quarters (in the rear), though clearly such housing would place whites and blacks in close proximity. To whites, housing blacks and whites on street fronts visually signaled equality; whites rejected blacks living on the same block unless blacks occupied a clearly subservient location—in an alley or behind the white employer. Races could be mixed front to back (house to alley dwelling or servants' quarters), but street *fronts* were not to be mixed. Plans to rebuild the lower Fourth Ward after two thousand homes had been lost to fire in 1917 likewise suggested concern about racially homogeneous street fronts and street lengths. One rebuilding proposal recommended that "Jackson Street from Houston to Irwin . . . be white on both sides, and also the Boulevard north of Houston . . . be white on both sides."[73] Here, the four-sided block was not the concern, but rather the homes that faced each other (i.e., the street front). This arrangement preserved and displayed a white facade—a visual performance of white power. Elites were not dictating the racial composition of whole blocks, which would have included back alleys and street faces not immediately visible. Rather, they sought to create a linear aesthetic—a uniformly white façade that mimicked the park-neighborhood streets of Druid Hills and Ansley Park. The proximity of African Americans mattered to white home-owning elites, but the street fronts—the facade—mattered more.[74]

Pro-segregation rhetoric confirms the relationship of park-neighborhood building fashions to demands for racial housing segregation. Attorney Eugene Mitchell, a resident of Jackson Hill, told the police committee, "The time is near when the negroes will be invading Ansley Park, Druid Hills, Boulevard and Brookwood sections."[75] Mitchell disregarded unplanned communities that lacked an overarching design. The *Atlanta Independent* picked up on this rhetoric as well, and Davis echoed the exclusive park-neighborhoods Mitchell cited: "The negro does not want to live on Peachtree Street, Druid Hills, or in any other exclusive white settlement."[76] In a follow-up editorial, Davis continued to focus on white elites' concerns about specific elite neighborhoods:

"The negro does not want a home in Ansley Park, Inman Park, Druid Hills, Peachtree Street, or any other exclusive settlement."[77] Mitchell's evocation of some of the most prestigious park-neighborhoods in the city reveals that white elite concerns about black invasion did not include *all* white-majority neighborhoods in the city—just the elite, white park-neighborhoods. Mitchell disregarded neighborhoods housing white skilled workers, clerks, or shop foremen and focused on the districts of lawyers, merchants, and bankers. Atlanta's civic elites were less concerned about "white purity" than about cultivating and protecting their own status good set, which in this era included exclusively white park-neighborhoods.

Since Jackson Hill had not been established as a park-neighborhood from the beginning, its white homeowners struggled to introduce practices associated with designed communities, such as aesthetic control through deed restrictions. Ultimately, Jackson Hill's white elites resorted to segregation by ordinances that regulated race throughout the city and then relied on other white elites to support the movement. Eugene Mitchell's reference to the new park-neighborhoods may well have enlisted support from white elites living outside Jackson Hill. Having faced the failure of two informal declarations and one city ordinance to control black presence in his own neighborhood, Mitchell adopted scare tactics suggesting that black families might soon attempt to move into the city's planned communities and lower property values.

✧

Although segregation ordinances failed in court, block sampling indicates that racial segregation did increase between 1891 and 1919. However, while neighborhoods changed their racial makeup over time, the direction of racial change was not a given. "White flight" out of neighborhoods was more likely than "black flight," but some neighborhoods that began as disproportionately black evolved into white strongholds within the core city.

City directories reveal that much of the racial succession prior to 1919 took place between 1909 and 1914, the earliest years of Atlanta's debates over racial boundary lines and residential segregation by law. The street length of McDaniel Street between Berkele Street and Rockwell Street (block 55; see fig. 3.4) moved from a population of ten African Americans, five whites, and three vacancies in 1909 to include seventeen African Americans and three whites in 1911. This pattern remained, with the street showing seventeen African Americans and three whites in 1913, and by 1918, seventeen African Americans and no whites. Bradley Street between Decatur Street and Edgewood Avenue (block 31), part of Atlanta's Fourth Ward, actually counted only 38 percent of its population as black in 1899. Change came dramatically between 1912 and 1913. In

A City Divided 97

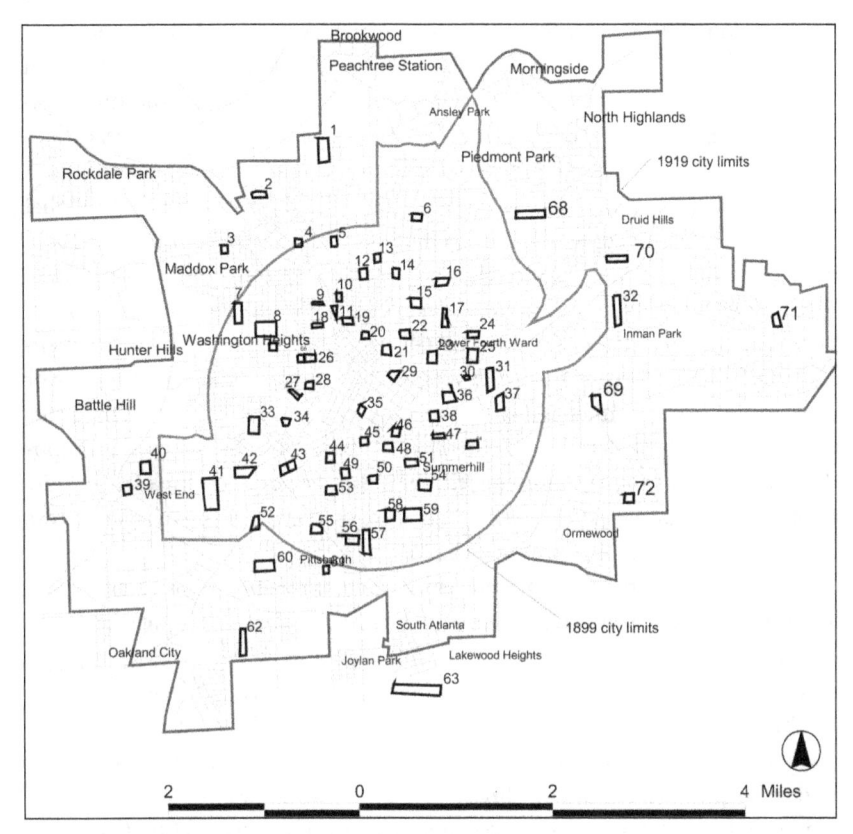

Figure 3.4. Block sample numbers.

1912, the area included twenty whites and three blacks, but one year later had virtually flip-flopped to four whites, fourteen blacks, and two vacancies. Similarly, Johnson Avenue between Boulevard and Howell Street (block 24) reordered quickly and dramatically. Counting thirteen whites and no blacks in 1909 and 1911, the single block counted seven blacks, one white, and two vacancies in 1912—an almost complete racial transition in a single year. The portion of Rock Street between Elliott Street and Mangum Street (block 18) turned quickly from six blacks and fourteen whites in 1909 to twenty-three blacks and one white in 1911. Similarly, Mitchell Street between Mangum Street and Haynes Street (block 28) counted eight whites and eleven blacks in 1909, but no whites in 1911. Change came more gradually on some streets. Hilliard Street between Decatur Street and Pittman Place (block 36) counted thirteen whites and three blacks in 1909. By 1911, the ratio had changed to eight whites and six blacks, and by 1913 the area counted thirteen blacks and one white. Although these changes occurred in a period of particularly intense debate about segregation, it does not appear that the rapid change was prompted by, say, the 1913 or the 1916 ordinance specifically. Changes occurred on different streets in different years.

These transitions are even more striking when rental practices are considered. The rapid change, combined with the fact that social custom dictated that once a home was occupied by blacks, the house typically would not (or could not) be rented by (non-Jewish) whites, suggests that after 1910 property owners and landlords made a conscious business decision to turn over individual homes or even entire street lengths racially. As discussed previously, while entire neighborhoods were less often identified as "black," individual homes or rows of shanties *were* intended for occupation by one race or another. Investors who owned multiple homes on a street could easily change the racial composition of a street front by "flipping" all their properties in the area from white to black. Firms handling rental property were in a position to advise investors when such a transition might be advisable.

It is clear that racial segregation and particularly white isolation increased as local segregation debates became heated and a clear regional movement gained momentum toward residential segregation by law. Also, segregation and white isolation expanded as park-neighborhoods and their associated elite cultural norms grew in popularity in Atlanta. As Ansley Park introduced covenants against "people of African descent," Claude Ashley led the Fourth Ward in declaring a racial boundary line. It is difficult to know what individual decisions led to the quick racial succession between 1909 and 1914 that is apparent in the block sampling, but likely the larger cultural movement demanding park-neighborhood conventions (including whiteness) informed them. Racial segregation may have been on the rise, but white elites pressed on, adopting riot imagery to persuade the state that it had an interest in imposing racial segregation.

⌘

As courts began overturning local and state segregation laws after 1913, white segregationists mobilized images of invasion and threats of public disorder to legitimate segregation ordinances. This is not to say that violence was not a real possibility—it most certainly was. Riots and lynchings were all too common in the South at the turn of the twentieth century, and Atlanta itself had suffered a devastating riot in 1906. But this does not preclude the use of threats and imminent danger as a means to introduce the police power of the state. When early attempts to effect residential segregation by law failed, white elites increased references to impending violence and called on the government to ensure stability and social order.[78]

The threat of interracial violence was a powerful device at the turn of the twentieth century, particularly after the 1906 Atlanta race riot. Rumors of the rape of white women by black men continued, as did race-baiting political campaigns, altercations between blacks and whites, and lynchings. Forty race riots occurred in U.S. cities between 1898 and 1908, events that Atlantans would have been well aware of. Many of Atlanta's leaders feared a resurgence of urban violence or anything that might damage the city's national reputation and ability to lure industry and finance. Atlanta's promoters of segregation thus embraced the fear of racial conflict and utilized it to their advantage.[79]

Whites did not directly reference the 1906 riot, but they alluded to mob rule and vigilantism, unruly acts that had shut down the city four years earlier. In 1913, three years after the failure of the informal racial boundary line, advocates of the Ashley segregation ordinance warned, "There is danger of a clash between the whites and blacks unless something is done." Realtor L. C. Green told the *Constitution* that he "was afraid trouble and bloodshed" would result if segregation ordinances were not imposed.[80] Councilman Claude Ashley, sponsor of the bill, described white-on-black violence as looming, explaining to the city council, "I have been out among the people of the lower part of the Fourth Ward every night for several weeks imploring them to calm themselves and let council act.... I am afraid that unless this ordinance is passed there will be trouble.... I'll tell you frankly that I don't want to go out there tonight and tell the people that council would not relieve them."[81] The June 13, 1913, *Atlanta Constitution* suggested potential violence by placing the story and its "Danger of Clash" headline just above a piece on impending race riots in Savannah. The 1913 ordinance itself opened with emphasis on looming disorder, asserting that the act was "for preserving peace, preventing conflict and ill feeling between the white and colored races, and promoting the general welfare of the city."[82] In 1915, after the courts ruled that the Ashley ordinance was unconstitutional, threats of violence resurfaced. The *Atlanta Independent* reported that four black families on Houston had been "ordered" to move, and that a "citizen vigilante committee" would enforce the order "by peaceable means if possible, but drastic ones if necessary."[83]

Initially, the rhetoric of disorder and impending white-led violence failed to persuade the courts to support the 1913 ordinance, but the courts found the language and imagery persuasive in 1917. In *Harden v. City of Atlanta*, the Georgia Supreme Court ruling directly cited potential conflict when it upheld the city's 1916 ordinance. Writing for the court, Justice P. J. Evans affirmed that the ordinance would "uphold the integrity of each race and ... prevent conflicts between them resulting from close association."[84] The argument failed in the U.S. Supreme Court, however, when the court ruled in *Buchanan v. Warley* that a Louisville, Kentucky, segregation ordinance was unconstitutional in 1917. The court responded to assertions that Louisville's ordinance was enacted to promote public peace by noting, "Desirable as this is, and important as is the preservation of the public peace, this aim cannot be accomplished by laws or ordinances which deny rights created or protected by the Federal Constitution."[85]

In 1917, the ability of white Jackson Hill property owners to control neighborhood character looked bleak. They had attempted to remove a major black institution, Morris Brown College, from the lower Fourth Ward in hopes that the black populace would follow. They had demanded the imposition of a racial boundary line. They had followed the lead of other cities in pushing for local racial segregation ordinances, only to have them struck down in court. In 1917, another opportunity presented itself for white elites to achieve class and residential segregation, but like the proposed Morris Brown move and segregation ordinances, this method of racial division was less effective than white elites had hoped.

On May 21, 1917, fire consumed black and white housing alike as it made its way through the lower Fourth Ward. Starting in a black hospital on Fort Street, the fire moved north, eating a swath of homes, businesses, and land stretching two miles. Newspapers reported that the conflagration destroyed the "negro section between Edgewood and Houston" as well as the area "straight along North Jackson Street and North Boulevard," which was described as "one of the most beautiful [areas] in the city."[86] Citizens as well as the city immediately pledged assistance to the ten thousand people left homeless and suffering. The city's aldermen promised fifteen thousand dollars to the Red Cross to provide relief. Hundreds of black residents found shelter in the Odd Fellows building on Auburn Avenue, and cots lined the roof garden and filled six lodge rooms.[87]

In describing the fire damage, the white newspapers portrayed Jackson Hill as historic, distinctive, and white. Writers waxed nostalgic about the "fine" and "distinguished" homes of Old Atlanta families that had been lost. Not simply homes, these were "landmarks." On North Jackson and North Boulevard, "other fine places went," such as the "old Akers place." Headlines such as "Old Boulevard-Jackson Stamping Ground Gone Forever" and "Famous Old Landmarks Can Never Be Replaced" suggested a longing for an idealized white past. Former Fourth Ward resident Ward Greene explained to *Atlanta Journal* readers that he had "known the neighborhood for the last twenty-five years," as he was born at the corner of North Jackson and North Avenue. Recalling the days when Jackson was little developed, he reported that the nearest house to his was "the residence of W. D. Williamson, a block away on the Boulevard." He continued that he had "seen a forest of trees and thickets change to vacant lots and later to houses . . . played baseball and football on the lots . . . been through some of the houses from garret to cellar . . . [and now] seen them all razed to an ash heap in a day." Greene went on to recall playgrounds and grocers, pioneer Atlantans and expositions and their relationship to the lower Fourth Ward. Blacks did not make it into Greene's reminiscences.[88]

The fire gutted the lower Fourth Ward, consuming two thousand homes and giving whites a blank slate on which to redesign the area and directly apply suburban park-neighborhood practices. White residents met immediately to discuss "the launching of a concerted building plan" that would "make that section of the city more beautiful than ever before."[89] Area architects, including civic-plaza designer Haralson Bleckley, offered a variety of suggestions to those considering rebuilding, including the incorporation of interested owners and the establishment of a "home park" in the district. Chamber of commerce president Ivan Allen suggested that the burned section be turned into a park or a series of parks and established a committee responsible for reviewing ideas for the area's reconstruction.[90] Engineer Charles W. Leavitt's presence garnered the most press attention, in part because he showcased his range of knowledge about city development around the world with lantern slides, but also because he was known locally for designing Georgia Tech's football stadium. Leavitt no doubt piqued further interest when he remarked that Kansas City had "forged ahead" of Atlanta in civic improvements.[91] By June 1917, whites had a variety of proposals that included parkways, minimum construction costs, property restrictions, and a stock company to rebuild Jackson Hill and the lower Fourth Ward as a park-neighborhood within the city.[92]

For the Fourth Ward's white elites, plans to beautify the section meant excluding blacks altogether. Although a range of proposals surfaced, all assumed the erection of firm, visible boundaries between the homes of whites and those of blacks. Jackson Hill resident and attorney Eugene Mitchell, who had been involved in proposals to move Morris Brown and to establish racial boundary lines, spoke at length about the "problem" of black residents and the value of a parkway in solidifying racial divisions.[93] County engineer Tom Wilson's plan included a series of one-hundred-foot-wide parks along Hilliard from Houston Street to North Avenue that would divide blacks from whites. At one public meeting, real estate agent R. B. Adair assured attendees that if "negro encroachment" were halted, "property in the burned district [would] double in value."⁹⁴ City attorney James L. Mayson discussed what could be done legally to restrict property.⁹⁵

Whites continued to debate the efficacy of such plans. One public-meeting attendee questioned whether Charles Leavitt's plan left sufficient space for black residential expansion. Noting that the space allocated would not provide enough room for population growth and that blacks would eventually "spread out," one attendee suggested that "some way should be provided for the negroes to move to another section of the city."⁹⁶ Other whites sought racial separation but also improved housing conditions for blacks in the process. New York architects Henry A. Smith and Edgar Chambless proposed homes for the "negro district" of fire-resistant quality with hot and cold running water and steam heat. They contended that such services would help stem tuberculosis and pneumonia and would net a return of 13 to 20 percent to (presumably white) investors. Healthful homes for blacks could be profitable for whites—and located far away.⁹⁷

It is less clear what black Fourth Ward residents initially sought in the rebuilding process, as they were not invited to the planning meetings nor were they initially consulted by area whites. Even so, blacks did respond to the actions of whites. Black leader Jackson McHenry lashed out at segregationists in an *Atlanta Independent* column, immediately after whites discussed building a parkway to impose segregation. He charged, "I understand from the papers that the white people [proposed] to segregate the colored people in the destroyed districts before the blaze had quit burning. The man who proposed this segregation, if he had it in his power on Monday, would have segregated the fire and would have burned only Negroes and not Whites."⁹⁸ Editor Benjamin Davis held off initially but then scored white leaders, using language that reflected the racial tensions of World War I:

> With great headlines, the dailies published columns of rot about parks; trained architects leveled their genius upon the smitten Negro district to figure out ways and means to inflict segregation upon the Gate City of the South; local preachers and deacons, councilmen and lawyers, merchants and whatnot, of our white citizens, held meeting after meeting, devising ways and means to segregate the loyal colored people of the Fourth Ward, who, but a few days after the fire, registered two thousand, four hundred and odd, of its young men in this very ward alone as their offering to the President to lay down their lives as soldiers for this very city and country.⁹⁹

Other complaints registered in the area papers, black and white, suggested that African Americans were less concerned about housing segregation than about the possibility that areas designated for blacks would be deficient in city services and infrastructure. African Americans had suffered such injustices for decades; sewage lines drained onto streets with a majority of black residents, and the city responded slowly to needed infrastructure and repairs in such areas. Black leaders were fully aware that despite white leaders' stated concerns about sanitary conditions and healthfulness, in reality blacks would be the last served, if served at all.[100]

The plans of white segregationists remained firm, though, and two weeks later an *Atlanta Journal* headline announced, "PLANS TO BEAUTIFY FIRE-SWEPT SECTION RECITED AT MEETING ... Agreement Signed to Exclude Negroes from Property." After protest by black leaders, whites attempted again to assuage tensions, and a June 20, 1917, *Atlanta Journal* headline asserted, "Negro Home Owners in Burned Area Will Be Accorded Consideration." White elites were entrenched when it came to housing segregation, though. Using practices that had successfully excluded groups labeled undesirable from Atlanta's and other cities' suburbs, white leaders required that renovated properties carry covenants preventing the transfer of property to blacks. Attorney James Key was specifically added to the commission to draw up appropriate legal documents.[101]

To strengthen their case, white elites used various scare tactics to garner funding for rebuilding to their plans, and their rhetoric affirmed and propagated a new construction of race, space, and housing. In this white view, the presence of blacks marred the neighborhood, visually and economically. Whites polarized the ward's options and equated black-populated neighborhoods with ruin, as Fourth Ward resident D. W. Yarbrough did at a July 1917 meeting: "If the plan is made effective, the Fourth Ward will be rebuilt into one of the most desirable residence sections in Atlanta. If it isn't, you will see Jackson Street turned over in five years to our colored population." Yarbrough reflected the sentiments of many of his neighbors when he associated white residents with a "good neighborhood" and black residents with a "bad neighborhood." He explained ominously, "Either the Fourth Ward is going to be rebuilt a great deal better than it was or a great deal worse. It rests with you to decide," and "the salvation of the Fourth Ward depends on this rebuilding plan being put through."[102] In another case, city attorney James L. Mayson addressed a circular to white Fourth Warders notifying them, "It has been decided that each [white property owner] agree to sell their property only to white people and in this way to protect each by the agreement of all from the *menace of negro neighborhoods*" (emphasis added).[103] One *Atlanta Journal* writer summarized the general sentiment of meeting attendees that "a failure to rebuild the burned district, or to permit the burned district to be taken over as a negro section, would give the whole city a black eye."[104] White ministers joined in the scare campaign that portrayed black presence negatively. Dr. A. A. Little, pastor of Westminster Presbyterian Church, asserted, "If some such plan isn't adopted to stop the encroachment on the Fourth Ward, the ward in ten or fifteen years won't be a place in which you [i.e., whites] can make your home."[105] By the summer, shelter and the restoration of homes and commerce were no longer the primary goals of the rebuilding effort. Rather, as one public-meeting attendee asserted, "The most important detail in the reconstruction of the burned area is to establish a line of demarcation between whites and blacks."[106]

Proposals to rebuild the lower Fourth Ward after the 1917 fire indicated a desire by whites to bring park-neighborhood design to the central city. For example, DeLos Hill constantly juxtaposed the investor-planned heterogeneous built environment to whites' new imaginary in the same manner used by park-neighborhood promoters. In discussing the creation of a stock company to rebuild the area, Hill contended that it was "the only feasible plan for rebuilding the burned district into a beautiful residence section, instead of a hodge-podge of structures." He returned to the unplanned landscape later in summary: "To leave it to build in any way that chance dictates means that a miscellany of structures will spring up which will kill that section—or at least a part of it—forever as a residence district." By contrast, he argued, a holding company or similar organization could assert architectural control and "prevent the encroachment of undesirable buildings" and "stipulate the style of residences to be built."[107] As in the covenant-protected subdivisions, it was not simply *practices* associated with the black and the poor that were targets of elite control; to whites, black *presence*—literally their visual presence—interfered with beautification efforts because, according to white-authored discourse, "beauty" encompassed whiteness.

✥

The plans suggested by whites for remaking Jackson Hill involved fashioning the *memory* of Jackson Hill and the lower Fourth Ward into the white haven they sought to rebuild. What had been a mixed-race, mixed-class neighborhood in the late 1800s was linguistically spun into an all-white section; blacks were erased from historical memory and then positioned as invaders and trespassers in a white-penned history. First, whites painted Jackson Hill as a white neighborhood, ignoring decades of black community building in the lower Fourth Ward. Newspapers referred to "white residential sections" as if the sections were 100 percent white and "black sections" as if they solely housed blacks. Then, having situated Jackson Hill as white, elites deployed the language of "encroachment." The verb *encroach* suggested active black movement past established limits, toward (static) whites and white-occupied homes. In adopting this language, whites defined particular black housing choices as *trespass*—movement into territory they had no right or access to. Moreover, whites often used *encroach* in the present progressive or present continuous tense, as "are encroaching," implying that blacks actively continued to *trespass*. Indeed, *encroach* originally was defined as "to take illegally" or "to seize." In using the term, whites criminalized blacks by classifying their housing choices as *trespass* or *taking*. The use of other terms such as *black tide* and *invasion* implied that the movement was rapid and widespread, and that defensive action must be taken.[108] Put forward by businessmen, preachers, and politicians, these statements stuck and held, influencing cultural understandings of people and places and shaping housing and land-use policy.

Just as Atlantans drew their inspiration for park-neighborhood communities from cities and suburbs in the Northeast and the Midwest, Atlanta's white civic elites implemented their segregation ideologies in partnership with urban elites throughout the Southeast (and later with cities in the North and the West). Language promoting segregation displayed white Atlantans' extensive knowledge of segregation practices and court cases around the country. When recommending the 1913 segregation ordinance to the city council, Claude Ashley explained that such ordinances "had been adopted in Richmond, Va, and Baltimore, Md and [were] working out admirably." And in what the *Atlanta Constitution* described as a "vigorous speech" before the city council, Ashley asserted that white Fourth Ward residents requested "relief similar to that given by the legislature of California to the people of that state to stem the tide of Japanese invasion."[109] Newspapers regularly educated whites about segregation practices throughout the United States and about court cases ruling on segregation. On April 11, 1917, for example, the *Atlanta Journal* carried the Associated Press update on *Buchanan v. Warley*. That same day, the *Atlanta Constitution* noted that the case "would settle the validity of like measure in Richmond, Baltimore, St. Louis and scores of other cities and towns in the South."[110] In this manner, Atlantans joined with other city builders in making exclusion a central component of the idealized park-neighborhood and in imposing racial segregation on the city.

The attempt of Jackson Hill's white homeowners to create the park-neighborhood they had come to admire was a failure. Throughout the second decade of the twentieth century, builders continued to crowd modest homes into the ward's undeveloped lots and empty back alleys. And despite the protest of white elites, agents sold and leased homes to blacks. Such challenges reinforced civic elites' conviction that they needed to find more-effective and enduring ways to regulate housing and neighborhood geographies. But despite continued failures, civic elites succeeded in keeping park-neighborhood ideals and attendant exclusionary practices circulating in local culture, poised to reemerge in the building boom of the 1920s.

CHAPTER FOUR

Homeownership and Park-Neighborhood Ideology, 1910 to 1933

In a 1945 review of John Dean's *Homeownership: Is It Sound?*, real-estate analyst Helen Monchow observed that Dean had set himself an unpopular task in examining "an institution so long established, so deep seated, and so widely accepted as a principle or ideal of the so-called American way of life." She continued, "Enthusiasm for homeownership—or at least equal opportunity for homeownership—amounts almost to a religion in this country."[1] But in 1945, the position of homeownership as a sacrosanct institution had only just reached maturity.

From 1910 to 1933, the federal government and the National Association of Real Estate Boards (NAREB) made a coordinated and concerted effort not just to encourage homeownership, but to give home buying more stature within mainstream American society. To be sure, as Donald Krueckeberg, Peter Dreier, J. Paul Mitchell, and others have shown, bias toward property ownership over tenancy has existed throughout the history of the nation.[2] But federal and housing industry desires to use property ownership to calm political turmoil and buttress and reinvigorate land markets prompted agents and federal officials to imbue *homeowner* and *homeownership* with specific meanings in order to entice Americans into adopting a particular set of housing and neighborhood practices. National real-estate organizations and local land dealers alike associated homeownership with thrift, good character, moral fiber, and citizenship. Conversely, the federal government and the housing industry aligned tenancy with negative imagery, such as bolshevism and radicalism. Together, federal agencies and real-estate agents and associations crafted, deployed, and reinforced rhetoric that encouraged men to protect their families and the nation through homeownership. Homeowners were held up as patriots and family providers, the bulwark of the nation-state. By creating and delivering status rewards to homeowners, federal officials and real-estate interests enticed tenants into seeking homeownership a generation before amortized mortgages, federal mortgage insurance, and the mass production of housing combined to make homeownership "affordable" to most Americans.

Despite the dedicated efforts of federal officials and the NAREB, Atlanta's real-estate agents declined to participate in the renewed Own Your Own Home campaigns from 1918 to 1921, choosing to keep their attention on the local (and lucrative) rental-housing market. Indeed, despite the growing popularity of and media attention given to park-neighborhoods, most of the city's population rented. And the local real-estate industry cultivated rental-housing investors and developed services that met investors' needs. In 1922, though, Atlanta's real-estate agents went full tilt, holding home expositions and hawking park-neighborhood amenities and class and racial exclusion.

Atlanta Real Estate

In 1910, 75 percent of Atlanta's households rented their homes, as compared to 60 percent nationwide (see table 4.1). The city's high tenancy rate may be attributed in part to Atlanta's large native-born population, who, as Olivier Zunz, John Bodnar, Roger Simon, and others have shown, practiced homeownership to a lesser degree than immigrants at the turn to the twentieth century. As historian Margaret Marsh argues, it was not low wages or lack of savings that prevented many old-stock Americans from buying homes; rather, buying simply was not that important to many families. There were few discernible advantages, and ownership worked against some Americans' desires for mobility. As elsewhere, persistence rates in the South's Gate City were low; southerners migrated regularly for jobs, whether they primarily worked in textile mills or sharecropped. Lack of comment, reporting, or other analysis of low homeownership and low persistence rates from the city's reformers, public policy makers, or real-estate interests suggests that there was little concern about this pattern.[3]

Atlanta's high tenancy rates encouraged the development of an active and lucrative rental-housing and property-management market. Sales to people seeking to purchase homes in new park-neighborhoods certainly took place, but owner-occupied housing was a small product line for agents until the early 1920s. Not surprisingly, when agent George Adair tried to lure the National Association of Real Estate Exchanges (NAREE)'s convention to the Gate City in 1911, he highlighted one of the city's firms that handled significant numbers of rentals, not sales. Adair urged the NAREE convention audience to visit his native city, promising the professionals:

Table 4.1. Housing Tenure, Atlanta (city)

	Households reporting tenure (1890 to 1930) or number of occupied dwelling units (1940 to 1960)	Owner-occupied (free and in mortgage)	% Homeowners	Total occupied units	Total owner-occupied units	White owner-occupied units	Nonwhite owner-occupied units	Nonwhite owner-occupied homes as percent of occupied units	White owner-occupied homes as percent of occupied units	White owner-occupied homes as percent of owner-occupied units	Nonwhite owner-occupied homes as percent of owner-occupied units	Owner-occupied homes as percent of occupied units	Nonwhite tenant-occupied homes as percent of occupied units	Change in number of occupied units
1890	13,315	3,009	22.6%											
1900			18.6%											
1910			24.7%											
1920	49,523	12,026	24.3%											
1930	67,118	19,675	29.3%	67,749	19,675									
1940	84,764	20,769	25.3%	82,000	20,769	17,215	3,554	4.3%	21.0%	82.9%	17.1%	25.3%	30.2%	14,251
1950	92,667	36,985	39.9%	92,667	36,985	29,491	7,486	8.1%	31.8%	79.7%	20.2%	39.9%	25.0%	10,667
1960	145,953	66,504	45.6%	145,953	66,504	52,447	14,057	9.6%	35.9%	78.9%	21.1%	45.6%	24.6%	53,286

Source: U.S. Census, with the exception of 1900 and 1910 data, which are drawn from John M. Gries and James S. Taylor, *How to Own Your Own Home: A Handbook for Prospective Home Owners* (Washington, D.C.: USGPO, 1923).

[I will show you] a rental agency that I believe will be interesting and instructive for you to visit—one that employs eighty-two men and has on its roll eight thousand tenants. Is there a larger one in any of these big cities? That proprietor of that business (it is not mine), one of our largest competitors there, however, authorized me to say that his books, his accounts, his statements, his bank book and everything that he has got is subject to your inspection when you are there next year, and it may be interesting to have a committee spend a little while in his office, to see how he has done and built it up in a town of a hundred and fifty-six thousand inhabitants.[4]

Adair clearly saw Atlanta's rental-housing industry as the business to showcase; the city's new park-neighborhoods, the home sales line, or any firm dealing in park-neighborhoods or home sales were left unmentioned. Instead, it was Atlanta's rental-housing investment and property-management sector that established the city's position in national real-estate circles.

By 1910, Atlanta's land agents contributed to a national real-estate network that stretched from coast to coast. George and Forrest Adair, M. L. Thrower, L. C. Green, and other prominent dealers traveled extensively, participated in numerous city-oriented expositions, and sought the company and advice of well-known city planners. Atlanta's membership in the NAREB was particularly important to the city's network of financial, real-estate, and urban relationships. Formed in 1908 as the National Association of Real Estate Exchanges (NAREE), the NAREB and the larger network of agents, lenders, and builders shaped property trends, disseminated knowledge, set standards, and otherwise cultivated a professional consciousness among agents. The organization's *National Real Estate Journal* (*NREJ*) kept members up to date on practices and innovations across the nation. One 1915 article, for example, explained "the planning of a low-cost house," and another detailed the "relation of real estate men to city planning."[5] Similarly, at the NAREB annual conventions, attendees could learn how Californians handled their race "menace"—Chinese immigrants and Chinese Americans. As historian Jeffery Hornstein suggests, the conventions and other association activities facilitated network development and allegiance to the profession, and enabled members "to do business outside their own communities and transcend the limits of localism."[6] Atlanta's builders drew on all these resources as they espoused their New South creed and scrambled to erect a city that lived up to its swagger.

Shortly after the NAREE's formation, Atlanta's agents nurtured ties to the organization's leadership by hosting its national officers and attending the organization's annual conference. Agents and city leaders Walter G. Cooper, the Adair brothers, and others were on hand in 1911 to entertain as well as educate the visitors about the Gate City's land markets and business practices. Over one hundred Atlanta businessmen attended the banquet and discussion, which covered such topics as absentee property ownership and commercial property taxation. A few months later, Atlantans attended the national convention, where George Adair invited the organization to hold the next national meeting in Atlanta. With other land dealers across the country, Atlanta's agents and builders would eventually join the NAREB's loosely formed Own Your Home campaign as it diffused throughout the country.[7]

To NAREB members, increased homeownership promised to ease housing shortages and energize property sales and home construction, which had slowed nationally from 1915 to 1918 as companies diverted material and production resources to meet World War I–related needs. The president of Spokane, Washington's realty board explained to *NREJ* readers that stimulating "an interest in real estate in times of comparative dullness [was] the big problem before realty dealers and investors everywhere."[8] T. P. Hay of the Birmingham Real Estate Board lamented in 1916, "Birmingham, like a good many other cities, has had a rather slow real estate market the past few years."[9] Agents encouraged citizens to purchase homes to counter local business decline, and one *NREJ* article warned readers, "Any serious curtailment of home building means stagnation of business in a vast variety of interlocking trades, vitally affecting practically every line of business in every community in America."[10]

Local Buy a Home and Own Your Home campaigns spread rapidly from town to town in 1915 and 1916 and then were quickly curtailed by war-related needs and a subsequent housing depression. Spokane, Washington, launched a drive in 1915, for example, and Atlanta's chamber of commerce and local real-estate board advertised a "build now" and "lend now" campaign in that same year. Birmingham, Alabama, followed in 1916. In 1918, as World War I drew to a close, the national NAREB office brainstormed ways it might revive the homeownership movement—and thus the construction industry—so as to stave off a postwar depression and housing shortage.[11]

Beginning in early 1918, the NAREB worked vigorously with local agents, builders, and building-material suppliers to revitalize land sales by organizing homeownership drives from the NAREB headquarters. Almost immediately, the NAREB succeeded in moving national management of the program to the U.S. Department of Labor while still maintaining control over the program's framework and initiatives. Oregon real-estate agent and park-neighborhood developer Paul Murphy, who led Portland's Own Your Home campaign and served on the NAREB's committee formulating a national operation, moved to Washington and helped staff the Own Your Home section of the Division of Public Works and Construction Development under the Department of Labor.[12]

The public-private partnership was not new in housing, though the topic had been hotly debated. In 1917, after much discussion over the role that government should play in housing, the newly created U.S. Housing Corporation (USHC) partnered with private developers to produce affordable housing for individuals and families who were migrating to manufacturing centers throughout the United States. The USHC and the later Division of Building and Housing at the Department of Commerce intentionally sought the expertise of private-industry leaders, and a number of well-known planners and architects became "dollar-a-year men" and moved to Washington to assist in the war effort. Frederick Law Olmsted Jr., for example, proposed the use of city-planning ideas for housing war workers and directed the housing construction program at the USHC. Although Congress only reluctantly approved monies to build housing for civilians, the USHC eventually funded the development of housing plans consistent with those put forward by community planners throughout the United States. But even as federal officials worked with private builders to relieve the wartime housing shortage, they continued to promote private building through Own Your Own Home campaigns in the 1920s.[13]

Even as home-construction initiatives moved back into the private sector after World War I, federal agencies buttressed private homeownership initiatives in the 1920s by providing research, conference opportunities, guidance, and standards to both builders and consumers. The Department of Commerce embraced homeownership as a national goal when Herbert Hoover took over that office in 1921, and Hoover continued to promote homeownership after he was elected president in 1928. In this manner, even after the Department of Labor ended the official Own Your Home and Own Your Own Home campaigns in the early 1920s, homeownership remained on the federal agenda.[14]

Despite the increased promotion of homeownership following World War I, those seeking to purchase homes had few financing options in this period. Atlantans interested in buying a home could obtain a short, usually six-month mortgage through sellers and agents. But short-term mortgages ran the risk of not being renewed, and borrowers' financial situations sometimes required the taking of a second (overlapping) mortgage. Some purchasers secured mortgages through building and loan associations. Membership was a reasonable one dollar a month, but high demand for the loans resulted in high premiums. Savings and loans and insurance companies held most Atlanta mortgages as homeownership grew through the 1920s, but lack of state support and regulation for such organizations limited their effectiveness until the 1930s. To invigorate individual interest in homeownership despite these home-financing challenges, federal and private interests worked to give homeownership more status within American society. From the NAREB's original foray into homeownership campaigns in the second decade of the century to the NAREB-federal government partnership forged during World War I and into the postwar building boom of the 1920s, homeownership campaigns consistently deployed a set of messages that linked homeownership to thrift, good citizenship, patriotism, masculinity, domesticity, and social order.[15]

Propaganda

Individual agents and town- and city-based real-estate organizations crafted and disseminated a new collection of homeownership rhetoric in the second decade of the twentieth century. Agents and builders launched campaigns to promote their own and related businesses, borrowing promotional tactics by reading other cities' newspapers and visiting one another's towns and offices. Also, the *NREJ* and national NAREB conventions gave voice to hundreds of local homeownership promotions and at the same time provided strategies and language to spark new and ongoing efforts. When the Department of Labor and the Department of Commerce joined the campaign in 1918, they expanded the cache of persuasive tactics.

Together, local homeownership campaigns, the NAREB, the Department of Labor, and the Department of Commerce generated publicity packages that iterated a discrete set of appeals from 1915 through the 1920s. The guides, posters, contests, radio announcements, and other materials collectively asserted the following:

- An owned home is the ideal environment for child rearing.
- An owned home is the ideal environment for family life.
- The ideal home is the single family home.
- The homeowner is thrifty.
- The homeowner is independent.
- The homeowner is committed to the community.
- The homeowner is committed to the American way of life.
- It is human nature to want to own one's home.
- Homeowners are not socialists.

Publicity rhetoric also assigned particular characteristics to tenants and rental housing:

- Apartment living is detrimental to family life.
- Apartment living is detrimental to child development.
- Tenants are prone to crime.
- Tenants cause social disorder.
- Rental housing brings social disorder to neighborhoods.

Often these assertions appeared together, which encouraged consumers (as well as policy makers and real-estate agents) to consider them as a single set of related ideas. With one came the others, though no doubt some justifications for home purchasing resonated with individual buyers more than others.

Some claims appealed to sentimentality and domestic ideals current in the early twentieth century. One 1914 *NREJ* article explained:

> When the children grow up and strike out for themselves they look back with tender memories to the old home, their own rooms, the pleasant evenings when everybody could dance without fear of the tenants upstairs pounding on the floor or of rebuke by the lordly janitor, and to the favorite nooks in the house and yard for study and peace.[16]

In 1921, then secretary of commerce Herbert Hoover attached homeownership to family and child welfare and morality when he asked rhetorically, "What greater incentive for saving is there than for the ownership of a home, the possession of which may change the very physical, mental and moral fiber of one's own children?"[17] The cover of the National Lumber Manufacturer's Association (NLMA) campaign pamphlet suggested that children demonstrated pride in family when the parents owned a home; its cover featured a young boy pointing to a house and exclaiming, "That's our home—my dad owns it!"[18] Other articles asserted that place attachment was unlikely in a rented home. One *NREJ* article, for example, contended, "No family can ever acquire that deep-seated regard and heartfelt affection for a rented house that is naturally developed for a home which they own."[19] Others stressed a relationship between ownership, the single-family home, and family life, as when land dealer Max Ragley explained to *NREJ* readers, "One cannot make a home for children in an apartment house—there is no room to play, [and children] are not wanted [in an apartment house]. . . . Is this not going to have some deleterious effect on family life?"[20] Similarly, in "The Joys of Homeownership," one writer explained that the male head-of-household, "takes comfort in the fact—and his wife sleeps better for it—that if he is taken away his wife and children will have a roof over their heads. The family is kept intact through the ownership of the modest home" (see fig. 4.1).[21] In short, private organizations, federal agencies,

Figure 4.1. "Why Not Make This the Official Design?" Source: National Lumber Manufacturers' Association, "'Own Your Home' Campaign Handbook," file: publicity material, box 6, RG3, Records of the U.S. Housing Corporation, 1917–1952, National Archives and Records Administration, College Park, Maryland.

and real-estate dealers insisted that homeownership was necessary to a proper domestic life.

Other ad writers and speakers directly attacked tenancy and housing commonly occupied by tenants: apartments. In campaign materials produced by the NLMA, Mississippi governor Theodore Bilbo asserted, "No man can take much, if any pride, in a rented home."[22] Similarly, the NLMA averred, "The home owner is permanent; the shifter does little good to his city or himself."[23] Wisconsin governor E. L. Philipp suggested that tenants lacked local commitment when he asserted that when a man owns his home, "he has actually become a part of the community in which he lives."[24] Such assumptions and appeals carried over into public policy. In a 1925 *Land Economics* article, for example, Gertrude Harley assumed that multifamily rental housing itself was problematic when she wrote, "A great many factors influence and determine the amount of home tenancy in American cities. This summary is an attempt to determine the significance of the multi-family structure as a factor *in this problem*" (emphasis added).[25] Similarly and combined with an appeal to patriotism, another *NREJ* article asserted, "Tenant housing and tenant farming, is rapidly becoming a *serious menace* in America; and any movement that will tend to abolish or reduce that *growing evil*, is one that should receive the support of every patriotic citizen and every loyal business organization in the land, and should be encouraged by every department of our government" (emphasis added).[26] The NLMA summarized this appeals set in their declaration, "No city of renters can ever succeed. No nation of tenants can ever become great."[27]

Other writers argued that it was human nature to want to own one's home. Real-estate agent Arthur Wenz told the Wisconsin Association of Real Estate Brokers in 1918, "A desire seems to be born in every one to have a home of one's own, to possess a little place, however small—to be one's own landlord."[28] A 1918 *NREJ* writer combined appeals to human nature with appeals to masculinity when he wrote, "The desire to own a home is one of the natural, primal instincts of every real man."[29] The 1918 Department of Commerce guide "How to Own Your Home" asserted without evidence that "the great majority of people have a strong desire to own their homes."[30] Such appeals not only promoted but naturalized homeownership, making it a cultural expectation.

Some appeals featured people with political or social power mobilizing sentimentality, tradition, or other notions. The NLMA, for example, solicited quotes from several governors—"statements of well-known executives on the value of owning your home"—and encouraged local campaign workers to adopt the quotes on posters and in advertising. The governors, then, appealed to patriotism, sentimentality, and tradition. Indiana governor F. P. Goodrich asserted,

"It is but a truism to say that the American home is the foundation of the Republic." Mississippi governor Theodore Bilbo contended that homeownership "brings the family closer together and focuses the talents and ambition of all the members to a common center—home." Kansas governor Henry J. Allen waxed sentimental: "About the home clusters the dearest memories of life and its ownership gives a peculiar and lasting significance." Deployed by people in power, such appeals took on even greater rhetorical force.[31]

World War I, the Red Scare, and Russia's political turmoil provided ample fodder for the NAREB's drive to load *homeowner* and *homeownership* with status and cultural power. As historian Janet Hutchison explains, government propagandists utilized homeownership as a symbol of an individual's commitment and loyalty to the United States.[32] *NREJ* writers and editorialists took advantage of the nationalist fervor aroused by World War I and appealed to patriotism. This rhetoric equated homeownership with love of country and then demanded that the citizen perform his or her patriotic duty by purchasing a home. One *NREJ* editorialist penned, "Yes, own your home and protect it with your life, and you will be a good citizen and patriot."[33] The forging of home purchasing into a nationalist act is likewise readily apparent in the *NREJ*'s declaration, "BE PATRIOTIC! BUY A HOME!"[34] According to this way of thinking, homeowners were not political radicals and posed no threat to the nation-state; on the contrary, they buttressed the nation-state as it was popularly understood in 1920. The *NREJ* hammered at this notion of homeowner-as-patriot, buffering its reports and stories and filling white space with aphorisms such as, "No man was ever an anarchist or participated in the destruction of property which he owned or in which he had an interest."[35] Another writer stated, "It is safe to predict that [the homeowner] will never be found in the Socialist ranks."[36] The NLMA Own Your Home campaign pamphlet recommended "Bolshevism doesn't thrive in homes" as a campaign slogan.[37] Invited to share his justification for homeownership, Georgia governor Hugh Dorsey contended, "[Homeownership is] the best plan suggested to insure the safety of this country against the ills that are now disrupting and disturbing many nations."[38]

The *NREJ* also deployed the converse of the homeownership-patriotism construction—the notion that tenants were not patriots and might well be political radicals. The editorial leading the June–July 1918 edition of the *NREJ* contended, "A nation of renters will always be lacking in patriotism."[39] Another NAREB story insisted that radicals embraced tenancy: "Scott Nearing, sensationalist, Socialist, I. W. W. leader and whatnot, recently declared that the man who rented was the best citizen."[40] Those who rented in order to maintain the ability to migrate for work, without the financial ability to purchase, or who simply chose not to purchase property were immediately suspect in an era of prodemocracy, procapitalist rhetoric, and 100 percent Americanism.

The NAREB, local real-estate organizations, chambers of commerce, and agents themselves blanketed the nation with simple yet effective rhetorical tactics throughout 1918 and thereafter. Journals and conventions helped transmit successful sales strategies from town to town and city to city. Real-estate dealers agreed on the messages they wanted to convey, and their campaigns embedded and reinforced a relationship between homeownership, domestic ideals, citizenship, Americanism, and emerging middle-class values.

Educating the Sales Force—and the Masses

From 1918 through the 1920s, the NAREB implored its members to "educate" local citizens about the value of homeownership and the single-family home. One February 1918 *NREJ* editorial implored agents,

> Realtors: You have a definite duty. Aside from your natural wish to dispose of property on your lists, you have a patriotic call. The nation looks to you for education! Put a shoulder to the wheel! Get into the human side of present conditions. Teach the nation that there is one duty none should shirk. Convince the nation that it will become greater when it owns its own home![41]

And educate they did. Realtors launched sixty-eight local Own Your Home campaigns around the country in 1918 alone, from major cities such as New Orleans and New York, to state capitals such as Omaha and Indianapolis, to small towns like Cumberland, Maryland, and Poplar Bluff, Missouri.[42]

The editors at the *NREJ* used the publication's national circulation to cheerlead for local campaigns, provide advice, and disseminate sales tactics across the country. This 1918 recommendation was typical: "We want to speed the day when every Realtor will have a rack outside his business door, filled with tracts on Home Ownership, The Folly of Renting." The journal included stories that described how to organize local campaigns and offered platitudes for further distribution, including, "The home will make the citizen, and the honest and patriotic will create the foundation on which the national security, the national indebtedness and the national honor may safely rest."[43] The *NREJ* advised local real-estate boards that were just beginning to think about a campaign to form a committee of their members and representatives from related industries, such as home furnishings and building materials.[44] "Success stories" penned by local agents and reprinted in the *NREJ* lent credibility to suggested sales tactics. S. E. Hege, president of the Spokane Realty Board, explained that his city's Realtors confronted a slowing building year by encouraging "a desire in the minds of non-homeowners that it [was] to their advantage to buy a home now." As part of the home drive, the *Spokane Daily Journal* held a contest for the letter—not to exceed three hundred words—that put forth the best argument for owning one's own home. It offered three prizes, the top being fifty dollars. Spokane's *Chronicle* then published a selection of letters, which encouraged even more contest participation and provided advertising for the real-estate campaign. Local high-school teachers encouraged their students to participate, which attracted two hundred more essays.[45] Similarly, T. P. Hay Jr. of Birmingham explained that, confronted with a slow real-estate market, the city's board sought "to drive home to the public in every way possible the phrase 'Buy a Home.'" To this end, the real-estate board purchased five hundred yellow window signs with BUY A HOME printed in red and asked area merchants to display them in shop windows. The board hired a sign painter to add any additional wording about the shopkeeper's own home-related wares. One furniture dealer finished off his sign with "BUY A HOME AND LET OSTER BROTHERS FEATHER YOUR NEST." A jeweler came up with "BUY A HOME AND PUT YOUR SAVINGS IN A DIAMOND." And the streetcar company posted the Buy a Home signs in the cars' front windows.[46]

The NLMA provided a service similar to the *NREJ* in its production of the "Own Your Home Campaign Handbook" in 1919. Besides outlining possible campaign organizational structures, the pamphlet recommended advertising in newspapers and on billboards, producing "model bungalows" and furnishings exhibits, and developing "moving picture slides." Either inspiring or borrowing directly from Birmingham and Spokane's campaign, the NLMA suggested displaying posters in streetcars and in the windows of businesses, offering children prizes for essays on "why families should own their homes," and commending preachers to hold "Own Your Home" Sundays.[47]

The Department of Labor's *Suggestions for Own-Your-Own-Home Campaigns*, produced in 1919 and distributed to over eight thousand civic leaders, augmented the NLMA's advice. Besides essay contests, the Department of Labor recommended distributing "we own our own home" buttons to children. It suggested that restaurants weave slogans into the daily menus, such as "Do you own your own home? If not, why not?" Prizes could be offered for the best "illustrated posters" that conveyed "the spirit of 'Own Your Own Home.'" Thus, businesses, industrial organizations, the NAREB, agents, and federal officials worked together, staying on message in a comprehensive educational and sales campaign that retooled cultural meanings of *homeowner* and *homeownership*.[48]

Despite the pro-homeownership barrage from Washington and the national real-estate ranks, Atlanta real-estate agents maintained their focus principally on rental-housing investment and property management for years. The city launched a short campaign promoting "Buy now" and "Build now" in 1915 but did not join the revived homeownership movement in 1918. However, in 1922 Atlanta's real-estate interests made a conscious decision to promote homeownership as an additional product line. The Atlanta campaign adopted the rhetorical practices honed by the U.S. government and the national real-estate network, selling not just shelter but homeownership ideology. Atlanta's experience within a national homeownership movement illustrates how homeownership tenets became embedded in local material experience and daily practice, and how such cultural texts transferred easily from city to city.

The Atlanta Campaign

The NAREB's executive committee met at Atlanta's Piedmont Hotel in January 1921, and 150 Realtors from across the United States joined the discussion on homeownership and ongoing challenges to financing. True to form, the housing subcommittee's report insisted that homeownership would promote a "more patriotic citizenship" and tethered homeownership to social improvement—family contentment, thrift, and reduced rates of suicide, divorce, and radicalism. But while the NAREB held tightly to homeownership's virtues, it slowly shed its wariness of government intervention in the private housing market. By 1921, agents and brokers openly advocated for federal assistance in supporting home mortgages. The lack of capital interfered with agents' self-interest and the NAREB's homeownership goals, and the NAREB's Own Your Own Home committee commissioned Holyoke National Bank to draft a financing plan for presentation to federal officials. The final report recommended that lending institutions finance home building for patrons with one thousand dollars in their savings department, and that Congress stimulate home building and respond to the acute housing shortage by exempting mortgage interest payments from taxation. A year later, in 1922, an *Atlanta Journal* editorial cartoon suggested that limited financing still hindered sales in Atlanta (see fig. 4.2).[49]

The 1921 NAREB meeting likely sold Atlanta's agents on the merits of homeownership (or at least on the merits of homeownership as an additional product line), for in early 1922, Atlanta Realtors launched an Own Your Home campaign—reportedly the first in the South in the postwar years. Agent R. W. Evans chaired the three-month drive, which culminated in an Own Your Home exposition in May. Agents and builders intended the expo to meet a number

Figure 4.2. Own Your Own Home campaign promotion. Source: *Atlanta Journal*, February 17, 1922.

of local needs: to jump-start home building, funnel customers to home-related businesses (such as interior decorators and lumber companies), reiterate city beautification themes, and promote home buying. The six-day exposition borrowed from other commercial and world fairs in giving each day a particular theme or target group. Monday was the grand opening (replete with speeches and other pomp and circumstance), Tuesday was businessmen and taxpayers' day, Wednesday women's club day, Thursday Federation of Trades day, Friday homeowners' day, and Saturday everybody's day. The city auditorium housed over fifty exhibitors ranging from local architect Leila Ross Wilburn to lumber companies and decorative stores. Businesses offered prizes to entice visitors, including lots in assorted local subdivisions. Other prizes included face brick, doors, tile, and monogrammed china. Newspaper ads placed by participating companies repeated the board's positions.[50]

A review of Atlanta newspapers during this period confirms that the federal government and the NAREB's pro-homeownership discourse and carbon-copy campaign strategies transferred smoothly and were scarcely altered to meet any regional particularities. The Atlanta National Bank took out a one-sixth-page ad in the *Atlanta Constitution* and filled it with appeals recommended by campaign booklets and the *NREJ*. The ad declared, "The man who owns his home is a better citizen than he would be otherwise"; it contended that homeownership defused radicalism when it added, "The pride of ownership is a wonderful antidote for the poison of bolshevism, and makes for stability and permanency" (see fig. 4.3).[51] Atlanta land investor Eugene R. Black recalled older power and landed relations in 1922 when he asserted, "A city of homes ... would be an

1865 — Oldest National Bank in the Cotton States — 1922

Who's Who at
The Atlanta National Bank

The Home Owner

THE MAN WHO OWNS HIS HOME IS A BETTER CITIZEN THAN HE WOULD BE OTHERWISE. The pride of ownership is a wonderful antidote for the poison of bolshevism, and makes for stability and permanency.

In the Heart of Atlanta -- The Heart of the South

ATLANTA'S ARMY OF HOME OWNERS is being constantly increased by people from other sections who are attracted by our wonderful climate, splendid schools, good water, progressive citizenship and the opportunity to find ample building space in any section of the city.

Atlanta is fortunate in that such a large percentage of its population live in their own homes. This number is constantly increasing — ELEVEN HUNDRED AND FORTY-EIGHT PERMITS FOR HOMES HAVING BEEN ISSUED SINCE JANUARY FIRST.

Many of these homes are being financed with money saved in the Savings Department of the Atlanta National Bank. Regular weekly deposits of a few dollars soon paid for a lot. Another year or two saw enough saved to make it possible to safely begin building.

If you, too, would like to join this army of home owners, why don't you open a Savings Account at the Atlanta National?

The Atlanta National Bank

Savings Department on Main Floor at Whitehall and Alabama

Active Designated Depository of
U. S. Government, State of Georgia, Fulton County
and City of Atlanta

Figure 4.3. Atlanta National Bank advertisement. Source: *Atlanta Constitution*, May 7, 1922.

independent city, every citizen the monarch of his own home."[52] The lead *Atlanta Constitution* ad for the city's second homeownership exposition reprinted the assortment of homeownership adages, including that it was the duty of every man to own his own home and to "plant the flag of personal liberty" on his own land (see fig. 4.4).[53] Thus, even in Atlanta—a city of renters—Realtors and news outlets equated homeownership with traditional American values; to be truly American, one needed to own his or her home.

Public testimonials about home buying by people with social standing helped cement homeownership as a status good in Atlanta. According to the *Atlanta Constitution*, Mayor James Key spent his opening remarks at Atlanta's home exposition sharing his and his wife's own story of home buying. Key explained, "When I took home the deed to my first little home months after I was married . . . it was one of the happiest moments of my life. My wife and I had struggled a long time in the purchase of our first home on the installment plan and when we finally were rewarded for our efforts by having the deed delivered to us, it was indeed a happy moment."[54] Key's narrative aligned homeownership with American values and the American experience. Initially marked by struggle and sacrifice, the indenture finally resulted in the newlyweds' triumph and reward. Being delivered by the city's mayor, a person with political authority and social standing, the narrative also associated homeownership with status. And the mayor's reference to buying on an installment plan assured reluctant buyers that it was socially acceptable to carry debt (at least on a home).[55]

Though tenancy seemed satisfactory to Atlanta's citizenry for prior decades, the real-estate board's 1922 campaign adopted the position that Atlantans *wanted* to purchase a home but simply did not know how to go about it or feared the difficulty of the process. The use of assumption—in this case, assuming one wanted to buy a home—was useful in persuading the audience to adopt homeownership ideology. It suggested that *everyone* wanted to buy a home and pressured the audience to conform.

Assuming all Atlantans wanted to own their own home, companies immediately moved to persuading readers that buying a home was a simple process, as when R. O. Campbell Company and Miller Lumber Company assured Atlantans in their ads, "IT'S EASY TO OWN YOUR HOME." The expo patron, one ad explained, would be walked through the entire planning and buying process: "The exposition exhibits cover everything from the lot itself to the last detail of the furnishings—from methods to provide funds with which to build to the insurance on the completed home." The *Atlanta Constitution* assured readers, "The many exhibits are all arranged to show just how to choose

Figure 4.4. Own Your Own Home campaign advertisement. Source: *Atlanta Constitution*, April 8, 1923.

a building site [and] an architect's plans."⁵⁶ Simultaneously, though, some companies contended that house planning was difficult enough to require trained expertise. Individual companies also underscored how they would bring their specialized skills to a case and help ease what was now positioned as a challenging process. "Here the family can gather around the various exhibits and plan their new home *with the assistance of highly trained experts,*" one ad explained (emphasis added).⁵⁷ West Georgia Land Company assured potential customers: "Own Your Home, We Will Help You."⁵⁸ Real-estate practitioners deployed a unified rhetoric telling consumers that land professionals possessed the knowledge base and professional status necessary to lead buyers down the path to homeownership.⁵⁹

Although some expo rhetoric echoed national publicity and linked homeownership to masculinity, patriotism, and protection of wife and children, a significant portion of the exposition targeted women and domestic ideals. "Club women day" in particular emphasized domestic themes common during the period. The Women's Club featured a cookbook at its display, and the Georgia Railway and Power Company held a cooking demonstration at its booth. Other club women highlighted "various phases of home work." Mrs. J. E. Carlisle hosted a lounge "fitted up especially for the ladies." Finally, local china dealer Mrs. William Lycott gave away a complete dinner service in white and gold monogram. The *Atlanta Constitution* assured readers that women had attended the expo and were welcome on other days of the exposition, but this particular day would have special attraction for "feminine minds." What is more, the paper appealed to popular belief and asserted, "The vast majority of women dream of the time when they may own their own home."⁶⁰

Just as the NLMA and the Department of Labor recommended in their campaign handbooks, land dealers worked to inculcate home-buying expectations in Atlanta's children. Not content with simply providing activities designed to settle impatient children while parents learned how to choose the right architect, expo promoters explained that "one of the most important features of the educational campaign . . . [was] to interest the children and make them see the value of home owning." Steel Realty Development Corporation sponsored a children's essay contest, and campaign organizers awarded fifteen prizes ranging from one to fifteen dollars for the "best" entries listing ten reasons why a person should own his own home. The expo also featured a life-size playhouse, "built exactly like a large dwelling, having two nice rooms where the youngsters can play at keeping house." One lucky child won the playhouse on the last evening. To agents, builders, and related businesses, children were important future consumers, a market to be not overlooked but cultivated.⁶¹

If Atlanta's Own Your Own Home expo welcomed labor, women, and children as would-be future buyers, it ignored the city's African American population. Indeed, much of the expo spectacle reflected and reinforced white privilege. The white Board of Realtors planned, managed, and hosted the event. White businesses and professionals planned and staffed the booths, displays, and workshops. Black builder Alexander Hamilton, subdivision builder Heman E. Perry, and agent and builder Walter H. Aiken did not appear on the list of exhibitors. With the exception of three hours on Friday morning—secured at the request of black residents—the expo was likewise shopped by whites. Despite the emphasis on white homeownership, two thousand blacks visited the exposition during the three hours available. Ignoring the interest and growing buying power of blacks, Atlanta's whites continued to position homeownership as a white practice. As homeownership became entangled with park-neighborhood expectations, these cultural relationships strengthened.[62]

Homeownership and the Park-Neighborhood

Nationally and locally distributed homeownership guides and campaign pamphlets worked with the park-neighborhood movement to solidify new ideas about "neighborhood character," which included design, material features, aesthetics, and demographics. Pamphlets and guides consistently recommended that home seekers gauge not only the quality of the home itself but aspects of the neighborhood. The Department of Commerce's 1923 guide *How to Own Your Home,* for example, advised readers to assess neighborhood character and went so far as to recommend that readers *not* use proximity "to family and friends" as a factor in housing choice. Rather, the department encouraged readers to consider the "general type of people living in the neighborhood."[63] Besides neighborhood residents, agents, federal officials, and builders also instructed shoppers to assess neighborhood design, including green spaces and landscapes. In other words, public and private interests encouraged home buyers and owners to develop a landscape way of seeing, a view that took in not just home but street lengths, not just material landscapes but people.

Besides emphasizing a landscape way of seeing and an understanding of "neighborhood character," Atlanta's homeownership campaign cultivated and reinforced an appreciation for the new park-neighborhood aesthetic. Companies utilized natural environments and single-family homes typical of park-neighborhoods in their ads while they simultaneously promoted homeownership. One Carey Shingles ad, for instance, showcased not the average Atlanta bungalow but rather a two-story estate set within a well-landscaped lot with no neighboring homes in view (see fig. 4.5). A second Carey Shingles ad featured a

Figure 4.5. Carey Shingles and R. O. Campbell Coal Company advertisement. Source: *Atlanta Constitution*, May 7, 1922.

sizable single-family home, situated on a curbed street with manicured shrubs and set against a mature wooded backdrop. The small home used in the S. B. Turman and Company's home exposition ad was more typical of the homes built in the small subdivisions that emerged throughout Atlanta in the 1920s. That said, the tableau, which included established trees and a generous lot, reflected the park-neighborhood aesthetic, not the more common five-foot side yards and high-density development in which such homes were usually found (see fig. 4.6). In this manner, and not necessarily intentionally, companies helped readers link the park-neighborhood aesthetic with single-family homes and homeownership—relationships reinforced at the homeownership expo.[64]

Booths and activities at the Atlanta Own Your Home exposition echoed these themes and asked visitors to consider park-neighborhood-propagated garden and lawn design and embellishments. C. A. Dahl Floral Company, for instance, erected a miniature estate, complete with houses, drives and walks, lawns, gardens, and shrubbery that spanned two booths. According to the *Atlanta Constitution*, the exhibit intended to "give a comprehensive idea of what [could] be achieved in this vicinity in the way of landscape gardening and the planting of decorative trees and shrubs."[65] University Land and Development produced a quarter-scale model of a home "with pergolas and a pool" that showed "the possibilities of using a low lot for a sunken garden."[66] Agents, builders, and businesses encouraged expo visitors to think not in terms of shelter or practicality but, as the *Atlanta Constitution* described it, "the very latest ideas in materials, ornamentation, interior decoration and design, color schemes and arrangement."[67] In this manner, exposition visitors were simultaneously exposed to and taught to appreciate park-neighborhood-inspired scenes and landscape design practices as they shopped for a home.

Although some park-neighborhood advertisements were not directly connected with the homeownership exposition, their appearance within the expo-week newspapers helped associate that particular aesthetic collection with homeownership. In the exposition week's *Atlanta Constitution*, for example, Burdett Realty advertised Brookwood Hills as "more than 500 acres," "original woodland," "exclusive," "adequate restrictions," "bounded south by Ansley Park," and "on and east of Peachtree Road." Similarly, L. W. Rogers advertised Virginia Highlands as having "substantially paved boulevards" and "an expert landscape architect."[68] When Atlanta held its second home exposition in 1923, the *Atlanta Constitution*'s promotional art featured a single-family home enhanced by mature foliage, a manicured lawn, and a curbed street (see fig 4.4).[69] Thus, in the early 1920s, Atlanta residents found homeownership regularly positioned alongside the park-neighborhood aesthetic, which highlighted a natural

Figure 4.6. S. B. Turman & Company advertisement. Source: *Atlanta Constitution*, May 7, 1922.

environment, boulevards, restrictions, exclusivity, and proximity to elite neighborhoods. The combination of homeownership and park-neighborhood aesthetics found in text and visual imagery, in advertising and expos, suggested that the viewer link the practices.

Through homeownership expositions, advertisements, and news media, agents, builders, and related businesses encouraged Atlantans to associate homeownership, family, citizenship, and park-neighborhood aesthetics. In doing so, Atlanta's local housing culture reflected a dialogue taking place in federal agencies and at national housing conferences. Although ordinary Atlantans would not necessarily be aware of these policy conversations, they certainly were influenced by their outcomes, which included public educational campaigns that associated particular virtues with homeownership, schoolbook lessons on the relationship between home buying and family, and lectures on the significance of neighborhood to family life.

◈

Buoyed by the success of homeownership initiatives in the early 1920s and the rapid growth of home building, federal and private interests combined efforts in the 1930s both to ramp up the homeownership movement and to consider how to promote homeownership through federal policies. As part of the federal initiative, President Herbert Hoover initiated the President's Conference on Home Building and Home Ownership in 1931 and charged twenty-five "fact finding" committees and six "correlating" committees with investigating "the problem presented in home ownership and home building."[70] Over five hundred conference members drawn from political leadership, academia, city planning, national and state-level civic groups, real estate and building industries, and even heavy industries such as car manufacturing worked on the investigations and resulting series of reports. Participants included some of the nation's most innovative thinkers on housing, including former Richard Ely student and mortgage expert Arthur Mertzke and nationally renowned urban planner Harland Bartholomew. The secretaries of major urban organizations such as the National Conference on City Planning, the Conference of Mayors, the American Civic Association, and the U.S. Department of Commerce served on and led committees. Academicians from and administrators of the United States' leading universities played a significant role, including the president of William and Mary, University of North Carolina sociologist Howard Odum, and Columbia University sociologist Robert Lynd. National Housing Association director Lawrence Veiller chaired the Committee on Standards and Objectives.[71]

The Conference on Home Building and Home Ownership continued circulating the pro-homeownership rhetoric adopted by the Departments of Labor and Commerce in the early 1920s. Herbert Hoover opened the conference by asking, "In what manner can we facilitate the ownership of homes and how can we protect the owners of homes?" Adopting the notions successfully mobilized by the Department of Commerce and echoing the attributes laid out in previous homeownership campaigns, the conference insisted that homeownership induced "a better home life for children; a feeling of security and permanence; a greater interest in and use of the home; better social standing; the pride of possession; greater interest in government; the habit of saving; something to rely on in case of need; stability of investment; and an incentive to work for."[72] Moreover, literature generated by the conference helped solidify the cultural linkages between homeownership and neighborhood landscapes. Just as John M. Gries and James S. Taylor's *How to Own Your Home* asked the average home buyer to assess "neighborhood character," *Planning for Residential Districts*, one of the eleven volumes produced by the conference, insisted to academicians, policy makers, and mortgage brokers that "the neighborhood is vitally important." The authors emphasized that the home did not simply shelter the privatized family but operated in network with other homes and families. "The building and owning of a home," the authors explained, "should be undertaken with the frank acceptance of the fact that it *is part of a community* and not something apart therefrom" (emphasis in original).[73] The individual house may be of good design and construction, *Planning for Residential Districts* asserted, "but in an unsuitable neighborhood it would be a bad investment." The City Planning and Zoning Committee was particularly attentive to "neighborhood character" and explained that zoning and city planning were specifically designed to deal with the "physical *environment*," which they contended reflected "the relation of *each* dwelling to its *community* instead of considering a dwelling as a separated and distinct unit" (emphasis in original). To control those who did not accept the individual home's relationship to the neighborhood character, *Housing Objectives and Programs*, another volume produced by the conference, suggested deed restrictions—safeguards against "careless, eccentric or greedy acts" by other residents. Deed restrictions and zoning laws, they argued, would help to maintain "good character."[74]

With the help of *Housing Objectives and Programs*, neighborhood character came to reflect the concerns of the park-neighborhood movement by encompassing a particular set of aesthetic expectations. This set included harmony in design, well-tended grounds, natural landscapes, and picturesque views.

For example, the committee asserted that neighborhoods "should have charm" and "be free from ugliness and monotony and other conditions that tend to depress or humiliate the family." Elsewhere the committee recommended, "Every American home should, where feasible, be situated in surroundings of natural beauty and make a fit setting for it." This included the designing of "home grounds," which would ensure "beauty, privacy, shade, [and] freedom from dust." If neighborhoods contained homes built from identical plans, the committee suggested "the use of window boxes, porch and garden furniture" to achieve individuality. The committee was careful to discourage "excessive ornamentation."[75]

The committee based its standards on neighborhood and domestic sensibilities expressed in and by elite park-neighborhoods. In discussing building setbacks, for example, the committee asserted, "*Peace and quiet and a pleasant and dignified mode of living* will be secured through the establishment of building lines which automatically result in the setting back of homes from the noise of the streets" (emphasis added). Home decorations, furnishings, and "embellishments" should be considered in home standards, and homes should be designed not for their exchange value, but as "a place of serene, peaceful, happy, and harmonious family life, where each member of the family will find rest and sanctuary from the stress of life outside." Reflecting elite expectations, the members went on to commend the home as a space for consideration of music, nature, literature, and art.[76]

Like Frederick Law Olmsted and the Olmsted brothers, the conference envisioned neighboring homes and lots as "one harmonious composition." Grounds did not simply accent an individual home but worked with adjacent property to produce a neighborhood landscape. As the committee explained, grounds should possess "harmony and proportion—not only with relation to the house as the central feature, but with consideration for neighboring and street conditions." So that house and grounds could "be designed as one harmonious composition," landscape planning should be done at the same time as the architectural plan. Drawing on Olmstedian thinking, the committee report contended that "for beauty, planting should blend with the landscape and the topography. It should avoid too great formality and symmetry and should give unobstructed views for traffic safety, and should frame vistas." Like the designers of park-neighborhood, the committees recommended parks, suggesting that at least 10 percent of a community's land should be given over to green space.[77]

Like popular literature and real-estate professional journals, the conference adopted a housing hierarchy that positioned single-family homes above apartments. In his address to the conference, Secretary of the Interior Ray Lyman

Wilbur insisted, "The one-family dwelling can be protected from the invasion of the multi-family dwelling or apartment house." To Wilbur, apartments ruined the "charm and integrity" of a neighborhood. The Standards and Objectives Committee expressed concern over the proliferation of apartment living, asserting, "There has been a startling trend in recent years in America away from the private house to the larger multiple dwelling." To the committee, the trend was "unfortunate." Indeed, the committee gave multifamily housing only negative attention when it gave it any attention at all; the committee provided guidelines and standards only for single-family and semidetached homes. As an illustration, under "types of homes" the report listed, "The one-family house, preferably detached, best serves the needs of families and children." The alternative to the family-focused single-family home was captured by the vague explanation, "Other types ranging from the one-family house to the multi-family house, and even the hotel, serve the needs of others."[78]

Conference members considered their catalog of housing recommendations a "housing movement" and, like the ownership campaigns, an educational initiative. The committee recommended infusing elementary, high-school, and college courses with housing material and even suggested providing material to textbook publishers. Popular audiences could be targeted with exhibits, public addresses, and radio programs. Feature films could incorporate home-planning scenes and juxtapose the effects of good and bad housing on children, youth, and adults. Home demonstrations, guided garden tours, "playlets," and dialogues could also illustrate ideas for both school and nonschool audiences. Mirroring practices honed by the real-estate industry, conferees proposed essay contests on "special aspects of home building and home ownership" to promote these interests in grammar and secondary schools. Lantern-slide presentations could "include examples of good houses, good yards and gardens, and pleasing parkways from other places," but should "contain a good number of local slides which the local people [would] recognize."[79] To conference attendees, homeownership and park-neighborhood sensibilities could *and should* be taught and iterated through schools, films, books, radio, and advertising.

As in other cities, Atlanta's land dealers had to sell not just homes but the *idea* of homeownership. Homeownership rhetoric crafted and widely disseminated by agents, builders, and federal officials reveals that lack of financing was not the only obstacle to selling more homes. Rather, agents, the NAREB, federal officials, and builders saw the need to increase desire and promote demand for homeownership itself. The resulting language focused less on shelter, health, or wealth building, and more on imagery intended to deliver status rewards and associate ownership with socially valued institutions, such as family, or other subjectivities, such as masculinity. Ownership expositions, speeches, and newspaper copy positioned homeownership as citizenship embodied. Government and business interests operating in and on Atlanta and elsewhere in the second and third decades of the twentieth century reworked the terms *homeowner* and *homeownership* and delivered status rewards to buyers by creating a system that offered land market predictability and a social order. To the federal government, homeownership promised political stability, an informed citizenry, and a responsible electorate.[80] The NAREB, federal agencies, and private industry celebrated homeowners as patriots and citizens, good family protectors and providers, thrifty and reliable. The association of homeownership with an individual's thrift and stability led to associations of homeownership with job stability and adulthood. Thus, such rhetoric encouraged young Americans to believe that homeownership was part of life's stages. Those adults who did not own a home or appear to be preparing to purchase a home signaled their instability and perhaps immaturity. As homeownership became part of the American life cycle, it became less necessary to persuade citizens that a relationship existed between Americanism and homeownership.

Besides intertwining homeownership and park-neighborhood fashions, white builders, agents, suppliers, bankers, and park-neighborhood residents assumed homeownership and park-neighborhood landscapes as the province of whites. That is, white elites largely cultivated homeownership ideology and park-neighborhood living for white consumption. The resulting collection of status markers encompassed the park-neighborhood aesthetic, homeownership, and whiteness. This is not to say that only whites owned homes or that black families were not interested in homeownership. That is, between 1915 and 1930, whites had come to associate a discrete set of property practices and material elements with each other—single-family homes, managed landscapes, harmonious neighborhood aesthetics, deed restrictions, and whiteness. Public and private initiatives combined to tutor whites in how to maintain this social and cultural landscape, a set of expectations that included a landscape way of seeing. While federal agencies, the NAREB, and local housing industries worked together to produce the park-neighborhood landscape, they simultaneously taught the consumer how to *read* that particular landscape. They taught members of the white middle class to appreciate harmony, tended (yet natural) landscapes—and whiteness.

CHAPTER FIVE

Exclusion and Park-Neighborhood Building, 1922 to 1929

In the 1920s, subdivision building drove Atlanta's largest housing boom to date. Established housing developers and new speculative builders alike platted, subdivided, graded, planted, and hawked new neighborhoods ranging from four square blocks to five hundred acres. Sales values peaked in Atlanta from 1922 to 1925; sales volume, in 1927. From 1924 to 1928, builders completed at least fourteen thousand units, and from 1925 to 1928, $23 million worth of housing. As a result, the city filled in and spread out. Some 1920s-era projects were entirely new, as when Sylvan Hills launched in 1922, or when J. P. King auctioned Roxboro Park's first forty lots in 1927. In other cases, developers announced expansions to already existing neighborhoods, as when Ansley Park advertised its "Annex Lots" in 1923. Like the prewar exclusive park-neighborhoods, those sweeping across Atlanta's suburbs in the 1920s promised natural settings, restrictions, and prestige. And they diffused racial and class exclusion across the landscape.[1]

As park-neighborhood building accelerated in the 1920s, restrictive covenants dictated the racial and class composition of more and more of the Atlanta landscape. Typically spelled out in a deed or subdivision plat, as in the covenants for Inman Park or Ansley Park in the 1880s and 1900s, such restrictions established minimum building costs or lot sizes, or specified use (e.g., residential, commercial) for a specific period of time (e.g., forty or sixty years). A subdivision developer could, for example, require that properties be used only for residential purposes or that buildings measure no less than, for instance, 1,500 square feet, or cost no less than two thousand dollars. Covenants could also, as discussed in chapter 2, regulate race. A developer could require that a property not be sold or leased to "Semites" or "people of African descent." However, restrictive covenants were less successful in controlling race, class, and housing practices in older, established areas of the city. Consequently, white elites cast about for ways to manage race and class across the whole city, in established neighborhoods as well as new suburban enclaves.

Comprehensive land-use zoning, unlike restrictive covenants, held the potential to order the entire city by class and race, and Atlanta's elites pushed for zoning's adoption in the early 1920s. To be sure, zoning could not ensure architectural harmony or designed landscapes, as protective covenants might, but it could establish lot sizes and building setbacks, regulate building heights, and control density. Black-occupied and multifamily housing could be assigned to less-desirable areas of the city, away from white-occupied park-neighborhoods or from older districts that whites had come to view as *white*. That is, protective covenants could *prevent* nonwhites (or people unable to afford minimum building costs) from living in park-neighborhoods, but they did not establish where, exactly, nonwhites or the poor or middle class could live within the city. Comprehensive land-use zoning had the power to assign people to particular places, across the whole city and even in the unincorporated areas. Moreover, unlike restrictive covenants, zoning did not expire, and it applied to neighborhoods that did not adopt covenants when property was originally subdivided. Thus, Atlanta's white elites decided not simply to institute zoning practices that were becoming increasingly accepted throughout the country, but opted to continue their racial segregation campaign by introducing racial classifications into the city's 1922 Comprehensive Land-Use Plan.[2]

Equally important, the public debates over comprehensive land-use zoning acted to further disseminate pro-segregationist rhetoric and normalize white park-neighborhood expectations in Atlanta. Texts generated as part of Atlanta's 1922 zoning proposal (including the plan itself, its promotional materials, media coverage, and public hearings) affirmed and publicly circulated park-neighborhood thinking and practices. Protests against requests for zoning variances that arose after 1922 suggest that many Atlantans had accepted the idea that apartments and single-family homes, businesses and residents should not be mixed.

The 1922 zone plan continued the ongoing quest of whites for racial housing segregation by classifying land use by race. Rapid park-neighborhood building inside and outside Atlanta's city limits augmented zoning's influence on residential geographies by developing more land into white-occupied park-neighborhoods; disseminating deed covenants that mandated class and racially exclusionary practices across the landscape; and producing and circulating advertisements selling and media stories detailing these housing landscapes and their attendant racial and class assumptions. That is, park-neighborhood practices and sensibilities—particularly race and class exclusion—spread via the rapid development of the material landscape itself as well as through the circulation of related texts such as plat maps, advertisements, and news coverage.

Park-Neighborhood Building

The park-neighborhood fashions launched in Atlanta by Edwin Ansley and Joel Hurt at the turn of the century lurched forward in 1922, consuming acres of suburban property and drawing whites further from the central city. While commercial, industrial, and residential activity still concentrated within Atlanta's two-mile radius immediately after World War I, investors and developers laid claim to land well outside the city center for new park-neighborhoods. White, restricted Lenox Park broke ground 4½ miles from the city center, northeast of Ansley Park. Peachtree Heights Park flanked Peachtree Road four miles north, and elite-dominated Tuxedo Park lay 8½ miles out. These enclaves expanded Atlanta's urbanized area; indeed, by 1930 the city encompassed only 34 miles, but the metropolitan area comprised 221.

Atlanta chased the suburbs, frequently annexing established towns and population centers. The city acquired Kirkwood and part of DeKalb County to the city's northeast in 1922, and then East Lake and the Flat Shoals portion of DeKalb County in 1926, bringing the city to thirty-four square miles. By 1930, between annexation and in-migration, the city's population reached 270,000, and the metropolitan area, which included DeKalb, Fulton, Clayton, and Cobb Counties, hit 370,000.[3]

The *Atlanta Constitution*'s "Views of Atlanta Home and Artistic Landscapes" illustrates how the popular media mirrored and propagated this elite-neighborhood ideal, particularly with regard to neighborhood landscapes and natural (if cultivated) environments. The writer explained that, besides being known as the city of homes, Atlanta was becoming "the city of magnificent landscapes." The three photographs accompanying the article signaled a departure from a narrow focus on houses (and domestic interiors). Rather, the photos featured long entry drives, ornamental lawns, and manicured hedges. The writer continued, "The beautiful gardens surrounding [the homes were] the work of well-known architects whose specialty is the ornamentation of landscapes about these handsome structures."[4] Other news stories featuring new park-neighborhoods similarly highlighted "architectural beauty and distinction" by including photographs of extensive, manicured grounds. Here, news stories recorded neighborhood fashions while simultaneously propagating new understandings of neighborhood practices and expectations.[5]

As earlier, white park-neighborhood developments that padded the city's edge in the 1920s celebrated natural landscapes and attempted to distinguish their settings from the urban environment. With over five hundred acres, Brookwood Hills trumpeted its "original woodland," and Tuxedo Park touted its "beautiful wooded hills and streams [that lent] naturally to artistic landscaping."[6] Peachtree Hills Place, Miramar, and other new subdivisions promised natural beauty, lovely settings, charm, and refinement.[7] Garden Hills went further, offering "up-to-date" landscape plans and children's playgrounds.[8] Thus, by the mid-1920s, manicured park-neighborhoods seemed everywhere, a stark contrast to the smoky, sooty Gate City of 1910.

Not surprisingly, many park-neighborhoods also emphasized status and exclusivity, a haven from, as Peachtree Heights Park explained, "the grim of the dense, soft-coal-burning population."[9] In 1922, the *Atlanta Constitution* described Brookwood Hills, directly north of Ansley Park, as "one of the city's most select residential communities." There, the city's "leading citizens" planned "fine residences."[10] Roxboro Park and Tuxedo Park emphasized their location on the city's "fashionable north side."[11] Others hitched their status to Peachtree Street's, as when Peachtree Heights Park described its location on "the most far-famed and attractive residence boulevard in the whole South."[12] Modest, less formally planned subdivisions used proximity to exclusive communities as a selling point. Agents explained that Johnson Estates was "just north of Morningside and adjoining Druid Hills."[13] Empire Trust did not simply emphasize that Highland Park was "heavily wooded" but pointed to its location "midway between Druid Hills and Ansley Park."[14] In bringing subdivision amenities and named, exclusive neighborhoods together in advertisements, real-estate dealers helped readers and buyers equate these elements. Buying a particular aesthetic, the ads suggested, spatially situated one within a particular cultural group or social stratum.

The park-neighborhoods emerging in the 1920s *were* exclusive—restrictive covenants limited who could live in these communities by stipulating minimum building costs or minimum lot sizes or by limiting property to residential use. Moreover, park-neighborhoods *sold* exclusion, highlighting it in their ads. Country Club Estates, for example, was "highly restricted against all developments but the mansion or estate type of homes."[15] Collins Park buyers were required to build residences costing no less than $15,000.[16] Brookwood Hills confined buyers to building "residences only" and maintained other restrictions "regarding the cost of the dwelling" (see figure 5.1).[17] Shadow Lawn insisted, "No homes have been or will be built that will tend to destroy the unusual prestige this community enjoys," while Tuxedo Park and Peachtree Heights Park assured buyers that they were safe from "undesirable" conditions.[18] Sylvan Hills insisted that neighbors would not "erect cheap 'shacks'" that would spoil the desirability of the location as a home section."[19] Thus, according to developers' ads, elites seeking a respite from the "soft-coal-burning population" could be

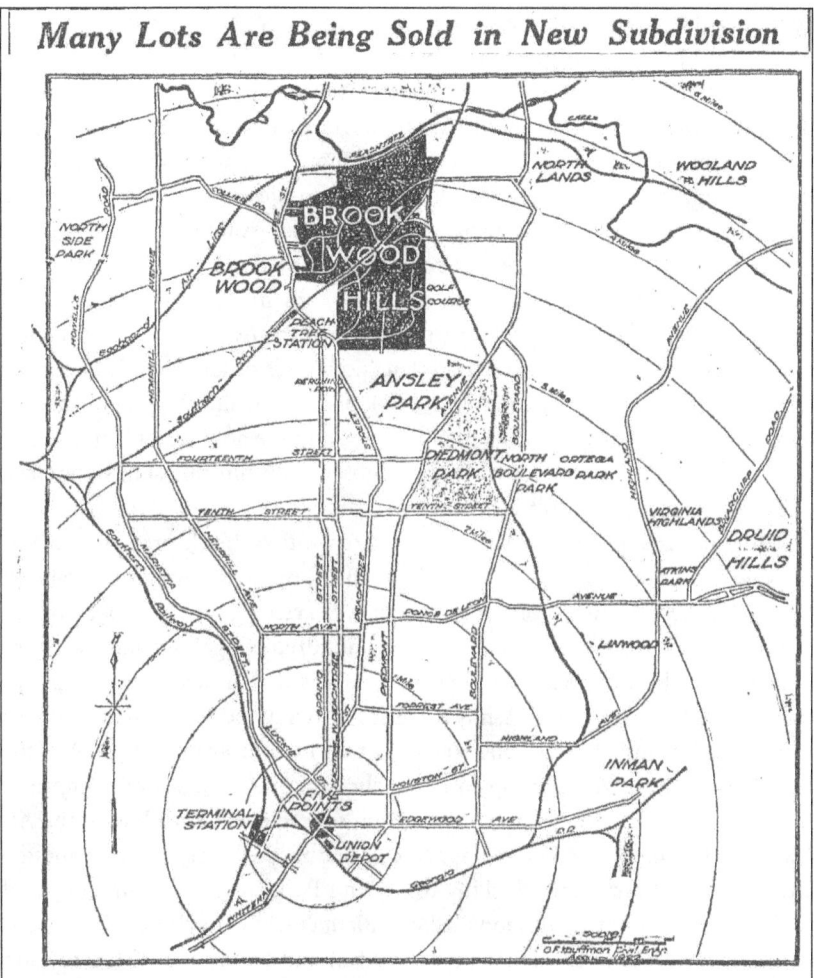

Figure 5.1. Brookwood Hills advertisement. Source: *Atlanta Constitution*, May 28, 1922.

confident that they would be safely distant from hodge-podge built environments, working-class neighbors, nonwhites, and other "undesirables."

Park-neighborhood restrictions favored the white and well off, implicitly and explicitly. Minimum building costs, minimum lot sizes, and other restrictions pushed up home costs in an era without federal subsidies and amortized mortgages, limiting entry to white-collar professionals, merchants, and others of means. In the 1920s, racial segregation was assumed (at least by white elites), though some developers specifically excluded blacks from new park-neighborhoods. Sylvan Hills, south of the city, for instance, stipulated on its plat map, "Lots shall not be sold, rented or leased to any person of African descent."[20] Tishomingo Park advertised that "no houses or lots [could] be sold to negroes."[21] Thus, park-neighborhood developers and white elites were encouraged to equate exclusivity, aesthetic harmony, and the absence of "undesirable conditions" with the absence of black neighbors. Within this status good set, one element accompanied the others.

While not covered extensively in the city's white or black press, black subdivision building, too, expanded in the 1920s, though at a far slower rate. In 1921, 2½ miles southwest of Atlanta's center, Service Company broke ground on a thirty-three-acre development for one hundred bungalows and two-story homes priced between $2,500 and $12,000. Subdivided in stages, the company's four blocks between C and Ashby Streets, Beckwith and West Hunter Streets comprised lots of 5,000 to 7,500 square feet on rectilinear streets. In 1923, the L. P. Flowers subdivision adopted a curvilinear street design and comprised thirty-nine lots ranging from 4,800 to 9,100 square feet. According to the *Atlanta Constitution*, "the better class of colored people" seeking to escape the city's noise and dirt were "flocking to Joyland Park" in 1926.[22] But compared to the park-neighborhoods launched on Atlanta's white north side, black subdivisions were modest, smaller in size overall and by individual lot. Joyland Park, for example, maintained a rectilinear street structure, and its lots measured about 4,000 square feet. Moreover, new black subdivisions of the 1920s were likely to be more centrally located than white subdivisions. Sited outside the central business district, black developments concentrated in a stretch of land between the city's two- and three-mile radius, primarily south and west of downtown. Pine Acres and Washington Park, for example, lay between mile markers two and three as measured from the city's center. And it was a three-mile trip to Joyland Park.[23]

Service and skilled workers largely populated Atlanta's black subdivisions, though professionals and white-collar workers remained scattered throughout neighborhoods, particularly near the black universities and in the lower Fourth

Ward. Service Company's black subdivision, located in a more-established area of Atlanta and within a few blocks of Atlanta University, housed porters, cooks, waiters, and skilled workers. Joyland Park, located south of the city and surrounded by undeveloped acreage, housed farmers, farmhands, and laborers. In contrast, white, exclusive Tuxedo Park and Haynes Manor, north of the city, housed primarily white-collar professionals and business owners.[24] In sum, black, predominantly working-class subdivisions remained close to the city's core, within two to three miles of the city's center. In the 1920s, though, white elites dominated the planned, exclusive park-neighborhoods that were consuming property outside the city's three-mile radius, especially to the city's north.

Thus, Atlanta's heterogeneous city, which had been punctuated by a few racially and class-homogeneous neighborhoods and blocks, grew denser and more segregated during the 1920s. By the end of the decade, the housing boom had filled in much of the empty space within the three-mile radius and lined the city's perimeter (from three to four miles out) with small to large subdivisions and—as far as nine miles out—with exclusive, restricted park-neighborhoods. Clearly, new construction and suburban amenities appealed to some Atlantans, and many fled the older, speculator-designed city when they could. As park-neighborhood advertisements suggested, the dirt, din, and activity of the urban environment intensified in early twentieth-century Atlanta. Indeed, Atlanta's heterogeneous core—*the city*—is what many elites sought to rein in and reorganize when they pursued comprehensive land-use zoning in the early 1920s. This planning innovation promised to discipline both land use and people. Through zoning, blacks and whites, businesses and residences could be assigned a place and limited to it.

Zoning a City

In the 1920s, white civic elites experimented with how to use comprehensive land-use zoning to solidify landscape preferences cultivated over the preceding twenty years. Segregating housing by race through protective covenants and zoning seemed particularly urgent to elites, as courts continued to rule against local segregation ordinances across the South, and migration to Atlanta accelerated after World War I, crowding the city. To be sure, "protecting" residential communities also meant preserving a particular landscape aesthetic— well-groomed lawns, homogeneous and tasteful architecture, and single-family homes. Zoning and planning also promised to rationalize city functions, such as the orderly movement of people and goods. In sum, zoning and city planning offered much to New South city leaders concerned about growing and maintaining Atlanta's urban status—and controlling "nuisance" populations.

Like city leaders and planners in most U.S. cities in the early twentieth century, Atlantans initially approached city planning in a piecemeal fashion. Concerned with rapid population growth, overcrowded streets, and the city's ability to attract business, industry, and tourists, civic elites and property investors such as Joel Hurt and Robert Otis pushed for the studies, improvements, and long-term goal setting modeled in Chicago. But, as was the case with parks, the challenge came in funding and implementation. The Atlanta Real Estate Board passed a resolution in 1915 urging the city council to establish a city planning board, but that effort apparently went unrealized. Disparate city-planning efforts continued for a few more years, with the park commission, street committees, and the like designing and realizing their own initiatives. But as Atlanta recovered economically from the post–World War I recession, more ambitious city plans surfaced. In early 1920, following a formal motion by the *Atlanta Journal's* John Cohen, the chamber of commerce approved the formation of a twenty-four-member planning commission.[25]

The resulting "Greater Atlanta" report of 1920 and the 1921 ad hoc planning committee combined to persuade city leaders to "rationalize" the city through comprehensive planning. Although not the first attempt at city planning, this particular combination offered a broader vision for city organization compared to previous efforts. "Greater Atlanta" outlined needed improvements in schools, parks, and roads. In 1921, Mayor James L. Key responded by charging an ad hoc body with planning for zoning, widening, and regrading of streets, construction of sewers, building of bridges and viaducts, regulation of heights and appearance of buildings, and "other kindred subjects."[26] To this end, the committee contacted planners and related professionals nationwide both to gauge their interest in working on an Atlanta plan and to solicit initial ideas about how such work might proceed.[27]

The ad hoc committee was decidedly business and elite oriented, making it consistent with planning projects across the nation. Robert Otis, who served as vice-chair, owned and operated his own real-estate firm, selling and managing business and industrial properties. Other members had personal interests in Atlanta's growth and business development. Fred Pittman operated a construction company, and Charles Wickersham owned the Atlantic and West Point Railroad and was a partner in other businesses. Joel Hurt, developer of Inman Park and Druid Hills, had a long-standing interest in the profitability of fashionable landscapes, park trends, and large-scale residential developments, as did former owner of the *Atlanta Journal,* U.S. senator, former governor, and attorney Hoke Smith, who had partnered with Joel Hurt in the Kirkland Land Company, which had launched Druid Hills. What is more, the committee's racial sensibilities resonated with Atlanta's jim crow traditions. In 1906, Smith and his *Journal* became deeply involved in a divisive, race-baiting fight for governor against Clark Howell, a battle that raised racial tensions and set the stage for Atlanta's multiday race riot later that year. Overall, the committee represented white elites' interests in economic and park-neighborhood development as well as class and racial exclusion.[28]

The committee immediately set about hiring a professional to develop a city plan, and some members already had their favorites. Joel Hurt suggested a continued concern with City Beautiful–inspired ideas when he wrote to Frederick Law Olmsted Jr. that the commission sought landscape artists who "had to do with city planning heretofore."[29] But Robert Otis favored Robert Whitten, who had previously prepared plans for Cleveland and New York. The commission ultimately recommended hiring a team—a landscape architect, a civil engineer, and a zoning expert—to direct plan development and procedures. The commission considered Frederick Law Olmsted, Nelson P. Lewis (a civil engineer), and Robert Whitten, but "on account of limited appropriation," finally opted to hire only Whitten.[30]

Widely regarded as a leading thinker on comprehensive zoning practices, Robert Whitten brought years of planning and zoning experience to Atlanta's new planning commission. Though trained in law, Whitten had developed an interest and expertise in municipal matters. He had served as secretary of the Commission on Building Districts in New York, coauthored New York's 1916 zoning ordinance, and authored precedent-setting zoning ordinances for Cleveland's upscale suburbs, including Cleveland Heights and Shaker Heights. Indeed, Whitten had some familiarity with racial housing issues from working with Cleveland in the second decade of the century, when Cleveland Heights had confronted blockbusting, racial strife, and the threat of riots. His plan for the Cleveland suburb of Lakewood had focused on controlling the presence of Jews. His ability to protect elite white homeowner interests in Cleveland's new suburbs and his success in designing a parkway system that enhanced area land values no doubt made him attractive to Atlanta's commission. Whitten's interest in stabilizing populations was especially appropriate given white homeowners' concern over the "invasion" of blacks, and his experience in zoning suburbs would aid their quest to institutionalize new neighborhood fashions of continuity and order. Finally, Whitten's legal background may have offered hope to white property owners tired of negative court reception of the city's segregation ordinances.[31]

Whitten's attention to controlling "nuisance populations" reflected established practice among zoning proponents. Indeed, from the beginning, land-use zoning involved the sorting of people across the city. California led the nation in instituting land-use restrictions intended to control "nuisances" in residential areas when, in the 1880s, a Modesto ordinance excluded laundries from some areas of the city. Since Chinese immigrants owned most of Modesto's laundries, the move appeared to be, as historian Marc Weiss writes, "a clear-cut proxy for Chinese exclusion from certain 'Caucasian' neighborhoods."[32] Whether Modesto whites intended to exclude Chinese or not, cities adopted such practices more frequently as designed neighborhood and park-neighborhood aesthetics gained importance around 1900. Proponents continued to obscure the issue of discrimination against individuals by actively associating particular groups with specific nuisance practices and then outlawing the practice instead of the person. According to historian Max Page, for example, New York City's Fifth Avenue Association (FAA) fought the introduction of lofts into the area in order to limit the presence of immigrant workers; to the FAA, the lofts were cheap, ugly, and poorly maintained—as were the "hoards" of immigrants.[33]

Californians may have been the early purveyors of restricted land use in the United States, but these were piecemeal efforts in that they did not attempt to dictate land use across an entire city. It was New York that introduced comprehensive—or citywide—land-use zoning in 1916. There, urban leaders and a new cadre of planning professionals created five districts that specified maximum building heights and two general-use districts that divided the city into residential and business/industry zones. After New York's implementation, zoning's popularity grew quickly. Indeed, a New York citizen's committee accelerated the diffusion, reasoning that if zoning were widely adopted, it would be protected against the courts. By the mid-1920s, over four hundred municipalities had instituted zoning. In 1922, Atlanta's white civic elites would attempt to combine the practices of California and New York by racializing the entire city without veil or apology.[34]

To be sure, Robert Whitten was concerned with more than the regulation of populations that whites sought to avoid, and his initial proposal to Atlanta's ad hoc committee incorporated practices typical of city plans produced in the 1920s. In his first report, "A Planning Program for Atlanta," Whitten advised the city to draft a seven-point schema for physical growth that addressed zoning, new development, streets, parks and recreation, street railways and busses, railroads and terminals, and public buildings (including spatial design and appearance). Conceding that it was not practical to tackle all these elements at once, he recommended that the city pursue planning and improvement work in the order listed. He suggested completing a preliminary study of existing conditions before any work commenced. Proposing that Atlanta undertake zoning first, he asserted, "While no part of a comprehensive plan can be worked out entirely independent of other features, zoning is the part that can be brought most nearly to perfection in Atlanta in advance of a *complete* working out of other features" (emphasis in original).[35]

At its most basic level, Robert Whitten's 1922 comprehensive zoning plan for Atlanta included classifications typical of those developed in other cities. Whitten segregated land uses into two residence districts and four business and industrial districts. Over these, he laid four height districts and five area districts. The U1 Dwelling House District included single-family and duplex (semidetached) homes. The U2 Apartment House District allowed all types of residential structures. Five area districts (A1 through A5) operated more as density requirements, allowing no more than one family for the specified square footage per lot. That is, A1 districts dictated that "no building shall be erected or altered to accommodate ... more than one family for each 5,000 square feet of the area of the lot." A2 designated one building per family for each 2,500 square feet, and so on. Although the area requirements did not establish minimum lot sizes or house sizes per se, they did require a certain amount of property per family and thus influenced where people of different income levels could live. Departing from standard zoning practice, Whitten also satisfied white Atlantans' desires to settle the racial segregation question once and for all by creating race districts. Race districts overlay other established districts and included R1, white; R2, "colored"; and R3, undetermined.[36]

If Whitten's categories and approach were typical of the era, this did not mean that zoning was an easy sell to (white) Atlantans, even if the plan did include racial restrictions. Gate City residents had become used to a real-estate market unbounded by regulations and open to speculation. Whitten expected resistance (indeed, cities throughout the United States—not just those in the South—questioned comprehensive zoning) and had arrived in Atlanta well armed with justifications for and defenses of zoning that had proven effective elsewhere.

✥

Whitten and Atlanta's pro-zoning contingent argued the need for zoning more broadly and Atlanta's 1922 zoning plan specifically by utilizing rhetoric adopted by the concurrent homeownership campaigns and park-neighborhood movements. In *The Atlanta Zone Plan: Report Outlining a Tentative Zone Plan for*

Atlanta (hereafter referred to as *The Atlanta Zone Plan: Tentative*), Whitten included "Five Illustrations of the Need for Zoning," which discussed and illustrated what he considered to be urban ills, such as the introduction of stores into residential areas and tall buildings that, according to many planners, robbed adjacent buildings of sunlight and air. Although *The Atlanta Zone Plan: Tentative* itself simply defined zone classifications and mapped these classes across the landscape, the accompanying educational materials iterated the argument that homeowners and single-family, owner-occupied homes should be protected; multifamily housing, tenants, and blacks should be avoided; and the neighborhood and the city alike should display an aesthetically pleasing facade that expressed harmony and balance.[37]

Whitten created a hierarchy between single-family and apartment homes by depicting multifamily housing in tragic terms. Tenement (apartment) house construction was "one of the most important *problems* in zoning" (emphasis added) because, according to Whitten, apartment buildings limited open space, potentially interfered with light and air for adjoining properties, and crowded neighborhoods.[38] Consistent with his concern for homogeneity, Whitten argued, "The apartment house and the one or two family house cannot exist side by side."[39] *The Atlanta Zone Plan: Tentative* utilized photos, drawings, and anecdotes to illustrate Whitten's points, and in the second of "Five Illustrations of the Need for Zoning" the plan described a formerly "well-kept" neighborhood that was "practically destroyed" when an apartment building was introduced. Other neighborhood residents, it noted, began to "fear" more apartment houses and fled. In this manner, the pamphlet instructed Atlantans that apartments were a menace to "residential" (i.e., predominantly single-family-home) neighborhoods. Should apartments be introduced into a neighborhood, the owner of a single-family home should move, lest real-estate values drop.[40] Put another way, Whitten and his colleagues contended that, to protect homeowners and their neighborhoods, apartments should be limited in number and segregated from single-family residential sections. "If Atlanta is to be preserved as a *city of homes*," Whitten explained, "we must protect the *homeowner* by establishing definite limits beyond which the apartment may not spread."[41] Zoning, Whitten concluded, would "keep the apartment out of the private home sections."[42]

Moreover, tenants themselves negatively affected neighborhood character, according to Whitten. His concerns encompassed not only property and the material environment but also people, a point he made clear in a 1920 article for the *Journal of the Western Society of Engineers*. Few planners or elites publicly spoke of tenants themselves as negative influences, but Whitten was unusually candid on this topic and stated that with the introduction of apartments, "degeneracy is certain." "The erection of a single apartment house in a block," he argued, "is almost certain to mean *a radical change in the residential population*, a decline in the value of the single family houses and a gradual replacement of such houses by apartment houses" (emphasis added). He concluded ominously, "Our civilization is at stake."[43]

Similarly, Whitten argued for the separation of businesses and residences because to him and some park-neighborhood developers, neighborhood stores did not offer convenience but marred streetscapes. Illustrations included in *The Atlanta Zone Plan: Tentative* encouraged readers to think of clustering businesses together as "common sense" (see fig. 5.2). Zoning and park-neighborhood design both, then, promoted hard separations between housing forms, land uses, and people.

In segregating people and land uses through comprehensive land-use zoning, Atlanta's elites performed their local cultural work in partnership with other civic elites around the country, in this case sharing appeals and justifications for zoning. Whitten himself facilitated the transmission of zoning ideas throughout the country through his work with different cities. He brought the device of "protecting the small property owner" with him from Chicago's zoning commission, for example.[44] Pittsburgh's city-planning commission likewise called its zoning plan a "Bulwark to Owners of Small Homes."[45] Pittsburgh's civic club ran a newspaper ad that, according to historian Janet Daly, "featured a picture of a charming cottage with a picket fence in the ominous shadow of a large factory to emphasize zoning's promise to protect the sanctity of the family home."[46] This phrasing could well have been used to describe the *Atlanta Journal*'s editorial cartoon on the same subject. In the *Journal*'s version, the homeowner lost his savings due to an encroaching "boiler factory," a rendering that painted the city and its leaders noble in their role of protector (see fig. 5.3).[47]

Curiously, Whitten and Atlanta's civic elite sometimes plucked tactics from other cities that did not resonate with Atlanta's reality. There is little evidence, for example, that Atlanta's factories threatened the city's homes. Neither zoning advocates nor newspaper accounts identified any specific industrial nuisances when justifying the need for zoning. The same was true for apartments. Neither newspapers, officials, nor Whitten himself named a specific example of an apartment "encroaching" on a single-family-home residential section. Finally, Whitten did not even use Atlanta photos to illustrate his educational materials; rather, the pamphlet credited the Cleveland City Planning Commission for all five illustrations. Thus, Atlanta's civic elites blindly copied other cities' justifications for zoning in their attempt to persuade citizens of its efficacy.[48] But *The Atlanta Zone Plan: Tentative* and the zone plan approved by the city offered more

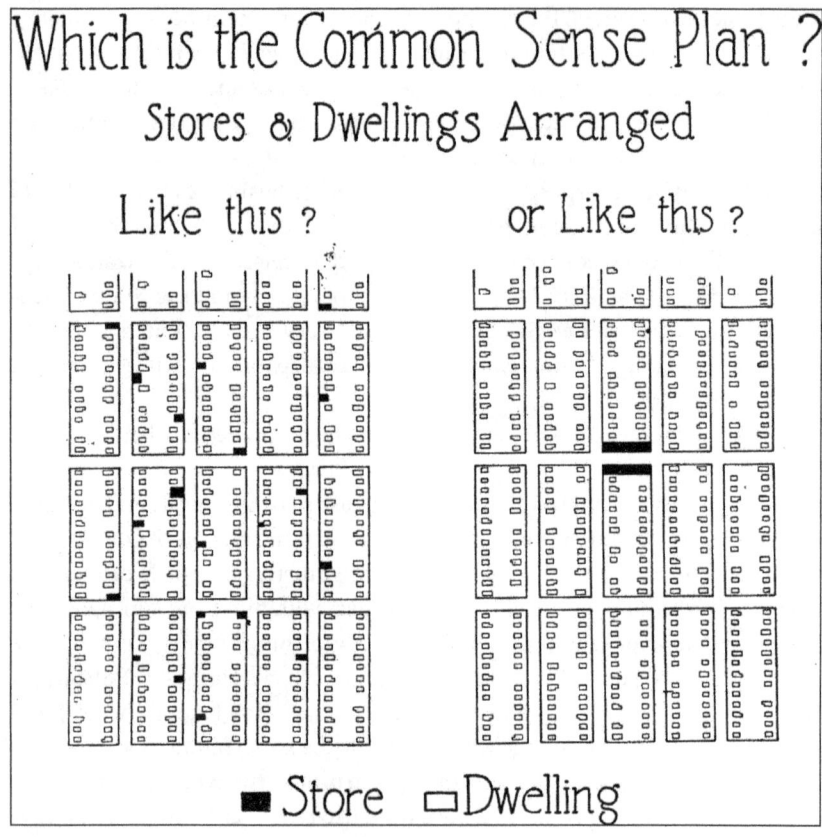

Figure 5.2. "Which Is the Common Sense Plan?" Source: Robert Whitten, *The Atlanta Zone Plan: Report Outlining a Tentative Zone Plan for Atlanta* (Atlanta: City of Atlanta, 1922), Robert H. Whitten Collection. Graduate School of Design, Frances Loeb Library Special Collections, Harvard University, Cambridge, Massachusetts.

Figure 5.3. Zoning scare tactics. Source: *Atlanta Journal,* March 30, 1922.

than persuasive text; in combination with other housing and zoning texts, it sorted people across the city by mapping class, housing form, and race.

In the 1920s, Whitten and other planners of his generation envisioned and worked toward goals that sorted residents by class across the city. Many well-known planners, including Whitten, promoted the clustering of homes based on size and cost, which effectively sorted people by class. J. C. Nichols, already famous in the 1920s for his Country Club District in Kansas City, had espoused such concepts nationally for years. As the developer explained in a 1912 speech to the National Association of Real Estate Boards:

> The space we set aside in our plats on record for the $3000 cottage is sufficiently removed from the houses of greater cost to prevent any disparagement in the cost and size of homes in their respective neighborhoods; but the entire district is characterized by conspicuous balance and symmetry in home groupings, the costly homes with spacious grounds being protected from the proximity of the less pretentious ones.[49]

Similarly, at the National Conference on City Planning in 1918, Whitten had recommended that residential sections be organized by type of dwelling; percentage of the lot that the dwelling could consume; and the number of houses or families per acre. Specifically, he suggested that zones designate a minimum land area for each family housed. His examples of 5,000, 2,500, 1,250, 625, and 312 square feet eventually made their way into Atlanta's zoning plan. Whitten justified these groupings by averring that they would secure an appropriate distribution of population, ensure the availability of recreational area, and prevent undue congestion in central areas.[50] But Whitten's attention to population distribution, recreation, and congestion masked his classist assumptions. According to Bruno Lasker, editor of the journal *Survey,* Whitten conceded to him in conversation:

> It is more desirable that bankers and the leading businessmen should live in one part of town, storekeepers, clerks, and technicians in another, and working people in yet others where they would enjoy the association with neighbors more or less of their own kind. . . . I admit the fact [that zoning segregates different economic classes] but do not consider this result either anti-social or undemocratic in its tendency. My own observation is that whenever you have a neighborhood made up of people largely in the same economic status, you have a neighborhood where there is the most independence of thought and action and the most intelligent interest in the neighborhood, city, state and national affairs.[51]

To Whitten, the organization of neighborhoods by class promoted "community" and "civic engagement." Planner John Nolen argued likewise, contending that city builders should use zoning to both decentralize the working class and separate the middle and working classes into garden cities and industrial villages, respectively. Nolen's choice of language and landscape is worth emphasizing: gardens were for the middle and upper classes; industry was allocated to workers.[52]

Class zoning met resistance in Atlanta, though, both for its segregating tendencies and its limits on free alienation. At one public hearing on the zoning plan, Judge Ernest C. Kontz complained that Whitten's plan gave "the commission power to classify the residents of different communities" and called the plan "un-American."[53] But agents William Ansley (brother of park-neighborhood and central-city rental-housing developer Edwin Ansley) and M. L. Thrower declared that the proposal infringed on property owners' "personal liberty" to develop land to what they considered to be the highest and best use, whether apartments, rental property, or tall commercial buildings.[54] Alderman J. L. Carpenter blasted the proposed zoning plan for "destroying the rights of people." Carpenter was particularly suspicious of the "experts" the city had hired, with their "hair parted in the middle" and "toothpick shoes." "Where do they come from?" he queried. "From the north," he responded, his final damning critique.[55] Others questioned whether stable property values were even desirable, as they would "destroy the speculative value of a piece of property" and "throttle Atlanta's growth."[56]

For all the talk about class segregation and declarations that the plan was, in Ernest Kontz's words, "monstrous," the draft zoning plan's area demands were relatively conservative compared to the lot sizes in new park-neighborhoods, particularly those to the city's north. The plan's most demanding category, A1, required 5,000 square feet per family. Garden Hills, in contrast, had lots ranging from 10,000 to 32,000 square feet intended for single-family homes, and Collins Park's lots measured from 7,075 to 30,000 square feet. Compared to these park-neighborhoods, Shadowlawn and Peachtree Hills seemed modest at 8,000 and 5,000 to 10,000 square feet, respectively. But if the plan was liberal with minimum lot sizes, it proved far more limiting regarding race.[57]

In assigning "white" and "colored" districts across the city, Atlanta's zoning plan continued white propertied elites' efforts to control the housing choices of African Americans. Unsuccessful in earlier attempts to create an informal racial boundary line in the Fourth Ward or to impose racial-segregation ordinances, segregationists would not accept defeat. Indeed, authors of the 1922 City Planning Commission *Annual Report* specifically cited racial issues as an inducement for formal city planning. In tracing the history of the planning commission, the report explained that, in 1917, the Real Estate Board had sought a planning commission "mainly" to convert part of the fire-damaged lower Fourth Ward "into an esplanade to separate the two races." After this effort foundered, "property damage, encroachment of the races," and other issues that consumed Mayor James L. Key's first administration prompted the creation of the commission in 1920. Thus, in white elites' view, the City Planning Commission and its 1922 zoning plan were intended specifically—though not solely—to manage racial residential issues.[58]

Curiously, although civic elites were bold enough to zone explicitly by race, they declined to produce educational materials that explained or defended that practice or to insert racial examples into *The Atlanta Zone Plan: Tentative*'s "Five Illustrations of the Need for Zoning." None of the materials directly addressed a need for "R" districts—R1 for white sections, R2 for "colored," and R3 for undetermined—even though Atlanta was setting a national precedent by introducing racial classifications into a comprehensive zoning plan. Perhaps white civic elites thought their desire for racial residential segregation required no defense. Or perhaps given the wave of court rulings defeating residential segregation efforts in the second decade of the century, Whitten and pro-segregationists decided not to draw unnecessary attention to the racial categories.

When asked at public meetings or interviews to justify the R1 and R2 race categories contained in *The Atlanta Zone Plan: Tentative*, Whitten echoed the same arguments put forward by Atlanta's segregationists and mobilized the race-riot trope. "A race riot is a terrible possibility in many southern cities," he warned in the journal *Survey*. "Atlanta in establishing colored residence districts has removed one of the most potent causes of race conflict."[59] Section 20 of the 1922 plan departed from the other sections of the ordinance by including an explanation for racial districting; other sections simply articulated requirements. The justification continued the public-welfare rhetoric of the previously unsuccessful segregation arguments, asserting that racial districts were established "for the promotion of the public peace, order, safety and general welfare." Whitten appeared persuaded by the white property owners who insisted on a racial boundary line in Jackson Hill, and he concluded his defense by recalling the higher "public good" of preventing disorder. A few Atlantans recognized the zoning plan as a thinly veiled segregation ordinance and, given the 1917 *Buchanan v. Warley* ruling, doubted the legality of the racial zoning portions. Attorney James W. Mayson, who had worked with the city to develop previous segregation ordinances, advised that the zoning law was unconstitutional in that it discriminated "against certain classes of people."[60]

Segregation proponents responded to these challenges by publicly reinforcing white segregationist ideology. When Judge Ernest Kontz pointed out at a public hearing that the Supreme Court had outlawed racial residential segregation, for example, Mayor James Key (who had assisted with the development of racial restrictions for the post-fire redevelopment of the Fourth Ward) immediately retorted, "Are you opposed to the separation of blacks and whites?"[61] Key's remark spoke to the beliefs and tactics of white propertied elites bent on building a spatial network of privilege. Key indirectly suggested that by *not* fighting the Supreme Court, Kontz promoted race mixing. Here, Key used his rhetoric and position as mayor to stifle challenge and to ensure the place of white propertied, white taste cultures in public policy.

Whitten may have repeated the oft-mobilized threat of a race riot to explain the plan's race categories, but he also relied on his own cache of strategies. Whitten and other zoning advocates contended that they were "building communities" by segregating blacks to particular neighborhoods, asserting, "Colored people in these large homogeneous districts are given a better chance for the development of a more intelligent and responsible citizenship than was possible under former conditions." Here the planner deployed the very same argument he had used to support class segregation; Whitten justified racial isolation by insisting that homogeneous neighborhoods fostered citizenship and social improvement.[62]

Despite Whitten's expressed concern for black community development, Atlanta's draft and final zone plans left little room for black neighborhood expansion. Areas zoned R2, "colored," in the draft zoning plan included sections of Jackson Hill, South Atlanta, Pittsburgh, and portions of Atlanta's west side, concentrations of black families that had developed and evolved for decades. Railroads, small commercial districts, or other barriers circumscribed almost all R2 districts, leaving majority-black neighborhoods no land on which to expand. Thus, the draft and final zone plans suggest that white civic elites had no plans, and indeed did not even consider the possibility of black residential expansion. Instead, white civic elites attempted to control and limit black residential growth by assigning blacks to particular areas of Atlanta's central city.

Changes made between the draft and the final zoning plan indicate that in areas where obvious barriers between black and white neighborhoods did not exist, whites still waged a block-by-block battle to curtail black movement into particular established sections of Atlanta. For example, between the draft and the final plan, one block of Jackson Hill that had been disputed since 1910— the section of Houston Street between Butler Street and Bedford Place—was reclassified from R2, "colored," to R1, "white." No discussion of this change surfaced, but given the very public debate regarding residential segregation in Jackson Hill in the second decade of the century, it is safe to say that Jackson Hill whites still intended to manage the area's racial identity and had likely requested the change. Although Fourth Ward whites had encouraged blacks to relocate to the city's west side, changes to the draft plan indicate that whites had firm ideas about the appropriate location for black housing on that side of town as well. Specifically, one multiblock section between Simpson Street and Bankhead Avenue, east of Maddox Park to Walnut Street, which was originally partially marked as R3 (neither black nor white) and partially marked as R2 (colored) was changed to R1 (white) in the final plan. With this change, the zoning plan indicated that no new construction of housing intended for black occupancy would take place in the city's northwest quadrant north of Simpson Street. Again, no discussion surfaced regarding this particular adjustment, though the change encompassed more land than any other revision in the zoning plan.[63]

Likewise, Whitten's requests for zoning reclassifications after the plan's approval in 1922 indicate the willingness of whites to fight for every street length if necessarily. In the Bedford Pine neighborhood of the Fourth Ward, for example, whites successfully petitioned for Bedford Place from Forrest Avenue to Angier Place to be reclassified from "undetermined" (R3) to R1, "white."[64] After it was clear that a proposed change to the zoning classification of Summit Avenue from Highland Avenue to East Avenue from R1 to R3 would pass, Fourth Ward councilman John White suggested closing down East Avenue from Summit to Jackson to "prevent the influx of negroes."[65]

Despite the efforts of white elites to maneuver around previous court rulings and manage Atlanta's racial geography through comprehensive land-use zoning, the Georgia Supreme Court declared the racial districting section of the zone plan unenforceable in *Bowen v. Atlanta* (1924). The case arose when, denied a permit to rezone a property from R1, "white," to R2, "colored," Annie Bowen sued the city, contending that section 20 denied her the right of free alienation. Bowen's investment property, located on the west side of Chickamauga Avenue, had been zoned "white," though blacks occupied the east side of the street. Bowen's husband, reasoning that blacks would be more likely to buy property and move onto streets that fronted homes already occupied by blacks, subdivided the property and advertised it as "choice property for colored people."[66] Luther J. Crittle, an African American, purchased a lot and subsequently constructed a dwelling on the property. The building inspector attempted to enforce the zoning ordinance, drawing the lawsuit. The court ruled in favor of Bowen.[67]

Although the racial elements of Atlanta's zoning ordinance were in force only from 1922 to 1924, the significance of the 1922 zoning plan lay not so much with its long-term influence, but rather with the fact that it continued the ongoing campaign of white elites to impose racial residential segregation across the city; the offensive helped sustain the ongoing public discourse explaining and defending white ideology. This public circulation of segregationist thinking and attempts to impose housing segregation continued practically uninterrupted from the second decade of the century through the 1930s. Again, in May 1929 the city council approved an ordinance brought by Fourth Ward council representative John A. White that stated, "A person could not live on those streets where a majority of the persons who resided on these streets were persons with whom one was forbidden to intermarry."[68] Borrowing language directly from a Richmond, Virginia, ordinance and echoing the rhetoric used to justify previous ordinances, the ordinance intended "to preserve the general welfare, peace, racial integrity, morals, and social good order of the city" by segregating housing by race. The city council unanimously approved the 1929 proposal, though city attorney James Mayson recommended against its passage. After Mayor I. N. Ragsdale vetoed the ordinance—stating that he supported it, but that he was confident it would be ruled unconstitutional—the council unanimously reversed the veto. The council's insistence on fighting a sure-to-be-lost battle, the 1929 action, and its surrounding rhetoric echoed themes of early segregation fights—a Fourth Ward representative led the fight, the proposal borrowed language from an ordinance generated by another city (suggesting that Atlanta still planned exclusion in partnership with other urbanites), and despite sound advice that the ordinance would not survive court challenge, advocates insisted on passing it.

Thus, throughout the 1920s, whites diligently pursued racial control of the residential landscape through multiple overlapping paths—restrictive covenants, ordinances, and zoning plans. Although efforts to segregate through ordinances and zone plans failed, elites continually diffused segregationist ideology across the landscape through public texts. Such language helped normalize neighborhood practices and gradually persuaded white Atlantans that segregation of land use and people was socially desirable, aesthetically superior, and financially stable.[69]

After the zoning plan's passage in 1922, requests to change zoning classifications of particular blocks suggest that by the mid-1920s, many Atlantans had accepted the idea that a city should be sorted into residential (that is, single-family home), business, and apartment districts, and that "mixed" land uses depreciated property values. In June 1925, for example, residents near Juniper and Fourth Street protested a request to change a corner lot to "business." Residents opposing the change contended that the neighborhood was largely residential, and zoning the lot for business would "cause a depreciation in property values."[70] Heated discussions surrounded apartment-building location as well, a housing form that pro-zoning materials had taught Atlantans to avoid. One petition requesting that Myrtle between Fourth and Fifth Streets be rezoned from residential to allow for an apartment building met with stiff opposition at the November 1924 planning commission meeting. Washington Street and Woodward Avenue residents resisted the "encroachment" of business by fighting a proposed classification change in October 1924. That same month, Jackson Hill residents also successfully fought the introduction of a store on North Jackson. In *Smith v. Atlanta*, the 1926 case that ultimately ruled the Zoning Ordinance for Atlanta unconstitutional, Chauncey Smith sued the city after being denied the right to erect businesses on her property on Piedmont Avenue, which was zoned residential. To many Atlantans, apartments, businesses, and single-family homes should have separate, assigned places in Atlanta's geography.[71]

Having no zoning plan in force after *Smith v. Atlanta* left white elites feeling anxious about their ability to control park-neighborhood access and the park-neighborhood aesthetic. Newspaper coverage incited fear of declining property values. Avondale Estates developer George Willis asserted, "Unless the residents of our beautiful residential sections can find some means to legally protect themselves against the encroachments of business and other establishments that detract from the value of their properties, this decision will have a most unhappy effect."[72] To some Atlantans, zoning's uncertain status affirmed the need for restrictive covenants. Garden Hills developer P. C. McDuffie explained to the *Atlanta Constitution* that the 1926 ruling "played into the hands of the modern residential developers" who "stipulate[d] certain restrictions and safe guards in every sales contract and deed."[73] Nonetheless, zoning proponents and park-neighborhood interests were panicky without zoning to "protect" elite communities. One *Atlanta Constitution* editorial complained, "Since the [1922] zoning law . . . was killed the suburbs of Atlanta—even close-in residence districts—have become a hodge podge with garages, grocery stores, filling stations and the like, destroying not merely the beauty of old residence sections but materially damaging the home owners."[74] Though the paper exaggerated, the *Atlanta Constitution* fairly expressed the fears of Atlanta's elites. Shortly after the *Smith* ruling, the Supreme Court upheld the constitutionality of zoning in *Euclid v. Ambler*, and Atlanta's elites turned their attention to crafting a new zoning code.[75]

Although Atlantans would have to redo the entire zoning code after 1926, civic elites could not consider the 1922 effort a complete failure. Zoning materials, the plan itself, and the public debates it prompted kept key ideas about housing landscapes and city and neighborhood organization—including defenses of class and racial housing segregation—in front of residents. Through these modes and others, ordinary Atlantans learned and later were required by public policy to concern themselves not just with their own homes and property but with adjacent property and people. They were urged to think in terms of *landscapes,* which in this case meant the totality of space, including the natural environment, buildings, and occupants. As noted, white elite homeowners—a minority of Atlanta's residents—pushed these beliefs and insisted on their adoption. By iterating particular arguments and defending segregation's "natural" underpinnings, cultural understandings about the relationship between race, class, housing, and landscape were woven into the cultural framework of not just a minority of residents but the bulk of the populace, white and black, working class, middle class, and elite. Through repetition, components within this constellation of artifacts, relationships, and meanings became interchangeable.

The decade's economic growth helped circulate new cultural norms by catalyzing the rapid production of park-neighborhoods, particularly for well-off whites. On the ground, this meant more planned neighborhoods featuring natural environments, deed restrictions, and whiteness. The sheer number of deed-protected, all-white park-neighborhoods and park-neighborhood-inspired communities normalized the residential form and its associated exclusionary practices. Moreover, as park-neighborhoods and park-neighborhood-inspired subdivisions consumed property outside Atlanta's city limits, space for more-modest developments decreased. As zoning and other edifying materials had taught them to do, park-neighborhood residents resisted the encroachment of more-modest neighborhoods, multifamily housing, and commercial areas. As historian Thomas Hanchett argues occurred in Charlotte, Atlanta's civic elites had made a "conceptual shift" during the 1920s in how they viewed their neighborhoods and the city at large. In the 1930s and 1940s, New Deal housing programs would transform these park-neighborhood preferences into national public policy.[76]

CHAPTER SIX

Park-Neighborhoods, Federal Policy, and Housing Geographies, 1933 to 1950

What had been the most productive period of home building in Atlanta's (and the nation's) history slowed and stalled by the late 1920s and then dropped precipitously as the Great Depression set in. Mirroring the decline occurring in other cities, property values had dropped 69 percent between 1929 and 1934. Just over 50 percent of Atlanta families had incomes of less than $1,000 in 1933, and the Home Owners' Loan Corporation (HOLC) estimated that three thousand Atlanta families defaulted on their mortgages in 1932. As a result of foreclosures and high rent-to-income ratios, nearly ten thousand families in the metropolitan area were "doubled up" with other families in 1934. Atlanta's blacks and poor—families who did not benefit from the park-neighborhood building wave of the 1920s—coped with particularly high rents, substandard housing, and aging and overcrowded neighborhoods in the 1930s. According to one study, tenants with annual incomes of less than $250 paid over 60 percent of their income toward rent in 1933, and those with annual incomes of between $250 and $500 devoted 38 percent to rent. Properties aged and decayed; the HOLC Real Property Inventory reported that 29 percent of Atlanta's homes needed major repairs or were simply unfit for use in 1934.[1] Not surprisingly then, and like residents of cities across the South, Atlantans adopted New Deal housing programs that promised to provide more, affordable, and healthy housing and that, in practice, helped impose racial residential segregation.[2]

Beginning in 1933, public and private building practices and policies combined to sharpen boundaries between black and white neighborhoods. Policies, studies, and guidelines issued by the HOLC, the Federal Housing Administration, and other New Deal Housing offices in the 1930s and 1940s indicate that federal agencies adopted elite park-neighborhood sensibilities and used them as the housing standard. Appraisal manuals, reports and surveys, workshops, and pamphlets instructed public and private housing professionals in these housing and neighborhood expectations and kept this new framework in circulation within bureaucratic circles. As a result, professionals and their agencies or businesses inculcated park-neighborhood fashions that celebrated owner- and white-occupied single-family homes, planned and designed neighborhoods, housing clustered by value or purchasing prices, and whiteness.

New Deal mortgage insurance programs gave whites incentives to embrace and perpetuate the park-neighborhood landscape and facilitated white movement to Atlanta's suburbs, while public-housing programs relegated black families to the urban core. The Public Works Administration, the U.S. Housing Administration, and the Public Housing Administration offered subsidies for low-cost housing production that, in the hands of Atlanta officials, improved urban housing conditions while concentrating black families in Atlanta's core and near west side in the 1930s and 1940s. Supported by federal mortgage insurance programs, white park-neighborhood building continued the 1920s pattern of consuming acre upon acre of suburban land around Atlanta, particularly to the city's north. Often "protected" by restrictive covenants or zoning ordinances, such communities became off-limits to nonwhites and the less well off.

After World War II, Atlanta's local black leadership confronted local and federal, public and private housing discrimination by drawing on its community resources to launch a sustained home-building movement. Building on successful private home-building efforts in the 1920s and 1930s, the Atlanta Urban League (AUL) and its partners outlined a plan for black housing expansion in Atlanta's central city and near west side that relied on the production of new homes targeted to black families and behind-the-scenes maneuvering that resulted in the turnover of white housing to blacks. As a result of these spatial and policy machinations, black Atlantans gained more housing, while lines between blacks and whites, homeowners and tenants sharpened, and racial and class distinctions across the metro area hardened.

New Deal Housing Programs

With 25 percent of the country's population out of work, worldwide market failure, and escalating foreclosures, President Franklin Delano Roosevelt's staff proposed aggressive programs for short-term relief and long-term market stabilization. The resulting agencies—Home Owners' Loan Corporation, Federal Housing Administration (FHA), Public Works Administration, U.S. Housing Administration, and Public Housing Administration—were designed to heal a range of housing market ills. For the private market, the HOLC, established in 1933, offered refinancing mechanisms to homeowners facing foreclosure, and the program's long-term amortized mortgage significantly influenced mortgage design thereafter. In this new form, the loan payment plan extended over longer terms (twenty to thirty years), and monthly payments included allocations for taxes and insurance. By extending payments over a longer period and restructuring the payment itself, the HOLC increased the likelihood that borrowers would meet their mortgage obligations. From its launch in 1933 to the agency's end in 1951, the HOLC refinanced over 1 million mortgages—14,850 in Georgia alone. Expanding on the HOLC's practices, the FHA, established in 1934, created and implemented a standardized home financing system and outlined home construction standards. Beginning in 1944, the Serviceman's Readjustment Act augmented FHA by offering similar subsidized housing programs through the Veterans Administration (VA), and its generous terms allowed lenders to cut payments further. Through these mechanisms, the federal government developed an entirely new kind of mortgage market, which included a dramatically expanded secondary mortgage market. Also, the FHA's building specifications helped ensure the production of safe and durable housing, which builders soon produced to these standards in nearly all residential construction. Through these practices and requirements, the FHA facilitated the production of more-affordable and better-quality housing and revitalized and stabilized the home-construction industry. Housing developers launched subdivisions targeted to middle-income buyers on a new scale, planning entire neighborhoods that incorporated park-neighborhood elements. In addition to revolutionizing home financing, the HOLC and (primarily) the FHA helped change the way Americans looked at and thought about homes and neighborhoods. First, the HOLC, the FHA, and other federal agencies circulated park-neighborhood sensibilities and a landscape way of seeing among their own staff and related policy makers and professionals.[3]

HOLC SECURITY MAPS AND AREA DESCRIPTIONS

New ways of looking at and thinking about neighborhoods circulated within policy documents, manuals, and reports, helping to inculcate such practices into bureaucratic structures governing home finance and construction. The preparation of HOLC security maps and their associated area descriptions, for example, involved teaching appraisers to assess housing and neighborhoods in a specific, standardized way. Intended to assist the HOLC in decision making about mortgages it granted or purchased, the HOLC security maps and associated area descriptions outlined neighborhood demographics (including race, occupation [in general categories], ethnicity, and rate of homeownership) and described what appraisers considered to be positive and negative influences on area property values. Significantly, the HOLC security maps and associated area descriptions demonstrate that HOLC staff had adopted a specific landscape way of seeing. In this case, they judged neighborhoods against an elite (and white) park-neighborhood standard that favored single-family, white- and owner-occupied homes, planned built environments, and natural settings.[4]

The HOLC ranked single-family detached houses highest in a residential property hierarchy. The HOLC actuated such hierarchies in Atlanta's survey when it contended that one housing form influenced another. In Collier Woods and Ansley Park (B12), for example, HOLC appraisers warned of "detrimental influences," including the "presence of multifamily structures in area."[5] The "presence of apartments" in the southern portion of North Boulevard Park (C11) likewise jeopardized that neighborhood's values. In other cases, the HOLC asserted that the conversion of homes to boardinghouses diminished C2's desirability and that portions of West End (D16) suffered from the "encroachment of boarding houses." The HOLC, like the NAREB and the Department of Commerce, consistently characterized multifamily housing in negative terms, as detrimental, encroaching, infiltrating, and damaging. In the process, single-family, owner-occupied homes became the standard against which all other property was measured. Similarly, whiteness became the "measuring stick" for residents themselves.[6]

The HOLC contended that people and property were so intimately connected that the presence of particular racial groups could positively or negatively influence the market value of white-occupied property, an ideology that historian David Freund refers to as a "racially constructed theory of property."[7] In favoring deed restrictions that limited the presence of people labeled "undesirable," the HOLC adopted and perpetuated a white elite and middle-class frame of reference that constantly subjugated blacks and black-occupied property. HOLC staff recognized that the Atlanta risk appraisals privileged elite white sensibilities and contended that two land markets existed—one black and one white. Ultimately, HOLC appraisers chose to assess risk from the standpoint of the white home buyer. The report explained, "In order to avoid the setting up of 2 grades of residential trends (one for white and one for negroes) when preparing the Atlanta security area map, it was decided to approach the city-wide pictures from the standpoint of trend of desirability of white-occupied residential property." That is, white-elite sensibilities and housing preferences became normalized. Black families suffered accordingly, as "all negro property in the community was given a D grade rating."[8] That being said, appraisers occasionally differentiated white markets and black markets within the one-page area descriptions. For example, staff marked the "trend for desirability" for the Bedford-Pine neighborhood (D20) as "down for white, static for negroes."[9] If neighborhood D17 (near Atlanta University) were graded "from a negro standpoint," the appraisers noted, the property "would rate as a high B grade, or possibly a low A grade."[10] The HOLC's white frame of reference extended beyond African Americans to encompass "mixtures of racial groups" and also Jews as threats to "white" property. According to the report, the "infiltration" of Jewish families negatively influenced values in Druid Hills, and West End's newly built section (C36) suffered from the "proximity to negro property." A mixture of racial groups threatened values in Avondale (D5) and Edgewood (D10). An increase in Jewish families in the DeKalb County portion of Lenox Park (A8) hurt values. Just as property values were no longer limited to what was contained within lot lines but took into consideration property's relationship to neighborhood, residential property and its value now encompassed who resided upon it. The HOLC helped solidify this relationship by giving it the weight of a federal standard and by investing based on those standards. After all, the HOLC itself purchased mortgages, using these very property ratings.[11]

The HOLC's social and physical appraisal standards helped cement associations between whiteness, park-neighborhoods, and suburbia. All A-rated park-neighborhoods were located outside the city limits, four to eight miles from the city center, on a substantial amount of land (at least one hundred acres). The park-neighborhoods—which included Tuxedo Park, Haynes Manor, Peachtree Heights Park, Ridgedale Park, Brookhaven Estates, Country Club Estates, Lenox Park, and Johnson Estates—were recently built, all white, restricted, and designed around or to feature natural environments.[12]

Though not distributed to the public, the HOLC reports circulated the constellation of park-neighborhood practices and expectations through the network of the HOLC's property appraisers, policy makers, and financial professionals. In doing so, the reports reinforced the relationship between homeownership, neighborhood, housing landscapes, whiteness, and exclusivity that had been promulgated by and throughout the real-estate industry in the previous decade's homeownership campaigns and private park-neighborhood building boom. The map and descriptions also worked in concert with other policy documents and instruction materials to actively circulate the park-neighborhood frame among professionals working directly or indirectly with real-estate markets. The FHA in particular continued the HOLC's cultural work by amplifying new park-neighborhood discourse and accelerating the dissemination of park-neighborhood practices and landscape ways of seeing.

THE FHA AND *THE UNDERWRITING MANUAL*

The FHA's policies disseminated park-neighborhood sensibilities and landscape ways of seeing, strengthened associations between whiteness and park-neighborhood landscapes, and rewarded their adoption. The agency's

Underwriting Manual, intended to teach appraisers how to gauge quality construction and "quality neighborhoods" and develop property risk ratings, reveals how the FHA viewed and valued particular forms of housing and related property practices.

First published in 1935 and revised periodically, the FHA *Underwriting Manuals* reified the relationship of individual properties to a larger neighborhood. The manual instructed appraisers to focus their risk assessments not just on individual homes and properties but on a variety of neighborhood and location characteristics. In outlining the philosophy of mortgage-risk procedures, for example, the 1936 manual explained, "A most important group of factors which affect mortgage risk is . . . the relationship between the physical property and the neighborhood in which it is located."[13] Echoing the aesthetic preferences of park-neighborhood designers and following NAREB-sponsored real-estate appraisal texts of the era, the manual asserted, "A beautifully laid-out area with adequate street improvements, good plot layouts, and well-planted shrubs and trees will tend to create strong appeal."[14] While L. Elden Smith wrote in *Insured Mortgage Portfolio* in 1938 that "the Federal Housing Administration had been a pioneer in placing emphasis on the neighborhood influence," the FHA actually expanded on the cultural work of the HOLC, housing conferences, and professional efforts by further instilling a particular landscape way of seeing property into bureaucratic practices.[15] Such training, in turn, had long-term financial implications for home developers and home buyers; developers and buyers, too, had to adopt a landscape approach to property or risk losing out on one of the nation's largest subsidy programs.[16]

Like the HOLC, the FHA rewarded neighborhoods with homogeneous neighborhood landscapes by assigning them favorable risk ratings.[17] Indeed, the first principle governing a valuator's judgment of location stated that the "homogeneous development of properties in any neighborhood tends to reduce mortgage risk." "Architectural designs," the manual explained, should "blend harmoniously." The FHA's preferences for homogeneity in architectural styles and form reinforced its disposition toward a narrow range of property values. The manual stressed that when values of individual properties varied little across a neighborhood, one was "likely to find people whose living standards likewise [were] substantially the same."[18]

The FHA affirmed the relationship between neighborhood occupants and property values, encouraging appraisers to see residents themselves as part of the landscape. The agency advised appraisers to assess the population of surrounding neighborhoods for "a declining population" and "incompatible racial and social groups." To the FHA, a neighborhood's desirability diminished "through the influx of people of lower living standards."[19] "If a neighborhood is to retain stability," the FHA reasoned, "it is necessary that properties shall continue to be occupied by the same social and racial classes. A change in social or racial occupancy generally leads to instability and a reduction in values."[20] Thus, working with other texts generated by federal agencies and private enterprise, the *Underwriting Manual* encouraged residents and developers alike to be sensitive to, assess, and categorize one's neighbors, as one would architecture and building quality.[21]

The FHA argued that neighborhoods with desirable characteristics needed to be protected from change, from influences that might alter the population characteristics or otherwise accelerate "decay." It sought to stall neighborhood change by financially rewarding housing and developments that adopted restrictive covenants. The FHA promoted protective covenants to set limitations on architectural practices and promote aesthetic "harmony," and the agency encouraged developers and residents to establish architectural review boards to vet plans and specifications for homes and landscapes. To the FHA, covenants contributed to, as assistant FHA commissioner for underwriting Curt Mack explained, "the establishment of the character of a neighborhood" and maintained property values by regulating lot sizes and the type, size, and placement of homes.[22] But covenants could also ensure a homogeneous population by preventing the intrusion of "incompatible racial and social groups." As historian David Freund notes, such practices lumped nonwhites into the category of property "nuisances," much like industrial properties and noisy traffic. Justifying such social exclusion as a means to preserve the physical character of neighborhoods, the FHA dehumanized nonwhites, treating them as material artifacts that should be controlled and removed.[23]

The FHA disseminated its racialized view of property not just by recommending the use of restrictive covenants in its *Underwriting Manual*, but by distributing the guide "Outline of Protective Covenants" to land dealers, appraisers, and builders across the United States. As the guide explained, the FHA recommended that subdivisions adopt covenants to "assure the continuing marketability of property," and it suggested the phrasing, "No person of any race other than the _____ shall use or occupy any building or any lot."[24] Developers readily adopted such deed covenants in order to meet FHA standards, propagating racial exclusion across new developments in cities throughout the United States. Economist John P. Dean's 1947 study showed that racially restrictive covenants spread rapidly after the FHA endorsed their use. In the large subdivisions that Dean surveyed, developers used racial restrictions more frequently than in developments of fewer than twenty homes. Of subdivisions counting seventy-five or more parcels, 83 percent employed racial restrictions, thus cutting white swaths across the nation's suburbs. As Dean noted, some covenants pointed directly to the FHA as the basis for the restriction.[25]

Assuming FHA appraisers followed *Underwriting Manual* directives and assigned more favorable risk ratings to homogeneous, planned communities that incorporated natural environments, architectural harmony, and restrictive covenants, the FHA gave these practices market value. That is, FHA mortgage insurance financially motivated builders and developers to adopt park-neighborhood subdivision styles, customs, and landscapes that had become widespread in the 1920s. As historian Thomas Hanchett explains, banks actively sought FHA-approved developments for lending, and developers responded by building larger and larger subdivisions.[26] Properties that met the FHA's standards and incorporated suggested practices were more likely to be approved for federal mortgage insurance, which meant easier sale *and* resale of homes. Because the FHA and the VA insured nearly 25 percent of newly constructed single-family homes from the 1940s to the 1960s, this was no small matter. Indeed, builders regularly advertised that they had built to FHA standards, as when D. L. Stokes explained that a Grove Circle property was "built under FHA specifications."[27]

Like the HOLC's security map descriptions, the *Underwriting Manual's* park-neighborhood expectations spread through networks of federal bureaucrats and policy makers, builders and developers, lenders and insurance institutions that sought to facilitate or exploit federal largesse. The FHA provided local offices with "Established Ratings of Locations based upon Outlined Neighborhoods" to guide appraisers who were learning new ways of viewing and assessing property. A series of federally sponsored land planning bulletins likewise helped developers understand FHA standards and expectations. "Successful Subdivisions," for example, reinforced the FHA's attention to neighborhood and asked developers to provide a holistic picture of their proposed neighborhood by packaging topographic maps, zoning maps, and sample restrictive covenants related to proposed projects. Similar advice was offered at speaker engagements, workshops, and professional meetings. In 1937, for example, FHA administrator William D. Burkheimer discussed "Risk Rating for Mortgage Insurance" at an Atlanta workshop on FHA procedures. In 1939, the Atlanta Society of Residential Appraisers hosted HOLC appraisal supervisor Paul Hathaway, who had helped originate the HOLC's "scientific" appraisal system.[28] As Charles Abrams observed in the *Nation,* real-estate agents used the FHA as a "sales tool"; they referred to the program and its standards to sell homes, as when two Lakeview Road homes were advertised as "new FHA-built homes for GI," and one three-acre property offered "FHA loan or will go GI comb[ination]."[29] Thus, while the FHA intended the manual and associated documents for dissemination to staff and related personnel, neighborhood expectations transferred easily into popular literature and public circulation as appraisers, agents, and developers educated the general public on home-buying practices and sold homes and neighborhoods.[30]

In this manner, the FHA's assumptions and expectations became part of the larger public discourse about neighborhood and suburban culture. Park-neighborhood practices were required by underwriters to obtain FHA (and later VA) mortgage insurance, and thus the agency powerfully influenced the landscape itself. Builders, agents, and appraisers learned and implemented the practices and disseminated them through the residential building industry. Moreover, because the FHA favored newly constructed, single-family homes in homogeneous, master-planned neighborhoods intended for white occupancy, the agency helped popularize a constellation of park-neighborhood practices and expectations that came to be associated with white-dominated suburban areas. In short, the FHA reshaped how white Americans looked at and thought about homes and neighborhoods. But more than this—beyond influencing policy making and popular understanding of neighborhood landscapes—the FHA and later the VA had a direct impact on the spatial organization of the city through their power to encourage or discourage particular building patterns and practices and their power to decide who did and did not receive mortgage insurance.

Because the FHA (and later the VA) catalyzed much of the private home building taking place after 1933, the agency's policies significantly influenced who had access to new, affordable housing in the Atlanta metro area. The FHA favored white-occupied housing, and FHA-backed developments for whites in Atlanta were hard to miss; they were documented in HOLC reports and ubiquitous in real-estate advertisements. The $2,000 to $4,000 single-family homes in the Pleasant Homesites subdivision were, according to the *Atlanta Constitution*, "being bought about like rent on the FHA plan."[31] A newspaper ad for Jefferson Mortgage insisted that readers "File Your Application with Us under the New FHA Plan."[32] Cascade Heights, on the city's west side, featured single-family homes priced from $6,000 to $8,000, with "most" financing from the FHA. The neighborhood boasted schools, the nearby John A. White Golf Course, and the swimming pool and tennis courts of Adams Park. The HOLC's

1938 report documented Oak Knoll (C28), whose FHA-insured, single-family homes were purchased by white factory and clerical workers who earned about $1,000 to $1,500 annually.[33] In contrast, the FHA only rarely insured black-occupied housing—even housing developments designed for and marketed only to black families and isolated from white development. Between 1934 and 1954, minorities accounted for less than 1 percent of the FHA's mortgage insurance nationally. As late as 1950, the FHA or the VA had insured mortgages on twelve thousand white, owner-occupied single-family homes nationally, but only 367 mortgages for black-occupied, single-family homes. This disparity in FHA financing was readily evident in Atlanta prior to the end of World War II. From the program's inception in 1934 to 1943, nonwhite Atlantans could claim only 323 FHA-supported single-family *and multifamily units*. Thus, from the FHA's birth and throughout the 1940s, it built its mortgage-insurance system around white expectations and indeed *established* white expectations by promoting white ways of seeing and practicing property.[34]

The FHA did insure mortgages on some black developments in Atlanta (as noted in the statistics above), though proportionally fewer than allocated to whites. In fact, the FHA's early relationship with builder Walter Aiken belied the racialized property philosophy that pervaded the agency. The FHA, for example, funded Aiken's building of "America's first and only all-colored modernized home" on Atlanta's west side in 1935. Part of the larger "Colored Better Housing Campaign," the home featured lighting fixtures by Atlanta Electrical Company and Sterch Brothers furniture. FHA officials John Millsaps and Harry Burns "heartily commended" Aiken and, along with thousands of Atlantans, toured the home that April.[35] Despite this promising start, FHA- or VA-backed black projects were rare, and each was a victory. Aiken's Fairview Terrace subdivision, built in 1944 as part of the National Housing Agency's push to build housing for war workers, was one such success. The project delivered 250 two-bedroom units, each with an electric refrigerator, gas range, and hot-water heater. The units came landscaped with shrubbery, dogwoods, and crepe myrtles, and lawns were "fully sodded with grass"—features not usually advertised for black housing in this period. But generally speaking, black families seeking new housing could not rely on the federal government for assistance, even during this period of rapidly expanding federal involvement in housing.[36]

Despite the lack of federal support, developers managed to provide some black housing and planned developments, even in the Depression. In 1933, for example, Johnson Realty auctioned 50 lots in the black subdivision Pine Acres at Simpson Road and Anderson, west of downtown. Ads for Hunter Hills promised building restrictions and featured homes of prominent black Atlantans (see fig. 6.1). In 1936, E. R. Craighead broke ground on Ezra Church Heights' 220 lots between Washington Park and Anderson Park on Atlanta's west side. Mirroring pro-homeownership rhetoric that had marked 1920s park-neighborhood building, Ezra Church Heights pledged to be one of the largest black subdivisions to that date with one hundred homes and "one of the leading sections of Atlanta for home owners of the race."[37] Adopting the park-neighborhood practice of providing status-reinforcing amenities, the subdivision promised tennis courts and a clubhouse modeled after the field house at Tuskegee Institute, with a gym, swimming pool, showers, and locker room for both men and women.[38]

Most new black subdivisions in the 1930s and early 1940s adopted at least some park-neighborhood components, though black homes tended to be modest in size (Joyland Parks' homes measured about 875 square feet) and moderately priced (homes in Ezra Church Heights started at $2,000), and they encompassed far less acreage than white elite park-neighborhoods. For example, Service Company's black subdivision measured only thirty-three acres; white Brookwood Hills, five hundred. Instead, most black subdivisions resembled working-class white developments in their embrace of only a few park-neighborhood attributes and their proximity to the central city.[39]

As in white subdivisions of the era, many residents of Atlanta's black subdivisions owned their homes, though at lower rates. On Ashby Terrace in Washington Heights, for example, nine out of twenty-one black households owned their homes in 1942, far exceeding the average black homeownership rate of 13 percent in 1940.[40] That same year, nine of eighteen black families on Eason Street in Hunter Hills owned their homes. According to the 1940 *Housing: Analytical Maps*, black Washington Heights, at the city's two-mile radius and west of Atlanta University, ranged between 40 and 80 percent homeowners.[41] In white Grove Park, forty-one West Lake Avenue residents owned, while nine rented. White Lakewood Heights counted between 60 and 80 percent homeowners. White Ansley Park's homeownership rates ranged widely, from 40 to 80 percent. In contrast, homeownership rates in the unplanned neighborhoods of the lower Fourth Ward (both black and white) stayed below 20 percent. Tenants included drivers, a machinist, postal carriers, and laborers. Significantly, many of the new black subdivision occupants were blue-collar and service workers, who, despite low wages, still sought and achieved homeownership. In black Hunter Hills in 1942, porters, carpenters, painters, chauffeurs, and drivers owned homes on Eason. In established Washington Heights, porters, a nurse, a cook, and a waiter owned their homes.[42]

Figure 6.1. Hunter Hills. Source: *Atlanta Daily World,* October 23, 1938.

Black subdivision building was slow-going, though, as white racism in federal programming and private industry limited both home financing and the land available for black housing. Whites exerted control over black geographies, particularly through zoning and the use of restrictive covenants. Since all home building within city limits required building permits, bureaucrats could control black plans by interfering with the application process.[43] Zoning also limited space for affordable housing. When Fulton County began zoning independently of Atlanta in 1938, citizens from Haynes Manor, Peachtree Heights, and Heights Manor successfully petitioned the county to zone a large portion of the white-elite-dominated Buckhead district for single-family homes, specifically excluding duplex homes, apartments, and businesses. In the revised 1946 zoning plan, minimum lot sizes in the unincorporated west side began at nine thousand square feet, well above the minimum lot sizes used in established black suburbs, such as Washington Heights or Hunter Hills. On Atlanta's north and northwest, lot sizes began at ten thousand square feet at the city's four-mile radius (the location of the Peachtree Heights subdivision) and reached one and two acres beginning at the five-mile radius (which included Buckhead and Tuxedo Park). Thus, local zoning, restrictive covenants, and FHA policies reinforced one another during the 1930s and 1940s, reserving suburban areas for whites and limiting blacks and the less well off to Atlanta's core city.[44]

As black housing developer W. H. Aiken explained to the U.S. Commission on Civil Rights regarding Atlanta's history of housing segregation, "[Black families are] fenced in, and when we move, we have to move in block by block in forbidden areas"—white neighborhoods. Indeed, Atlanta's racial-segregation ordinances and racial zoning may have been ruled unenforceable by courts, but racial boundaries were widely acknowledged by both blacks and whites. When asked about Atlanta's racialized areas, Atlanta Savings and Loan Association President W. O. Du Vall told the U.S. Civil Rights Commission, "There is more or less a general understanding or agreement between the races that this area is colored and this is white. It is a nebulous kind of thing." Land to be used for black housing had to be "cleared politically," as black home builder T. M. Alexander explained it. That is, Atlanta's Board of Aldermen or the city's zoning board approved land for black housing projects and used zoning reclassifications and other such methods to deny proposals they considered inappropriate. But if local whites acted to limit black housing opportunities and if the federal government and its state and local offices were reluctant to extend FHA benefits to black families, federal agencies and local civic elites targeted African Americans with public-housing programs.[45]

PUBLIC HOUSING

As outlined by historian Karen Ferguson, Atlanta's civic elites used public housing and slum clearance to actively manipulate the city's racial geography in a period of rapid urban change. After the passage of the National Housing Act of 1937, federal public-housing officials accepted local control and bowed to the white South's preference to separate blacks and whites. Neighborhood-composition guidelines dictated that public housing not alter prevailing neighborhood demographics. In practice this meant that projects intended for black occupancy could not be placed in predominantly white areas, such as Atlanta's largely white north side. In contrast to FHA practices, though, black families were allocated a "fair share" of public housing. That is, blacks were entitled to a portion of units consistent with their representation in substandard housing. In Atlanta, that meant blacks were entitled to just over 50 percent of new public-housing units. In the 1930s and 1940s, civic elites and agencies used slum clearance and public housing to eliminate mixed-race neighborhoods, raze small concentrations of black housing that still punctuated the predominantly white north side, establish buffers between black and white neighborhoods, and concentrate black families in the city's core and west side.[46]

The 1933 National Industrial Recovery Act augmented local efforts to clear slums and answer housing shortages for low-income families by supporting slum-clearance projects and the construction or renovation of low-cost housing. States, cities, and other public entities could apply for grants, and Congress appropriated just over $3 billion for distribution. After trying a limited dividend program to produce low-cost housing, Secretary of the Interior Howard Ickes looked for better solutions. The subsequent direct-build program within the Public Works Administration (PWA) completed fifty-one housing projects, providing over twenty thousand dwelling units nationally in the four years it operated. Program leaders and housing advocates argued over the central purpose of low-cost home building, but Ickes saw slum clearance as a primary goal, and PWA located twenty-seven projects on former "slums."[47]

The public-housing programs that emerged from the Housing Act of 1937 had features that made them attractive to civic elites seeking to rework the urban landscape. Federal agencies allocated funding directly to locally organize housing authorities, and the public-housing agencies lent up to 90 percent of capital costs and subsidized construction and maintenance. But cities and counties decided whether they needed low-income development; the federal government did not mandate a local commitment to public housing. As a result, local decision making allowed suburbs to avoid public housing (and thus low-income families) by not indicating a "need." In doing so, suburbs relegated low-income housing to urban cores and the few suburbs that utilized the program. Moreover, local authorities maintained power over site selection. The U.S. Housing Administration (USHA) and the subsequent Public Housing Administration (PHA) continued the PWA's practice of assigning projects to a particular race and then locating projects based on preexisting—or desired—racial patterns.[48]

Hoping to buffer Atlanta's central business district from the city's housing sores—the pockets of "unfit" housing that had been allowed to decline for decades—and seeking to establish or fortify divisions between black and white residential areas, Atlanta's civic elites joined city leaders around the country in instituting slum clearance and public-housing programs. To ensure public support for proposed revitalization plans, Atlanta's white leaders actively managed how neighborhoods marked for slum clearance appeared to the public and the private sector. Atlantans' perceptions of targeted neighborhoods were crucially important. If portrayed as homes of workers and families, such neighborhoods might have garnered sympathy. Painted as diseased and threatening, the neighborhoods demanded eradication. In 1935, Atlanta's Municipal Housing Authority and the City Planning Commission distributed maps of Atlanta's "slums" and "blight," areas that businessmen and slum-clearance promoters referred to as "deficit districts." In a well-orchestrated public-information campaign designed to persuade citizens to fund clearing these areas and building public housing, white elites reworked predominantly black neighborhoods from homes of working, if poor, families into, in the words of one Atlanta Housing Authority film, "a jungle world breeding jungle life."[49] Augmenting such metaphors, the film used scare tactics that suggested contamination, disease, and crime were poised to attack the balance of the city. "These areas breed a group . . . that obviously has a degrading influence on the body politic," the film warned. It advised, "A slum like any other blight must be treated as a disease . . . must be wiped from the face of the earth." The film was less clear if the "disease" to be eliminated was the built environment or the black residents themselves. As historian Karen Ferguson observes, "The fear of disease extended to a fear of the black population in general." Through the mobilization of such imagery, city elites succeeded in drumming up popular support to establish the city housing authority necessary to initiate slum clearance. At the same time, they tethered imagery of disease and criminality to blacks and black-occupied housing.[50]

Despite the advantages public housing offered to white elites attempting to manage the central-city landscape, locations that whites considered acceptable for black housing were hard to find. When it was announced in 1939 that

John Eagan Homes would provide 1,200 units to black families at the division between largely white West End and the growing black west side, over 3,800 whites petitioned the city council, wrote congressional leaders, and held meetings to fight the proposal. The housing authority responded by proposing a white project and a black project, each with approximately 400 units. In a further concession to white demands and mirroring earlier concerns about racial facades, the authority altered site plans so that the project's white units faced white-occupied West View and the black homes faced black-occupied Hunter Street. Businessman and chair of the Atlanta Housing Authority Charles Palmer promised whites at a 1,000-strong public meeting at Joel Chandler Harris High that "a wide area" would separate the two projects and ten acres of land would be devoted to a park for white children. Further white protest pushed the black project away from West End and toward Connolly Park. As the Eagan Homes fight illustrates, city officials and bureaucrats used public housing to hone and remake borders between blacks and whites.[51]

Similarly, city leaders used the city and country's first public-housing project to eliminate a mixed-race neighborhood. In 1930, prior to razing, the Techwood Flats neighborhood was 72 percent white and 28 percent black; the resulting housing project, Techwood Homes, was for whites only. As civic elites eliminated mixed-race Techwood Flats, they rehoused that neighborhood's black families in University Homes, near Atlanta University on the city's increasingly black west side. As the Council on Human Relations representative described to the U.S. Civil Rights Commission in 1959, such programming "not only created a rigid segregated pattern where none had existed but cloaked it with official respectability."[52]

In this manner, whites used public housing in the 1930s to shunt black families to the segregated areas within the city's core and near west side by providing more black housing in those areas. The "slum clearance" and subsequent building of John Eagan and John Hope Homes resulted in a net gain of 575 black homes on the city's near west side. By 1940, 40 percent of Atlanta's black population lived just west of downtown. In Atlanta, then, as in Chicago, Philadelphia, and many other cities, public-housing placement increased black concentration in the central city and intensified residential segregation.[53]

Whites may have used public housing to refine racial segregation, but publicly whites positioned the public-housing program as their visible commitment to improving the city's poor housing conditions. Indeed, public housing was one of few initiatives that the city could tout as disproportionately benefiting blacks. Twenty years later, M. B. Satterfield, director of the Atlanta Housing Authority, explained to the U.S. Civil Rights Commission, "The nonwhite have fared well under this policy," as 51 percent of public housing built in the South had been assigned to African Americans.[54] Locally, the Atlanta Housing Authority allocated 59 percent of public housing to blacks by the end of the city's second wave of building in 1941 (and 66 percent by 1956). Rhetoric like Satterfield's served white purposes in that it assured the public that government offices actively responded to black demand for more and better housing while masking the intention of civic elites to manage racial housing geographies.[55]

In this manner, local officials implemented public-housing programs to further define "white" and "black" neighborhoods. What is more, public-housing implementation strategies combined with FHA policies to assign most black families to housing in or near Atlanta's core and eliminate housing opportunities in the city's whitening north side.

NEIGHBORHOOD GEOGRAPHIES

By the end of the 1930s, a decided shift had occurred toward racial and class residential segregation and isolation in Atlanta, a phenomenon illustrated by the 1940 U.S. Bureau of the Census *Housing: Analytical Maps* and the 1938 HOLC risk-assessment maps and related descriptions.[56] The HOLC maps, forms, and explanations—prepared after the 1920s building boom, but deep within a stagnant building period in which few developers added homes to the landscape, and prior to the dramatic wave of federally subsidized home building after World War II—are some of the best neighborhood-level descriptions of the housing patterns and human landscape that emerged from the 1920s building frenzy. Certainly, city-planning and housing-policy philosophies current at the time biased the descriptions, but, used carefully, the maps and accompanying descriptions also reveal racial and class geographies, the material landscape, and the workings of urban housing markets.[57] The 1940 *Housing: Analytical Maps* complement the HOLC maps by graphically representing specific housing characteristics by block, including average rent, year built, tenure status, persons per room, mortgage status (for structures containing four or fewer dwelling units), and nonwhite households (which comprised "Negro, Indian, Chinese, Japanese, Filipino, Hindu, Korean, and other nonwhite races," and persons of mixed white and nonwhite parentage).[58] Together, the analytical block maps and the HOLC data reveal the emergence of small, single-race subdivisions within the city's three-mile radius, the enlarging elite park-neighborhood landscape at the city's perimeter (including, to some degree, the unincorporated suburbs), and the persistence of Atlanta's variegated racial, class, and neighborhood landscapes within the central city.[59]

As in 1899, Atlanta's workers remained scattered throughout the city and just outside the city limits in the late 1930s. The neighborhood between Ashby and

Marietta Streets near Atlanta University (D18), for example, housed "mill workers, factory workers, laborers and domestics" earning between six hundred and nine hundred dollars a year, as well as many families on relief.[60] To the city's south, Lakewood Heights housed factory workers, skilled mechanics, and clerical workers. Workers still found some housing just southeast of downtown in Summerhill (D12), the neighborhood that HOLC staff referred to as Capitol Avenue. Southern Railway employees had, since 1910, come to dominate the Pittsburgh neighborhood, southwest of downtown (D15). But even though railway workers had a significant presence in Pittsburgh, the neighborhood still housed employees of other companies, as well as some low-white-collar workers.[61]

In contrast, the park-neighborhood boom of the 1920s concentrated high-white-collar households in wholly contained neighborhoods such as Morningside (B13) to the city's northeast and Peachtree Park and Haynes Manor (A3) to the city's north. All-white, restricted, and residential, Lenox Park and its adjacent subdivisions (A8), boasted rolling and well-wooded land, and the neighborhood's residents—"executives, business and professional men"—earned between three thousand and six thousand dollars a year. The HOLC reported that the neighborhood's brick, one- and two-story homes had all been constructed since 1929 and were all owner occupied. In Peachtree Heights Park (B2) to the north of downtown, one- and two-story brick homes housed white businessmen, executives, and professionals who made at least five thousand dollars a year. Consistent with the park-neighborhood segmentation encouraged by Robert Whitten and J. C. Nichols, some differentiation was evident among neighborhoods housing white-collar workers; Peachtree Park (A4), for example, housed "smaller business men," as did Ridgedale Park (A5).[62]

As encouraged by the FHA and park-neighborhood fashions, the new suburban communities utilized protective covenants to manage lot sizes, ensure consistent design, and limit residency to middle- and upper-middle-class buyers. County property records reveal that Haynes Manor advertised itself as "among the hills" and "highly restricted."[63] Glenwood Park demanded minimum lots of 7,500 square feet, housing design approval, and minimum building costs of two thousand dollars. Redland Road and Dellwood Drive in Collier Heights required 8,000-square-foot lots.[64] In fact, those subdivisions submitting covenants with their plats from 1939 to 1940 clearly patterned their restrictions on the same model. Restrictions did not always limit the same things, but when developers decided to control a particular element, they adopted language strikingly similar to other subdivisions' covenants. For example, some subdivisions included easements for utilities, and others declined to include minimum building costs. But covenants that forbade "noxious or offensive trade" used nearly the exact same language in each instance. One such restriction read, "No noxious or offensive trade shall be carried on upon any lot nor shall anything be done thereon which may be or become an annoyance or nuisance to the neighborhood."[65]

Following the recommendations of the FHA, subdivisions filing plats with Fulton County after 1939 commonly included racially restrictive covenants that limited residency to whites. Glenwood Park's covenants, for example, stated:

> All lots in described tract are intended to be used solely by the Caucasi[a]n race, and no race or nationality other than those for whom the premises are intended, shall use or occupy any building on any lot, except that this covenant shall not prevent occupancy by domestic servants of a different race or nationality employed by an owner or tenant.[66]

Restrictions included in subdivisions platted from 1939 to 1941 vary only in the way they phrase race. That is, while Glenwood Park articulated that the lots were "intended to be used solely by the Caucasi[a]n race," Victory Heights stated that its lots were "intended to be used solely by the white race."[67] Like Glenwood Park, Richland Park limited its occupants to "Caucasians," but Moreland Drive Subdivision outlined that "no member of the black race" could live in the area.[68] Lake Forest deviated from the norm by specifically targeting "the Semitic race" (though it went on to state "or by anyone other than a member of the Caucasian race").[69] By 1939, it appears, racially restrictive covenants had became standard practice when filing plats in Fulton County. A survey of plats filed between 1939 and 1941 shows that Longwood Subdivision, College Hills, Tuxedo Park, Grove Park, the Liddell Estate Subdivision, the Morris Brandon Estates, the A. B. Suttles Property, Collier Hills, Collier Heights, Peachtree Hills, Northwood, Rugby Estates, J. M. Karwisch's subdivision on Habersham Road, Morningside Hill, and Ferstwood—neighborhoods in all directions around Atlanta but primarily in the north and northwest—all filed restrictive covenants reserving their homes for whites only. Class restrictions often accompanied racial restrictions and included minimum lot sizes, design approvals, and minimum building costs that excluded families of moderate (or lower) incomes. In sum, land beyond Atlanta's three-mile radius was increasingly reserved (and marked, in the case of zoning) for white, park-neighborhood, and park-neighborhood-inspired development. Property within the three-mile radius, on the other hand, remained the locus of black development, though building proved challenging in the core city as well.[70]

Closer to the core, black-occupied housing had both spatially expanded *and* become more concentrated by the late 1930s, particularly immediately west and east of the central business district. By 1940, two hundred contiguous blocks on the city's west side were disproportionately nonwhite (that is, with greater than 50 percent nonwhite heads of household), while east of downtown, nearly one hundred contiguous blocks were disproportionately nonwhite (see fig. 6.2). South of downtown, black families dominated the Pittsburgh neighborhood between Stewart Avenue and the Southern Railway (D15)—about seventy square blocks. Racial homogeneity marked street lengths, blocks, and whole sections of the city. Compared to the turn of the twentieth century, racial segregation had spread, leading to greater racial isolation.[71]

While the city overall tended toward racial segregation by the end of the 1930s, some heterogeneous racial patterns persisted, particularly in neighborhoods established prior to World War I.[72] Of the 111 areas rated and described by the HOLC, 14 were mixed race, though 6 of the 14 were disproportionately white or black (that is, greater than 60 percent black or greater than 90 percent white).[73] The lower Fourth Ward and Bedford Pine (D20), for example, measured 95 percent black, while the neighborhood surrounding Techwood Homes (D19) counted 85 percent white. The Summerhill neighborhood (D12) immediately southwest of downtown Atlanta and the Scottsdale and Ingleside sections of DeKalb County (D4) were both approximately 40 percent black—close to the city's proportions of 35 percent black, 65 percent white. Generally speaking, poor conditions marked the 14 mixed-race blocks, including poorly maintained property, unpaved streets, aged buildings, proximity to rail lines or industrial sites, and, in the case of Summerhill (D12) and the lower Fourth Ward (D2), high mortality and tuberculosis rates. Families in the mixed-race neighborhoods often had lower or unstable incomes (five hundred to seven hundred dollars annually in Hillcrest and Avondale Estates in DeKalb County [D5]), which meant some residents could not always pay rent, as was noted in many of the reports.[74]

Despite the HOLC's and the FHA's insistence that homogeneity stabilized property values, the HOLC maps also indicate that, as in earlier decades, Atlanta's pockets of dilapidated, black-occupied or mixed-race housing remained safe sites for financial investment, even during the Depression. The Summerhill neighborhood (D12), consisted primarily of single-family and duplex rental housing described as "antiquated and in poor repair." The mixed-race neighborhood had a high infant-mortality rate and incidents of tuberculosis, and many of the families received government support. Even so, according to the HOLC, demand for black rental properties in the area was fair, and appraisers noted the "slight demand for negro property on investment basis." That is, people seeking to purchase black-occupied rental property found the neighborhood a good investment, even within an economic depression and stagnant

a

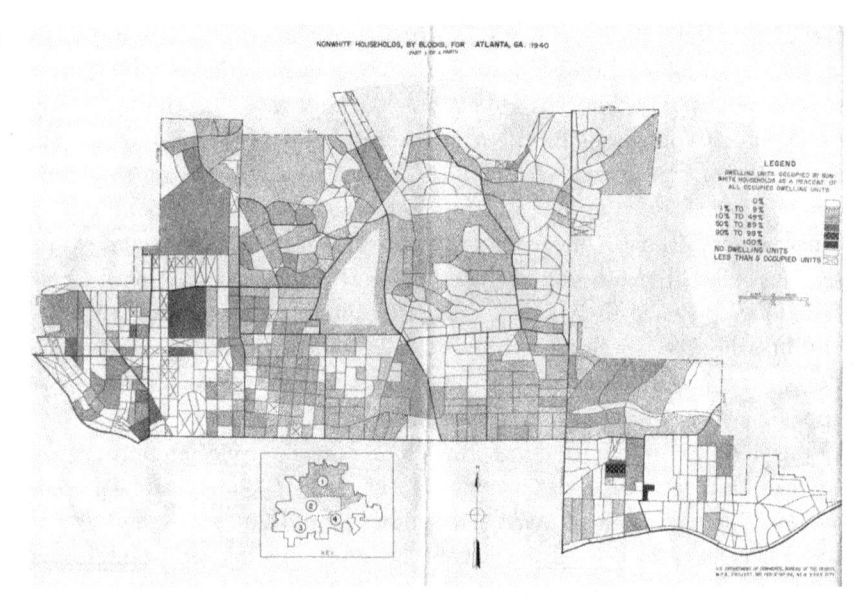

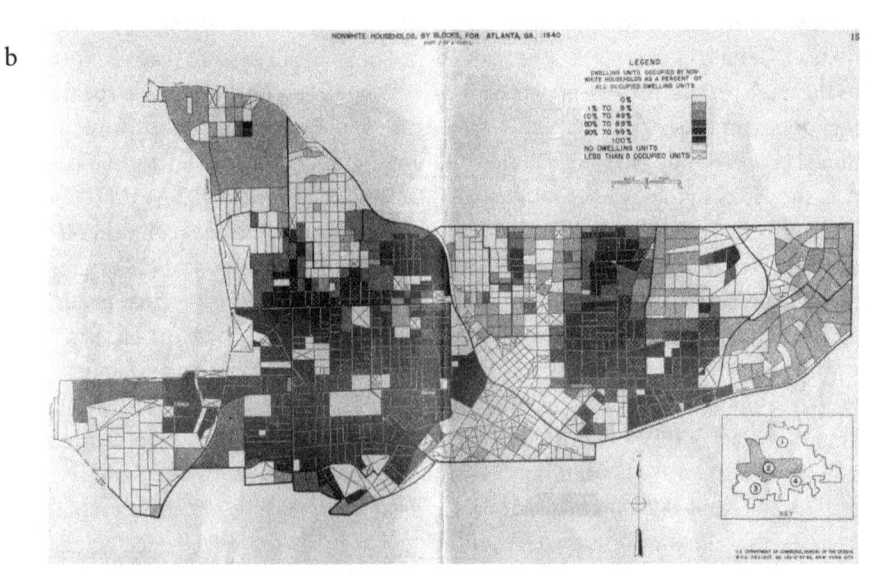

b

Figure 6.2. a through d. U.S. Bureau of the Census. *Housing: Analytical Maps; Atlanta, Georgia; Block Statistics* (Washington, D.C.: United States Bureau of the Census, 1940).

c

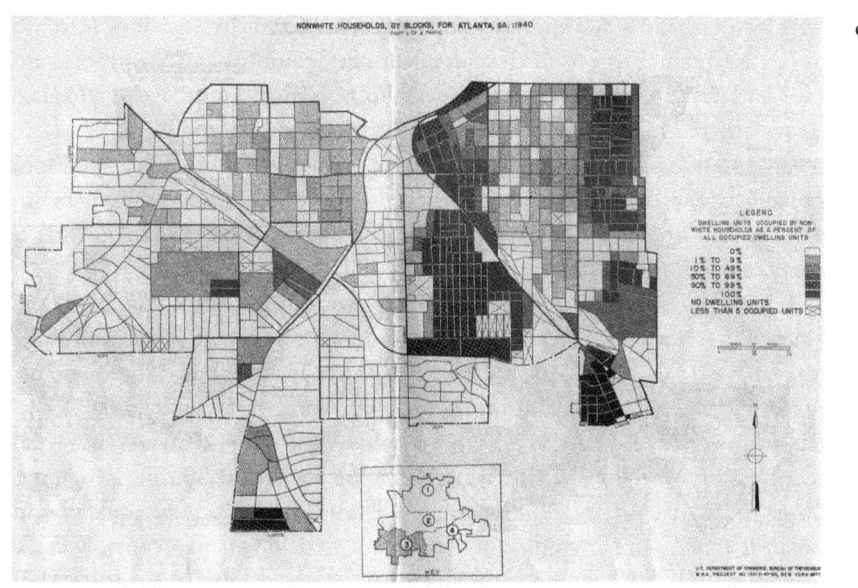

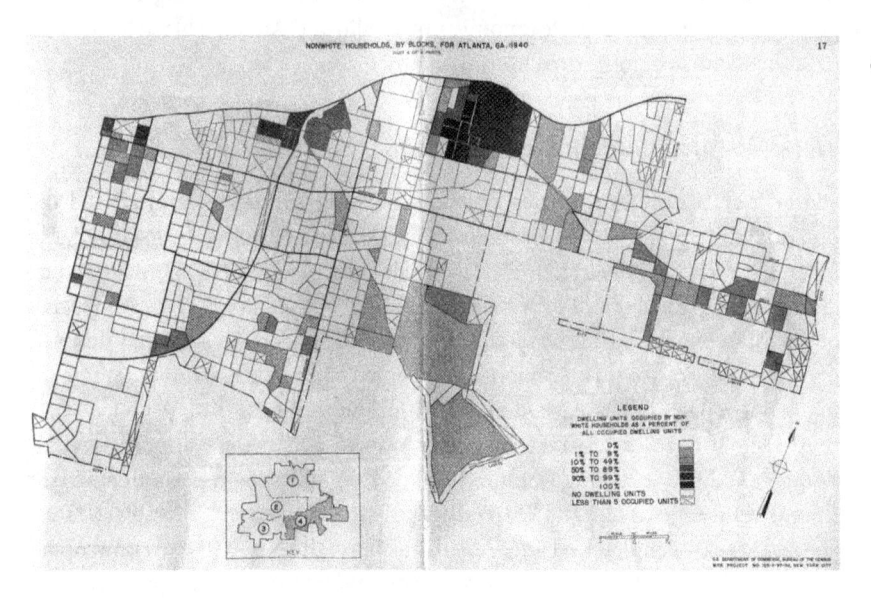

d

housing market. HOLC appraisers likewise considered Bedford-Pine (D20) "a good negro rental area from an investment standpoint." Such statements, common in HOLC surveys, reveal that neighborhoods with aged and dilapidated structures and high infant-mortality, tuberculosis, death, and crime rates still meant profit for rental-housing speculators. Likely, given the poor conditions noted in the security area descriptions, profit came by limiting property maintenance and improvements, a widespread practice that no doubt was further encouraged by the 1930s depression.[75]

Thus, white Atlantans joined with other civic elites around the nation and entered the World War II years by using federal programs to install and shore up racial and class exclusionary devices. However, black political and economic power increased dramatically during and after World War II, providing a foundation from which major civil rights organizations could demand faster and more-sustained actions against discrimination in federal housing programs. Though civil rights organizations focused litigation on school equality and policy demands on fair employment practices, housing access frequently made headlines and remained on local and national organizations' agendas. Also, growing black political and economic power allowed Atlanta's black leadership to launch and sustain its own housing plans.

World War II and the Immediate Postwar Years

World War II only exacerbated crowded housing conditions and slowed the potential of federal housing programs to provide more and safer housing. The federal government diverted materials and labor to war efforts, and nationwide, annual housing starts still only reached 114,000 by the end of 1946. About half of Atlanta's married white veterans and married black veterans lived doubled up with family or friends. About half of married black vets lived in homes needing major repairs or that lacked major plumbing facilities.[76]

At the national level, black civil rights groups such as the National Association for the Advancement of Colored People (NAACP) and the National Urban League refused to accept the FHA's discriminatory policies against black families and black-occupied housing. As early as 1940, the NAACP had complained that the FHA's "Outline of Protective Covenants" recommended practices that were "not only unreasonable and unjust" but also unlawful.[77] Shortly thereafter, FHA administrator Stewart McDonald responded, "[I am] ordering the restrictive covenant about which you protested removed from our 'Outline of Protective Covenants.'"[78] But by 1944, the NAACP was not only insisting that the FHA end discriminatory policies in the *Underwriting Manual*, but also that the agency proactively respond to black housing needs. As explained by historian

Arnold Hirsch, FHA officials initially stalled in the face of acute black housing needs, both denying that the agency discriminated and contending that it was only responding to (white) market forces.[79] But as the United States moved toward, into, and out of a war against fascism, the federal government found it increasingly difficult to simultaneously maintain discriminatory practices while projecting a message of equality and democracy for everyone around the world. Black servicemen and veterans demanded victory at home and abroad, and this meant equal access to employment, the ballot box, and housing opportunities and subsidies. Faced with growing black power and mounting pressure to live up to American tenets, the FHA reluctantly agreed to remove racial language from its *Underwriting Manual* in 1947. Still, as National Urban League officer Reginald Johnson pointed out to Housing and Home Finance Agency (HHFA) commissioner Raymond Foley, the *Underwriting Manual*'s new phrasing left room for "errors"; according to Johnson, the remaining references to "compatibility among neighborhood occupants" and "mixture of user groups" were vague and subject to racist interpretations. Johnson suggested stronger, plainer language regarding protective covenants and recommended a new statement asserting that the desirability of property covenants was not a recognition of racial property covenants.[80] The revised manual, published in 1949, may have deleted direct racial references, but as housing advocate and attorney Charles Abrams contended in the *Nation*, it was clear from the new wording "that the discrimination policy [was] unchanged."[81] And as historian John Kimble observes, the manual continued to encourage racial discrimination through expressed preferences for homogeneity.[82]

The FHA's concession to black demands for proactive development of black housing opportunities prompted the appointment of five race-relations officers in 1947 and the launching of an educational campaign to demonstrate the buying power of the black community. But such national-level actions appear to have had little direct impact on Atlanta, at least initially. Like black housing developers in other cities, the Gate City's home builders struggled to secure primary and secondary mortgage financing and faced white resistance to enlarging black-occupied areas. In practice, the AUL, and Robert Thompson specifically, appeared to serve the role intended for the Region II race relations officer, working directly with developers and municipalities to make site selection and approval as smooth as possible under a system of white control of space and housing.[83]

Black economic advances and continuing civil rights victories encouraged Atlanta's black community to exploit its local resources and launch a sustained movement to increase the supply of and access to housing. The *Atlanta Daily World* contributed to the atmosphere of achievable, impending change, alerting black Atlantans to court rulings advancing civil rights, strikes, and new black ventures, implicitly inviting participation in the growing number of regional and national actions demanding access to the vote, public facilities, fair employment practices, and quality housing and education. But Atlanta's black housing advocates faced a formidable challenge: whites who expressed a willingness to forego federal housing subsidies if using such programs meant giving up their "right" not just to "choose their neighbors" but to determine appropriate sites for black housing within the metropolitan area.

White Atlanta and the South's ongoing commitment to racially segregated housing—and the city and the region's ability to assert and impose their political will—is illustrated by the local and regional uproar that followed the 1948 *Shelley v. Kraemer* Supreme Court decision. Ruling racially restrictive covenants unenforceable, *Shelley* triggered heated debates nationally and locally over how the decision applied to private, publicly owned, federally subsidized, or federally insured housing.[84]

White southerners responded to *Shelley* with threats to ax federal housing programs while simultaneously looking for loopholes in the ruling. Senator Olin Johnston of South Carolina publicly promised, "I certainly am not going to vote for any more housing if this business continues."[85] Georgia Senator Walter George asserted, "I don't see how I can support any of these programs when the expressed policy of this administration is predicated on the violation of state law."[86] Georgia Governor Herman Talmadge rose to the occasion and, writing in his weekly paper, the *Statesman*, reminded the public that attempts "to mix the races" had resulted in riots elsewhere. He rallied the troops and implored white Georgians to "stand solidly together on this issue and fight as one to maintain [their] established traditions in the South."[87] The president of Atlanta's home builders' association, R. Hallman, asserted that court rulings mandating open housing interfered with "states' rights."[88] James Marlow, writing for the Associated Press, was unwilling to label housing segregation a southern issue, but still appealed to tradition when he contended, "It has been a widespread practice in this country for property owners in a community to discriminate against whole groups of people because of their race, religion or color, particularly Negroes and Jews."[89] Marlow carefully explained to his readers how restrictive covenants on the record prior to the implementation deadlines were to remain in effect.[90] In a follow-up article, Marlow instructed readers on how to get around the FHA regulations:

> Suppose you haven't signed or agreed to a restrictive covenant of any kind, get the FHA loan, and then it comes time to rent or sell the house you refuse to let it go to a Negro or a Jew because he's Negro or a Jew. Can the FHA do anything about that?

No. That's up to you. The FHA says it can't interfere with a person's right to refuse to rent or sell to anyone for any reason.

To sum up: Under the new rule you can get FHA help and discriminate, in renting or selling, for racial or religious or any other reasons, provided you haven't agreed to do so in a covenant made a matter of record after Feb. 15.[91]

NBC journalist David Brinkley advised white viewers to "let Negroes know when they [were] not wanted in a community."[92]

Rulings like *Shelley* and the federal power to regulate racial geographies by allocating or withholding funds threatened white power in Atlanta and throughout the nation, but whites fought federal imposition. Faced with what they considered to be punitive federal actions, southern whites exerted their considerable political influence and forced federal bureaucrats back to a "local control" position. Assured that housing programs were safely in the hands of local white power structures, officials continued using tax dollars and housing programs to manipulate racial and class housing geographies.

After asserting that the FHA would deny insurance to properties carrying racially restrictive covenants, the FHA's Franklin D. Richards wilted under mounting pressure and white threats to undermine federal housing programs and almost immediately reversed himself. He soothed ruffled white feathers by explaining that the policy would "not bar a property owner from selecting the tenants he want[ed]," and that the agency would not interfere with an individual's right to dispose of his property as he saw fit. In response, a coalition of forty organizations, including the NAACP, the American Council of Human Relations, and the National Urban League, insisted that President Harry Truman remove HHFA head Raymond Foley from office. The coalition's protests appeared successful; by the end of the month, the FHA had directed all field and underwriting offices to disregard racially restrictive covenants.[93]

White Atlantans also fought black housing choice on the ground, resurrecting tactics used in Jackson Hill and mirroring actions taken in cities throughout the country. When black families violated white-imposed racial borders to seize better housing and the opportunities it offered their families, whites resisted with actions ranging from verbal protests and harassment to violence. In March 1949, for example, white neighborhood representatives Joe Wallace and H. C. Harris Jr. threatened a new black resident in West End. That night, the house was bombed, but no charges resulted. When Rosa Mae Williams moved into the Ashby Street home in April, she was immediately met with threats. In May that year, approximately two hundred men went door to door on Ashby Street between Greensferry Avenue and West End Avenue demanding that blacks move out of the homes. Whites went on to destroy at least twelve black homes in Atlanta in the 1950s, five within a three-month period. Reflecting on an earlier spate of violence against black home buyers, black home builder Walter Aiken insisted to the Joint Committee on Housing in 1947, "Those things are going to happen unless we have planned areas."[94]

Buoyed by the economic and civil rights gains of the 1940s and confronted by an increasing number of returning war veterans, yet largely ignored by the FHA and facing violence when moving into predominantly white areas, Atlanta's black leaders worked tirelessly to develop new black housing opportunities in such "planned areas." The AUL's Robert Thompson and other community leaders knew the buying power of Atlanta's black community and the extent of unmet housing need. As Thompson frequently pointed out, literally thousands of black families earned incomes over $3000 a year in the late 1940s and could afford to pay more for housing if the opportunities were available. Planning consultant Philip Hammer confirmed Thompson's assertion in his 1954 report on the black rental-housing market, noting that black incomes had tripled from 1936 to 1949. Appealing to patriotism, Thompson asserted to the joint committee investigating the late 1940s housing crisis that the majority of black veterans were forced to live in homes deemed "substandard." Seeking federal programs that would help produce low- to middle-income housing, Thompson explained that the majority of black vets had registered their desire to purchase a five-room house at payments of $31 a month, but that construction projections predicted that most builders planned to produce $5,800 to $8,000 homes—homes outside the price range of the city's black veterans.[95]

To meet Atlanta's housing needs, housing developer Walter Aiken and the AUL's Robert Thompson formed the Temporary Coordinating Committee on Housing (later renamed the Atlanta Housing Council) in 1946. Intending to erect more quality housing as quickly as possible, the AUL and its partners quietly located land appropriate for the building of multifamily complexes and single-family-home subdivisions, charting properties owned by blacks adjacent to established black neighborhoods or distant from white residential areas. The Housing Council's 1947 report, "Proposed Expansion Areas for Negroes," identified six potential areas in which to expand housing for blacks. Most were located on the city's near south and west sides, but the committee also suggested property adjacent to small, historically black neighborhoods to the city's north (see fig. 6.3).[96]

Forwarded to white and black civic leaders across the city for comment, the plan was met with ringing endorsements from some and ambivalence from others. Forrester Washington of Atlanta University's School of Social Work, for example, pledged support to Thompson, but added that he would oppose

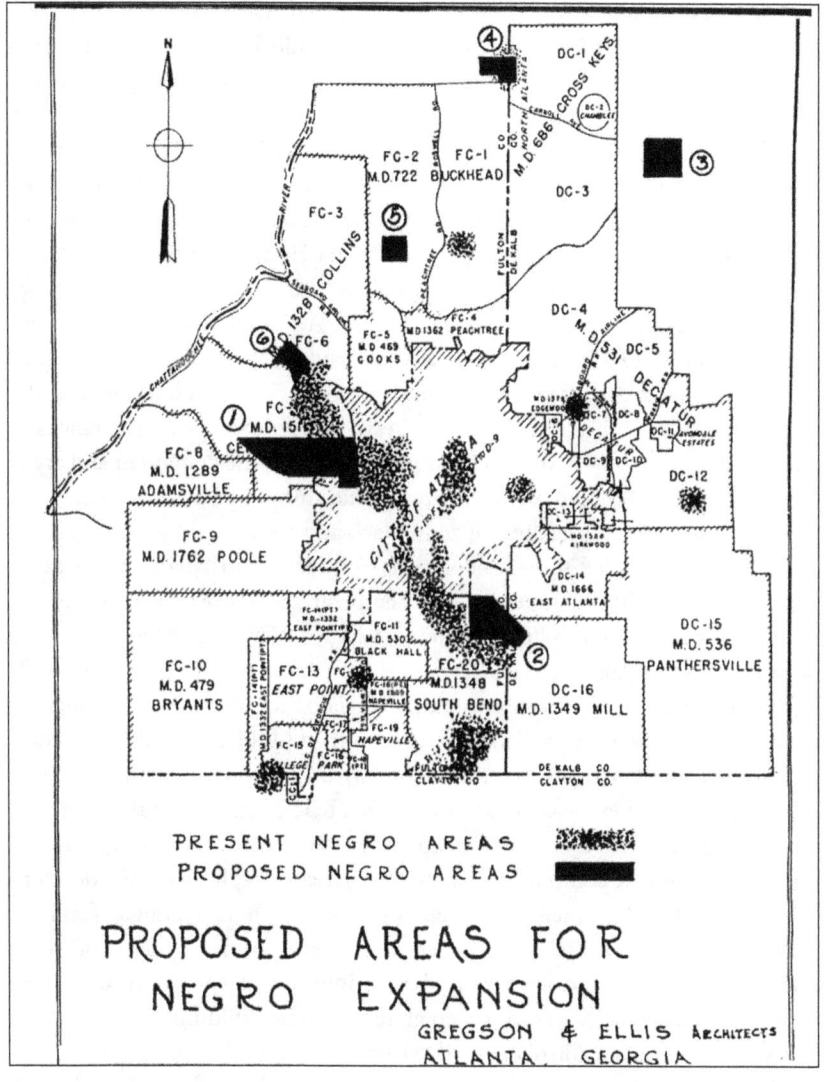

Figure 6.3. "Proposed Areas for Negro Expansion," Atlanta Housing Council, 1947, attached to letter from R. A. Thompson Jr. to James H. Therrell, July 29, 1947, folder 1, box 252, Atlanta Urban League Papers, Robert W. Woodruff Library of the Atlanta University Center.

such schemas if they "were done by law" or by "so-called 'gentlemen's agreements.'" He concluded, "Of course, the ideal would be not to have any specific Negro communities in Atlanta."[97] Thompson circulated the proposal not just among black leadership but to white social, business, and political leaders, and the bureaucracies that governed land use, including the Atlanta Chamber of Commerce, the Buckhead Trade Association, area colleges and universities, as well as neighborhood associations. Among whites endorsing the plan were James Therrell, executive director of the Atlanta Housing Authority, and Wilfred Gregson, president of the Brookhaven Civic Association.[98]

The plan, though not legally binding, and the AUL's method of gaining comment and "approval" from a variety of white and black entities were designed to help ease land purchases and zoning approvals for new black housing development. That is, if faced with white resistance to the housing of blacks in particular areas, the AUL or developers could point to the document and argue that it—and therefore the particular area in question—had been circulated and "approved" by Atlanta's leading citizens, black and white.

The report appealed to white concerns and fears, particularly about racial segregation and slum conditions, and demonstrated the AUL's ability to use park-neighborhood sensibilities to their advantage. New housing for blacks, the document explained, would be developed "in complete self-contained neighborhoods" and would "make possible the reclamation of the present blighted areas." In discussing the particular areas identified for black housing, the committee noted that African Americans already occupied land in the proposed expansion areas; there was no suggestion that black housing would replace or even locate near white-occupied neighborhoods. Finally, the proposal incorporated fashionable community-planning practices, emphasizing the development of "individual integrated neighborhoods" with recreational facilities, commercial areas, and schools. "Greenbelts" would delineate roads and separate neighborhoods. Lot sizes would be a minimum six thousand square feet with standard setbacks and lot coverage restrictions. Buildings and structures would be "carefully controlled by deed restrictions and zoning." The report downplayed apartments, though it suggested mixing housing stock. By implying that blacks embraced the same housing expectations as elite and middle-class whites, the report sought to allay white fears of black housing, not for the purposes of securing civil rights, necessarily, but so as to ease white-imposed barriers to black expansion and to provide more high-quality housing for the black community. The strategy worked, and by February 1949, twenty-one organizations had endorsed the recommendations. According to the AUL, the consents signaled that "both racial groups fully understand that Negro citizens may live and build additional houses [in the areas designated] without intimidation or fear."[99]

The concessions of civic elites to black demands no doubt resulted in part from the rapid growth in black voting power in the mid-1940s. After the 1944 *Smith v. Allright* U.S. Supreme Court ruling outlawed the white primary and Governor Ellis Arnall repealed the poll tax in 1945, Atlanta's black civic leaders launched a voting drive that raised black registration to six thousand in 1945. In 1946, after the *Chapman v. King* ruling outlawed the white primary in Georgia, black-led organizations launched a two-month door-to-door registration push that brought the voting rolls to over twenty-five thousand. At that point, as the AUL's Robert Thompson explained to the U.S. Civil Rights Commission, "the social climate of Atlanta changed very definitely with respect to the Negro getting the amenities and facilities needed for housing."[100] Insurance and real-estate agent T. M. Alexander affirmed, "Before we were voting in larger numbers we did not get the type of cooperation from the previous city administration that we are getting now."[101] Moreover, police became more responsive to black needs, and neighborhood services improved.[102]

The AUL used the "Proposed Areas" as its blueprint and brought together resources to produce durable, safe housing for black occupancy. When the AUL identified property it considered appropriate for single-family or multifamily homes, it approached the landowner and offered to sponsor a new housing development. When Robert Thompson invited investor George Wilson to consider using his Willis Mill Road property for black housing, for example, he explained that the AUL would secure a builder and construction loans, identify a life insurance company that would purchase the mortgage, seek FHA and VA approval for the site and insurance, lobby city officials for the quick provision of services, provide information on the homes to be built to potential buyers or tenants, and assist in the sale or leasing of homes.[103]

In some cases, housing facilitated by the AUL kept to plan and adopted park-neighborhood practices such as setbacks and planned green spaces. Fair Haven subdivision, as historian Andrew Wiese explains, included a "uniform streetscape of front lawns, concrete steps, and wrought-iron railings," creating "a residential landscape that would have been immediately familiar to middle-class suburbanites anywhere in the United States."[104] Other developments deviated from the schema outlined in "Proposed Expansion Areas." Apartments, not single-family homes with six-thousand-square-foot lots and standard setbacks, were the central component of many projects. Highpoint, Magnolia, and Ire-Ron Apartments, for example, provided 452, 16, and 44 units, respectively, to the city's south and west. Other projects took the form of infill development rather than wholly designed neighborhoods, including the Richardson Road and Simpson Road projects, which delivered 12 and 7 units, respectively.[105]

To accomplish its goals, the AUL relied heavily on Atlanta's cadre of black builders, black housing developers, and its black-owned financial institutions. Indeed, Atlanta's black-led financial institutions fulfilled much of the community's mortgage needs when many white-owned institutions would not issue first mortgages or purchase or insure mortgages for black housing. By 1955, black-owned Atlanta Life Insurance Company, Citizens Trust Company, and Mutual Federal Savings and Loan had 24 percent of their total assets in first-mortgage loans. That said, Thompson doggedly pursued all lenders, white or black, identifying those who had previously financed black housing and inviting their participation in the AUL project. Thompson enjoyed some success; white lenders Atlanta Federal Savings and Loan Association and the Life Insurance Company of Georgia financed Walter Aiken projects. Besides applying to local institutions, Thompson sought mortgage originators and investors outside Atlanta, particularly in the Northeast. Able to call on local financial resources, black-owned businesses, and a network of institutions outside the region, the AUL facilitated the construction of 1,276 owner-occupied dwellings and 2,862 rental units between 1945 and 1956, or 56.2 percent of all new black-occupied housing produced in that period. But while financing black housing in Atlanta may have been easier than in many southern cities, and while the AUL's "Proposed Areas" had received the endorsement of white civic elites, finding locations for black housing that met white approval proved challenging.[106]

"Proposed Expansion Areas" failed to quell protest from residents, even if the report had "endorsements" from city officials and civic elites. The AUL met with the white Grove Park Civic Association in 1949 when the civic association raised concerns about the county's sale of 145 acres for the purpose of housing black veterans. DeKalb County residents, to the city's east, objected to the proposed 26-acre Wesley Heights and Hardee Court Apartments. Housing, Inc.'s experience with Highpoint Apartments illustrates the manifold difficulties associated with siting new black housing in race-conscious Atlanta. White investors Morris Abram and Hugh Howell envisioned Highpoint as a multifamily housing community for the black middle class. Working with the AUL, Abram and Howell proposed an 800-unit complex for Pryor Road, near the established black neighborhood known as South Atlanta. The FHA rejected the project, though, contending that the proposed rents—forty-nine to fifty-nine dollars a month—were too high for black occupants. The AUL, which had carefully studied Atlanta's black population and housing markets, contested the decision and demonstrated black middle class demand for units in this price range. The

FHA reversed its decision and insured the project. In the meantime, though, nearby white Lakewood Heights residents protested the proposed complex, and black expansion in south Atlanta in general. Tensions escalated as black businessmen involved in the project accused whites of lobbying for the relocation of a future expressway over the project site. Black housing advocates successfully appealed to Washington officials to prevent the expressway's change, and ultimately the Fulton County Planning Commission accepted the project. To address white protests, though, the commission agreed to establish a buffer between the black and white residential areas, cut the number of units in half, and zone 27 acres of project land for industrial development. Even at its reduced size, Highpoint's 452 units made it the largest FHA-insured black project in the South. But such ongoing land disputes, the FHA's recalcitrance on the question of race, and slow financing waylaid new home production for blacks, and Atlantans continued to rely on the turnover of white housing to answer some housing needs.[107]

Housing competition reached a crescendo as black families expanded into the city's mixed-race west side in the late 1940s. Black families had been moving westward for two decades, filling new subdivisions such as Bennett and Simpson Heights as well as formerly white-occupied housing. In 1948, housing shortages forced some black families to gradually move nearer (and eventually into) white-occupied Mozley Park. White residents threatened black property owner William A. Scott Jr., but he declined to move, and whites in the nearby blocks began placing their homes on the market. (At least one black real-estate agent, John Calhoun, encouraged the process by informing other area whites that their neighbors were fleeing.) Black migration to the area continued, and blacks families gradually encircled Mozley Park over the next two years. By 1951, despite the defensive tactics of the Mozley Park Home Owners Protective Association, a number of white-occupied Mozley Park homes were listed for sale in the black-owned *Atlanta Daily World*. Soon thereafter, and in order to avoid the tensions and violence that were manifested in Mozley Park, Mayor William Hartsfield created a biracial West Side Mutual Development Committee (WSMDC) to mediate housing issues between blacks and whites. As white business owner and president of the Southwest Citizens Organization Carroll Barfield explained to the U.S. Civil Rights Commission, simply forming the committee helped ease tensions, as it gave white residents someone to complain to.[108]

The high rate of black building within and just outside Atlanta's city limits should not be read as willingness by black developers or the AUL to forego housing in the burgeoning areas surrounding Atlanta. Robert Thompson was acutely aware of housing need further out, but he also understood the extent of white resistance. (Apparently in response to his information request made at Atlanta's Southeastern Fair, Thompson received a notice from Kennesaw Acres subdivision in Cobb County indicating he had won the opportunity to purchase a lot for only sixty-four dollars. The letter stipulated that Thompson needed to "be of the white race" to claim his lot.)[109] But the AUL pursued suburban housing opportunities when it could. In 1952, when an Atlanta attorney contacted Thompson about the possibility of building housing for Lockheed and air force personnel, Thompson responded that to date, "no attention [had] been given to the housing conditions of Negroes in Marietta and Cobb County."[110] Thompson immediately went to work making contacts. He also appealed for FHA financing for Lynwood Park in DeKalb County, to the city's northeast. DeKalb had consistently resisted black housing, and J. W. E. Bowen explained in his letter of support to the FHA, "Nothing is being done in this section for our people."[111] Although AUL board chair and attorney A. T. Walden asserted that Buckhead "afford[ed] practically no living accommodations for Negroes," he was also careful to note that the proposed black development was three miles from the prestigious white section of north Atlanta.[112] By the mid-1950s, some applications for federal insurance for black housing in the outer suburbs were successful. Parsons Village erected nineteen "Atomcrete" homes in Doraville, to the city's northeast. FHA- and VA-approved, the two-bedroom homes started at $8,990 and were convenient to the Naval Air Station and industries accumulating in the Chamblee-Doraville section.[113]

In this manner, from 1922 to 1950—with federal subsidies, private development of multi-acre subdivisions (black and white), zoning, and restrictive covenants—Atlanta's formerly mixed-race blocks gave way to multiblock subdivisions and public-housing projects that targeted particular racial groups. Whereas from the 1880s to about 1910, builders and investors produced housing in lengths of one to five homes, subdivisions of ten to two hundred homes emerged in the 1920s and became common building practice. Churned out in a period of white power, park-neighborhood sensibilities, and black actions to mitigate the housing shortage, these development practices rarely resulted in mixed-race blocks. Public housing exacerbated segregation, as each project contained twice the number of units of most black park-neighborhoods—hundreds (and in the 1950s, thousands).

New public and private building practices combined to racialize much larger spaces than forty years prior. The largest FHA-financed black project in the South to date, Highpoint Apartments placed about 450 black units on about thirty-five square blocks. Next door, Carver Homes assigned 990 units to black

Figure 6.4. Fairview Terrace. Source: Long-Rucker-Aiken Collection, Atlanta History Center.

families in 1953 on an equivalent amount of land. Thirty years earlier, no cluster of seventy square blocks of 100 percent black-occupied homes existed in the city. To be sure, not all housing projects were as large as Highpoint Apartments, but small projects accumulated, adjacent to each other, resulting in a similar pattern. Walter Aiken's Fairview Terrace subdivision assigned approximately seven square blocks to black families (see fig. 6.4), and the abutting black-occupied Hunter Hills doubled the area occupied by blacks. E. R. Craighead's Hunter Hills and Ezra Church Heights subdivisions, west of Washington Park, comprised five hundred lots. Smaller black subdivisions were located nearby, including Service Company's thirty-three acres, on which it intended to house about one hundred black families, Pine Acres, which comprised fifty lots, and Fair Haven's 233 homes. White subdivisions amassed in a comparable way to the city's north, stacking acres of whites-only subdivisions one atop another. Peachtree Hills Place, Peachtree Terrace, and Peachtree Heights embedded whiteness north through the city, one subdivision atop another, in large assemblages of restricted housing (see fig. 6.5). Garden Hills gathered about 300 homes in 14 "clusters," Peachtree Hills delivered 200-plus homes to white families, and Peachtree Heights contributed 120 homes.[114]

As figure 6.6 illustrates, even while black families consumed more land, they remained confined and concentrated, largely in Atlanta's near west and

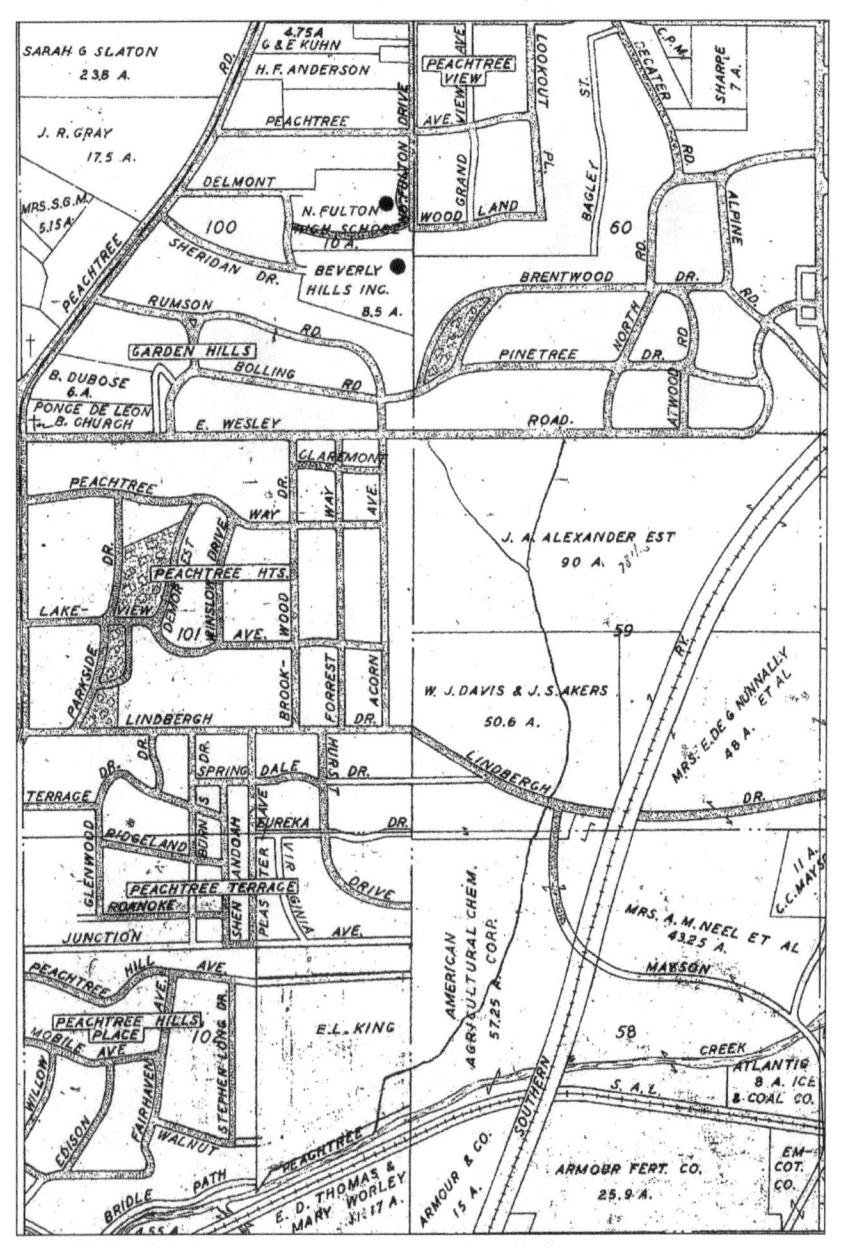

Figure 6.5. North Atlanta white subdivisions. Source: Robert and Robert, *Land District Nos. Six & Seventeen, Fulton County,* GA (Atlanta: Fulton County Commissioners of Roads and Revenues, 1939).

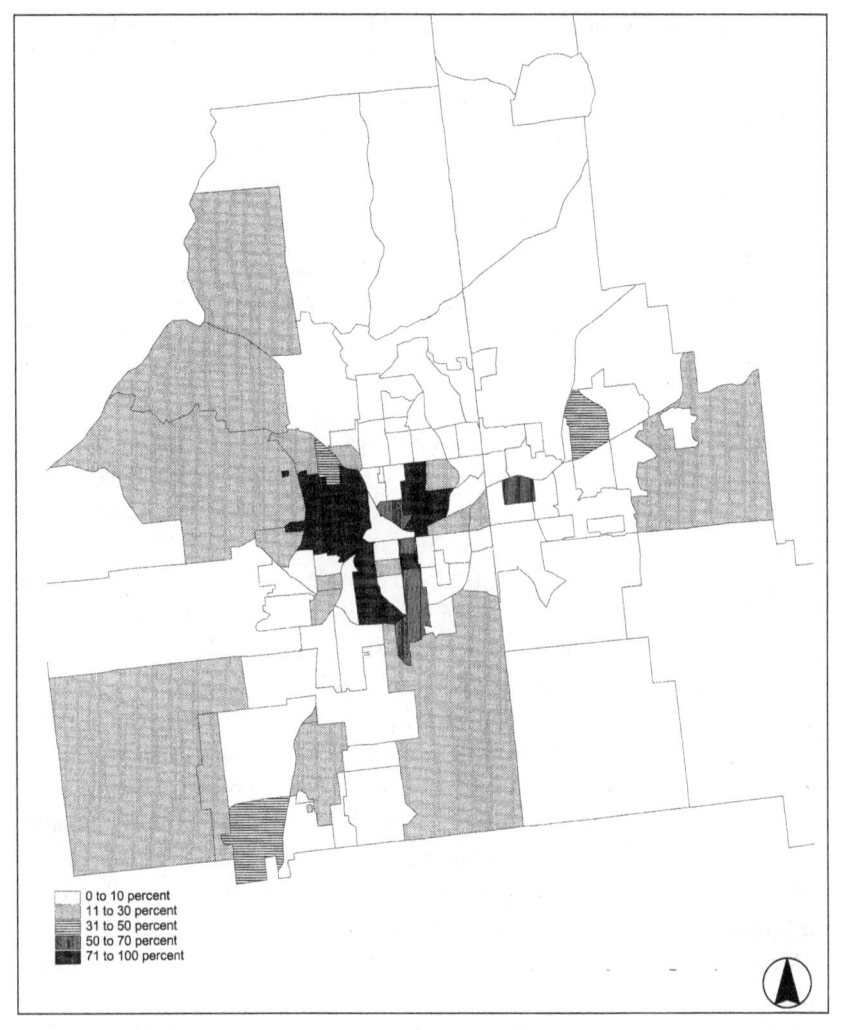

Figure 6.6. Nonwhite occupied dwellings, 1950. Census data and shape files: Minnesota Population Center. *National Historical Geographic Information System: Pre-release Version 0.1* (Minneapolis: University of Minnesota, 2004), http://www.nhgis.org.

Table 6.1. Population Changes between 1940 and 1950, Metropolitan Atlanta, by Race

	White increase	White increase, percent	Black increase	Black increase, percent
City of Atlanta	12,200	6.2%	16,800	16.1%
Outside city	119,100	67.3%	5,600	14.5%
Metropolitan total	131,300	35.0%	22,400	15.6%

Developed from table 1, "The Market for Negro Rental Housing in Metropolitan Atlanta," May 5, 1954, folder 45, Philip Gibbon Hammer Collection, Southern Historical Collections, University of North Carolina–Chapel Hill, p. 3.

southwest. This is not to say that black families did not spread into more areas; they did. Rather, the spatial area accessible to black families remained tightly constrained when compared to the space to which whites had access. After World War II in particular, white families moved rapidly into Atlanta's undeveloped perimeter, consuming more land and expanding the metropolitan boundaries. Blacks, in contrast, remained relegated to a corridor on the west wide, the central city core around the central business district, and then in tightly controlled clusters near the two- and three-mile radius. Put another way, between 1940 and 1950, the nonwhite population increased in the northwest and southwest 82 percent, but only 23 percent in the city's northeast and southeast. The AUL's efforts to open up more land for black home building worked to some degree, but by 1949, Atlanta's blacks, who comprised one-third of the city's population, still occupied only one-fifth of the city's land. Not surprisingly, between 1940 and 1950, black population growth within the city limits tripled the growth rate in the balance of the metro area (see table 6.1).[115]

A comparison of the proportion of black-occupied dwellings by census tract confirms that portions of central Atlanta, particularly on the west side, became "blacker," while six suburban census tracts became "whiter" from 1940 to 1950 (see fig. 6.7 and table 6.2). To the city's northeast, in DeKalb County, tract DC0002 decreased its proportion of black-occupied dwellings by 17.6 percent, largely because of the scale of white housing production in the area. In contrast, F0008, just northwest of Atlanta's downtown, increased its proportion of black-occupied housing by 40 percent. Since the tract did not lose much housing overall from 1940 to 1950, most of this transition is likely explained by the turnover of white housing to black families. Adjacent F0022, on the other hand, increased its proportion of black-occupied housing by 11 percent, largely through new construction. FC0004, directly north of the city, increased its proportion

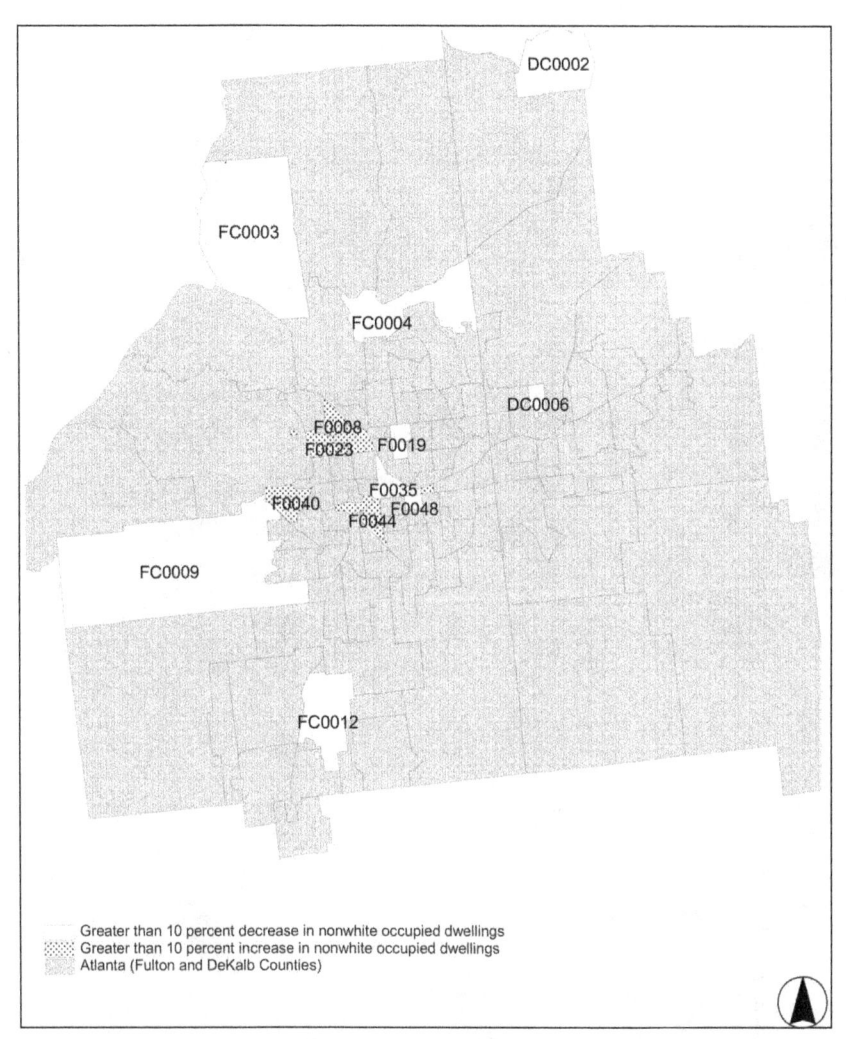

Figure 6.7. Change in proportion of nonwhites and whites in occupied dwellings, 1940 to 1950. Census data and shape files: Minnesota Population Center. *National Historical Geographic Information System: Pre-release Version 0.1* (Minneapolis: University of Minnesota, 2004), http://www.nhgis.org.

Table 6.2. Tracts Showing Greater than +/-10 Percent Change in Proportion of Nonwhite-Occupied Dwellings, 1940 to 1950

Census tract	Occupied dwelling units total	1940 Nonwhite occupied	1940 White occupied	Nonwhite occupied percent	White occupied percent	Occupied dwelling units total	1950 Nonwhite occupied	1950 White occupied	Nonwhite occupied percent	White occupied percent	Change in proportion of nonwhite occupied	Possible cause of change
DC0002	264	50	214	18.9	81.1	824	11	813	1.3	98.7	-17.6	New white construction
F0008	1,278	113	1,165	8.8	91.2	1,184	576	608	48.6	51.4	39.8	Turnover
F0019	1,174	330	844	28.1	71.9	542	52	490	9.6	90.4	-18.5	Demolition (F0019 losing housing overall)
F0022	873	755	118	86.5	13.5	1,210	1,180	30	97.5	2.5	11.0	New nonwhite construction
F0023	826	561	265	67.9	32.1	935	808	127	86.4	13.6	18.5	Turnover, new nonwhite construction
F0034	255	143	112	56.1	43.9	114	89	25	78.1	21.9	22.0	Demolition (F0034 losing housing overall)
F0035	279	64	215	22.9	77.1	524	54	470	10.3	89.7	-12.6	New white construction
F0040	912	81	831	8.9	91.1	1,153	241	912	20.9	79.1	12.0	New white and black construction

F0043	717	606	111	84.5	15.5	1,116	1,061	55	95.1	4.9	10.6	Turnover, new nonwhite construction
F0044	1,704	1,279	425	75.1	24.9	1,545	1,319	226	85.4	14.6	10.3	Turnover
F0048	1,202	1,088	114	90.5	9.5	1,494	911	583	61.0	39.0	-29.5	Demolition, new white construction
FC0003	321	87	234	27.1	72.9	641	80	561	12.5	87.5	-14.6	New white construction
FC0004	979	152	827	15.5	84.5	1,613	40	1,573	2.5	97.5	-13.0	Demolition, new white construction
FC0009	643	125	518	19.4	80.6	1,685	122	1,563	7.2	92.8	-12.2	New white construction
FC0012	1,100	446	654	40.5	59.5	3,000	662	2,338	22.1	77.9	-18.5	New black and white construction

Calculated from census data made available by the Minnesota Population Center, *National Historical Geographic Information System: Pre-release Version 0.1* (Minneapolis: University of Minnesota, 2004), http://www.nhgis.org.

of white-occupied housing by 13 percent. Part of this can be explained by the addition of at least nine hundred white-occupied homes, but the decrease in black-occupied homes and the fact that social practice usually precluded turnover of black homes to white families suggests that a little over one hundred black-occupied homes were demolished or perhaps lost to fire.[116]

FHA housing program mandates, the local implementation of federal public-housing projects, and the AUL's housing program worked together to sharpen distinctions between white and black residential areas in metropolitan Atlanta. The FHA influenced segregation by subsidizing whites and ignoring blacks and by favoring new construction in racially homogeneous planned communities. Whites took advantage of subsidized and unsubsidized development at the city's edge and grew Atlanta's urbanized area and marked it for whites only by installing racial covenants. By June 1947, Atlanta developers intended over 90 percent of the 11,065 planned housing units for white occupation. As a result, between 1940 and 1950, white population growth was nine times higher outside the city limits than within. Black housing areas grew, too, but largely within the city's three-mile radius, limited by public-housing location, financing mechanisms available to black home builders and buyers, and white notions of the appropriate locations for black housing.[117]

From the early 1930s to 1948, when the U.S. Supreme Court ruled racially restrictive covenants unenforceable, an array of local and federal policies and private practices circulated new thinking about the organization of cities and neighborhoods by race and class and propagated a landscape way of seeing residential landscapes. Even while black families adopted park-neighborhood practices, media and policy texts associated that residential landscape with whiteness and civic elites. Indeed, federal policies encouraged whites and discouraged blacks from partaking in exclusive neighborhood living. Thus, residential landscapes did not simply reflect popular assumptions about class and racial organization but imposed racial and class divisions and inculcated a particular way of seeing, understanding, and practicing property.

CHAPTER SEVEN

White Property and Homeowner Privilege

Atlanta exemplified the problem of urban inequality at the turn to the twenty-first century. As economist David Sjoquist outlines in a May 2000 Russell Sage–funded study titled *The Atlanta Paradox,* poverty was highly concentrated and largely located in the older urban core. Despite the city's reputation as a magnet for black business and the black middle class, white household income was over twice the average black household income. Jobs had moved to the suburbs, while many of the poor and working class remained confined to the central city.[1]

The Russell Sage Foundation series investigating economically and racially divided cities continued a twenty-five-year run of urban decline literature, a trend that accelerated in the 1960s as the nation's cities exploded with racial and economic tensions. The riots and protests that spawned the analysis of the "urban crisis" capped four generations of urban development that had rent the city into zones of economic homogeneity—wealthy, middle class, working poor, destitute—that overlay a more pervasive geography of black and white. But for all the studies and policy initiatives, as the publication of *The Atlanta Paradox* indicates, Atlanta still carried the burden of a divided city. A core city of decaying infrastructure, economic devastation, poor schools, and unhealthy, unsafe, and unaffordable housing remained surrounded by a ring (a *sprawling* ring) of affluence marked by stable public schools and a vibrant economy. Atlanta wasn't alone. American cities remained so racially segmented at the end of the twentieth century that social scientists Douglas Massey and Nancy Denton boldly label the issue "American Apartheid" in their 1993 analysis of the pervasiveness of racial segregation. If anyone wondered why our "city too busy to hate" was rent into giant swaths of black and white, rich and poor, he or she didn't have to look far for at least part of the answer.[2]

As Atlanta's Russell Sage study moved through its last stages of publication, housing developer Tim Jones filed suit against Henry County, Georgia's Board of Commissioners, contending that the county's zoning plan discriminated against low- to moderate-income home buyers. "Exclusionary zoning," his lawyer charged. Jones's proposal to build 400 homes on his 103 acres in Atlanta's suburbs near Interstate 75 and Jonesboro Road drew protests from neighbors in nearby, higher-priced subdivisions. Jones acquiesced and lowered his proposal to 296 homes ranging in size from 1,300 to 1,700 square feet on 6,000-square-foot lots. Henry County's commissioners modified their classification to require that 75 percent of properties have a minimum 1,300 square feet on 18,000-square-foot lots, but Jones took the issue to court. Henry County attorney Wade Crumbley told the *Atlanta Journal-Constitution,* "The notion that Henry County is discriminating against the working class is not only not supported by the record, it's absurd."[3] Jones's attorney Douglas Dillard disagreed and asserted that local governments throughout Georgia were using minimum lot sizes and house sizes as a way of excluding low-income people. The courts found in Jones's favor. The case was appealed, but the ruling was upheld. Indeed, policy analysts no longer bother with proving whether exclusionary zoning is used in the United States but simply move on to discussing how it is effected or outlining the extent of the practice.[4]

The exclusionary Atlanta of the early twenty-first century contrasts sharply with the Gate City of the 1880s and 1890s. Then, residences abutted businesses. Some blocks were mixed by race, and many were mixed by class. These uses existed without threat to adjacent properties' values, at least for a time. But by the end of the 1920s, white homeowners increasingly approached housing and neighborhoods with a new collection of desires and sensibilities. White, owner-occupied neighborhoods were marked by architectural and landscape continuity, a narrow range of housing values, and some form of buffer that separated the area from undesirable land uses—*and undesirable people.* These shared understandings about residential landscapes emerged between 1900 and 1915, took hold in the wave of suburban park-neighborhood building in the 1920s, and were embedded into local public policy in the 1920s and federal public policy in 1930s. Thereafter, this tangle of raced and classed landscape understandings powerfully influenced succeeding generations of white working- and middle-class city and suburban residents. They helped maintain class and racial divisions after racial segregation was outlawed, even after racist rhetoric became taboo. Although Americans maintained a belief that theirs was a classless society, these shared understandings became naturalized, embedded in public policy. The transformations we have examined are worth a recap before moving on to discuss the legacy of this landscape of power.

❧

From 1900 to World War I, grand structures, green and manicured thoroughfares emerged in urban rhetoric and imagery. City Beautiful ideals combined with the park-neighborhood aesthetic cultivated by suburban designers to produce a greater appreciation and desire for parkways, plazas, monuments, and homogeneity, at least among civic elites. Planning-by-speculation and infill development were out, and Atlanta's haphazard array of people and housing had to be cleaned up, reorganized, and disciplined. The city-planning proponents of the era encouraged a managed, rational landscape.

White residents of Atlanta's new park-neighborhoods and park-neighborhood-inspired communities carried these ideas into their neighborhoods and demanded more distance between themselves and land uses that they perceived as disturbing to their neighborhood ideal. That meant limiting the entry of black residents to particular areas, and (in the case of the lower Fourth Ward in the 1910s) removing those already living there. But informal "whites only" spatial agreements failed. Institution moving failed. Threats of violence failed. Segregation ordinances failed. As white elites attempted stronger controls over the urban environment, land developers continued lacing Atlanta's blocks with a variety of housing, from rooming houses to "painted ladies." Tenants and black home buyers moved nearer. Unable to control what they perceived as "their" neighborhoods, white, propertied elites attempted to enlarge and solidify property buffers by adopting comprehensive land-use zoning, which had the dual advantage of controlling class as well as race. The racial elements of this tactic, too, failed. But if political maneuvers fell short, cultural machinations did not. Confronted with such challenges, well-off white homeowners launched and continually fortified a campaign that linguistically turned housing and land-use incongruity, blacks and tenants into "undesirables." It was this strategy that, over time, proved most effective.

Exclusive park-neighborhood building accelerated as Atlanta and the United States recovered from World War I and captured the white imagination. Whereas only a handful of such developments marked Atlanta's perimeter before the war, elite-oriented subdivisions rapidly consumed the countryside beginning in 1922. Developers of Garden Hills, Peachtree Hills Park, Sylvan Hills, Tuxedo Park, and other subdivisions seized one hundred to five hundred acres beyond the city's limits, marked off lots of nine thousand square feet and more, laid out streets, trees, and parks, and tagged their communities "exclusive" and "restricted." Ads celebrated the park-neighborhood experience, newspapers waxed eloquent about the newest subdivisions and record-breaking land sales, and plat maps hawked natural environments and notable neighbors. If advertisements were to be believed (and census records suggest that they were), park-neighborhoods were "the place to be."

The park-neighborhood imagery animated and illustrated the post–World War I homeownership campaigns. Advertisements, "how-to" manuals, and policy documents incorporated park-neighborhood ideals of neighborhood, single-family homes, pastoral imagery, and whiteness. *Homeownership* was foregrounded, but homogeneity and the park-neighborhood aesthetic were all part of the package on display. The whole package was what was bought, intentionally or unintentionally. As homeownership increased, park-neighborhood sensibilities (racial and class housing segregation, manicured lawns, orderly street fronts) spread with it. Thus, the white elite–birthed practices diffused through both the textual and visual imagery associated with sales campaigns and government-led promotions, but were likewise transmitted across the landscape—literally *in and on the ground*—as homeownership increased through the 1920s onward. Moreover, these practices and sensibilities became associated; homeownership, whiteness, and the park-neighborhood aesthetic merged in popular texts and policies.

Comprehensive land-use zoning solidified segregated land-use patterns and exclusionary practices in the 1920s. In Atlanta, the 1922 *Zone Plan* favored homogeneous spaces and planned neighborhoods. Zoning materials instructed readers that mixed-use and heterogeneous built environments decreased property values, and that single-family, owner-occupied homes ranked highest in a property hierarchy. Like park-neighborhoods, comprehensive land-use zoning encouraged and taught a landscape way of seeing that encompassed not the single house and property, but the neighborhood and streetscape. What is more, comprehensive land-use zoning encouraged greater attention to neighborhood occupants' race and class—it classified all residential property as white, "colored," or undetermined, and sorted housing into apartments and single-family home districts with density requirements. Thus, unsuccessful in their earlier attempts to control property use and transfers, white elites found a convenient and potentially legal device to control property use in the 1920s zoning trend.

Throughout the early 1900s, public policies and homeownership campaigns linguistically created a host of "undesirables" that civic elites utilized to justify segregating and zoning. Blacks promised neighborhood "ruin," and black men threatened white womanhood. Black housing, in turn, became a "menace." Apartments were "to be avoided," and tenants jeopardized civilization. Such language and imagery spread through newspaper accounts, public-policy justifications, advertisements, and casual conversations and created the "fear" that Robert Fogelson contends informed the creation and rapid spread of restrictive covenants in the twentieth century. Such uninformed and unexamined anxiety fed white desires to erect walls, gates, or simply put distance between themselves and others. This greater distance only exacerbated phobias, as it physically prevented social, economic, and political engagement that might have broken down perceived barriers and promoted interaction. Because much of the physical distance that had been built between groups was tied to housing investment, many whites were reluctant to take a financial risk to allow "others" to enter white-majority neighborhoods or white-majority schools.[5]

Besides influencing how residents looked at and understood property and property organization, zoning worked "on the ground," sorting people and land uses. Here, zoning and restrictive covenants together acted to organize people across Atlanta's landscape. Both utilized minimum lot sizes, race, and land use (residential versus commercial) to assign people to particular areas of the city. Covenants "protected" exclusive park-neighborhoods from the intrusion of undesirables and helped maintain the park-neighborhood landscape aesthetic that visually marked an exclusive community. In the 1920s, zoning, on the other hand, allowed elites to control the location of particular groups across the whole city. Nonwhites, for example, could be assigned to particular areas where they were less likely, in white elites' thinking, to disturb property values or challenge emerging notions of who did or did not belong in a particular housing landscape.

While zoning withstood a court challenge in *Euclid v. Ambler* in 1926, the courts ruled the racial portions of Atlanta's plan unenforceable in 1924. But even without racial specifications, minimum lot or building sizes served the same end as did restrictive covenants. Property owners remained relatively secure within their property buffers. Even while Atlanta's white elites continued pressing the issue and insisting on segregation ordinances or the adoption of racially restrictive covenants, residential racial segregation by law became less and less necessary. The efforts of white elites to reshape thinking about residential geography, class, and racial landscapes had taken root. To civic elites (and increasingly to middle- and working-class residents), whiteness, designed residential landscapes with a narrow range of housing forms and people, homeownership, single-family homes, restrictive covenants, natural environments, and suburban locations all were related. With one element came the others.

In the 1930s, the HOLC and the FHA had little problem working these equivalencies—homogeneity, whiteness, and stability—into reports, guidelines, and policy documents in the 1930s. The underwriting practices of the New Deal's HOLC and FHA gave federal mandate to assumptions that mono-racial, mono-ethnic, mono-class communities were more economically stable than mixed-race, mixed-class neighborhoods. The HOLC produced residential security maps for 239 cities that assigned grades to thousands of neighborhoods based on the "desirability" of those areas. Although it is not clear how widely distributed or used these maps were, the maps and guides indicate that federal officials and local real-estate interests maintained and enacted the white elite preference for homogeneity and thought in terms of neighborhood effects—not simply about the quality of an individual property. The FHA *Underwriting Manual*, first produced in 1935, followed the same pattern of focusing on neighborhood as well as structure. These federal-policy documents contributed to the exclusionary park-neighborhood ideology in two ways. First, the HOLC documents and the FHA *Underwriting Manual* worked with other policy documents to constantly circulate park-neighborhood sensibilities among policy makers and bureaucrats. In doing so, these documents helped naturalize class and racial exclusion among the purveyors of federal standards and policies and instruct them in a landscape way of seeing and evaluating property. Second, FHA and VA mortgage subsidies provided white home buyers with incentives to adopt exclusionary property frameworks. To qualify for federal mortgage insurance, white home buyers accepted the FHA's landscape and housing preferences and purchased homes in newly constructed, planned subdivisions at the perimeters of cities—subdivisions that carried restrictive covenants limiting facade and landscape changes as well as nonwhite residents. Making the largest and most important investment of their lives, white home buyers had little reason to challenge these mandates, and, indeed, the FHA encouraged whites to defend them. Blacks, on the other hand, were largely ignored by the FHA and the VA, at least until the early 1950s. Black families, instead, were offered public housing, which, prior to 1950, was relegated to Atlanta's core city.

Although federal and local policy favored the development of whites-only park-neighborhoods, the assignment of black families to Atlanta's central city and near suburbs, and the shift of Atlanta's outer suburbs to house the white and well-off, in the 1940s, black leaders organized a home-building plan that ultimately seized portions of the city previously considered for whites only and built new housing for blacks. While black subdivision building had taken place on a limited scale in the 1920s and expanded slowly through the early 1940s, the economic gains from World War II buttressed a new level of neighborhood building after 1945. Beginning in 1947, the Atlanta Urban League worked with bankers, the FHA and the VA, landowners, builders, and home buyers to finance and build single-family-home subdivisions and apartment complexes to meet the acute black housing shortage. Managing and at times manipulating white racism, black leaders secured acres of lands in west Atlanta previously zoned for whites and otherwise worked political and private networks to open up new housing opportunities. Constrained by white power and ideas about the appropriate location for blacks and black housing, though, black families largely remained relegated within Atlanta's three-mile radius. Public-housing policies exacerbated this pattern by siting new projects on Atlanta's west side or adjacent to established black neighborhoods. As a result, from 1900 to 1950,

Atlanta's core city became blacker as whites marked proportionally more of the suburbs for white occupancy through park-neighborhood building and by relying on the class-regulating components of zoning plans and restrictive covenants.

⬥

From 1900 to 1950, Atlanta worked closely with cities across the nation to hone new cultural understandings of residential landscapes and shape white homeowner privilege and power. Increased cooperation between urban leaders during these years did not preclude competition between cities, of course. As the century advanced, cities' concern with image only heightened. As the swapping of city building ideas matured into professional structures and formal exchanges, national patterns of urban development became evident. Cities followed one another in establishing infrastructure or revamping government, fearing that by not keeping up with the latest innovation they would lose industry and people to a nearby rival. Such fears pervaded chamber of commerce and council conversations, and planners learned to use comparisons with other cities to argue for their interests. Atlanta's white elites worked with urbanites across the nation formally through organizations that ranged from the American City Planning Institute to the National Chamber of Commerce. Real-estate dealers read about activities elsewhere through the NAREB journals and attended question-and-answer sessions at land conventions. The federal government provided "how to" and "best practice" pamphlets and hosted Senate hearings and conferences on different housing issues. In the process, urban leaders spread more than best pavement practices, but also discussed the best ways to word segregation ordinances to evade federal court rulings. They collectively developed methods of dividing and controlling property owners and tenants, and they cultivated discursive practices that placed white elites atop an emerging hierarchy of race, property, and performance. Atlanta, then, was not exceptional in its adoption of park-neighborhood and exclusionary ideology from 1900 to 1950. Although the city certainly was informed by New South thinking, in many ways it was representative of what was happening in cities throughout the country.

Legacies

Spatial isolation by race, income, and housing tenure continued to escalate from 1950 onward, a result of policy machinations, the acceleration of subdivision building and related mobilization of park-neighborhood sensibilities, the acceptance of class-based zoning and protective covenants, and the willingness of whites to pack up and move when they thought their property values (or cultural values) were threatened. Racial segregation at the block level remained stable and high in Atlanta from 1940 to 1970. Segregation indices moved from 87.4 in 1940 to 93.6 in 1960, meaning that 93.6 percent of blacks would have had to move to achieve a residential configuration consistent with the regional population demographics. At 93.6, Atlanta was the third most segregated city in the nation in 1970. By 1980, only Cleveland, Chicago, Philadelphia, and St. Louis were more segregated than Atlanta. As Douglas Massey and Nancy Denton note, this meant that in Atlanta, whites and blacks were living in wholly distinct neighborhoods from 1940 onward, a point confirmed by the Institute on Race and Poverty's recent work on white and black neighborhood segregation between 1980 and 2000 (see fig. 7.1).[6]

School desegregation and integration frightened Atlanta's whites and became closely intertwined with concerns about property and property values. Faced with a growing black population and insisting on maintaining racially separate schools, whites worked diligently to maintain whites-only neighborhoods. At the same time, working-class and middle-class whites fought desperately to maintain their "communities" and property values by resisting any population change in their neighborhoods. Whites expanded their use of urban infrastructure and federal programs to buffer white-owned housing from uses and people that middle- and upper-income whites devalued. Unlike zoning or protective covenants, such practices eased white fears through the presence of visible, physical barriers. In 1954 the city had planned to extend one access road in an attempt to physically divide Center Hill and Grove Park from black movement west. By 1960 it was publicly acknowledged that Interstate 20 West was established, in part, as a boundary between white and black communities. In one of the most famous performances, the white residents of Peyton Forest received city approval to erect a concrete and steel roadblock in an attempt to halt black movement into the subdivision. Mayor Ivan Allen Jr. explained that the wall would calm whites and secure land on the wall's north side for much-needed black housing. In other cases, neighborhood "improvement" organizations encouraged whites not to sell or rent to black families, as in the case of West Side Mutual Development Association. Other, more radical whites threatened black newcomers and bombed homes.[7]

Local black leadership and many black residents refused to accept white claims to particular neighborhoods. The Atlanta Urban League worked tirelessly to secure more west-side land for black development, moving steadily into areas whites had refused to concede in the 1922 *Zone Plan*, and, at times, forced the turnover of white homes to blacks. Black leaders and residents alike appeared at public hearings to review the city's *Up Ahead* plan and complained

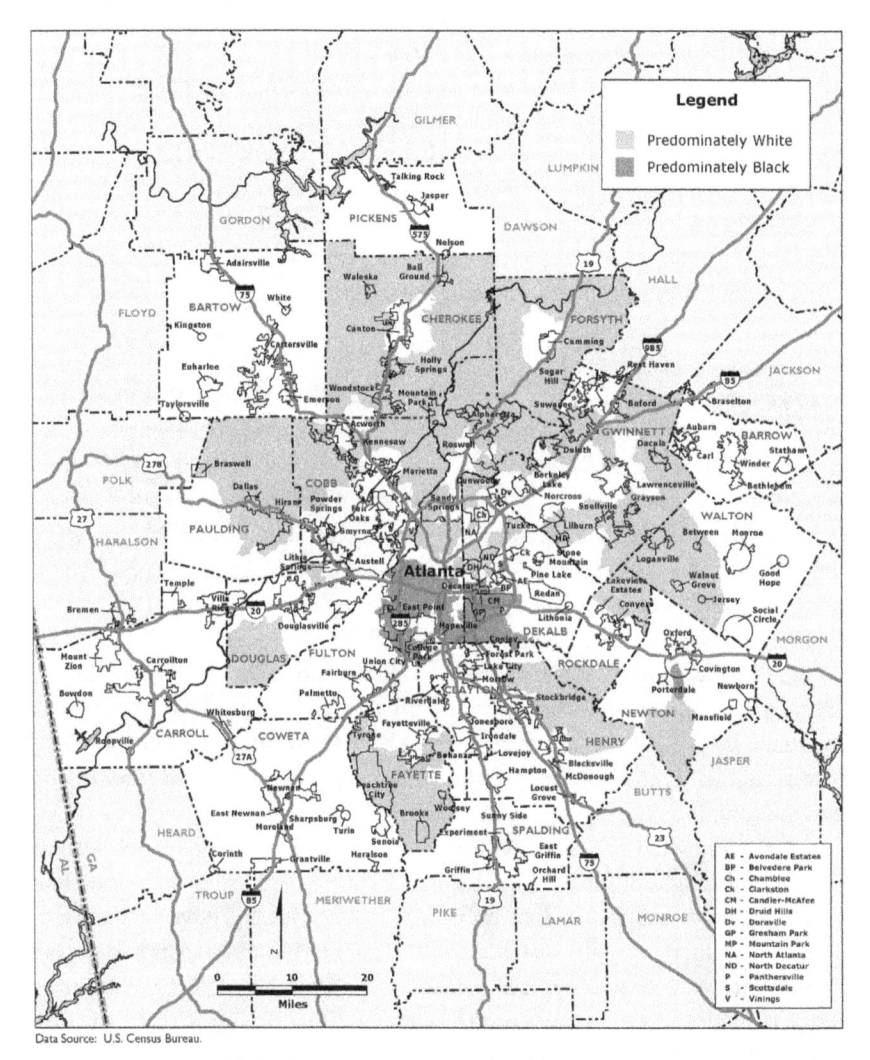

Figure 7.1. "Segregated Neighborhoods: 1980 through 2000." Source: Institute on Race and Poverty, University of Minnesota Law School, Minneapolis.

loudly about planned areas for black housing. Certainly, blacks did not win every battle. Despite various protests, Bedford-Pine lost a significant amount of housing in one phase of urban renewal, for example, and the new "domed stadium" wiped out Lightning and part of Vine City.[8]

Ultimately, whites who insisted on maintaining the racial "integrity" of their neighborhood (or practicing "freedom of association," as they sometimes put it) in the 1960s and later had to do so by moving to new all-white neighborhoods. In the 1960s and 1970s, 160,000 whites fled to the suburbs. From beyond I-285, whites reworked their power strategy. As historian Kevin Kruse elucidates, in the 1960s and 1970s, white suburbanites normalized their racism by infusing the national political structure with their values.[9]

✥

Segregation by income in Atlanta is similarly discouraging. The Brookings Institution found that as income levels bifurcated nationally after 1970, low-income families became more likely to live in lower-income neighborhoods and higher-income families in higher-income neighborhoods. Although the Atlanta metro area experienced new levels of economic growth in the 1980s, the metropolitan area gained more upper-income housing than lower-income housing, which increased housing pressure on the poor. As media outlets covered the city's "resurgence," the share of neighborhoods classified as very low income in the central city expanded. From 1970 to 2000, the proportion of very-low-income neighborhoods in the urban core increased 22 percent, and the share of very-low-income housing rose by 9.3 percent. As recently as 2006, researchers asserted that "the gulf between very low-income neighborhoods and the rest of the city may have widened."[10]

Often overlooked by researchers, tenure status also spatially divides Atlanta and cities throughout the nation. The Joint Center for Housing Studies at Harvard University has shown that homeowners continue to move further outside the city, increasing the distance between themselves and tenants. Whereas homeowners nationally increased their median distance from central business districts (CBD) from 9.8 miles to 13.8 miles over the last thirty years, the distance renters lived from CBDs increased only slightly, from 7.4 miles to 9.4 miles. In Atlanta, rental housing concentrations in the core city often meant poor living conditions; in the mid-1980s, one-fifth of the city's rental properties were substandard. If landlords failed to maintain property, tenants simply could not afford to take action—27,000 families paid more than 35 percent of their income on housing. To be sure, apartment building has increased outside of CBDs, but suburban multifamily housing rents have been weighted toward the high end, meaning this construction does not necessarily meet the needs of median, much less low-income, families. In fact, *affordable* rental housing currently is on the decline.[11]

Atlanta's core city became the repository of the poor even while the amount of low-cost housing decreased, rents increased, and incomes stagnated in Atlanta's central city. Urban renewal programs gutted urban neighborhoods of affordable housing—nine urban renewal projects in the 1960s took nine hundred acres of land for a civic center, a stadium, and business development. Rents rose throughout the 1960s and 1970s (a result of inflation and the tightening housing market), throwing more families into poverty. In the 1970s alone, poverty rates within the city almost doubled. By 2000, housing consumed 34 percent of even median-income households in the ten-county region, regardless of tenure status. But tenure status mattered: 36.9 percent of tenants paid more than 30 percent of their income toward housing, as opposed to only 24.4 percent of owners. Indeed, as the Atlanta Neighborhood Development Partnership (ANDP) observes, lower-income households are "double-burdened"; low-income households have less than 70 percent of their lower-than-average incomes to spend on nonhousing necessities, and fewer housing units are available in the low-income price range. What is more, a discriminatory lending system exacerbates public-policy effects—in the 1980s, five times as many home loans were made in white-majority areas as in black-majority areas.[12]

❖

From the 1930s to the 1980s, white power successfully concentrated its principal fears in the core city, but the post-1990 immigrant influx did not let that power rest easy. Attracted by the job market "outside the perimeter," immigrants from East Asia and Latin America have filled apartments as well as single-family homes and condominiums. Since 2000, Cobb County's immigrant population has increased 45 percent, and Gwinnett County's has increased 72 percent. In 2000, 93 percent of the metro area's Hispanics lived in the suburbs. As in many cities, metro Atlanta's white population has declined as a percentage of the total population. Of the United States' 361 metro areas, 111 saw white population drop from 2000 to 2004. In Atlanta's case, part of the racial and ethnic change is a result of "reverse" black migration, the movement of African Americans from northern and western cities to the South, a phenomenon that began in the 1970s and accelerated in the 1990s. Metro Atlanta had the largest gains in black population of any metro area from 1990 to 2004. An increase of nearly 184,000 between 2000 and 2004 meant that Atlanta had the nation's third-largest black population.[13]

Metro-area home-owning whites entrench when they perceive that their suburban enclaves are threatened. Various incidents highlight how whiteness and privilege remain intertwined not just with tenure status, but with housing performances, and the materiality of the single-family home. Mirroring actions taken from the 1920s through the 1940s, white homeowners respond to "threats" to their property and lifestyle by attacking and attempting to outlaw particular housing practices and particular housing landscapes.

Cracking down on "overcrowding" became the method of choice for eliminating people and practices considered disagreeable by white middle- and upper-class residents. Fulton County pursued one Alcott Drive home after complaints that the home was being used as a rooming house. The head-of-household countered that the home housed his wife, five children, two cousins, and aunt, not nonfamily tenants. But charges against the home and residents appeared more concerned with Hispanic presence than with health; county officials explained that complaints about overcrowding had come from areas where housing had turned over to rental property, "often occupied by immigrant laborers and their families."[14] Similarly, Cobb County code enforcement official Rob Hosack told the *Atlanta Journal-Constitution*, "Ninety-five percent of the complaints I get are white folks complaining about Hispanic folks" (it is not clear how he ascertained race or ethnicity). Like Jackson Hill's whites in the 1910s, Fulton County's whites narrated their neighborhood's history as white with particular housing landscapes and practices—Hispanic extended families did not fit white expectations for housing landscapes.[15]

Such housing performances could be found throughout the metro area (and beyond) in the early years of the twenty-first century. In 2005, Gwinnett County residents complained of overcrowding in one Beaver Bend Estates home. In September, the county restricted homes to eight residents, regardless of family relationship. Again, health did not seem to be the main concern, as one subdivision resident, Jan Marencin, explained to the *Atlanta Journal-Constitution* that she thought the "fleet of pick ups" in the home's driveway "would hurt property values." The home's resident Yolanda Martinez responded to complaints by explaining that their home was a gathering place for family members who live in the area. Just as Atlanta Urban League members used white neighborhood expectations to secure more and better quality housing in the 1940s and 1950s, Martinez mobilized white homeowner expectations to try to deflect criticisms about the number of vehicles parked near her house—she pointed out that her lawn and house were well maintained. Accused of racist and anti-Mexican sentiment, Marencin had the white flexible frame to fall back on, allowing her to adopt particular language and constructs in order to avoid appearing prejudiced. "It's not that we don't want Hispanic residents," she said. Rather, "we don't want 12 cars in a driveway." The white-homeowner practices of Marencin and others had the effect of eliminating nonwhites through seemingly raceless demands about housing performances and proper neighborhood landscapes.[16]

Those People

Housing landscapes and crime, race, ethnicity, and tenure status are linked frequently in popular discourse. In late 2006, when Lawrenceville established a quality of life unit within its police force, *Atlanta Journal-Constitution* writer George Chidi interspersed his story on driver's-license checkpoints with remarks on neighborhood aesthetics. His comments that "a few lawns looked like they needed cutting, if not weeding," helped readers equate safety with proper home and yard maintenance.[17] Similarly, writer Mary Lou Pickel assisted readers in associating day laborers, petty crime, and (again) overcrowding when she noted that police roadblocks and code-enforcement sweeps were "the kind of police attention many residents hope to see in neighborhoods that have attracted large numbers of immigrant day laborers with crowded dwellings."[18] Elsewhere, municipal texts suggested that immigrant presence ruined neighborhoods of single-family homes. In June 2006, the Roswell city council approved an ordinance that limited the number of unrelated people who could live together in a single-family-home neighborhood to three. Officials, adopting language almost to the word of pro-zoning advocates of the 1920s, argued that they "must protect the integrity of single-family neighborhoods."[19] In another case, Richard Whitt's *Atlanta Journal-Constitution* article was structured so that non-middle-class, nonwhite practices were the article's "hook." Whitt opened, "Manuel Flores rents a house in a tidy south Cobb neighborhood, where he lives with his wife, five children, two cousins and the mother of a cousin—10 people in a three-bedroom, one-bath home." Whitt's opener both played to white fears of immigrants (signaled by the use of the householder's Hispanic name) and stereotypes of nonwhite, non-middle-class practices (large families occupying an average-sized home) *and* transmitted white, middle-class practices by emphasizing that housing a sizable extended family was *not* a white, middle-class practice. If officials or neighbors were concerned for the health and welfare of the "overcrowded," that went unstated. Rather, regulations were created and enforced to address the concerns of white homeowners distressed about the proximity of nonwhite families and housing practices they perceived to be inconsistent with homeownership standards. Officials (and the *Atlanta Journal-Constitution*'s journalists) had no problem giving primacy to these concerns at the expense of the nonwhite and the nonpropertied.[20]

Janet Frankston began her 2003 article on housing in the *Atlanta Journal-Constitution* by posing the question, "What's the quickest way to pack a county commission meeting with angry homeowners? Put a rezoning application for an apartment complex on the agenda."[21] By the early twenty-first century, white homeowners had accepted the dictum that multifamily housing was a nuisance and damaged park-neighborhood and single-family-home values. Cherokee County homeowners, for example, fought a proposed 337-unit multifamily project because it purportedly would decrease property values, erode the community, and bring congestion. Marietta officials became alarmed in 2003 when they found that over half the households within city limits rented. City officials set out to increase homeownership—even putting a statement to that effect into their vision statement—and set a homeownership rate goal of 50 percent by 2008.[22]

Responding to what seemed to be a rise in fear of immigrants and tenants in Atlanta's suburbs, *Atlanta Journal-Constitution* editorialist Jim Osterman unmasked the euphemisms used by what he called "cocktail party bigots." "The new slurs," he explained, are "those people" and "apartment people," and they are adopted in social settings where people are not sure whether they can truck out more traditional slurs. He explained that "the truly ingenious thing about these words is you can make your point and still be able to have plausible deniability about using hot-button words. Indeed, if you press someone to explain whom 'apartment people' or 'those people' are, most get flustered and fall into panic-speak. 'You know,' they say, dropping their voice into a stage whisper. 'Those people.'"[23] Osterman's commentary demonstrates the continued prevalence of what Toni Morrison calls "racetalk," the everyday rhetoric by which whites insert racial signs and symbols into conversations that continually position nonwhites at the lower end of the racial hierarchy. In Osterman's telling, such talk continually inserted tenure status into American hierarchies and often blurred the categories between it, race, and ethnicity.[24]

Once school funding became linked to property values and residential geography, school performance became an effective veil for discrimination, a socially acceptable trope that works with tenure status to control space and maintain white privilege.[25] In 2003, Gwinnett County Planning Commissioner Lorraine Green explained that many in her district opposed apartment building because "people associate, rightly or wrongly, that apartments won't be typical middle-to-upper class. . . . You get too many kids in multifamily dwellings, and it tends to lower the performance in the schools." Apartment opponent Cindy Faulkner asserted that apartment dwellers "aren't interested that much in PTAs, the schools, because they know they'll be gone in a year or two."[26] A blog titled "White Flight & Schools," hosted by the *Atlanta Journal-Constitution*, drew many comments asserting that flight to the suburbs was no longer "white," but the language adopted suggests that bias against low-income groups and rental housing remains a constant. One writer lamented, "It's too bad that counties like Dekalb and Athens-Clarke don't stop building lower-income housing. That is what happens. The more lower-income housing you have, traditionally, the poorer the schools in that district perform."[27]

Whites actively defended their white propertied space by cloaking prejudice in socially acceptable terms. By outlawing *apartments* but not *tenants,* homeowners could achieve the same result without appearing prejudiced against particular *people*—in this case, tenants. Then, by deploying a property-values defense ("apartments will lower the value of my house"), homeowners mobilized reasoning associated with neoliberal American values of property and capital accumulation. In practice, these discursive frameworks were multilayered and relied on different ideologies that resonated with different groups.

By the end of the twentieth century, most white Americans believed that the state had a legitimate role to play in protecting the property values of white homeowners. And protecting property values continued to be buttressed by exclusion, the landscape white elites had created in the second and third decades of the twentieth century. Zoning by property size, coupled with restrictive covenants, solidified divisions between classes and, by extension, race and ethnicity. Only heated court battles would open some suburban areas to housing for lower- and middle-income groups. Mount Laurel, New Jersey, spent the 1970s and 1980s fighting the introduction of housing for low- and middle-income groups, a battle that produced a landmark case challenging such zoning regulations. Bedminster, New Jersey, one of the areas in question, required five acres for each single-family home. Chief Justice Robert N. Wilentz spoke to the moral issues at hand when he wrote the New Jersey Supreme Court's opinion for the 1983 ruling, a ruling that upheld a 1975 decision mandating that municipalities' land-use regulation provide a realistic opportunity for low- and moderate-income housing. Wilentz asserted, "The state controls the use of land, *all* of the land. In exercising that control, it cannot favor the rich over the poor. It cannot legislatively set aside dilapidated housing in urban ghettos for the poor and decent housing elsewhere for everyone else."[28] Such battles over housing and economic and racial integration were waged in cities and towns throughout the United States.

Just as white elites successfully manipulated popular understandings of "proper" neighborhood aesthetics and geographies, so too did they manage the discourse around white homeowner privilege. Homeowner subsidies, such as tax write-offs or FHA loan guarantees, are not "welfare" in the American lexicon. The term *welfare* carries the ugly connotation of "freeloader." Such is the case with the label "welfare mother," which is taken to mean someone who takes advantage of government subsidies or someone who sponges off "the system." Whites controlled this imagery, and in doing so white homeowners portrayed themselves as not just elite, but as the *deserving* elite, worthy of entitlements. As historian Kevin Kruse notes, at the end of the twentieth century white elites continued to manufacture simplistic and often aesthetic justifications (deployed as "middle-class values") for their exodus to the suburbs and then their eventual dominance of the Republican Party. Central Atlanta was tagged a "welfare state" by Newt Gingrich, and he explained that Cobb County residents desired neighbors who would "keep their lawn cut." White Cobb County residents worried because "the parents that live in the apartment complexes don't care that the kids don't do well in school and the whole school collapses."[29] The nonwhite and nonpropertied were categorized and labeled in such a way that white homeowners could justify actions and various "protections" that, in reality, served to maintain their position of power in the American economy and social structure. The nonwhite and nonpropertied—welfare mothers, apartment dwellers—were effectively prevented from being assessed on individual merit, and their assigned epithet justified white-imposed actions.

Housing location is no small matter. Where one lives today has great implications for life opportunities. It gives or restricts access to schools, to jobs, to transit. One's neighborhood could be beset with crime, with disease, or with cultural opportunity and community support, all of which have been shown to influence children's intellectual development. Where one lives can be limiting or liberating. Resource distribution varies across the urban landscape, a phenomenon well documented by social scientists. Public-school allocations, for example, are neither equal nor fair. As shown by UCLA policy analysts Meredith Phillips and Tiffani Chin, poor schools have more buildings in need of repair, fewer support staff, and are often overcrowded. Past discriminatory housing practices mean that people of color have to play catch-up in terms of wealth accumulation. Housing segregation past and present means that blacks cannot expect housing investment values to rise as quickly in predominantly black neighborhoods. Lack of savings and credit stifle college opportunities for children. Segregation by race, class, and housing tenure means that metro-area nonwhites are seven times more likely to attend schools in areas of highly concentrated poverty. Less than 10 percent of whites endure this burden.[30]

The crisis wrought by the hyperconcentration of the poor, people of color, and tenants is well documented in the 2004 Annie E. Casey Foundation study of the five Atlanta neighborhoods of Pittsburgh, Mechanicsville, Summerhill/ Capitol Homes, Adair Park, and Peoplestown. In 2000, the child poverty rate of the area reached 59.3 percent—37 points higher than the county's poverty rate. African Americans comprised 92 percent of the area's population, and 66 percent of households rented. (Citywide, 51 percent rented.) The area housed 475 active probationers. Urban renewal ate through this collection of neighborhoods for interstate and other highway construction and then used new urban-entertainment structures such as Turner Field to "buffer" the city from the remaining families.[31]

Purported solutions to urban inequality sustain segregation by class and race and help constitute white power and neoliberal structures. The Atlanta Housing Authority's widely touted program to replace public-housing units with mixed-income, privately managed developments, for example, reportedly was designed to offer healthier and better-serviced housing opportunities for low-income Atlantans. But the plan realized few of its goals beyond helping meet the housing needs of the city's middle-income residents. The authority didn't replace lost units on a one-to-one basis, instead substituting Section 8 vouchers for some units. In an ideal world, the rental vouchers would allow residents to move wherever they liked in the metro area, close to work or to needed services, or to extended family members. But landlords don't have to accept the certificates. Then the certificate pool was depleted. The housing authority failed to effectively track the location of displaced residents, but they do track Section 8 vouchers. One such report showed that most voucher holders remain concentrated in the highest-poverty census tracts in the city. In 2008, voucher recipients are geographically concentrated in predominantly black, high-poverty clusters with unemployment reaching 19 percent.[32]

Protecting Privilege

White homeowners are keenly aware of the value of their spatial location and refuse to give ground, even if expanses of poverty mean economic devastation for a city, even if they mean poor educational opportunities for other children, even if they mean that elderly residents must endure declining infrastructure. Why, despite study after study and court case after court case, do white elites allow hypersegregation by race to continue? Why does class-based exclusion continue?

The "possessive investment in whiteness," as historian George Lipsitz phrases it, is in operation in Atlanta and throughout the United States. Faced with study after study that confirms the inequitable distribution of resources across our nation's cities, white home-owning Americans are unwilling to acknowledge that they actively maintain a system that artificially positions them at the top of a wealthy nation and intentionally positions the nonwhite and nonpropertied below them. When confronted with evidence of systematic and policy-based segregation, white homeowners consistently return to a flexible rhetorical frame of individual achievement and hard work and liberal constructions of equal opportunity. Sociologist Eduardo Bonilla-Silva demonstrates how well-schooled even young whites are in these discourse practices. The college-age students he studied repeatedly deployed phrasings that masked racist beliefs in nonracist language. Karyn McKinney's college-student subjects had moved so far away from understanding the workings of white privilege and structural racism that many saw whiteness as a liability; they were convinced that nonwhites demanded and garnered awards in American society today. But the system of privilege still operates, even if its major players do not recognize it. Sociologists Heather Beth Johnson and Thomas M. Shapiro used in-depth interviewing to show how race remains integral to what whites consider to be a "good school" and a "good neighborhood." But even the few students in McKinney's study who recognized the privileges of whiteness could not offer remedies to structural inequalities, in part because they did not realize that racial inequality as experienced in the United States was, as McKinney says, "much more than a list of inconveniences."[33]

White home-owning Americans resist acknowledging that they benefit from inequality for several reasons. Many simply are not willing to risk their position in American society. Having worked hard all their lives, whites are reluctant to give up a comfortable lifestyle to ensure equal access to countless unknown others. Other whites are unwilling to risk the futures of their children, preferring to let them benefit from the privilege their racial status delivers. This is particularly true when we look at education. As Jonathan Kozol notes in his recent book on the United States' apartheid education system, white elites are unwilling to allow any resource reallocation that threatens the educational opportunities currently afforded *their* children, even if it means claiming resources from other schools. Like Bonilla-Silva's college-age subjects, Kozol's interviewees adopted a flexible rhetorical framework. While the white-dominated schools he examined commonly received significantly higher funding per student than did the minority-dominated schools, the whites questioned balked at reallocating funding more equitably. "Throwing money at the problem" won't solve it, they claimed. Ensuring equality of education belongs on someone else's watch, with someone else's kids. Finally, expectations regarding landscapes and segregation became perceived by many, particularly property-owning whites, as "natural." Bonilla-Silva notes that this is not surprising, this is a "'natural' consequence of a white socialization process." That is, whites teach whites (and nonwhites) these values through formal and informal educational and social structures—and through housing and neighborhood discourses.[34]

Housing Justice

A housing-justice movement requires more than producing more-affordable housing. As long as we tie resources as critical as education to property, we must ensure an equitable spatial distribution of housing types (rental, owned, single-family homes, multifamily housing, studio apartments to three-thousand-square-foot McMansions) across the city. This means rethinking residential zoning. And it means unmasking and breaking down cultural understandings that support and cement racial and class divisions in housing and social practice.

Such proposals are seldom raised. In Atlanta, the Atlanta Neighborhood Development Partnership (ANDP), a collection of housing advocates, university researchers, and social-service providers, has launched a campaign promoting mixed-income housing and new urbanism. Their strategy is not to change extant neighborhoods but to introduce mixed-income communities as new developments are planned and built. Their reasoning is based on metro-area studies of the high cost of commutes for low-income families who are forced to live long distances from work as well as for those middle- and upper-income families who commute in their own vehicles to affordable housing outside the city.[35]

The ANDP does not argue that mixed-income housing is a corrective to spatial injustice. This is a rational choice on their part; such moral arguments fail to persuade. Calls for equitable distribution of resources or equal access to housing don't resonate with most of the populace, particularly white property owners who may stand to lose some of the gains they've made. Rather, their pitch focuses on economics, particularly the white privileged pocketbook, which means pointing out the high cost of transportation and time spent commuting. But high transportation costs hit the average consumer whether he or she is purchasing gas or a Marta card. And they are felt through increased taxes. Leveraging the high day-to-day time and monetary cost of commutes may be the appeal necessary to deliver tangible resources. If effective, such plans could have the effect of balancing resource allocation across the city—providing low-income families with business services, jobs, and good schools; chipping away at the isolation of low-income people of color; and erasing spatial disparities between tenants and property owners.

In the end, such strategies may end up like Morris Brown's bold decision to remain in the Fourth Ward in 1910. Leadership in that case won the battle, defeating property-oriented whites in their attempt to control and remake Jackson Hill into a white park-neighborhood. But white elites reworked their approach and exerted their power elsewhere, never securing the Fourth Ward in the way they had planned but working cultural understandings to attach negative imagery to black housing and black neighborhoods, raise the status of all-white areas and homogeneity in general, and ultimately manufacture other ways to "protect" their neighborhoods from undesirables. New strategies to provide affordable housing in a mixed-income setting may provide real, tangible results for the time being, but they may well leave white homeowner privilege intact, to assert its power in other ways.

Perhaps the greatest challenge is unmasking how cultural power is created, disseminated, and made hegemonic. Here, part of the problem is our own classrooms. Instances of discrimination and the creation, perpetuation, and stabilization of inequitable political, social, cultural, and economic systems are struck from state curriculum and sometimes erased from our textbooks (particularly those that serve precollegiate markets). That said, most curricula are written broadly enough to allow the examination of structural racism and economic inequality within lesson plans. Most curricula allow us to help students trace the impact of jim crow practices through time, to assist students in understanding how federal housing policy had a larger influence on metropolitan racial patterns today than individual failure to achieve the "American dream." These themes do not make their way into precollegiate classrooms in part because we do not introduce them in the college classroom. Or because the students leave the university with a single class in race or multiculturalism. Or because they have only heard scattered references to inequality, and the college curriculum failed to provide any sustained attention to structures of power.

Scholars, teachers, and policy makers have failed to bring this agenda into the schools and into citizens' lives. We have retreated in the face of culture wars and the promotion of hero-based curriculum. We have shrunk in the face of classroom challenges by students who have never heard this narrative and have consequently responded with denial or with accusations of liberal or antiwhite bias. We have retreated to the comfort of writing books to other scholars instead of addressing the greater challenge of popular education and social change. Our unwillingness to confront these challenges in the classroom and in the public arena leaves discourses and landscapes of whiteness and power intact.

APPENDIX

Discerning Atlanta's residential class and racial geography with an eye to street-level organization was the first task in this project. A variety of methods have been used by scholars to assess how groups segregate themselves or others residentially. The index of dissimilarity, for example, measures the extent to which groups inhabit different areas by assessing the fraction of one group that would have to change areas to achieve a distribution consistent with the population distribution city- or regionwide. Social scientists have developed other models, but the census block or tract usually is the smallest area of analysis.[1] But as sociologist Rick Grannis has asserted, community relationships are more often based on street relationships, and racial segregation patterns specifically "reflect an attempt to separate races along the residential street network, not to keep them spatially distant."[2] Olivier Zunz has recognized the importance of neighborhood or block-level organization historically and built his analysis of industrializing Detroit around the street blocks and facing streets that constitute a citizen's immediate environment. Although certainly more difficult and time consuming than studies that use census blocks and tracts, studies based on block and street-front sampling more effectively reflect residential clustering by race, ethnicity, class, and occupational type. Such detail is integral to establishing and detailing which factors become more or less important in neighborhood formation historically. Using blockfront sampling over time, for example, Zunz found that while Detroit's neighborhoods initially formed loosely around ethnic identity, large-scale industrialization at the turn of the century made class a more apparent sorting factor after 1900.[3] Since the 1980s, Geographic Information Systems (GIS) has helped ease the drudgery of such block-level, longitudinal investigations.[4] But although GIS helps facilitate data analysis, historians are still often burdened with building databases of historical information or recreating historical maps.

I used a combination of methods to trace Atlanta's changing human geography over the late 1800s and early 1900s. I used GIS to implement a block-level study of Atlanta from 1891 to 1919. Limitations to the data and changes in the city made any later block sampling too difficult, as I will discuss. Therefore, to discern Atlanta's human and material geography in the late 1930s, I drew on the *Housing: Analytical Maps* (which is based on the U.S. Census block statistics) and the HOLC city survey. Finally, I used the National Historical GIS data and shapefiles to map racial patterns for 1950.[5] Each tool has its own set of limitations. The GIS study is largely limited to data within the city limits, for example. The HOLC city survey provides information on suburban developments as well as the material environment, but does not contain block-level data. In the end, the combination of resources seemed the best route to unmasking Atlanta's changing residential landscape in the early twentieth century.

The balance of this appendix will discuss the design and implementation of the block study from 1891 to 1919.

To understand the street-level organization of Atlanta's population, I located heads of household by "block sampling," that is, taking a sample of city blocks. Blocks, usually consisting of four street fronts but sometimes consisting of only three, were outlined and numbered on a 1920 map. Then sample blocks were selected using the Rand table of random numbers. Once sample blocks were chosen, opposing street fronts were added. The four- (or sometimes three- or five-) sided block and the opposing street fronts served as the unit of analysis (see fig. A1).[6]

Heads of household were located spatially using city directories.[7] A directory's street index organizes information (head-of-household name, race) by street name and address number and indicates cross streets. Thus, with the street index, one can identify the persons who lived on Elm Street between First Street and Second Street with relative ease. The name index can then be used to find the head of household's occupation and place of employment (when available). Critically important, too, the directory indicates whether the household head was identified as "colored."[8] In sum, for any given block in the sample, the city directories reveal who lived on both sides of a street, his or her occupation and place of employment, and whether her or she was "colored" or white.[9]

The disadvantage of using city directories instead of census manuscripts is that *only* the name of the head of household is given; other family members are not included.[10] Consequently, only the residential patterns of the head of household are tracked in the block

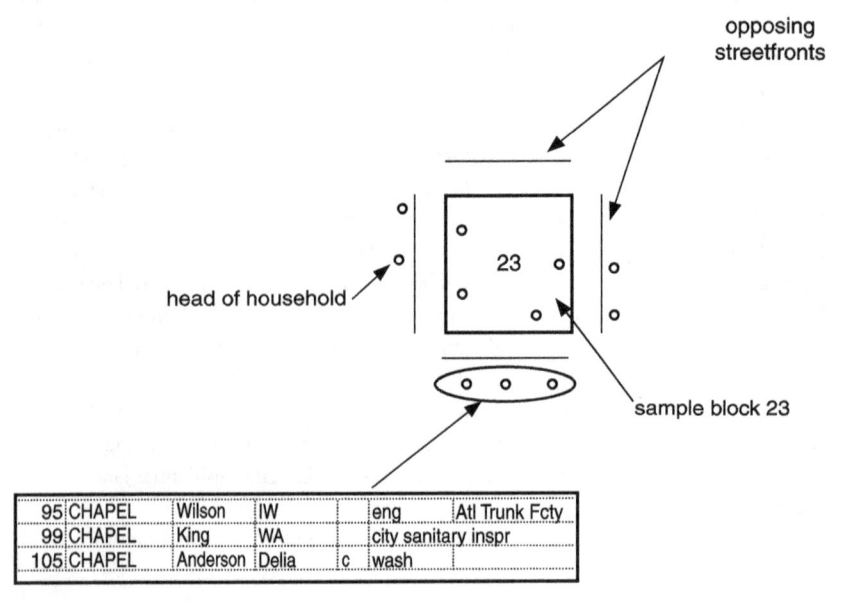

95	CHAPEL	Wilson	IW		eng	Atl Trunk Fcty
99	CHAPEL	King	WA		city sanitary inspr	
105	CHAPEL	Anderson	Delia	c	wash	

Figure A1. Block sample unit

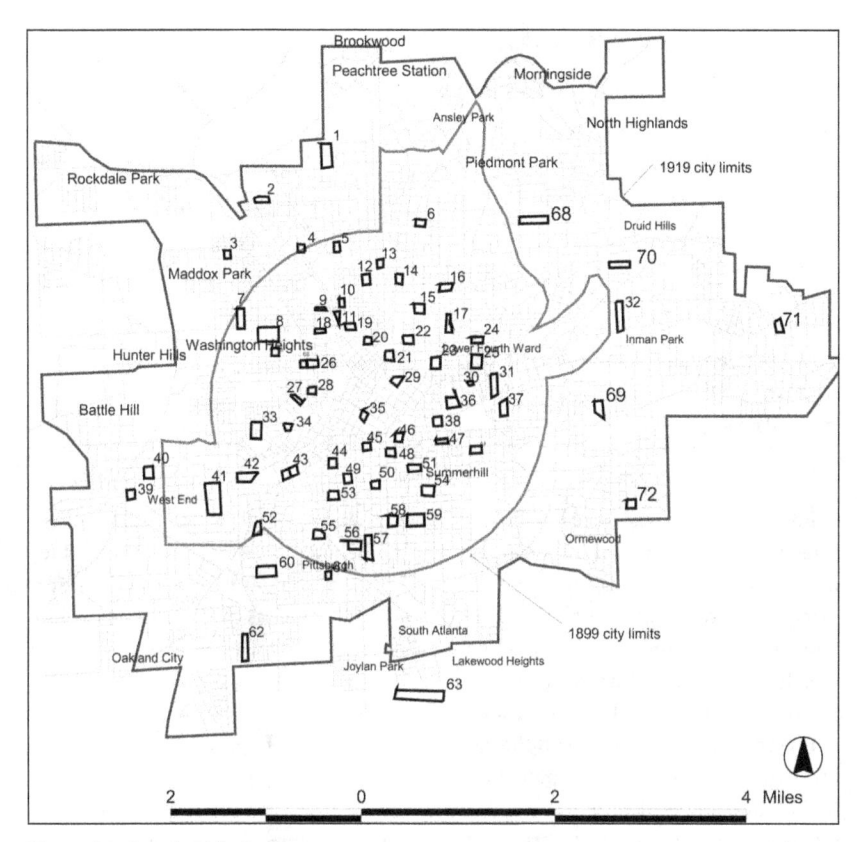

Figure A2. Sampled blocks

study. The project was originally designed to compare residential geographies for 1880, 1900, and 1920. Missing or unavailable directories forced a project change to compare 1891, 1899, and 1919.

Block samples took into consideration the change in city limits over the period studied. In 1880, the city had a circular shape measuring one and one-half miles out from the city center. By 1895, the city measured about two miles out from the city center, but with suburban additions (Inman Park and West End) that jutted from the formerly circular limits. By 1919 the circular city-limit pattern had been eliminated altogether, and the city's limits had more than doubled to include about twenty-six square miles. Samples for 1899 contained the same blocks sampled for 1891 but included additional blocks to account for the increased area of Atlanta after city-limit extensions. Likewise, the samples for 1919 and 1929 included the same blocks included in the 1899 and 1891 samples, plus additional blocks to account for the additional area added to the city. Block samples for each additional area were drawn using the Rand table of random numbers (see fig. A2).[11]

Table A1. Summary of Data Samples

	1891	1899	1919
Dwellings in city (approximate)	13,300	16,500	49,000
Number of blocks sampled that produced reliable occupational data	40	50	63
Number of blocks sampled that produced reliable racial data	39	52	67
Number of points producing occupational data (occupational data set)	649	1,262	2,591
Number of points producing racial data (racial data set)	998	1,644	3,356

Information on heads of household were not available for all sample blocks. To ensure an adequate sample size, blocks and their household data were added to the study until there was racial data returned on at least 6 percent of heads of household.[12] For example, there were approximately 13,300 residences inside Atlanta's city limits in 1891. Block sampling was repeated twice to produce a final sample of 998 data points (a 7.5 percent sample). Some data returned vacancies and businesses, and those data were eliminated. The final data point and block totals are shown in table A1.

I recently attempted to extend the block study to 1929 by simply adding on a decade. (That is, I tried to simply integrate the 1929 data for the already established blocks into the database rather than proceeding through the iterative, data-correction process just discussed.) However, by 1929, Atlanta's street layout and names had changed to the point that I was not confident that particular blocks sampled in 1929 truly matched blocks sampled in 1919 or before. Also, missing data, street name changes, and related issues caused a significant reduction in data returned. After dropping data in which I was not completely confident, the 1929 sample produced data for only 65 percent of the residences captured in the 1919 racial data set, or 3.3 percent of occupied dwellings in 1929. Because of the low return, I decided not to include the 1929 data in the summaries and opted to use other sources to discern post-1930 human geography. Although introducing 1929 data ultimately was a failed project, I explain the attempt here to reiterate the importance of pre- and overall planning of such GIS studies. The year 1929 (or any other years I wanted to study) should have been included in the plan from the beginning so that sample blocks could have been adjusted to return sufficient data for all years under study.

Since Atlanta's street and residential structure changed significantly over the last eighty to one hundred years, a modern Atlanta map would not work for the study. A 1920 Atlanta city map was digitized for use as the map base in the GIS.[13] Because of the excess "dirt" and "noise," the map was redrawn by hand onto vellum and then scanned into a format transferable to computer-aided drafting software (AutoCAD). In AutoCAD, street segments were redrawn. In ESRI ArcInfo, streets were "rubbersheeted" and standardized to a known longitude and latitude.[14]

Heads of household were entered into the GIS as points, in the correct order along a street length, and assigned a unique identification number. Standard street numbering practice placed odd numbers on the right as one proceeded (chronologically) down a street, and this convention was followed. However, directory publishers noted and Sanborn Fire Insurance Company maps confirm that, on occasion, the converse was followed. As such, this is a source of potential error in residence placement. In no cases was it found that odds and evens existed on the same side of the street. Thus, while there is a small possibility that a residence point may be located on the incorrect side of the street, the relation of the houses to one another remains correct—street faces would simply be reversed. In sum, the residence points are located in correct order on their respective street fronts, between the correct intersecting blocks, but not with exact distances between structures. Therefore, distance is accurate to a block length, a measurement suited for this study's potential measurements (distance to work, distance to streetcar lines, and the like).

A database for each sample year includes head of household name, the unique identification number used on the map, and socioeconomic information culled from city directories on that individual—occupation, place of employment, race, and an occupational classification.[15] The identification number linked the database to the head of household points on the map. Starting from the occupational categories produced by Olivier Zunz for his survey of Detroit in 1880 and 1900, a "class" category was added to the database. I sorted occupations into four classifications—high white collar (HWC), low white collar (LWC), skilled (S), and semiskilled and unskilled (L). Job titles found in Atlanta directories but not listed in Zunz's schema were added to the categories based on the following: high white collar included corporate officers, owners of companies requiring large investments of capital, and the heads of household who practiced medicine, dentistry, architecture, or law; low white collar included jobs that did not involve manual work or services; skilled included jobs that required hand production of products or services or that otherwise required training, education, or experience; semiskilled and unskilled included jobs requiring little or no training. Because of the various names used by directories for jobs within a single directory and over time, it became increasingly difficult to maintain the differentiation between skilled, semiskilled, and unskilled worker categories. Thus, I later aggregated those categories into a larger "working class" category (as shown in the table and maps). There were a few cases in each data sample where a classification could not be assigned because of the ambiguity of the job description, and these data were discarded.[16]

Limitations of Data and Structure

In addition to nonstandard street numbering, other circumstances or practices may also have introduced error into the data. In particular, incomplete directory information hampered sampling.[17] In some cases, the directory agent may not have been able to obtain the occupational or employment information. Other factors were apparent, though. In the

1891 sample (the most troublesome of the city directories), scores of black females appeared in the street index (indicating them as head of household), but they were often not included in the person index, and consequently occupation and place of employment were not available. Furthermore, the ubiquitous "washerwoman" who appeared in censuses and later directories was not to be found in the 1891 directory. This oversight of black working women was less apparent in the 1899 and 1919 directories, though it undoubtedly existed. The sources used also did not adequately detail suburban residential patterns. Some suburban residents are mentioned in city directories, but residential listings are usually very general, such as "East Point" or "in country." Also, Atlanta's city maps for that era include very little street geography for areas outside the city limits. Finally, census manuscripts often do not include street or house numbers for suburban residents (and in many cases, streets and house numbers probably did not exist, even in villages and towns). Given these problems, the discussion of the GIS study's findings are limited to the residential geography within the city limits.

Other smaller problems also complicated data collection. Directory agents often spelled names differently on the street and name indexes or used initials sometimes and full names others. Occasionally street intersections were not included. Sometimes the dividing point could be discerned (if a church or business had marked the division in the previous sample, for example). If this was not possible, though, a potential street front of data had to be discarded, which introduced error into the total population of the block.

Finally, it is important to recognize that these aggregated data do not indicate the specific geographic pattern below the four paired block faces composing a neighborhood. That is, the sample block may fall on a dividing line between entirely homogeneous black and white districts; contain black residences behind white residences or along alleyways; include black occupants on one side of the street and white occupants opposite; or contain white and black residences interspersed throughout the block.

Table A2. Working Class by Head of Household

Block	1891	1899	1919
1			100.0%
2			85.7%
3			95.0%
4		76.9%	78.0%
5		88.5%	94.2%
6		0.0%	8.7%
7		84.0%	95.9%
8		66.7%	81.1%
10	66.7%	61.1%	55.6%
11	43.8%	47.8%	50.0%
12		66.7%	57.1%
13	40.0%	0.0%	29.4%
14	0.0%	6.3%	11.8%
15	50.0%	52.0%	6.1%
16	66.7%	57.1%	90.0%
17	65.0%	76.5%	
18	76.0%	86.1%	94.4%
19	60.0%	57.6%	81.4%
20	40.0%	40.0%	60.0%
21	15.0%	11.8%	30.8%
22	85.7%	71.7%	77.9%
23	63.0%	88.3%	94.5%
24	66.7%	36.4%	60.7%
25	76.9%	72.2%	73.7%
26	84.6%	93.0%	100.0%
27		77.0%	87.8%
28	47.6%	61.5%	96.2%
29	28.6%	38.5%	60.0%
30	75.0%	63.6%	90.9%
31	90.5%		
32			27.5%
34	71.4%	65.2%	50.0%
35	16.7%	14.3%	0.0%
36	63.9%		
37	83.3%	81.3%	91.2%
38	70.0%	64.7%	65.0%
39			0.0%
40			36.4%
41			24.0%

Table A2 (*continued*)

Block	1891	1899	1919
42		0.0%	24.5%
43	70.0%	78.7%	88.2%
44	22.2%	53.3%	53.5%
45	18.8%	10.0%	34.5%
46	33.3%	42.4%	62.5%
47	75.9%	55.3%	48.6%
48	61.5%	59.0%	69.4%
49	14.3%	37.5%	42.9%
50	46.7%	46.7%	33.3%
51	100.0%	100.0%	98.2%
52			63.6%
53	82.6%	87.5%	91.4%
54	33.3%		63.6%
55		91.7%	100.0%
56		62.5%	81.4%
57		28.6%	43.7%
58	40.0%	54.5%	60.0%
59	100.0%	94.7%	91.3%
61			38.6%
63			64.3%
64			37.0%
65		100.0%	96.0%
66	94.1%	73.9%	69.2%
67	100.0%	71.4%	83.3%
68			12.5%
69		100.0%	100.0%
70			0.0%

Based on data available in *Atlanta City Directory*. Block nine was eliminated from occupational analysis.

Table A3. Percent White and Nonwhite by Head of Household

Block	% White by head of household 1891	1899	1919	Block	% Nonwhite by head of household 1891	1899	1919
1			100.0%	1			0.0%
2			33.3%	2			66.7%
3			100.0%	3			0.0%
4		100.0%	100.0%	4		0.0%	0.0%
5		100.0%	100.0%	5		0.0%	0.0%
6		100.0%	100.0%	6		0.0%	0.0%
7		100.0%	93.9%	7		0.0%	6.1%
8		100.0%	52.4%	8		0.0%	47.6%
9	25.8%	25.0%	5.3%	9	74.2%	75.0%	94.7%
10	95.0%	91.2%	95.8%	10	5.0%	8.8%	4.2%
11	87.5%	96.8%	100.0%	11	12.5%	3.2%	0.0%
12		3.7%	4.5%	12		96.3%	95.5%
13	83.3%	100.0%	100.0%	13	16.7%	0.0%	0.0%
14	87.5%	100.0%	100.0%	14	12.5%	0.0%	0.0%
15	52.2%	63.6%	100.0%	15	47.8%	36.4%	0.0%
16	53.8%	44.4%	16.5%	16	46.2%	55.6%	83.5%
17	38.5%	28.6%	0.0%	17	61.5%	71.4%	100.0%
18	64.0%	54.2%	2.5%	18	36.0%	45.8%	97.5%
19	93.9%	90.2%	100.0%	19	6.1%	9.8%	0.0%
20	87.9%	97.3%	96.8%	20	12.1%	2.7%	3.2%
21	96.3%	100.0%	100.0%	21	3.7%	0.0%	0.0%
22	37.2%	36.4%	44.7%	22	62.8%	63.6%	55.3%
23	22.2%	23.6%	2.4%	23	77.8%	76.4%	97.6%
24	81.5%	94.4%	6.7%	24	18.5%	5.6%	93.3%
25	46.3%	31.4%	4.2%	25	53.7%	68.6%	95.8%
26	32.6%	25.0%	7.9%	26	67.4%	75.0%	92.1%
27		46.7%	1.0%	27		53.3%	99.0%
28	72.0%	58.5%	18.9%	28	28.0%	41.5%	81.1%
29	95.0%	75.0%	100.0%	29	5.0%	25.0%	0.0%
30	46.7%	62.5%	0.0%	30	53.3%	37.5%	100.0%
32			100.0%	32			0.0%
33		25.0%	37.2%	33		75.0%	62.8%
34	81.8%	89.3%	91.2%	34	18.2%	10.7%	8.8%
35	93.8%	100.0%	100.0%	35	6.3%	0.0%	0.0%
37	95.6%	100.0%	100.0%	37	4.4%	0.0%	0.0%
38	83.3%	100.0%	100.0%	38	16.7%	0.0%	0.0%

Table A3 (*continued*)

Block	% White by head of household 1891	1899	1919	Block	% Nonwhite by head of household 1891	1899	1919
39			100.0%	39			0.0%
40			100.0%	40			0.0%
41			100.0%	41			0.0%
42		100.0%	100.0%	42		0.0%	0.0%
43	35.0%	46.6%	48.3%	43	65.0%	53.4%	51.7%
44	91.7%	94.4%	100.0%	44	8.3%	5.6%	0.0%
45	95.0%	95.5%	100.0%	45	5.0%	4.5%	0.0%
46	67.5%	77.8%	58.8%	46	32.5%	22.2%	41.2%
47	82.0%	100.0%	100.0%	47	18.0%	0.0%	0.0%
48	57.1%	48.1%	30.2%	48	42.9%	51.9%	69.8%
49	100.0%	93.8%	95.8%	49	0.0%	6.3%	4.2%
50	61.9%	66.7%	100.0%	50	38.1%	33.3%	0.0%
51	5.0%	0.0%	2.6%	51	95.0%	100.0%	97.4%
52			100.0%	52			0.0%
53	45.9%	39.0%	41.2%	53	54.1%	61.0%	58.8%
54	100.0%	100.0%	75.9%	54	0.0%	0.0%	24.1%
55		75.0%	0.0%	55		25.0%	100.0%
56		100.0%	100.0%	56		0.0%	0.0%
57		100.0%	100.0%	57		0.0%	0.0%
58	57.1%	100.0%	96.0%	58	42.9%	0.0%	4.0%
59	0.0%	0.0%	0.0%	59	100.0%	100.0%	100.0%
60			100.0%	60			0.0%
61			68.6%	61			31.4%
63			100.0%	63			0.0%
64			100.0%	64			0.0%
65		0.0%	0.0%	65		100.0%	100.0%
66	95.5%	90.3%	88.9%	66	4.5%	9.7%	11.1%
67	100.0%	50.0%	76.9%	67	0.0%	50.0%	23.1%
68			100.0%	68			0.0%
69			100.0%	69			0.0%
70			100.0%	70			0.0%

Based on data available in *Atlanta City Directory*.

NOTES

Abbreviations

ACCM	Atlanta City Council Minutes
AHC	Kenan Research Center, Atlanta History Center Archives, Atlanta
MARBL	Manuscripts, Archives, and Rare Book Library, Emory University, Atlanta
LOC	Library of Congress, Washington, D.C.
NAR	National Association of Realtors Archives, Chicago.
NARA	National Archives and Records Administration, College Park, Maryland
NREJ	*National Real Estate Journal*
NUL-SRO	National Urban League, Southern Regional Office Collection
OA	Records of the Olmsted Associates, Manuscripts Division, LOC
RWWLA	Robert W. Woodruff Library Archives, Atlanta University Center, Atlanta
SFIM	Sanborn Fire Insurance Maps, City of Atlanta, Ga. (Teaneck, N.J.: Chadwick-Healey, 1983), microfilm

Introduction

1. Annie E. Casey Foundation, Atlanta Civic Site, *Neighborhoods Count;* Logan, *Ethnic Diversity Grows; Atlanta Journal-Constitution,* January 14, 2001. The story of post-1950 redevelopment and the removal of the poor and black from near Atlanta's central business district is told in L. Keating, *Atlanta.* See chap. 5 in particular.

2. U.S. Census Bureau, DP-1, Profile of General Demographic Characteristics: 2000; U.S. Census Bureau, DP-3, Profile of Selected Economic Characteristics: 2000.

3. Atlanta was similar to many cities in its heterogeneity prior to 1920. See Gotham, *Race, Real Estate,* 27–32; Hanchett, *Sorting Out,* 48–67; Katzman, *Before the Ghetto,* 67–80; Kusmer, *Ghetto Takes Shape;* Osofsky, *Harlem,* 83–85; Spear, *Black Chicago,* 41–43; G. C. Wright, "NAACP and Residential Segregation," 39.

4. On the move within history to address questions of hegemony as well as everyday enactments of power and resistance, see Gunn, "From Hegemony to Governmentality."

5. Kruse, *White Flight;* Lassiter, *Silent Majority;* Warner, *Streetcar Suburbs;* Zunz, *Changing Face of Inequality.*

6. Kirby, *Darkness at the Dawning;* Silver, "Racial Origins of Zoning"; Silver, *Twentieth-Century Richmond.*

7. Power, "Apartheid Baltimore Style"; Rice, "Residential Segregation by Law"; G. C. Wright, "NAACP and Residential Segregation." See also Grossman, *Land of Hope;* and Sides, *L.A. City Limits.* On the role of housing inequality in urban riots and civil disturbances, see, for example, Tuttle, *Race Riot.* The Atlanta riot did cause a backlash against

blacks, but in the form of social reform, segregated streetcars, and restriction of voting rights. "Reformers" targeted saloons and brothels, and housing "reform" was not proposed. See Bauerlein, *Negrophobia*; Crowe, "Racial Massacre in Atlanta"; Crowe, "Racial Violence and Social Reform"; Godshalk, *Veiled Visions*; Mixon, *Atlanta Riot*.

8. Garb, "Drawing the 'Color Line.'" On race and real-estate practices, see also Gotham, *Race, Real Estate*.

9. Hirsch, "Choosing Segregation"; Hirsch, "'Containment' on the Home Front"; Hirsch, "Less than *Plessy*"; Hirsch, *Making the Second Ghetto*.

10. Hillier, "Residential Security Maps"; Jackson, *Crabgrass Frontier*. Hillier challenges the argument that the HOLC maps were used widely in redlining. Hillier, "Redlining." David Freund discusses the continuing popular resistance to the idea of federal involvement in housing segregation. See Freund, *Colored Property*, chap. 3 in particular. See also Kimble, "Insuring Inequality."

11. Kruse, *White Flight*; Wiese, *Places of Their Own*. On the intersections of class, race, and housing, see also Lassiter, *Silent Majority*; Seligman, *Block by Block*; Sugrue, *Origins of the Urban Crisis*.

12. Nicolaides, *My Blue Heaven*; Freund, *Colored Property*. Geographers Marc Choko and Richard Harris have also traced how cultures of property vary across time and space. See their "Local Culture of Property."

13. Bonilla-Silva, *Racism without Racists*; Duncan and Duncan, *Landscapes of Privilege*; Roediger, *Wages of Whiteness*. On the construction of race in the post-Reconstruction South, see Hale, *Making Whiteness*; and Ritterhouse, *Growing Up Jim Crow*.

14. On color-blind racism, see Bonilla-Silva, *Racism without Racists*. See also Freund, *Colored Property*; Kimble, "Insuring Inequality"; Kruse, *White Flight*.

15. Blomley, "Mud for the Land," 557.

16. Bonilla-Silva, *Racism without Racists*; Duncan and Duncan, *Landscapes of Privilege*; Feagin, *Racist America*; Lipsitz, *Possessive Investment in Whiteness*.

17. On the development of elite suburban neighborhoods, see Sies, "'God's Very Kingdom'"; Sies, "Paradise Retained"; Sies, "Toward a Performance Theory." On suburban park-neighborhood design, see Fishman, *Bourgeois Utopias*; Fogelson, *Bourgeois Nightmares*; Jackson, *Crabgrass Frontier*, 87–102; Lyon, "Frederick Law Olmsted," 166–67.

18. My definition of a *landscape way of seeing* is informed by various works exploring cultural landscapes, including Cosgrove, *Social Formation and Symbolic Landscape*; Duncan, *City as Text*; Duncan and Duncan, *Landscapes of Privilege*. While most geographers use the phrase "landscape way of seeing" to discuss larger, natural environments and social systems, I find the concept appropriate for explaining how civic elites began to look at, shape, and/or appropriate residential landscapes and neighborhoods.

19. Federal interest in homeownership dates to the early formation of the United States, when Thomas Jefferson articulated a desire for a country of independent yeomen. See Cullen, *American Dream*, 138–41.

20. On the variety of American suburban patterns, see Archer, *Architecture and Suburbia*; Hayden, *Building Suburbia*; Stilgoe, *Borderland*.

21. Kruse, *White Flight*, chap. 6.

22. Bourdieu, *Practical Reason*, in particular chap. 2 and the appendix. See also Swartz, *Culture & Power*, in particular chap. 5.

23. As Eduardo Bonilla-Silva and David G. Embrick argue, *white habitus* produces group (white) identity while simultaneously masking whites' racialization of their own group. Moreover, white *habitus* internalized in childhood is likely to carry over into adulthood, despite any change in one's racial milieu. See Bonilla-Silva and Embrick, "'Every Place Has a Ghetto'"; Bonilla-Silva, Goar, and Embrick, "When Whites Flock Together." David Freund also argues that housing policies helped reshape white thinking about property. See Freund, *Colored Property*, 4–10.

24. Constance Perin argues that rather than the possession of property itself, it is the status incurred by qualifying for credit sufficient to purchase a home that confers status. Thus, indebtedness has become a social good, and, in Perin's words, "one's credibility as a fully social person is enhanced by the long-term obligation represented in homeownership" (*Everything in Its Place*, in particular chap. 2, quote from 76).

25. See Mills, "White Supremacy as Sociopolitical System," 45–46.

26. Freund, *Colored Property*, in particular chap. 6.

27. Duncan and Duncan, *Landscapes of Privilege*, 184–85.

Chapter One. Housing the City, 1865 to 1910

1. Trowbridge, *South*, 458.

2. Reid, *After the War*, 356.

3. Andrews, *South since the War*, 838.

4. Hubner, "Atlanta," 377. Andrews also noted that the streets were narrow and irregular (*South since the War*, 840).

5. Atlanta was similar to many cities in its heterogeneity prior to 1920. See Gotham, *Race, Real Estate*, 27–32; Hanchett, *Sorting Out*, 48–67; Katzman, *Before the Ghetto*, 67–80; Kusmer, *Ghetto Takes Shape*, 12–13; Osofsky, *Harlem*, 83–85; Spear, *Black Chicago*, 41–43; G. C. Wright, "NAACP and Residential Segregation," 39. Tera W. Hunter discusses the geography of Atlanta washerwomen and other African American household workers in *To 'Joy My Freedom*.

6. Hammond to Adair, February 10, 1865, quoted in Garrett, *Atlanta and Environs*, 1:671.

7. *Daily Intelligencer*, July 21, 1865, July 25, 1865; Ingersoll, "City of Atlanta"; Humphreys, *Yellow Fever and the South*.

8. Belissary, "Rise of Industry," 197.

9. Don Doyle refers to the years between 1880 and 1940 as a "crucial intermediate stage" in southern urban development. Only 8.7 percent of the South's population lived in urban places in 1880. By 1920, the South's urban population approached 20 percent. The region suffered uneven development, though, and not all southern cities experienced growth (*New Men, New Cities*, 3, 9–10).

232   Notes to Chapter One

10. Garrett, *Atlanta and Environs*, 1:712.

11. On organizing for business development in Atlanta, see Doyle, *New Men, New Cities*, 139–44.

12. ACCM, Annual Reports, 1889, AHC.

13. ACCM, Annual Reports, Report of Committee on Manufacturing and Statistics, 1889, AHC.

14. ACCM, Annual Reports, Report of the Committee on Manufactures, Statistics, Freight Rates, and Transportation, 1895, AHC

15. Deaton, "Atlanta during the Progressive Era," 101–2; Doyle, *New Men, New Cities*, 143. Word of the city and its advantages also spread informally by way of conventioneers attending national and regional meetings held in the growing city, including the International Cotton Spinners Conference (1907), the National Society for the Promotion of Industrial Education Conference (1908), the Conference for Education in the South (1909), and the Boll Weevil Conference (1910). ACCM, Annual Reports, Committee on Manufactures, Freight Rates and Statistics, 1903, AHC.

16. ACCM, Annual Reports, Committee on Manufactures, Freight Rates and Statistics, 1903, AHC

17. Wotton, "New City of the South," 148–49, 152; J. M. Russell, *Atlanta*, 14–37. On railroad development in the immediate postwar South, see Woodward, *Origins of the New South*, 120–24.

18. Map of Atlanta, 1889, H. G. Saunders, AHC. The map collection is organized by decade.

19. ACCM, August 7, 1882, AHC; ACCM, October 2, 1882, AHC. Smoke problems continued to plague the city, however.

20. ACCM, July 16, 1883, AHC; ACCM, December 3, 1883, AHC.

21. ACCM, November 3, 1884, AHC; ACCM, July 7, 1884, AHC; ACCM, Annual Reports, Report of Chief Sanitary Inspector, 1890, AHC.

22. United States Department of Labor, *Bulletin* 22 (Washington, D.C. 1899), 406, quoted in McLeod, "Black and White Workers," 29.

23. Quoted in Maclachlan, "Women's Work," 49.

24. Hickey, *Hope and Danger*, 16, 26–27.

25. Garrett, *Atlanta and Environs*, 1:713; McLeod, *Workers and Workplace Dynamics*, 8–9, 29, 57, 73, 81, 152.

26. J. M. Russell, *Atlanta, 1847–1890*, 164–65, 169–231.

27. On Atlanta's "new men," see Doyle, *New Men, New Cities*, 99–103; J. M. Russell, *Atlanta, 1847–1890*, 161–68.

28. Kuhn, *Contesting the New South Order*, 21.

29. Ibid., 20, 24–25.

30. Dittmer, *Black Georgia*, 32; Kuhn, *Contesting the New South Order*, 26–29; Mixon, *Atlanta Riot*, 11; J. M. Russell, *Atlanta, 1847–1890*, 213–15.

31. J. M. Russell, *Atlanta, 1847–1890*, 213–15.

32. Trowbridge, *South*, 455.
33. Reid, *After the War*, 357.
34. *Atlanta Constitution*, January 2, 1880.
35. Such building is readily visible on 1891 Sanborn Fire Insurance Company maps.
36. Homeownership is discussed further in chap. 4. In 1900, 18.6 percent of Atlanta households owned their home. In contrast, homeownership rates were 38 percent in Dayton, Ohio; 39 percent in Detroit; and 27 percent in Pittsburgh (Gries and Taylor, *How to Own Your Home*, viii).
37. *Atlanta City Directory*, 1867, 1870, 1890.
38. *Curbstoner* was a disparaging term, rooted in the mid-nineteenth century, for a broker without an office, or one without training or experience. On the professionalization of the real-estate industry, see Fishman, *Bourgeois Utopias*, 121–54; Hornstein, *Nation of Realtors*. The National Real Estate Association fell apart in 1894 and regrouped as the National Association of Real Estate Boards in 1908.
39. *Atlanta Constitution*, January 4, 1891.
40. *Atlanta Constitution*, March 11, 1892; March 20, 1892.
41. Vol. 11, p. 66, 1892, land district 14, land lot 12, G. W. Adair Plat Map Books, AHC.
42. *Atlanta Constitution*, July 9, 1882.
43. *Atlanta Constitution*, July 8, 1869.
44. *Atlanta Constitution*, July 9, 1882.
45. *Atlanta Journal*, May 14, 1884.
46. *Atlanta Constitution*, April 12, 1885.
47. *Atlanta Constitution*, September 2, 1868.
48. Rental advertisement and price list, box 3, MSS 23 Jack Adair Collection, AHC.
49. Quoted in Davies, *Real Estate*, 32.
50. *Atlanta Constitution*, November 17, 1890.
51. Robson and Rivers invoice to A. H. Benning, July 24, 1905, MSS 60, box 7, folder 1, AHC.
52. G. W. Adair ledger for W. A. Russell, MSS 71, box 3, folder 7, AHC.
53. T. J. Cheshire to Mrs. M. R. Benning, October 21, 1916, MSS 60, box 7, folder 1, AHC.
54. Robson and Rivers invoice to A. H. Benning, July 24, 1905, MSS 60, box 7, folder 1, AHC.
55. Compiled from Atlanta building permits (microfilm), AHC and Atlanta city directories.
56. City of Atlanta, Building Permits (microfilm), 74, 76, 78, and 80 Rawson Street, August 11, 1905, AHC. City of Atlanta, Building Permits (microfilm), 68 and 70 Hayden Street, May 16, 1906, AHC. The building permit collection is organized by address. Race and occupation can be found in the Atlanta city directories. On builder Alexander Hamilton, see Dorsey, *To Build Our Lives Together*, 50.
57. City of Atlanta, Building Permits (microfilm), AHC. The building permit collection is organized by address.

58. Board of Trade, *Cost of Living*, 56–58; Warner, *Streetcar Suburbs*, chap. 5.

59. SFIM, 1899, 1911.

60. SFIM, 1899.

61. Vol. 9, p. 68, land division 87, land lot 14, G. W. Adair Plat Books, AHC. Today the phrase "south Atlanta" is used to describe much of the metropolitan area south of I-20. This is not to be confused with the subdivision South Atlanta that was developed in the 1880s. SFIM, 1892, 1899, 1911.

62. The primary exception to this statement is the northern corridor flanking Peachtree Street. Upscale, all-white development of this rather narrow sector until the turn of the twentieth century suggests that it was (officially or unofficially) considered off-limits for the development of worker housing.

63. Scholars have examined the concentration of textile workers in Atlanta's Cabbagetown neighborhood, the neighborhood adjacent to the Fulton Bag and Cotton Mills. See Grable, "Other Side of the Tracks."

64. *Atlanta City Directory*, 1899; SFIM, 1899.

65. For further discussion of washerwomen, their work, and their social and residential patterns, see Maclachlan, "Women's Work." Also on the geography of women and their work, see Board of Trade, *Cost of Living*, 57. *Negro tenements* and *Negro shanties* were terms commonly used on Sanborn Fire Insurance Maps. See SFIM for the variation in housing. As will be demonstrated, however, this variegated housing pattern was much less prevalent toward the 1920s.

66. *Atlanta Journal*, January 15, 1905.

67. *Atlanta Journal*, July 7, 1907.

68. *Atlanta Constitution*, October 9, 1910.

69. *Atlanta Journal*, April 16, 1905.

70. *Atlanta Journal*, May 18, 1911.

71. *Atlanta Journal*, January 15, 1905.

72. *Atlanta Journal*, April 12, 1903.

73. *Atlanta Journal*, January 1, 1905.

74. Board of Trade, *Cost of Living*, 56.

75. Ibid., 56.

76. Because city directories commonly overlooked alley dwellers (whom narrative sources often identify as black), these figures are likely conservative regarding the number of black households.

77. In 1890 and 1900, blacks comprised between 40 and 43 percent of the population. I arbitrarily established that greater or equal to 65 percent was "disproportionately black" for city blacks in this period.

78. Manuscript Census, City of Atlanta, Fulton County, Georgia, U.S. Census of Population (1900), microfilm.

79. *Atlanta City Directory*, 1899; Manuscript Census, City of Atlanta, Fulton County, Georgia, U.S. Census of Population (1900), microfilm.

Chapter Two. Atlanta, Park-Neighborhoods, and the New Urban Aesthetic, 1880 to 1917

1. Cooper, "Beautification of Cities," 274.
2. Ibid., 285.
3. H. Johnson, "Atlanta." See also *Atlanta Constitution*, March 13, 1909, for Coca-Cola magnate and chamber of commerce president Asa Candler's discussion of his visits to and observations of Los Angeles, San Antonio, San Francisco, and New Orleans.
4. I use the term "taste culture" instead of simply "taste" to emphasize the development of a collective understanding by a particular group.
5. Sies, "North American Suburbs," 328–30; Sies, "Paradise Retained," 168–69.
6. Gwendolyn Wright, *Building the Dream*, 82.
7. Fishman, *Bourgeois Utopias*, 123; Gwendolyn Wright, *Building the Dream*, 82–89; Gwendolyn Wright, *Moralism and the Model Home*, 10. Other authors who discuss the ideal housing landscape as developed and experienced in the nineteenth and early twentieth century United States include Handlin, *American Home*; Jackson, *Crabgrass Frontier*, particularly chaps. 3 and 4. Other authors detailing subdivision building include Burgess, *Planning for the Private Interest*; Fogelson, *Bourgeois Nightmares*; A. D. Keating, *Building Chicago*; Weiss, *Rise of the Community Builders*; Worley, *J. C. Nichols*.
8. Jenkins, *Lawn*, 21, 31, quote from 21.
9. Fishman, *Bourgeois Utopias*, 125, 129–32, quote from 130. On the development of elite suburban neighborhoods, see Sies, "'God's Very Kingdom,'" 3–31; Sies, "Paradise Retained," 165–91; Sies, "Toward a Performance Theory," 197–207. On suburban park-neighborhood design, see Fishman, *Bourgeois Utopias*; Fogelson, *Bourgeois Nightmares*; Jackson, *Crabgrass Frontier*; Lyon, "Frederick Law Olmsted and Joel Hurt," 166–67.
10. Quoted in Garrett, *Atlanta and Environs*, 2:69–70.
11. On the relationship between transportation networks and suburban development in Atlanta in this period, see Klima, "Breaking Out." Historian Robert Fishman notes that railroad developers identified land profits as a major driver of railroad building rather than the efficient transfer of people and goods (*Bourgeois Utopias*, 142–45). Here I draw on Jon Peterson's assertions regarding Frederick Law Olmsted, whom Peterson contends believed that comprehensive planning could encompass any restricted physical area, not just a city. See Peterson, "Frederick Law Olmsted," 47.
12. Klima, "Breaking Out."
13. Burnham suggested that Hurt consider hiring Frederick Law Olmsted to design Hurt's second development, Druid Hills. Lyon, "Frederick Law Olmsted and Joel Hurt," 166–67. On Burnham, see Hines, *Burnham of Chicago*; C. S. Smith, *Plan of Chicago*.
14. Quoted in Beard, "Hurt's Deserted Village," 196.
15. Beard, "From Suburb to Defended Neighborhood: Change in Atlanta's Inman Park and Ansley Park," 52; Beard, "Hurt's Deserted Village," 196.
16. Beard, "From Suburb to Defended Neighborhood: Change in Atlanta's Inman Park and Ansley Park," 44–45, 47–49.

17. *Atlanta Journal,* May 6, 1889.

18. Beard, "From Suburb to Defended Neighborhood: Change in Atlanta's Inman Park and Ansley Park," 89–93.

19. Beard, "From Suburb to Defended Neighborhood: The Evolution of Inman Park and Ansley Park," 118.

20. Beard, "From Suburb to Defended Neighborhood: Change in Atlanta's Inman Park and Ansley Park," 29, 99, 86–87; Beard, "From Suburb to Defended Neighborhood: The Evolution of Inman Park and Ansley Park," 118, 120; Beard, "Hurt's Deserted Village," 203; Lyon, "Frederick Law Olmsted and Joel Hurt," 165–93. Rick Beard concludes that the financial depression of the 1890s and subsequent design decisions altered the character of the area and caused the neighborhood's demise ("Hurt's Deserted Village," 195–221).

21. SFIM, 1911.

22. Sies, "Toward a Performance Theory," 199. Other scholars dispute that a consensus emerged regarding suburban preferences by this period. See Wiese, "Stubborn Diversity."

23. John Olmsted to Joel Hurt, April 4, 1902, job file 71, "Kirkwood Land Company," microfilm reel 10 (container B13), OA.

24. Hurt formed the Kirkwood Land Company in the 1890s and hired Frederick Law Olmsted to develop a preliminary plan for Druid Hills in 1893. Financial setbacks stalled the project, and Hurt relaunched in 1902 by inviting John C. Olmsted to consult with him and Atlanta engineer Solon Z. Ruff. The Olmsted Brothers firm revised and implemented the plans over the next few years. Olmsted retired in 1895 and died in 1903. Lyon, "Frederick Law Olmsted and Joel Hurt," 171, 173, 176–77.

25. Richard Peters, George Adair, Hannibal Kimball, and Edwin Ansley appeared to think similarly to Hurt. However, these developers left few manuscript resources that would reveal their development or investment philosophies.

26. Lyon, "Frederick Law Olmsted and Joel Hurt," 178.

27. John Olmsted to Joel Hurt, April 4, 1902, job file 71, "Kirkwood Land Company," microfilm reel 10 (container B13), OA.

28. *Atlanta Journal,* May 19, 1908, quoted in Lyon, "Frederick Law Olmsted and Joel Hurt," 179.

29. According to historian Elizabeth Lyon, Hurt only planned to develop four hundred to six hundred acres but was later persuaded by the Olmsteds to plan to develop the entire tract ("Frederick Law Olmsted and Joel Hurt," 171, 178). Different sections of Druid Hills opened periodically over the next few years. Druid Hills Heights set up in booth 88 at the Own Your Own Home exposition in 1922, advertised "winding drives, shrubs, and trees," and specified that the prices of new homes ranged from $5,000 to $10,000. *Atlanta Constitution,* May 7, 1922.

30. John S. Olmsted notes, July 25, 1902, job file 71, "Kirkwood Land Co.," microfilm reel 10 (container B13), OA.

31. *Atlanta Constitution,* April 27, 1904.

32. *Atlanta Constitution,* March 22, 1908; Beard, "From Suburb to Defended Neighborhood: Change in Atlanta's Inman Park and Ansley Park," 110, 113, 118–19; Preston, "Parkways, Parks," 230. Whitten is discussed in greater detail in chap. 5.

33. *Atlanta Constitution,* April 27, 1905.

34. *Atlanta Constitution,* April 20, 1909.

35. Beard, "From Suburb to Defended Neighborhood: Change in Atlanta's Inman Park and Ansley Park," 155–56. Another gauge of status, documented by historian Rick Beard, is the fact that one out of six Ansley Park residents built servants' quarters; in contrast, about one in ten Inman Park residents included servants' quarters in their plans (173).

36. *Atlanta Constitution,* April 27, 1904; Sies, "City Transformed," 84–85.

37. I use the terms *deed restrictions, covenants, deed covenants,* and *restrictive covenants* synonymously. Subdividers used deed restrictions to maintain the character of the neighborhood at least until all the lots were sold.

38. John Olmsted to Joel Hurt, May 13, 1905, job file 71, "Kirkwood Land Company," microfilm reel 10 (container B13), OA.

39. That is, as long as the deed restrictions were in force. Beard, "From Suburb to Defended Neighborhood: Change in Atlanta's Inman Park and Ansley Park," 116, 203; Lyon, "Frederick Law Olmsted and Joel Hurt," 181–82. For the most extensive analysis of such restrictions, see Fogelson, *Bourgeois Nightmares.* Nationally, such restrictions could be found in the early 1800s, but they were rare until the 1880s and did not become widespread until the building boom of the 1920s. See also Stach, "Deed Restrictions."

40. Fogelson, *Bourgeois Nightmares,* 137–50.

41. *Proceedings of the First Annual Convention Conferences of the Homebuilders and Subdividers Division of the National Association of Real Estate Boards* (Omaha: NAREB, 1923), 71.

42. Robert Fogleson argues that restrictive covenants were an attempt to ensure permanence, and that such covenants were insurance against unwanted change (*Bourgeois Nightmares,* 32).

43. Joel Hurt to Messrs. Olmsted Brothers, May 13, 1905, job file 71, "Kirkwood Land Company," microfilm reel 10 (container B13), OA.

44. Olmsted Brothers to Joel Hurt, May 16, 1905, job file 71, "Kirkwood Land Company," microfilm reel 10 (container B13), OA; Beard, "From Suburb to Defended Neighborhood: Change in Atlanta's Inman Park and Ansley Park," 56.

45. Olmsted Brothers to Joel Hurt, April 4, 1902, job file 71, "Kirkwood Land Company," microfilm reel 10 (container B13), OA; Lyon, "Frederick Law Olmsted and Joel Hurt," 181–82; Beard, "From Suburb to Defended Neighborhood: Change in Atlanta's Inman Park and Ansley Park," 49, 56.

46. Olmsted Brothers to Joel Hurt, April 4, 1902, job file 71, "Kirkwood Land Company," microfilm reel 10 (container B13), OA.

47. Draft deed restrictions, stamped received May 16, 1905, job file 71, "Kirkwood Land Company," microfilm reel 10 (container B13), OA According to historian Robert Fogelson, restrictions limiting sale or rental of properties to nonwhites were still rare in the 1890s (*Bourgeois Nightmares,* 95). Patricia Stach found likewise in her study of Columbus; racially restrictive covenants become much more evident after World War I ("Deed Restrictions," table 1). However, as late as 1935, Druid Hills excluded apartments and demanded minimum buildings costs, but did not specifically exclude nonwhites. See Warranty Deed,

Druid Hills to R. C. Avrett, May 23, 1935, folder 8, box 6, Asa Griggs Candler papers, MARBL.

48. Other agents raced property as well, some more than others. One typical investment property ad concluded with "white tenants, on car line with paved streets" (*Atlanta Constitution,* December 1, 1907). However, Ansley's attention to race should not be read as a belief in limiting black access to particular parts of the city; Ansley publicly, vocally opposed the racial zoning plan proposed in 1922 because it would interfere with the free operation of real estate markets.

Real-estate agent George Adair did not finance elite park-neighborhoods, but like Ansley, he invested extensively in elite property as well as property intended for rental-housing development for black and white tenants. His holdings in Druid Hills can be seen on plats held in the Asa Griggs Candler Papers, MARBL. Other details of his investments can be found in deed records, building permits, and tax records. Unfortunately, historians have failed to investigate how real-estate financiers, agents, and owners may have dealt in both rental and owner-occupied markets that marketed housing by race and class, so it is difficult to assess if Ansley is exceptional in this practice or if his practices reflect a larger trend.

49. *Atlanta Constitution,* July 15, 1923.

50. *Atlanta Constitution,* April 20, 1909.

51. Quoted in Schuyler, *New Urban Landscape,* 65–66.

52. Baldwin, *Domesticating the Street;* Schuyler, *New Urban Landscape,* 66.

53. On urban competition and the image of the city as circulated through the media, see Brownell, *Urban Ethos in the South,* 58–60, 81–95.

54. Mayfield, "Progress in Lynchburg, Virginia," 135.

55. Annual Address of Mayor Livingston Mims, Annual Reports, 1901, ACCM, AHC.

56. *Atlanta Constitution,* April 6, 1902; ACCM, September 2, 1907, AHC; *Atlanta Constitution,* October 2, 1907. On urban tourism, see Cocks, *Doing the Town.*

57. "California's Exhibit at the Atlanta Exposition," *Overland Monthly and Out West Magazine* 27 (April 1896): 396.

58. ACCM, May 23, 1907, AHC; ACCM, June 3, 1907, AHC; ACCM, November 17, 1902, AHC; ACCM, November 18, 1907, AHC; ACCM, November 23, 1903, AHC; ACCM, February 1, 1904, AHC; ACCM, April 4, 1904, AHC; ACCM, May 16, 1904, AHC; Cronon, *Nature's Metropolis,* 343.

59. ACCM, Report of the Building Inspector, 1901, AHC.

60. H. Johnson, "Atlanta," 3.

61. John MacVicar, "The League of American Municipalities," *10th Annual Convention of the League of American Municipalities* (1906), n.p.

62. ACCM, August 19, 1901, AHC; ACCM, July 7, 1902, AHC; ACCM, July 21, 1902, AHC; ACCM, August 21, 1905, AHC; ACCM, September 17, 1906, AHC; ACCM, August 19, 1907, AHC; ACCM, August 21, 1905, AHC; *Atlanta Constitution,* December 6, 1907; "Annual Meeting of the National Tuberculosis Association," *City Builder* 1 (1916): 14; Clinton Rogers Woodruff to Ernest Kontz, May 1, 1906, MSS 545, Kontz Family Papers, box 1, folder 4, AHC. The Kontz scrapbooks (contained in the same manuscript collection)

indicate that Ernest Kontz actively followed and publicly commented on civic affairs, including Atlanta's consideration of the commission form of government, the Bleckley civic plaza proposal, and zoning.

63. On the "park ideology" within the United States, see Schuyler, *New Urban Landscape*, particularly chaps. 4 through 7. On parks as precursors to City Beautiful, see Peterson, *Birth of City Planning*, particularly 39–47. On the City Beautiful movement, see Boyer, *Dreaming the Rational City*; Peterson, *Birth of City Planning*; Wilson, *City Beautiful Movement*. Although scholars and contemporaries declared City Beautiful over by about 1910, as David L. A. Gordon notes, planners like Edward Bennett (who worked with Daniel Burnham and was appointed consultant to the Federal Plan Commission) worked in the City Beautiful tradition for four decades afterward ("Introducing a City Beautiful Plan").

64. N. A. to Joel Hurt, March 13, 1902, job file 2740, "Atlanta Park System," microfilm reel 97 (container B131), OA. Hurt was appointed to head Atlanta's park commission in 1903.

65. Joel Hurt to Olmsted Brothers, January 26, 1905, job file 2740, "Atlanta Park System," microfilm reel 97 (container B131), OA. Although Atlanta's park commission reportedly had been in operation since around 1880, it had generated little activity, and even the Olmsteds had trouble securing early reports of commission work. Notes from March 14, 1901, job file 2740, "Atlanta Park System," microfilm reel 97 (container B131), OA.

66. Joel Hurt to Olmsted Brothers, January 4, 1905, job file 2740, "Atlanta Park System," microfilm reel 97 (container B131), OA.

67. Joel Hurt to Olmsted Brothers, January 26, 1905, job file 2740, "Atlanta Park System," microfilm reel 97 (container B131), OA.

68. Joel Hurt to Olmsted Brothers, March 7, 1905, job file 2740, "Atlanta Park System," microfilm reel 97 (container B131), OA; Joel Hurt to Olmsted Brothers, January 4, 1905, job file 2740, "Atlanta Park System," microfilm reel 97 (container B131), OA. Woodward had opposed the granting of franchises to Hurt's Atlanta Railway and Power Company. Deaton, "James G. Woodward," 13, 14. See also D'Avino, "Atlanta Municipal Parks," 111. St. Louis also experienced tension between the working class and the middle class on City Beautiful "reform." See Rafferty, "Orderly City, Orderly Lives."

69. Joel Hurt to Olmsted Brothers, January 4, 1905, job file 2740, "Atlanta Park System," microfilm reel 97 (container B131), OA.

70. Brownell, *Urban Ethos in the South*, 47–60.

71. Watts, "Characteristics of Candidates," 196.

72. Quoted in Watts, "Characteristics of Candidates," 52, 53, 143, 203.

73. W. G. Cooper to Frederick Law Olmsted, September 21, 1906, job file 2740, "Atlanta Park System," microfilm reel 97 (container B131), OA.

74. *Atlanta Constitution*, January 1, 1908.

75. *Atlanta Journal*, January 24, 1908.

76. *Atlanta Constitution*, January 1, 1908; "Atlanta Spirit," 48.

77. Quoted in Preston, "Parkways, Parks," 231.

78. *Atlanta Constitution*, April 1, 1907; November 17, 1907.

79. Schuyler, *New Urban Landscape*, 65–66. Similarly, Janet Daly found that Omaha "reformers" were more interested in combating "ugliness" than in social reform ("Early City Planning Efforts").

80. Dan Carey to Hon. George Eubanks, March 27, 1911, box 4, folder 6, MSS 70, Aldine Chambers Collection, AHC.

81. Schuyler, *New Urban Landscape*, 59–64.

82. *Atlanta Journal*, April 29, 1908.

83. *Atlanta Journal*, March 7, 1910.

84. *Atlanta Journal*, March 6, 1910.

85. *Atlanta Constitution*, May 21, 1911.

86. *Atlanta Journal*, March 4, 1910.

87. *Atlanta Constitution*, May 21, 1911.

88. *Atlanta Journal*, February 27, 1910.

89. *Atlanta Journal*, March 2, 1910.

90. H. Johnson, "Atlanta," 4.

91. *Atlanta Journal*, March 6, 1910.

92. *Atlanta Journal*, February 27, 1910.

93. See the descriptions in, for example, *Atlanta Journal*, March 3, 1910; March 6, 1910; March 2, 1910; February 27, 1910.

94. Otis, "Atlanta's Plan," 3–5, 9, 10, AHC. Various correspondence related to these later proposals can be found in box 1, MSS 18, Bleckley Family Papers, AHC. *Atlanta Constitution*, August 21, 1927; March 20, 1930.

95. *Atlanta Journal*, March 6, 1910.

96. Scholars have used the term *planning* to mean many different things. In this work, it is used broadly, to indicate the process of establishing any city function, by any type of actor—business person, politician, engineer, etc.

97. Here Atlanta's elites are consistent with Charlotte's elites, who, as described by Thomas Hanchett, shifted their expectations of park-neighborhood communities in the early 1900s (*Sorting Out*, 146–64).

Chapter Three. A City Divided, 1910 to 1917

1. M. M. Smith, *How Race Is Made*, chap. 3, particularly p. 54. For a description of dance halls and other businesses on Decatur Street, see Goodson, *Highbrows, Hillbillies, and Hellfire*. As in other cities, blacks regularly protested streetcar segregation in Atlanta. Dittmer, *Black Georgia*, 16–17, 234–37; Hunter, *To 'Joy My Freedom*, 99.

2. Dittmer, *Black Georgia*, 20–21.

3. M. M. Smith, *How Race Is Made*, chap. 3.

4. Allen, *Without Sanctuary*; Litwack, *Trouble in Mind*, 280–325; Williamson, *Crucible of Race*, 84–85.

5. Baker, *Following the Color Line*, 39–44; Meier, "Negro Class Structure"; Meier and Lewis, "History."

6. Mixon, *Atlanta Riot*, 28–33, quote from 32–33. After blacks successfully challenged white Democratic and Republican attempts to eliminate blacks from the state legislature, whites intermittently erected barriers to black voting, depending on whether they sought to use or to exclude the black vote. Democrats imposed whites-only primaries in 1872 and again in 1892, and poll taxes were implemented in 1868 and 1877. The 1908 Felder-Williams bill introduced "good character" and property ownership requirements. As historian Allison Dorsey observes, the good-character requirements allowed whites to use their stereotypes of black males as lewd and immoral to prevent blacks from voting. Dorsey, *To Build Our Lives Together*, 128–30.

7. Dittmer, *Black Georgia*, 96–104, quotes from 65 and 101; Mixon, *Atlanta Riot*, 53–60.

8. Goodson, *Highbrows, Hillbillies, and Hellfire*, 148–49.

9. On the Atlanta race riot, see Bauerlein, *Negrophobia*; Crowe, "Racial Massacre in Atlanta"; Crowe, "Racial Violence and Social Reform"; Godshalk, *Veiled Visions*; Mixon, *Atlanta Riot*.

10. Mixon, *Atlanta Riot*, 116–27. James English chaired the biracial "committee of ten" that formed to shape postriot news about Atlanta, ensure calm, and negotiate black-white relations.

11. McElreath, *Walter McElreath*, 145.

12. Ibid., 146. The *Atlanta Constitution* referred to the neighborhood as "Jackson Hill" and "the Jackson Hill section." The paper documented improvements to the area in the May 16, 1886, edition.

13. Quoted in Porter, "Black Atlanta," 89, 92.

14. SFIM, 1899, 1911. Grace Methodist Church moved to a larger building one block north on Highland and Boulevard in 1906. Regarding Auburn Avenue, see Alexa Henderson and Eugene Walker, *Sweet Auburn: The Thriving Hub of Black Atlanta* (Atlanta: Martin Luther King Jr. National Historic Site and Preservation District; U.S. Department of the Interior, n.d.); White, "Black Sides of Atlanta," 216–18.

15. *Atlanta City Directory*, 1899; SFIM, 1899, 1911.

16. On the teaching and learning of racial etiquette, see Ritterhouse, *Growing Up Jim Crow*.

17. McElreath, *Walter McElreath*, 149.

18. *Atlanta City Directory*, 1906; SFIM, 1899, 1911;

19. Building Permits (microfilm), AHC. The building permit collection is organized by address. *Atlanta City Directory*, 1909; *Atlanta City Directory*, 1910.

20. *Atlanta Constitution*, March 4, 1910.

21. *Atlanta Journal*, January 12, 1910; March 1, 1910. Caused by faulty wiring, the fire damaged the top floors of Gaines Hall, displaced female dormitory students, and caused $25,000 in damage. Insurance covered the building repairs, and local residents assisted the young women in recovering lost possessions.

22. Sewell, "Morris Brown College," 136; Sewell and Troup, *Morris Brown College*, 61; *Atlanta Journal*, January 12, 1910; Rothman, "Curriculum Formation," 13, 16; Dorsey, *To Build Our Lives Together*, 97–98. The African Methodist Episcopal conference supplied

the school's first land and buildings. Intended for any African American seeking an education, the school accepted students of all levels and served about one thousand students annually in the early 1900s.

23. On the development of black colleges in Atlanta, see Dorsey, *To Build Our Lives Together*, 95–100.

24. Vol. 14, p. 78, G. W. Adair Plat Books, AHC.

25. ACCM, Annual Reports, Sanitary Committee, 1896, AHC; ACCM, Inaugural Address of Mayor Evan P. Howell to the General Council of the City of Atlanta, 1903, AHC. By 1899, Mayor James G. Woodward was able to celebrate the completed Mitchell Street viaduct, exclaiming that the event "marked an epoch in the history of the western portion of the city" (ACCM, Annual Reports, 1899, AHC). ACCM, Address by Mayor Woodward, City of Atlanta, Annual Reports, 1904, AHC.

26. *Atlanta Journal*, January 28, 1910.

27. *Atlanta Constitution*, February 5, 1910.

28. *Atlanta Journal*, January 28, 1910.

29. *Atlanta Constitution*, February 3, 1910.

30. *Atlanta Constitution*, February 5, 1910.

31. *Atlanta Georgian*, February 19, 1910. Stinson's attacks were constant. In a letter to the *Atlanta Constitution* (February 3, 1910), Stinson averred, "[Smith] has played the role of firebrand, destructionist and hinderer in the communities where he has gone since becoming Bishop."

32. *Atlanta Journal*, January 28, 1910.

33. English was a partner in the Kirkwood Land Company, which established Druid Hills. Samuel Inman and Walker Inman helped Joel Hurt acquire the land for Inman Park. Beard, "From Suburb to Defended Neighborhood: Change in Atlanta's Inman Park and Ansley Park," 41–43.

34. *Atlanta Journal*, March 2, 1910.

35. E. W. Lee to E. T. Ware, March 18, 1910, Atlanta University President Records, folder 1, box 34, RWWLA; *Atlanta Journal*, March 1, 1910; March 2, 1910; ACCM 22 (March 7, 1910), 333, AHC; *Atlanta City Directory*, 1910.

36. E. W. Lee to E. T. Ware, March 18, 1910, Atlanta University President Records, folder 1, box 34, RWWLA. Morris Brown was owned and administered by Georgia's AME Church, which meant that land transactions and other such decisions had to be approved by the council bishops, who were spread across the state. E. V. Carter to C. S. Smith, April 9, 1910, C. S. Smith Papers, microfilm reel 5, "Morris Brown College, 1908–10," Center for Archival Collections, Jerome Library, Bowling Green State University, Bowling Green, Ohio.

37. *Atlanta Independent*, April 23, 1910; June 4, 1910. Stinson took his industrial interests elsewhere and founded the Atlanta Normal and Industrial Institute in 1914. Sewell and Troup, *Morris Brown College*, 134.

38. *Atlanta Constitution*, October 10, 1910.

39. *Atlanta Constitution*, October 12, 1910.

40. *Atlanta Georgian,* October 12, 1910.

41. *Atlanta Constitution,* October 12, 1910.

42. *Atlanta Constitution,* October 10, 1910; *Atlanta Independent,* October 15, 1910; *Atlanta Georgian,* October 12, 1910. If Mitchell and McElreath were correct, streetcar development helped the black middle class as well as the white middle class to access new housing. Scholars have cited tight housing markets as well as economic status change as reasons blacks moved into formerly white-occupied housing. See Klima, "Breaking Out."

43. *Atlanta Independent,* October 15, 1910. Despite Davis's choice of words, blacks did not *own* much of that property, but they rented it. Manuscript Census, City of Atlanta, Fulton County, Georgia, U.S. Census of Population (1910), microfilm T-624.

44. *Atlanta City Directory* 1911; *Atlanta City Directory,* 1912.

45. On racial social codes, see Litwack, *Trouble in Mind.*

46. This change was calculated using the 1899 and 1910 *Atlanta City Directory.*

47. *Atlanta Constitution,* September 16, 1906.

48. *Atlanta Journal,* April 2, 1910.

49. The *Atlanta Constitution* covered the passage of the Baltimore ordinance and then its later court challenges. See the December 20, 1910, edition. The newspapers also covered other cities' ordinances and court challenges. On St. Louis, for example, see *Atlanta Constitution,* April 18, 1916.

50. Petition to the Mayor and City Council, Baltimore City Archives, Mahool Files, file 406 (July 5, 1910), quoted in Power, "Apartheid Baltimore Style," 298–99. Nightingale, "Transnational Contexts," 667; Boger, "Meaning of Neighborhood"; Rice, "Residential Segregation by Law," 181–84. Louisville adopted a segregation ordinance in 1914. See Blum, "Race"; G. C. Wright, "NAACP and Residential Segregation," 44.

51. *Atlanta Independent,* June 14, 1913; June 21, 1913.

52. *Atlanta Constitution,* June 17, 1913; December 20, 1910; City of Atlanta, Ordinance Book, vol. 11, pp. 250–51, 263, AHC. The city amended the ordinance a few months later to forbid the introduction of blacks into white blocks or whites into black blocks without the approval of the people living in the "adjoining houses or buildings." The ordinance allowed for blacks to live on "white blocks" if they resided in servants quarters.

53. Booker T. Washington to Benjamin Jefferson Davis, June 19, 1913, in *Booker T. Washington Papers,* vol. 12 (Chicago: University of Illinois Press, 1982), 201–2. What is more, Washington's phrasing in his opening line, "I see that the city government of Atlanta has just passed a segregation act," and the fact that there are no references to Atlanta's segregation history elsewhere in his papers suggests that Washington was unaware of the movement toward residential segregation in Atlanta. If there was a response by the city's African American community to the Jackson Hill agreement, it had not been loud enough to draw Washington's attention.

Historian Louis Harlan notes that toward the end of Washington's life he moved toward the NAACP position against segregation laws, noting that Washington went so far as to pen, "my view of segregation laws" (published posthumously in the *New Republic*), in

244   Notes to Chapter Three

which he "opposed residential segregation laws so forthrightly that the NAACP Board of Directors voted to reprint [the article] as a pamphlet" ("Secret Life of Booker T. Washington," 413). Booker T. Washington, "My View of Segregation Laws," *New Republic* 5 (September 1915), 113–14.

54. The *Crisis,* the *Chicago Defender,* and the *Pittsburgh Courier* regularly reported black news from other cities, towns, and counties. And the *Crisis* regularly listed civil rights violations throughout the country.

55. *Atlanta Constitution,* June 13, 1913.

56. *Atlanta Journal,* June 13, 1913; *Atlanta Constitution,* June 13, 1913; February 13, 1915; Flint, "Zoning and Residential Segregation," 309–10; *Carey v. Atlanta* 143 Ga. 192 (1915).

57. *Atlanta Independent,* October 15, 1910; *Atlanta Independent,* June 14, 1913; *Atlanta Independent,* June 21, 1913; *Atlanta Independent,* October 9, 1915. Davis also pointed out that a small number of people were driving the racial segregation movement. *Atlanta Independent,* October 23, 1915.

58. *Atlanta Constitution,* October 6, 1915.

59. *Atlanta Constitution,* October 9, 1915. This agreement evolved into an Atlanta ordinance that Georgia courts upheld in 1917.

60. *Atlanta Independent,* October 16, 1915.

61. *Atlanta Independent,* October 9, 1915; October 16, 1915; *Atlanta Constitution,* October 9, 1915.

62. *Atlanta Independent,* October 23, 1923.

63. *Atlanta Independent,* October 16, 1915; October 23, 1915.

64. *Atlanta Independent,* October 23, 1915.

65. *Atlanta Constitution,* April 2, 1916; April 4, 1916; *Atlanta Journal,* August 31, 1917; *Atlanta Constitution,* November 6, 1917. The Georgia Supreme Court upheld the 1916 segregation ordinance in *Harden v. Atlanta* in 1917. City of Atlanta, Ordinance Book, vol. 11, pp. 391–93, AHC; *Harden v. Atlanta,* 147 GA 248 (1917). In 1917, the U.S. Supreme Court ruled that Louisville's segregation ordinance, and other cities' ordinances by extension, were unconstitutional in *Buchanan v. Warley.* Flint, "Zoning and Residential Segregation," 318. *Buchanan v. Warley,* 245 U.S. 60 (1917). On *Buchanan v. Warley,* see Power, "Apartheid Baltimore Style," 311–14; Rice, "Residential Segregation by Law," 179–99; G. C. Wright, "NAACP and Residential Segregation," 39–54.

66. Variations in housing stock can be readily seen in Sanborn Fire Insurance Maps. SFIM, 1899, 1911. See the appendix for a complete explanation of the city block sampling method. It is also important to remind readers that although the city was more mixed by race in 1891, that does not mean that blacks could live where they pleased. While entire neighborhoods were less often identified as "black," individual homes, or rows of shanties, *were* intended for occupation by one race or another.

67. Manuscript Census, City of Atlanta, Fulton County, Georgia, U.S. Census of Population (1910), microfilm. Baltimore's segregation campaign, in contrast, was pushed by the city's "middling stratum." See Boger, "Meaning of Neighborhood," 238.

68. Quoted in G. C. Wright, "NAACP and Residential Segregation," 42.
69. Quoted in "The Ghetto," *Crisis* 1 (January 1911), 11.
70. Laurenti, "Effects of Nonwhite Purchases," 324.
71. Long and Johnson, *People vs. Property,* 5–6.
72. Helper, *Racial Policies,* chaps. 4 through 6.
73. *Atlanta Journal,* June 17, 1917.
74. *Atlanta Constitution,* June 17, 1913; City of Atlanta, Ordinance Book, vol. 11, pp. 250–51, 263, AHC.
75. *Atlanta Constitution,* June 13, 1913.
76. *Atlanta Independent,* June 14, 1913.
77. *Atlanta Independent,* June 21, 1913.
78. On Baltimore's use of conflict rhetoric to buttress the case for segregation, see Nightingale, "Transnational Contexts," 675–76. George Wright argues likewise regarding Louisville's ordinance. The ordinance's preface stated that it was "an ordinance to prevent conflict and ill-feeling between the white and colored races in the city of Louisville, and to preserve the public peace and promote the general welfare" ("NAACP and Residential Segregation," 45). Daniel Kelleher also notes that while St. Louis appealed to fears of race riots, community concerns were largely economic ("St. Louis' 1916 Residential Segregation Ordinance").
79. Bauerlein, *Negrophobia,* particularly 3–132; Crowe, "Racial Violence and Social Reform," 254; Dorsey, *To Build Our Lives Together,* chaps. 5 and 6; Goodson, *Highbrows, Hillbillies, and Hellfire,* 42–43 and 148–49.
80. *Atlanta Constitution,* June 17, 1913.
81. Ibid.
82. Quoted in *Carey et al. vs. Atlanta,* 143 GA 192 (1915).
83. *Atlanta Independent,* October 9, 1915.
84. *Harden v. City of Atlanta,* 147 GA 248, 93 SE 401 (1917).
85. *Glover et al. v. City of Atlanta,* 148 GA 385, 96 SE 562 (August 13, 1917); *Buchanan v. Warley,* 245 U.S. 60 (1917).
86. *Atlanta Journal,* May 22, 1917.
87. *Atlanta Journal,* May 23, 1917; *Atlanta Independent,* May 26, 1917.
88. *Atlanta Journal,* May 23, 1917; May 22, 1917.
89. *Atlanta Journal,* May 24, 1917.
90. *Atlanta Journal,* May 13, 1917; June 9, 1917.
91. *Atlanta Journal,* June 16, 1917.
92. *Atlanta Journal,* May 27, 1917.
93. *Atlanta Journal,* May 26, 1917.
94. Ibid.
95. *Atlanta Journal,* June 10, 1917; May 24, 1917; May 25, 1917.
96. *Atlanta Journal,* June 16, 1917.
97. *Atlanta Journal,* June 5, 1917.
98. *Atlanta Independent,* May 26, 1917.

99. *Atlanta Independent*, June 23, 1917.
100. *Atlanta Journal*, June 22, 1917.
101. *Atlanta Journal*, June 17, 1917. Key would later be elected mayor of Atlanta.
102. *Atlanta Journal*, July 17, 1917.
103. Quoted in *Atlanta Independent*, June 30, 1917.
104. *Atlanta Journal*, May 26, 1917.
105. *Atlanta Journal*, July 17, 1917.
106. *Atlanta Journal*, June 3, 1917.
107. *Atlanta Journal*, May 27, 1917.
108. *Atlanta Constitution*, June 11, 1913; June 13, 1913.
109. *Atlanta Journal*, April 11, 1917; *Atlanta Constitution*, June 11, 1913; June 13, 1913.
110. *Atlanta Constitution*, April 11, 1916; November 6, 1917.

Chapter Four. Homeownership and Park-Neighborhood Ideology, 1910 to 1933

1. Monchow, "Review of John P. Dean."
2. Dreier, "Status of Tenants," 181–82; Krueckeberg, "Grapes of Rent"; Mitchell, "Historical Overview of Federal Policy," 39–40.
3. Richard Hopkins found that in the late 1800s, just over half of male workers left Atlanta within the first ten years after their arrival ("Status, Mobility"). On residential mobility, see also Tobey, Wetherell, and Brigham, "Moving Out," 1404–5. One *Atlanta Constitution* writer blamed Atlanta's low homeownership rates on the city's high black population, "among which homeownership [was] rare." However, homeownership rates among both blacks and whites during the early twentieth century are difficult to locate. Nationally, the *Negro Year Book* estimated that 23 percent of black-occupied homes were owned by their residents in 1910, 28 percent in 1930. The first time specific census data is available, 1940, only 4.7 percent of Atlanta's total number of occupied dwellings were owned by blacks, and 12.5 percent of black-occupied homes were owned outright or in mortgage by their residents. *Negro Year Book* data given in Burroughs et al., *Negro Housing*, 79; U.S. Bureau of the Census, *Sixteenth* Census, vol. 2; *U.S. Census of Housing: 1940*, vol. 2. On homeownership, see Bodnar, Simon, and Weber, *Lives of Their Own*, 153–55; Choco and Harris, "Local Culture of Property"; Simon, "City-Building Process," 18; Zunz, *Changing Face of Inequality*, 152–61. Margaret Marsh argues that the suburban placement of the home carried more symbolic meaning than homeownership. See Marsh, *Suburban Lives*.
4. *NREJ* 3 (August 15, 1911): 428.
5. *NREJ* 12 (October 15, 1915): 289; *NREJ* 11 (January 15, 1915): 8.
6. Hornstein, *Nation of Realtors*, 30.
7. *NREJ* 3 (March 15, 1911): 21–22; *NREJ* 3 (August 15, 1911): 428–29.
8. S. E. Hege, "Own Your Own Home," *NREJ* 11 (May 15, 1915): 274.
9. T. P. Hay Jr., "A 'Buy a Home' Campaign," *NREJ* (November 14, 1916): 209.
10. K. V. Haymaker, "How Building Associations Can Aid the 'Own Your Home' Movement," *NREJ* 17 (June–July 1918): 263; "'Own Your Home' Campaign," *New York Times*, August 11, 1918.

11. *Atlanta Journal*, January 14, 1915; *NREJ*, May 15, 1915; Hay, "'Buy a Home' Campaign," 209.

12. "Report of Activities in the Own Your Own Home Section of the Division of Public Works and Construction Development," May 1, 1919, RG3, box 6 of 6, file: Report of Own Your Home Section, NARA; Terry O'Donnell, "Report," Own Your Own Home Section, Homes Registration Service, Housing Corporation, U.S. Department of Labor, May 1919, RG3, box 6 of 6, file: Report of Own Your Home Section, NARA; Mr. [Paul] Murphy to Mr. [Franklin] Miller, March 4, 1919. RG3, box 6 of 6, file: James Ford, Manager, NARA. On the ties between NAREB and the federal homeownership movement, see also Dunn-Haley, "House That Uncle Sam Built," 107–12.

13. Scott, *American City Planning*, 170–72; Weiss, *Rise of the Community Builders*, 28. On the building of war housing, see also Karolak, "'No Idea,'"; Macieski, "Home of the Workingman."

14. Hutchison, "Building for Babbitt," 190.

15. Gries, Ford, and Taylor, *Home Ownership*, 24. By 1925, Georgia had twenty-one associations with $1.25 million in assets. (Five years later, the state had thirty-seven associations with $6 million in assets.) Bodfish, *History*, 631; Report of Survey: Atlanta Georgia, June 25, 1938, folder: Atlanta, GA, box 37, RG 195, Records of the Federal Home Loan Bank Board, 1933–1983, City Survey Files series, NARA; *Atlanta Constitution*, October 27, 1932. On building and loans, see Bodfish, *History*; Daunton, "Rows and Tenements," 258–62; Garb, *City of American Dreams*, 47–48; Weiss, *Rise of the Community Builders*, 32–33, 62.

16. "The Joys of Home Ownership," *NREJ* 9 (June 15, 1914): 431.

17. Herbert Hoover, "Home Ownership Will Develop Citizenry," *NREJ* (July 18, 1921): 20.

18. National Lumber Manufacturers' Association, "'Own Your Home' Campaign Handbook," file: publicity material, box 6, RG3, Records of the U.S. Housing Corporation, 1917–1952, NARA.

19. "The 'Own Your Home Movement' the Crying Need of the Nation," *NREJ* 17 (June–July 1918), inside front cover.

20. Max Ragley, "Why Every Man with a Family Should Own a Home," *NREJ* 12 (October 15, 1915): 276.

21. "Joys of Home Ownership," 431.

22. National Lumber Manufacturers' Association, "'Own Your Home' Campaign Handbook," p. 13.

23. Ibid., p. 15.

24. Ibid., pp. 12–13.

25. Harley, "Multi-family Housing Units," 371.

26. "'Own Your Home Movement' the Crying Need of the Nation."

27. National Lumber Manufacturers' Association, "'Own Your Home' Campaign Handbook," p. 15.

28. Arthur Wenz, "The 'Own Your Home' Campaigns," *NREJ* 17 (June–July 1918): 260.

29. "'Own Your Home Movement' the Crying Need of the Nation."

30. Gries and Taylor, *How to Own Your Own Home*, 1.

31. National Lumber Manufacturers' Association, "'Own Your Home' Campaign Handbook," pp. 12, 13.

32. Hutchison, "Building for Babbitt," 187.

33. Edward Newton Haag, "Reasons for 'National Home Day,'" *NREJ* (December 1918): 164–65.

34. "Many 'Own Your Home' Campaigns Being Planned for 1918," *NREJ* (February 1918): 71.

35. *NREJ* (January 5, 1920): 10.

36. *NREJ* (June 15, 1914): 421.

37. National Lumber Manufacturers' Association, "'Own Your Home' Campaign Handbook," p. 11.

38. Ibid., p. 13.

39. "'Own Your Home Movement' the Crying Need of the Nation."

40. "Many 'Own Your Home' Campaigns Being Planned for 1918," *NREJ* 17 (February 1918): 71.

41. Ibid.

42. Ibid., 72.

43. N. T., *NREJ* 18 (December 1918): 165.

44. "Many 'Own Your Home' Campaigns Being Planned for 1918," *NREJ* 17 (February 1918): 71.

45. S. E. Hege, "Own Your Own Home," *NREJ* 11 (May 15, 1915): 274.

46. T. P. Hay Jr., "A 'Buy a Home' Campaign," *NREJ* 14 (November 1916): 209.

47. National Lumber Manufacturers' Association, "'Own Your Home' Campaign Handbook," pp. 6, 11–12.

48. U.S. Department of Labor, *Suggestions for Own-Your-Own-Home Campaigns* (Washington, D.C.: USGPO, 1919), 31, file: publicity material, box 6, RG3, Records of the U.S. Housing Corporation, 1917–1952, NARA. Dunn-Haley discusses a range of homeownership propaganda as well; see "House That Uncle Sam Built", 107–29.

49. *Atlanta Journal*, January 12, 1921; *Atlanta Constitution*, January 13, 1921. The NAREB also recommended amending the Federal Reserve Act to allow banks to (1) accept home mortgages as collateral from member banks and (2) loan some of their savings on homes. *Atlanta Constitution*, January 15, 1921. Kenneth Jackson notes that interest on debt has been part of the income tax code since its establishment in 1913. The deduction became more important when taxes increased substantially for World War II (*Crabgrass Frontier*, 293–94).

50. *Atlanta Constitution*, May 7, 1922; May 9, 1922; January 13, 1921.

51. *Atlanta Constitution*, May 7, 1922.

52. *Atlanta Constitution*, May 9, 1922.

53. *Atlanta Constitution*, May 8, 1923.

54. *Atlanta Constitution*, May 9, 1922.

55. Key also foreshadowed homeownership's position in family lifecycles. See Perin, *Everything in Its Place*, particularly chap. 2.

Notes to Chapter Four   249

56. *Atlanta Constitution,* May 7, 1922; *Atlanta Journal,* May 7, 1922.

57. *Atlanta Constitution,* May 7, 1922.

58. *Atlanta Journal,* May 7, 1922.

59. On the professionalization of the real-estate industry, see Hornstein, *Nation of Realtors,* particularly chap. 3. On owner building, see Harris, *Unplanned Suburbs.*

60. *Atlanta Constitution,* May 3, 1922; May 7, 1922. See also *Atlanta Journal,* May 10, 1922.

61. *Atlanta Journal,* May 7, 1922.

62. *Atlanta Constitution,* May 12, 1922. Participating businesses and expo management were listed in expo ads and newspaper stories.

63. Gries and Taylor, *How to Own Your Own Home,* 11.

64. *Atlanta Constitution,* May 7, 1922; *Atlanta Journal,* May 7, 1922.

65. *Atlanta Constitution,* May 8, 1922.

66. *Atlanta Constitution,* May 12, 1922.

67. *Atlanta Constitution,* May 7, 1922.

68. Ibid.

69. *Atlanta Constitution,* April 8, 1923.

70. Gries and Ford, *Housing Objectives and Programs,* vol. 11, xv–xvii, quote from xv.

71. Weiss, "Richard T. Ely," 118; Gries and Ford, *Housing Objectives and Programs,* xvi–xvii. Committees and participants are described in Gries and Ford, *Housing Objectives and Programs.*

72. Gries and Ford, *Housing Objectives and Programs,* 1, 161–62.

73. Gries and Ford, *Planning for Residential Districts,* 3, 6.

74. Ibid., 3, 6; Gries and Ford, *Housing Objectives and Programs,* 182–83. Compiled by the six correlating committees and published in 1932, *Housing Objectives and Programs* outlined the intent of future national housing and home-building policy as well as standards for American homes. The transfer of homeownership ideology from 1918 and 1919 homeownership campaigns to the president's conference is hardly surprising. John Gries, who served as executive secretary for the president's conference, had, with James Taylor, prepared the Department of Commerce's *How to Own Your Home* pamphlet. Gries edited the conferences' final reports with Better Homes executive secretary James Ford. James Taylor, chief of the Division of Building and Housing with the Department of Commerce, also worked on the president's conference planning committee and served as one of three secretaries to the correlating committee on research. Thus, Hoover, Gries, Taylor, and Ford remained in positions to iterate a particular homeownership ideology from 1918 to at least 1932.

75. Gries and Ford, *Housing Objectives and Programs,* 160, 168, 182–83.

76. Ibid., 158, 161, 188.

77. Ibid., 160, 183–87.

78. Ibid., 7, 150, 156.

79. Ibid., 161, 210, 212, 215.

80. Gries, Ford, and Taylor, *Home Ownership,* 30.

Chapter Five. Exclusion and Park-Neighborhood Building, 1922 to 1929

1. Report of Survey: Atlanta Georgia, June 25, 1938, folder: Atlanta, GA, box 37, RG 195, Records of the Federal Home Loan Bank Board, 1933–1983, City Survey Files series, NARA; *Atlanta Constitution,* May 8, 1927; May 10, 1927; April 2, 1922. Several park-neighborhoods were subdivided from 1900 to 1915 but suffered slow development due to the 1907 panic or the World War I–related building slowdown. Many, such as Peachtree Heights, reemerged after 1922. *Atlanta Constitution,* August 21, 1923.

2. In the late 1920s, Atlanta worked with Fulton County to zone unincorporated areas of the county.

3. Transitions in Atlanta are summarized in Report of Survey: Atlanta Georgia, June 25, 1938. The growth of Atlanta's outer suburbs can best be seen on the Home Owners' Loan Corporation survey map and on "Map of Greater Atlanta and Suburbs," Gilmore's Map Company, 1947, AHC.

4. *Atlanta Constitution,* July 22, 1923.

5. *Atlanta Constitution,* November 17, 1929; May 12, 1929.

6. *Atlanta Constitution,* May 28, 1922; April 14, 1929.

7. Peachtree Hills Place, plat map, AHC; Miramar, plat map, AHC. At the AHC, plat maps not included in the Adair Plat Maps collection are organized by land district and land lot.

8. *Atlanta Constitution,* May 22, 1925.

9. Peachtree Heights Park, plat map, AHC.

10. *Atlanta Constitution,* May 28, 1922.

11. *Atlanta Constitution,* May 8, 1927; April 14, 1929.

12. Peachtree Heights Park, plat map, AHC.

13. *Atlanta Constitution,* May 19, 1929.

14. *Atlanta Constitution,* January 14, 1923; July 21, 1923.

15. *Atlanta Constitution,* November 17, 1929.

16. *Atlanta Constitution,* July 30, 1922.

17. *Atlanta Constitution,* May 28, 1922.

18. *Atlanta Constitution,* June 21, 1925; April 14, 1929; Peachtree Heights Park, plat map, AHC.

19. *Atlanta Constitution,* April 2, 1922.

20. Sylvan Hills Addition, 1922, plat map, Fulton County, Clerk of Superior Court, book 9, p. 170.

21. *Atlanta Constitution,* May 30, 1924.

22. *Atlanta Constitution,* October 3, 1926. At the same time, the paper noted that the "development of a negro subdivision on a high-class plan" was "a new departure in the real estate business." Joylan Park, plat map, 1923, Fulton County, Clerk of Superior Court, book 9, p. 130. Plat maps filed with Fulton County refer to this subdivision as "Joylan Park." The Atlanta Urban League occasionally referred to the subdivision as Joyland Park.

23. Joylan Park, plat map, 1923, Fulton County, Clerk of Superior Court, book 9, p. 130. The *Atlanta Independent* (published until 1927) did not cover black home and subdivision building extensively. The *Atlanta Daily World* launched in 1928, too late to provide much information on 1920s black home building. Service Company, plat map, 1922, Fulton County, Clerk of Superior Court, book 9, p. 32; L. P. Flowers, plat map, 1923, Fulton County, Clerk of Superior Court, book 9, p. 155; Joylan Park, plat map, 1923, Fulton County, Clerk of Superior Court, book 9, p. 130.

24. Report of Survey: Atlanta Georgia, June 25, 1938; *Atlanta City Directory*, 1928. Despite the *Atlanta Constitution*'s teaser that people were "flocking" to Joyland Park, the neighborhood grew slowly. By 1928, *Polk's Atlanta City Directory* listed only eight residents.

25. Atlanta City Planning Commission, Annual Report, 1922, p. 3, AHC; *Atlanta Constitution*, January 6, 1920; *Atlanta Journal*, January 6, 1920; December 29, 1919; December 30, 1919. On the development of comprehensive city plans, see Peterson, *Birth of City Planning*, 49. On Daniel Burnham and Chicago's city plan, see C. S. Smith, *Plan of Chicago*. Otis, "Atlanta's Plan," 6–7.

26. Mayor Key's address to the city suggests that the January 1920 committee was always intended to be temporary. Robert Otis recalled the committee disbanding "for want of funds." See *Atlanta Journal*, January 3, 1921; Otis, "Atlanta's Plan," 6–7.

27. *Atlanta Journal*, December 29, 1919; December 30, 1919; January 6, 1920; Joel Hurt to Frederick Law Olmstead, marked received November 1, 1920, microfilm reel 97 (container B133), job file 2746, "Atlanta City Plan," OA; Flint, "Zoning and Residential Segregation," 51; Otis, "Atlanta's Plan," 3. Atlantans appealed to national urban trends to justify comprehensive planning, just as they had done in parks and housing segregation initiatives. A 1920 city-planning committee pointed to over 230 cities that already had plans in place in their appeal to the city council and voters for a comprehensive city plan. Not only had Seattle appointed a commission that operated under the city council, for example, but their council had appropriated sixty thousand dollars to the "proper study" of the city's requirements. A promotional article penned by planning commission vice chair Robert Otis emphasized that "St. Louis, Cleveland, Detroit, Pittsburgh and Others [were] Widening Their Streets." As in other urban initiatives, Atlanta's civic elites made sure that the Gate City adopted the latest planning fashions. "City Planning Committee Urges Survey," *City Builder* 3 (January 1920): 12–13; Otis, "Atlanta's Plan," 18.

28. Atlanta City Planning Commission, Annual Report, 1922, p. 3, AHC; ACCM, October 21, 1920, AHC. Occupations were culled from city directories. Smith lost his seat in the U.S. Senate to Tom Watson in 1920.

29. Joel Hurt to Frederick Law Olmsted [Jr.], marked received November 1, 1920, microfilm reel 97 (container B133), job file 2746, "Atlanta City Plan," OA.

30. Atlanta City Planning Commission, meeting minutes, April 18, 1921, microfilm reel 97 (container B133), job file 2746, "Atlanta City Plan," OA. "Report of Special Committee to the City Planning Commission of Atlanta," April 18, 1921, microfilm reel 97 (container B133), job file 2746, OA.

31. Scott, *American City Planning*, 154; "Report of Special Committee to the City Planning Commission of Atlanta," April 18, 1921, microfilm reel 97 (container B133), job file 2746, "Atlanta City Plan," OA; Meck, "Zoning and Anti-Semitism"; Randle, "Professors, Reformers, Bureaucrats, and Cronies," 38–39; Revell, "Regulating the Landscape," 19.

32. Weiss, *Rise of the Community Builders*, 84.

33. Page, *Creative Destruction of Manhattan*, 64–65.

34. Los Angeles's 1908 districting plan, which limited industry in residential areas, was less controversial but equally significant to zoning's continued adoption. The 1908 plan established three classifications that specifically excluded industries but allowed a range and intermingling of housing (from single-family detached to apartment homes) and business (from movie theaters to commercial offices). A second ordinance classified and fixed seven industrial districts. Business and factory owners challenged such laws, but in *Hadacheck v. Sebastian* (1915), the U.S. Supreme Court ruled that zoning served a legitimate public need. Other cities followed Los Angeles and Modesto in implementing zoning ordinances to meet different cities' definitions of "nuisance." As David Freund explains it, rapid suburban development, the expanding technical nature of zoning, and whites' desire to impose or maintain racial divisions cannot be easily separated (*Colored Property*, 215–16). *Hadacheck v. Sebastian*, 239 U.S. 394 (1915); Flint, "Zoning and Residential Segregation," 20; Peterson, *Birth of City Planning*, 309; Weiss, *Rise of the Community Builders*, 81, 84, 87. Jon Peterson discusses Los Angeles's industrial districting but not its residential zoning; see *Birth of City Planning*, 309, 311. Power, "Advent of Zoning," 1, 3–4. On New York, see Boyer, *Dreaming the Rational City*, 91; Page, *Creative Destruction of Manhattan*, 61–65; Peterson, *Birth of City Planning*, 311–15; Revell, "Regulating the Landscape," 19–45.

35. Robert Whitten, "A Planning Program for Atlanta," is reprinted in Atlanta City Planning Commission, Annual Report, 1922, AHC.

36. Robert Whitten, *The Atlanta Zone Plan: Report Outlining a Tentative Zone Plan for Atlanta* (Atlanta: City of Atlanta, 1922), 9-10, Robert H. Whitten Collection, Graduate School of Design, Frances Loeb Library Special Collections, Harvard University, hereafter cited as *The Atlanta Zone Plan: Tentative*. The final zoning plan approved by the city council is titled *Zoning Ordinance for Atlanta, Georgia* (Atlanta: City of Atlanta, 1922), hereafter cited as *Zoning Ordinance*, and can be found in Robert H. Whitten Collection, Graduate School of Design, Frances Loeb Library Special Collections, Harvard University; Atlanta City Planning Commission, Annual Report, 1922, AHC; City of Atlanta, *Ordinance Book*, vol. 22, April 10, 1922, pp. 285–86, AHC. The tentative and final zoning maps are also available in the maps collection at the AHC. The map collection is organized by decade.

37. Whitten, *Atlanta Zone Plan: Tentative*.

38. Whitten, "City Zoning," 3.

39. Ibid., 4. Whitten's opposition to apartment houses within single-family home neighborhoods was consistent with emerging urban planning thought of the period, and these theories permeated local and national literature. A 1914 *NREJ* reported that the Rochester, New York, chamber of commerce, for example, was proposing an amendment to the New

York housing law that would allow apartments to be excluded from selected residential areas. "Protecting Residential Streets from Apartments and Factories," *NREJ* 9 (April 15, 1914): 279.

40. Planners and policy makers ignored rapid abandonment as a cause of declining real-estate values.

41. Only the draft zoning plan included materials justifying the need for zoning and the examples discussed. The final report only contained the zoning map and the explanations of categories and regulations. Whitten, *Atlanta Zone Plan: Tentative*, 3–8.

42. Ibid., 5.

43. Whitten, "City Zoning," 4–5.

44. Flint, "Zoning and Residential Segregation," 69.

45. Lloyd, "Pittsburgh's 1923 Zoning Ordinance," 297.

46. Daly, "Zoning," 122–23.

47. Ibid.; *Atlanta Journal*, March 31, 1922.

48. Whitten, *Atlanta Zone Plan: Tentative*, 5.

49. Pearl Davies, "Real Estate Achievement in the United States," MS, vol. 1, chap. 3, pt. 3, p. SS-4, NAR.

50. Robert H. Whitten, "The Zoning of Residential Sections," typescript available in Robert H. Whitten Collection, Graduate School of Design, Frances Loeb Library Special Collections, Harvard University. Notations on the paper indicate that it was read before the American City Planning Institute in St. Louis, May 27, 1918. Whitten's follow-up discussion suggests that he assumed lots of 1,250 square feet or less would be used for multifamily housing requiring a smaller footprint. For example, in his explanation of a 312-square-foot lot, he comments that a sixteen-family house would be appropriate.

51. Lasker, "Atlanta Zoning Plan," 114.

52. Macieski, "Home of the Workingman." The question of class segregation and the tendency "of people of one sort to flock together" was also introduced at the National Conference on Housing in 1913. See "Housing Problems in America," Proceedings of the Third National Conference on Housing, Cincinnati, (December 3–5, 1913): 153. On J. C. Nichols, see Worley, *J. C. Nichols*. Nichols's practices were often cited by other real-estate developers and agents. See, for example, Richard B. Watrous, "The Relation of Real Estate Men to City Planning," *NREJ* 11 (January 15, 1915): 10.

53. *Atlanta Constitution*, March 11, 1922. Opponents nationwide expressed similar arguments. In Pittsburgh, Senator David Reed contended that his city's minimum lot size discriminated against those of moderate means who could not afford the smallest lot sizes in "A" districts. Lloyd, "Pittsburgh's 1923 Zoning Ordinance," 298.

54. *Atlanta Constitution*, March 10, 1922; *Atlanta Journal*, March 10, 1922.

55. *Atlanta Constitution*, April 11, 1922.

56. *Atlanta Constitution*, March 10, 1922; March 17, 1922.

57. Peachtree Hills, plat map, AHC; Garden Hills, plat map, AHC. *Atlanta Constitution*, July 30, 1922; June 21, 1925; March 11, 1922.

58. Atlanta City Planning Commission, Annual Report, 1922, p. 3, AHC.

254 Notes to Chapter Five

59. Whitten, "Social Aspects of Zoning," 418.
60. *Atlanta Journal*, February 17, 1922.
61. *Atlanta Constitution*, March 11, 1922.
62. Whitten, "Social Aspects of Zoning," 418–19.
63. A few blocks between Ashby and Newport, south of Neal, continued with their original classification. Whitten, *Atlanta Zone Plan: Tentative; Zoning Ordinance*.
64. *Atlanta Constitution*, May 2, 1924.
65. *Atlanta Constitution*, October 3, 1924.
66. Chickamauga Avenue plat map, AHC.
67. *Atlanta Constitution*, October 18, 1924. *Bowen et al. v. City of Atlanta* (159 GA 145; 125 SE 199).
68. City of Atlanta, *Ordinance Book*, v. 26, May 20, 1929, p. 373, AHC.
69. *Atlanta Constitution*, May 21, 1929; *Atlanta Journal*, May 21, 1929; Flint, "Zoning and Residential Segregation," 342; Gilbert Jonas, *Freedom's Sword: The NAACP and the Struggle against Racism in America, 1909–1969* (New York: Routledge, 2005), 118–19. *City of Richmond v. Deans* (1930).

Undaunted by the numerous rulings against residential segregation at home and throughout the county, Atlanta's whites attempted to skirt the court bys creating an ordinance that dealt primarily with schools and children's education. The 1931 city ordinance argued that city growth pressed school needs, and that education—and enrollment—must be carefully regulated. Foreshadowing the links between housing and school geographies and school that would dominate the 1960s and 1970s, the council authorized the building commission to require occupancy permits for people intending to move within fifteen blocks of a public school intended for another race. Mayor James Key approved the measure. This new mechanism allowed white leaders to sort populations until 1939, when it was ruled unenforceable in Fulton County court. Flint, "Zoning and Residential Segregation," 327–28, 342–43. *Marisue v. Fulton County Superior Court* (1939); City of Atlanta, Ordinance Book, vol. 27, March 18, 1931, pp. 12–13, AHC.

70. *Atlanta Constitution*, June 9, 1925.
71. *Atlanta Constitution*, November 11, 1924; October 28, 1924; October 14, 1924; May 6, 1926; May 11, 1926; July 20, 1926; *Smith v. Atlanta*, 126 SE 66 (1926).
72. *Atlanta Constitution*, May 23, 1926.
73. Ibid. But planning commission secretary R. W. Torres found the "crazy quilt" of private deed restrictions frustrating. To Torres, large developments failed to account for residents' needs for local business establishments, and at some point, restrictive covenants would expire. *Atlanta Constitution*, November 4, 1928.
74. *Atlanta Constitution*, June 10, 1927.
75. *Village of Euclid, Ohio v. Ambler Realty Co.*, 272 U.S. 365 (1926).
76. Hanchett, *Sorting Out*, 169–70.

Chapter Six. Park-Neighborhoods, Federal Policy, and Housing Geographies, 1933 to 1950

1. As quoted in Report of Survey: Atlanta Georgia, June 25, 1938, folder: Atlanta, GA, box 37, RG 195 Records of the Federal Home Loan Bank Board, 1933–1983, City Survey Files series, NARA.

2. U.S. Bureau of the Census, *Sixteenth Census*; Report of Survey: Atlanta Georgia, June 25, 1938.

3. Freund, *Colored Property*, 118–28; Hanchett, "Other 'Subsidized Housing,'" 164; Jackson, *Crabgrass Frontier*, 196, 204–5; Richards, "How FHA Mortgage Insurance Operates," 6; Tough, "Life Cycle," 327–28. On federal housing programs in the 1930s and 1940s, see also Davies, *Housing Reform*; Gelfand, *Nation of Cities*; Hays, *Federal Government and Urban Housing*; Jackson, *Crabgrass Frontier*; Radford, *Modern Housing for America*.

4. The HOLC assigned four risk grades. The HOLC described A areas as the city's "hotspots"—new, well planned, and homogeneous. B areas were similar to A but completely developed. C areas were aging, obsolete, lacked transportation facilities, and sometimes "lacked" homogeneity. D areas had showed low maintenance, low rates of homeownership, unstable incomes, and could be characterized as "slums." "Security Area Descriptions: Atlanta, Georgia," folder: Atlanta, box 82, RG 195, Records of the Federal Home Loan Bank Board, 1933–1983, NARA. The HOLC only originated mortgages from 1934 to 1937.

5. The security map descriptions are mapped and organized by their rating and neighborhood number. All neighborhoods were assigned a risk rating and then numbered, so each neighborhood carries a unique designation. Thus, D18 carries a D risk rating. References to text within the report are hereafter cited by rating-neighborhood number combination. "Security Area Descriptions."

6. David Freund describes how local land-use zoning also contributed to such hierarchies and the establishment of the single-family home as the "superior type of residence" (*Colored Property*, 91).

7. Ibid., 128–33.

8. Report of Survey: Atlanta Georgia, June 25, 1938. Charlotte, for example, did not acknowledge two land markets in its HOLC report introduction. However, it still rated all black neighborhoods "D".

9. It is not clear, however, if such statements influenced the HOLC's decisions regarding mortgage purchases.

10. Report of Survey: Atlanta Georgia, June 25, 1938.

11. "Security Area Descriptions." The HOLC had closed on fifty thousand loans by 1933, and by 1936 the agency held at least 20 percent of mortgages on nonfarm dwellings. See Freund, *Colored Property*, 112.

12. "Residential Security Map, Atlanta Georgia," folder: Atlanta, box 82, RG 195, Records of the Federal Home Loan Bank Board, 1933–1983, NARA; "Security Area Descriptions."

13. Federal Housing Administration, *Underwriting Manual*, pt. 1, sec. 210.

14. Ibid., pt. 2, sec. 249.

15. Quoted in Kimble, "Insuring Inequality," 407.

16. On the influence of Richard Ely, his institute, the institute's textbooks, and other texts on mortgage structures and appraising practices, see Freund, *Colored Property,* 103–11; Weiss, "Richard T. Ely." Freund also describes the *Underwriting Manual's* assumptions, particularly with regard to race. See *Colored Property,* 156–62. Federal Housing Administration, *Underwriting Manual,* pt. 1, secs. 209, 221; Hillier, "Residential Security Maps," 212.

17. Like the HOLC, the FHA assigned four risk grades. A areas were new, well planned, and homogeneous. B areas were similar to A but completely developed. C areas were aging, obsolete, lacked transportation facilities, and sometimes "lacked" homogeneity. D areas had showed low maintenance, low rates of homeownership, unstable incomes, and could be characterized as "slums."

18. Federal Housing Administration, *Underwriting Manual,* pt. 2, secs. 210, 210(d), 251, 316.

19. Ibid., pt. 1, sec. 306(2). The FHA failed to clarify phrases like "lower living standards," assuming that the appraiser shared the same cultural norms and understandings.

20. Federal Housing Administration, *Underwriting Manual,* pt. 2, sec. 233.

21. The FHA's concern with racial mixing extended to schools serving a neighborhood's children. The manual advised appraisers that schools "should not be attended in large numbers by inharmonious racial groups," and it counseled appraisers to take school makeup into account when assessing neighborhoods. The manual cautioned that even when a neighborhood appeared favorable, if the residents were "compelled to attend school where the majority or a goodly number of the pupils represent[ed] a far lower level of society or an incompatible racial element," the neighborhood was far less desirable. Federal Housing Administration, *Underwriting Manual,* pt. 2, secs. 233, 266, 284(3)(g), 289(1).

22. Mack, "Covenants for New Subdivisions," 9–11. On restrictive covenants, see Fogelson, *Bourgeois Nightmares,* 1870–1930.

23. Federal Housing Administration, *Underwriting Manual,* pt. 1, sec. 306(2); Freund, *Colored Property,* 95–97.

24. Quoted in *Atlanta Daily World,* August 22, 1940, and August 7, 1940. See also *Atlanta Daily World,* August 28, 1940.

25. Dean, "Only Caucasian," 430.

26. Hanchett, "Other 'Subsidized Housing,'" 165.

27. Ibid., 165–67; *Atlanta Constitution,* April 24, 1949.

28. The FHA eventually explained its practices directly to the public. One October 19, 1957, United Press release explained to readers that appraisers took into account the "effect of surrounding areas" and "characteristics of the neighborhood." The story alerted readers to look for "non-conforming uses" such as rooming houses or a "nearby invasion" of industry. *Atlanta Journal-Atlanta Constitution,* October 20, 1957.

29. *Atlanta Constitution*, April 24, 1949; Charles Abrams, "Race Bias in Housing, I: The Great Hypocrisy," *Nation*, July 19, 1947, 69.

30. The "Established Ratings," the FHA contended, would help speed processing and ensure consistency of ratings. The agency suggested analyzing the economic background of neighborhoods, directions of growth, areas of competition, age, and quality, and recommended using a combination of maps and cards to convey the findings and ratings. Once staff completed the process, ratings of new areas could be made through comparison to the "Established Ratings." To assist valuators in preparing the local gauge, the FHA Mortgage Insurance Division's Underwriting Section assembled and distributed "illustrations of correctly rated cases for the guidance of the Underwriting Staffs in the Insuring Offices." The FHA expected underwriting staff to consult the illustrations and "make comparisons between them and current cases to seek analogies and cognate situations." Federal Housing Administration, *Underwriting Manual*, pt. 1, secs. 207–10, 237. Freund, *Colored Property*, 195–96; *Atlanta Constitution*, April 6, 1937, and June 11, 1939.

31. *Atlanta Constitution*, July 31, 1938.

32. *Atlanta Constitution*, February 8, 1938.

33. *Atlanta Constitution*, September 25, 1938; "Security Area Descriptions."

34. Kimble, "Insuring Inequality," 429; Wiese, *Places of Their Own*, 140. FHA and VA statistics were developed from the following sources: U.S. Bureau of the Census, *Census of Housing: 1950*, vol. 1, *General Characteristics*, pt. 1, "United States Summary"; Hammer and Company, "The Market for Negro Rental Housing in Metropolitan Atlanta," May 5, 1954, folder 45, Philip Gibbon Hammer Collection, Southern Historical Collections, University of North Carolina–Chapel Hill; untitled report on minority housing commitments by zone, RG31, box 2, file: minority group housing reports, Records of the Federal Housing Administration, 1930–1965, NARA (the report does no break down allocations by single-family home mortgages and multifamily housing); untitled report showing FHA commitments and rejections, September 17, 1943, box 2, Correspondence and Subject Files, 1938–1958, RG 31, Records of the Federal Housing Administration, 1930–1965, NARA.

35. *Atlanta Daily World*, April 9, 1935.

36. Ibid.; *Atlanta Daily World*, September 8, 1935, February 3, 1944. On the FHA's Better Housing Campaign, see Freund, *Colored Property*, 165–71. On Walter Aiken, see Silver and Moeser, *Separate City*, 55; Wiese, *Places of Their Own*, 182–83.

37. *Atlanta Daily World*, August 14, 1936.

38. *Atlanta Constitution*, October 27, 1933; October 23, 1938; August 2, 1936; *Atlanta Daily World*, August 14, 1936; July 28, 1936; August 2, 1936.

39. On the characteristics of working-class suburbs in this era, see Harris, *Unplanned Suburbs*; Nicolaides, *My Blue Heaven*; Wiese, "Other Suburbanites."

40. According to planning historians Chris Silver and John Moeser, 13 percent of black households and 32 percent of white households were owner occupied in 1940. See Silver and Moeser, *Separate City*, 37 and map 5. My calculations, based on the 1940 *Census of Housing*, indicate that blacks owned 4.3 percent of Atlanta's occupied units in 1940. Put

another way, blacks comprised 17 percent of Atlanta's homeowners. U.S. Bureau of the Census, *U.S. Census of Housing: 1940.*

41. U.S. Bureau of the Census, *Housing.* The report aggregated homeownership in increments of 20 percent.

42. U.S. Bureau of the Census, *Housing; Atlanta City Directory,* 1942.

43. Thus, even after the racial elements of the 1922 zoning plan was ruled unenforceable, and even after the 1948 *Shelley v. Kramer* case ruled racially restrictive covenants unenforceable, white officials could still manage land allocation by utilizing the zoning plan's density requirements, which could force up the lot size per family and thus housing costs, or by stalling the permit application process.

44. *Atlanta Constitution,* April 7, 1938; "Map of Zoning Districts," sheet 1, 1946, AHC. Sheet 2, which showed the zoning designations for Fulton County to the south of the city's limits, was not found in the map collection.

45. U.S. Commission on Civil Rights, "Housing," 459, 495, 521, 543, 561, 566.

46. The South uniformly separated whites and nonwhites in public housing. Most cities outside the South did as well, though seventeen mixed-race complexes existed outside the region in the late 1930s. See Bauman, *Public Housing, Race, and Renewal,* 37; Hirsch, "'Containment' on the Home Front," 161; Thompson, Lewis, and McEntire, "Atlanta and Birmingham," 21. Karen Ferguson provides the most complete treatment of 1930s and 1940s public housing in Atlanta; see her *Black Politics in New Deal Atlanta,* 179–82. On post-1949 public housing and slum clearance in Atlanta, see Bayor, *Race;* L. Keating, *Atlanta;* Keating and Flores, "Sixty and Out"; Stone, *Economic Growth and Neighborhood Discontent.*

47. Jackson, *Crabgrass Frontier,* 221–28; Radford, *Modern Housing for America,* 85, 89, 91, 101, 103.

48. Hirsch, "'Containment' on the Home Front," 161; Jackson, *Crabgrass Frontier,* 224–25; Radford, *Modern Housing for America,* 191.

49. Atlanta Housing Authority, "... And the pursuit of happiness," film (ca. 1940s), Charles F. Palmer Papers, MARBL, quoted in Ferguson, *Black Politics in New Deal Atlanta,* 174.

50. Ferguson, *Black Politics in New Deal Atlanta,* 172–75.

51. *Atlanta Constitution,* May 31, 1939; *Atlanta Daily World,* March 3, 1940; June 8, 1939; Ferguson, *Black Politics in New Deal Atlanta,* 180–81. On Charles Palmer, see Ferguson, *Black Politics in New Deal Atlanta,* 169–72; Palmer, *Adventures of a Slum Fighter.*

52. Atlanta Housing Authority, *8th Annual Report of the Atlanta Housing Authority* (Atlanta: Atlanta Housing Authority, 1945–46); U.S. Commission on Civil Rights, *Housing,* 612; Keating and Flores, "Sixty and Out."

53. Statistics were compiled from the Atlanta Housing Authority annual reports. Bayor, *Race,* 80; Ferguson, *Black Politics in New Deal Atlanta,* 190; Silver and Moeser, *Separate City,* 23–24. The PWA noted which projects were replacing "slums" and which were built on vacant property. See Radford, *Modern Housing for America,* 100–101. On public housing and Philadelphia, see Bauman, *Public Housing, Race, and Renewal.* On public housing

and Chicago, see Hirsch, *Making the Second Ghetto*. On federal policy and public housing, see Hirsch, "'Containment' on the Home Front"; Jackson, *Crabgrass Frontier*, chap. 12.

54. U.S. Commission on Civil Rights, *Housing*, 488.

55. Figures calculated from Atlanta Housing Authority annual reports.

56. The maps created as part of the FHA's Real Property Survey provide data similar to the 1940 analytical block maps. Occasionally, data results vary slightly between the two sets of maps. U.S. Bureau of the Census, *Sixteenth Census*.

57. "Security Area Descriptions." The HOLC only originated mortgages from 1934 to 1937. From 1934 to 1951, the agency forestalled foreclosures by purchasing mortgages from lending institutions. See Tough, "Life Cycle." HOLC staff consulted several Atlanta agents and mortgage grantors in the creation of Atlanta's report and related security map, including C. D. LeBay, whose company represented Metropolitan Life Insurance; Alvin Cates and Henry Robinson, real estate agents and "HOLC Contract Brokers"; and William Logan Jr., agent, broker, and president of the Atlanta Real Estate Board.

58. U.S. Bureau of the Census, *U.S. Census of Housing (1940)*.

59. Where appropriate, I also use plat maps and city directory and census manuscript data to explain particular patterns.

60. The security map descriptions are mapped and organized by their rating and neighborhood number. All neighborhoods were assigned a risk rating and then numbered, so each neighborhood carries a unique designation. Thus, D18 carries a D risk rating. Cited hereafter by rating-neighborhood number combination.

61. "Residential Security Map"; "Security Area Descriptions"; U.S. Bureau of the Census, *Housing*.

62. "Residential Security Map"; "Security Area Descriptions."

63. Haynes Manor, plat map, 1939, Fulton County, Clerk of Superior Court, book 21, p. 23.

64. Willie Mae Whitten [Collier Heights], plat map, 1939, book 21, p. 43.

65. Glenwood Park, plat map, 1939, Fulton County, Clerk of Superior Court, book 21, p. 27. The restrictive covenants are included in the plat book.

66. Ibid.

67. Victory Heights, plat map, 1939, Fulton County, Clerk of Superior Court, book 21, p. 62;

68. Richland Park, plat map, 1939, Fulton County, Clerk of Superior Court, book 21, p. 29; Moreland Drive Subdivision, plat map, 1939, Fulton County, Clerk of Superior Court, book 21, p. 3.

69. Lake Forest, plat map, 1939, Fulton County, Clerk of Superior Court, book 22, p. 1.

70. Ferstwood, plat map, 1941, book 23, p. 75; Morningside Hill, plat map, 1940, book 23, p. 73; J. W. Karwisch Property, 1941, book 23, p. 72; Collier Hills, 1941, book 23, p. 71; Rugby Estates, 1941, book 23, p. 66; J. J. Williamson and Sons, plat map, 1941, book 23, p. 54; Northwood Subdivision, 1940, book 23, p. 33; E. L. King Property [Peachtree Hills], 1940, book 23, p. 22; Collier Hills, 1940, book 23, pp. 5–6; A. B. Suttles Property, 1940, book 23, p. 4; Morris Brandon Estate, 1940, book 22, pp. 71–72; Liddell Estate, 1940, book

22, p. 62; Grove Park Development Company, 1940, book 22, p. 36; C. L. DeFoor [Tuxedo Park], 1940, book 22, p. 35; Collier Hills, 1939, book 22 p. 5; Longwood Subdivision, 1939 book 22, p. 2; Lake Forrest Development Corp., 1939, book 22, p. 1; W. B. Hardman, 1939, book 20, p. 37; Moreland Drive Subdivision, 1937, book 20, p. 3; Victory Heights Subdivision, 1939, book 21, p. 62; all filed with Fulton County, Clerk of Superior Court.

71. U.S. Bureau of the Census, *Housing*. Atlanta's black population measured 35 percent in 1940. I arbitrarily established "disproportional" as ± 25 percent for use in this study's demographic analysis. However, the analytical block maps categorized as 1 to 9 percent, 10 to 49 percent, and 50 to 89 percent. Thus, when examining race as presented in the analytical block maps, I consider "disproportionately black" to be ± 50 percent in 1940.

72. It is important not to misread what initially appears as "mixed race." On the analytical block maps, Ansley Park, northwest of Piedmont Park, shows some black population on about half its blocks. However, since Ansley Park had installed covenants prohibiting blacks from the beginning, except as servants, it is possible that the black residents may have lived in servant's quarters or some similar arrangement.

73. Atlanta's black population measured 35 percent in 1940. I arbitrarily established "disproportional" as ± 25 percent.

74. "Residential Security Map"; "Security Area Descriptions." Mixed-race patterns can also be seen in U.S. Bureau of the Census, *Housing*.

75. "Security Area Descriptions." The HOLC originated mortgages only from 1934 to 1937.

76. U.S. Department of Commerce, Bureau of the Census, "Survey of World War II Veterans and Dwelling Unit Vacancy and Occupancy in the Atlanta Area, Georgia," December 16, 1946.

77. Quoted in *Atlanta Daily World*, August 7, 1940.

78. Quoted in *Atlanta Daily World*, August 28, 1940. See also *Pittsburgh Courier*, December 22, 1945.

79. Hirsch, "'Containment' on the Home Front," 162–63.

80. Reginald A. Johnson to Raymond H. Foley, June 2, 1947, folder: "1947—Housing Expansion, Plans for," box A85, NUL-SRO, LOC.

81. Charles Abrams, "Race Bias in Housing, I: The Great Hypocrisy," *Nation*, July 19, 1947, 69.

82. *Pittsburgh Courier*, November 11, 1944. On civil rights and World War II, see Sullivan, *Days of Hope*, chap. 5. On the FHA's response to charges of racial discrimination, see Kimble, "Insuring Inequality," 399–434.

83. Atlanta race-relations officer Albert Thompson's work was more evident in Savannah, for example. This interpretation of the race relations officer's activity in Atlanta is based on my reading of correspondence, or lack thereof, in the Atlanta Urban League Collection and the National Urban League, Southern Regional Office Collection. As historian John Kimble notes, the race relations officers' powers were limited by HHFA from the start. The office was understaffed, and officers were charged with working "behind the

scenes" to facilitate FHA programs. Kimble, "Insuring Inequality," 427. On the RRS, see also Wiese, *Places of Their Own*, 138–40.

To provide more financing for black and open housing projects—housing open to occupancy without regard to race—the FHA launched public and professional educational campaigns to persuade bankers and developers to invest in black housing. Educational strategies would work slowly, at best, but had the advantage of causing few tensions with local white power structures. The FHA had publicized improved black economic circumstances since the beginning of World War II, hoping to persuade builders and agents to develop the private market for black-occupied housing. The *Insured Mortgage Portfolio*, for example, noted that "about 16 percent of the nonwhite families received incomes of $3,000 and over," which equated to "a substantial market for higher-priced properties among minority groups." In an attempt to overcome financial institutions' fear of investment, the FHA highlighted successful all-black subdivision and apartment projects. Kane, "Opportunities in a Neglected Market," 6. See the following articles stressing the growing black market in housing: Margaret Kane, "A Wider Field for Mortgage Lending," *Insured Mortgage Portfolio* 14 (4th qtr. 1949): 15–18; Margaret Kane, "Opportunities in a Neglected Market," *Insured Mortgage Portfolio* 13 (4th qtr. 1948), 6–8, 32–33.

84. On *Shelley v. Kraemer*, see Kimble, "Insuring Inequality," 413–15.

85. Quoted in *Atlanta Journal*, December 16, 1949.

86. Quoted in *Atlanta Journal*, December 3, 1949.

87. Quoted in *Atlanta Journal*, December 9, 1949.

88. Quoted in *Atlanta Journal*, December 3, 1949.

89. Quoted in *Atlanta Journal*, December 3, 1949.

90. Ibid.

91. *Atlanta Journal*, December 16, 1949.

92. Quoted in *Atlanta Daily World*, March 15, 1948. The *Washington Post* suggested forming property clubs whereby only persons who met state qualifications could purchase property.

93. *Atlanta Journal*, December 6, 1949; Hirsch, "'Containment' on the Home Front," 163–65; *Pittsburgh Courier*, February 5, 1949; February 26, 1949; February 8, 1949; *Atlanta Daily World*, December 11, 1949; December 8, 1949; November 8, 1949; *Pittsburgh Courier*, March 5, 1949. Similarly, Public Housing Administration commissioner John Taylor Eagan assured Atlantans concerned with public-housing allocations that the ruling and subsequent regulations applied to the FHA and "had nothing to do with public housing." Quoted in *Atlanta Journal*, December 5, 1949.

94. *Atlanta Daily World*, April 27, 1949; May 5, 1949; Joint Committee on Housing, *Study and Investigation of Housing*, 1254; Kruse, *White Flight*, 55–57; Wiese, *Places of Their Own*, 182.

95. Hammer and Company, "Market for Negro Rental Housing"; Joint Committee on Housing, *Study and Investigation of Housing*, 1263, 1265. On the AUL's Robert Thompson, see Wiese, *Places of Their Own*, 184–88.

96. "A Report of the Housing Activities of the Atlanta Urban League," June 18, 1951, p. 1, folder 5, box 244, AUL Collection, RWWLA; Thompson, Lewis, and McEntire, "Atlanta and Birmingham," 22–23; Minutes of Atlanta Urban League Board of Directors, June 3, 1948, file: 1948 Atlanta, GA, box A-92, NUL-SRO, LOC; Silver and Moeser, *Separate City,* 139; Wiese, *Places of Their Own,* 181–82.

97. Forrester B. Washington to R. A. Thompson, July 30, 1947, folder 22, box 240, AUL Collection, RWWLA.

98. On the AUL and the expansion plan, see Bayor, *Race,* 59–60. Wiese, *Places of Their Own,* 174–96; "Report of the Housing Activities of the Atlanta Urban League," November 28, 1950, folder: 1950—Atlanta Urban League, box A115, NUL-SRO, LOC; Robert A. Thompson to Arthur Shephard, November 10, 1947, folder 26, box 239, AUL Collection, RWWLA.

99. "Report of the Housing Activities," November 28, 1950; Bayor, *Race,* 59, 71; U.S. Commission on Civil Rights, *Housing,* 473; Wiese, *Places of Their Own,* 181–82; "Report of the Committee on Housing for Negroes," February 15, 1949, folder: 1949—Housing, box A107, NUL-SRO, LOC; "Proposed Areas for Expansion," included in R. A. Thompson Jr. to James H. Therrell, July 29, 1948, folder 61, box 239, AUL Collection, RWWLA. This is not to say that black families did not embrace park-neighborhood practices and expectations; many certainly did. See Wiese, *Places of Their Own,* 188–91.

100. U.S. Commission on Civil Rights, *Housing,* 526–27.

101. Ibid., 459.

102. Ibid., 585; Wiese, *Places of Their Own,* 182–83.

103. R. A. Thompson to George L. Wilson, November 10, 1954, folder 43, box 240, AUL Collection, RWWLA.

104. Wiese, *Places of Their Own,* 189.

105. R. A. Thompson to Hugh Howell, April 13, 1953, folder 3, box 245, AUL Collection, RWWLA; "Report of the Housing Activities," June 18, 1952; "Roster of Non-White New Owner-Occupied Dwelling Units," folder 5, box 244, AUL Collection, RWWLA.

106. Thompson, Lewis, and McEntire, "Atlanta and Birmingham," 29, 41–42; Wiese, *Places of Their Own,* 183. The AUL collection contains several letters from Thompson soliciting mortgages from firms throughout the East and the Northeast. "Nonwhite Housing Activities in Metropolitan Atlanta between 1945–1956," folder 6, box 244, AUL Collection, RWWLA.

107. "Report of the Housing Activities," June 18, 1951. In 1957 Thompson explained to urban-planning consultant Philip Hammer, "The mitigating factor against the nonwhite population moving into DeKalb County during the past 10 or more years has been the general attitude of the white population toward the non-white population living in the general area." R. A. Thompson to Phillip Hammer, June 25, 1957, folder 2, box 243, AUL Collection, RWWLA; *Atlanta Daily World,* July 11, 1950; *Atlanta Journal-Atlanta Constitution,* July 30, 1950; *Atlanta Daily World,* January 7, 1950; Atlanta Urban League "Occasional Papers," undated, folder 6, box 245, AUL Collection, RWWLA; R. A. Thompson Jr. to Albert H. Cole, August 19, 1955, folder 23, box 235, AUL Collection, RWWLA; Bayor, *Race,* 63; U.S. Commission on Civil Rights, *Housing,* 568–71; Thompson, Lewis,

and McEntire, "Atlanta and Birmingham," 24–25. On the financing and building of Highpoint Apartments as well as the concessions made to whites, see Wiese, *Places of Their Own*, 183–84.

108. U.S. Commission on Civil Rights, *Housing*. On Atlanta's post-1950 battles over housing and education, see Kruse, *White Flight*, chaps. 2 and 3; Wiese, *Places of Their Own*, 184–96. On the WSMDC and its ongoing negotiations over white and black housing in the 1950s and 1960s, see Bayor, *Race*, 59–60, 64–65; Silver and Moeser, *Separate City*, 136–44.

109. Universal Land Company to Robert Thompson, February 29, 1956, folder 1, box 236, AUL Collection, RWWLA.

110. R. A. Thompson to Pearce Matthews, May 30, 1952, folder 11, box 238, AUL Collection, RWWLA.

111. J. W. E. Bowen to John F. Thigpen, February 17, 1953, folder 1, box 240, AUL Collection, RWWLA.

112. A. T. Walden to John F. Thigpen, February 6, 1953, folder 1, box 240, AUL Collection, RWWLA.

113. "Parsons Village" advertisement, attached to R. A. Thompson to Sally Parsons, January 6, 1954, folder 54, box 238, AUL Collection, RWWLA.

114. *Atlanta Daily World*, May 14, 1939; January 8, 1922; *Atlanta Constitution*, October 27, 1933; Garden Hills, plat map, AHC; Peachtree Hills, plat map, AHC; Peachtree Heights, plat map, AHC.

115. R. A. Thompson to J. P. Whittaker, June 2, 1954, folder 32, box 240, AUL Collection, RWWLA; Bayor, *Race*, 83.

116. Census data and shape files courtesy of Minnesota Population Center, *National Historical Geographic Information System: Pre-release Version 0.1* (Minneapolis: University of Minnesota, 2004), http://www.nhgis.org.

117. Joint Committee on Housing, *Study and Investigation of Housing*, 1265; Joint Center for Housing Studies at Harvard University, *State of the Nation's Housing 2006*; U.S. Bureau of the Census, *U.S. Census of Housing: 1950*. Some respondents did not report race. Hammer and Company, "Market for Negro Rental Housing."

Chapter Seven. White Property and Homeowner Privilege

1. Sjoquist, *Atlanta Paradox*, 1–15.

2. Massey and Denton, *American Apartheid*. Other recent policy studies include M. Orfield, *Metropolitics*; and Rusk, *Cities without Suburbs*.

3. *Atlanta Journal-Constitution*, June 25, 2000.

4. Ibid. Appealed and upheld in *Henry County et al. v. Tim Jones Properties, Inc. et al.* 273 Ga. 190, 539 S.E. 2d 167 (November 30, 2000). On exclusionary zoning, see Downs, "Policies in the New Millennium." The National Low Income Housing Coalition compiled reports of exclusionary zoning ("not in my backyard") up until mid-2005 in their NIMBY report, available at http://www.nlihc.org/nimby/.

5. Fogelson, *Bourgeois Nightmares.*

6. Bayor, *Race,* 84; Institute on Race and Poverty, University of Minneapolis, *Minority Suburbanization;* Massey and Denton, *American Apartheid;* Sorensen, Hollingsworth, and Taeuber, "Indexes of Racial Residential Segregation," available at http://www.irpumn.org/uls/resources/projects/Minority_Suburbanization_full_report_032406.pdf.

7. Bayor, *Race,* 61–69.

8. *Atlanta Daily World,* June 26, 1952; May 27, 1952; Bayor, *Race,* 85–87.

9. Bayor, *Race,* 74; Kruse, *White Flight,* 4–5, 52, 56, and chap. 6.

10. Booza, Cutsinger, and Galster, *Where Did They Go?* 6–11; Institute on Race and Poverty, University of Minneapolis, *Minority Suburbanization;* Orfield and Ashkinaze, *Closing Door,* 49.

11. Orfield and Ashkinaze, *Closing Door,* 87–88; Joint Center for Housing Studies of Harvard University, *America's Rental Housing,* 23–24.

12. Atlanta Neighborhood Development Partnership, Inc., *Making the Case,* 14–17, available at http://www.andpi.org/uploadedFiles/pdf/03MICI%20MTC%20Report_CNT.pdf; Bayor, *Race,* 69–76; Orfield and Ashkinaze, *Closing Door,* 52–53, 74, 78.

13. *Atlanta Journal-Constitution,* August 15, 2006; Institute on Race and Poverty, University of Minneapolis, *Minority Suburbanization,* 7, 17; Frey, *Diversity Spreads Out,* 1–13. Interstate 285 rings the city and is referred to locally as "the perimeter." OTP is local slang for "outside the perimeter."

14. *Atlanta Journal-Constitution,* June 20, 2005; June 23, 2005.

15. *Atlanta Journal-Constitution,* June 20, 2005.

16. *Atlanta Journal-Constitution,* September 10, 2006. On the idea of a "flexible frame" and "frames of color-blind racism," see Bonilla-Silva, *Racism without Racists,* chap. 2.

17. *Atlanta Journal-Constitution,* November 4, 2006.

18. *Atlanta Journal-Constitution,* November 13, 2006.

19. *Atlanta Journal-Constitution,* June 12, 2006.

20. *Atlanta Journal-Constitution,* June 23, 2005; June 20, 2005.

21. *Atlanta Journal-Constitution,* February 3, 2003.

22. *Atlanta Journal-Constitution,* December 16, 2006; December 13, 2006; February 3, 2003; December 6, 2006; November 19, 2006; June 30, 2003. Minority share of renter households increased from 31 percent in 1990 to 43 percent in 2004. Anti-tenant and anti-apartment campaigns thus became effective, coded ways to control race/ethnic presence. See Joint Center for Housing Studies at Harvard University. *State of the Nation's Housing,* 21.

23. *Atlanta Journal-Constitution,* November 7, 2005.

24. Toni Morrison, "On the Backs of Blacks," *Time,* December 2, 1993, available at http://www.time.com/time/community/morrisonessay.html.

25. Johnson and Shapiro, "Good Neighborhoods, Good Schools."

26. Quoted in *Atlanta Journal-Constitution,* February 3, 2003.

27. Posted by Vermin8, November 16, 2005, 11:36 a.m., downloaded November 17, 2005, 7:30 a.m., copy in possession of the author.

28. *Southern Burlington County NAACP v. Township of Mt. Laurel*, 92 NJ 158, 456 A/2d 390 (1983), quoted in G. Orfield, "Minorities and Suburbanization," 225-26.

29. Quoted in Kruse, *White Flight*, 261.

30. Phillips and Chin, "School Inequality," 25. Dalton Conley demonstrates how wealth inequalities perpetuate racial inequality over time (*Being Black*). Thomas Shapiro contributes to our understanding of the continuing significance of race by moving beyond salary figures to examine the role of asset wealth in perpetuating inequality. See Shapiro, *Hidden Cost*, 339; Oliver and Shapiro, *Black Wealth/White Wealth*. See also Institute on Race and Poverty, University of Minneapolis, *Determining Equity*.

31. As reported in *Atlanta Journal-Constitution*, December 22, 2004. Annie E. Casey Foundation, *Neighborhoods Count*, 5.

32. Mara Shalhoup, "Locked Out," *Creative Loafing*, May 8, 2002; Matthew Cardinale, "AHA Demolition Applications Raise Questions," *Atlanta Progressive News*, March 9, 2008.

33. Bonilla-Silva, *Racism without Racists*, particularly chap. 3; Johnson and Shapiro, "Good Neighborhoods, Good Schools," 173-87; McKinney, *Being White*, 191-92. See also Maria Krysan, Reynolds Farley, and Mick P. Cooper, "In the Eye of the Beholder: Racial Beliefs and Residential Segregation," *DuBois Review* 5, no. 1 (2008): 5-26.

34. Bonilla-Silva, *Racism without Racists*, 36-39, quote from 39; Jonathan Kozol, *The Shame of the Nation: The Restoration of Apartheid Schooling in America* (New York: Crown, 2005), in particular see 244-60.

35. Atlanta Neighborhood Development Partnership, Inc., *Making the Case*.

Appendix

1. On methods of measuring and analyzing segregation, see Massey and Denton, *American Apartheid*, 74-78.

2. Grannis, "Importance of Trivial Streets." See also Grannis, "T-Communities."

3. Zunz, *Changing Face of Inequality*.

4. For an overview of the use of GIS in historical geography, see Knowles, "Emerging Trends in Historical GIS"; Knowles, "Introduction to 'Historical GIS.'"

5. U.S. Bureau of the Census, *Housing*; "Security Area Descriptions: Atlanta Georgia," and map, folder: Atlanta, box 82, RG 195 Records of the Federal Home Loan Bank Board, 1933-1983, NARA. The HOLC only originated mortgages from 1934 to 1937. Minnesota Population Center, *National Historical Geographic Information System: Pre-release Version 0.1* (Minneapolis: University of Minnesota, 2004), http://nhgis.org.

6. Rand Corporation, *Million Random Digits*.

7. Atlanta did not have a street atlas that included building footprints for the years after 1878. Such atlases contained building footprints and locations as well as other directory-type information.

8. "Colored" meant black or mulatto. People of Asian descent, for example, were not identified as "colored." Later city directories also note tenure status.

9. *Polk's Atlanta City Directory* (Richmond: R. L. Polk, 1891); ibid. (1899); ibid. (1919). Available at Robert W. Woodruff Library, Emory University, Atlanta.

10. Hereafter *household* will be used to mean "head of household." Nowhere should *household* be taken to mean the entire housing unit or the entire family. In some city directories, the name of the wife of the head of household is shown, though no other information about her is given.

11. Rand Corporation, *Million Random Digits*.

12. Some blocks returned no residential data, either because no building had yet occurred in the area, or because the directory agent failed to gather the names on that block.

13. City of Atlanta, 1920, Southern Map Company, AHC.

14. In rubbersheeting a digital map is "forced," mathematically, to fit a set of known coordinate values.

15. Although maps could be scanned and transferred into machine-readable format, scanning data from city directories was more problematic. "Noise" and the particular fonts used by directory publishers prevented the optical character recognition (OCR) software available at that time (approximately 1999) from picking up data without substantial error.

16. Zunz, in turn, based his scheme on those developed by Thernstrom, *Other Bostonians*, 290–92. For discussion of various occupational coding schemes, see Zunz, *Changing Face of Inequality*, 420–33. See also Hershberg and Dockhorn, "Occupational Classification."

17. Problems with the use of city directories are discussed in Knights, "City Directories."

SELECTED BIBLIOGRAPHY

Allen, James. *Without Sanctuary: Lynching Photography in America.* Santa Fe, N.M.: Twin Palms, 2000.
Andrews, Sidney. *The South since the War, as Shown by Fourteen Weeks of Travel and Observation in Georgia and the Carolinas.* Boston: Ticknor and Fields, 1866.
Annie E. Casey Foundation. *Neighborhoods Count:* NPU-V. Atlanta: Annie E. Casey Foundation, Atlanta Civic Site, 2004.
Archer, John. *Architecture and Suburbia: From English Villa to American Dream House, 1690-2000.* Minneapolis: University of Minnesota Press, 2005.
Atlanta Neighborhood Development Partnership, Inc. *Making the Case for Mixed-Income and Mixed Use Communities.* Atlanta: Atlanta Neighborhood Development Partnership, 2004.
"Atlanta Spirit." *Manufacturer's Review* (1908): 47-48.
Ayers, Edward L. *Promise of the New South: Life after Reconstruction.* New York: Oxford University Press, 1993.
Baker, Ray Stannard. *Following the Color Line: An Account of Negro Citizenship in the American Democracy.* New York: Doubleday Page, 1908.
Baldwin, Peter C. *Domesticating the Street: The Reform of Public Space in Hartford, 1850-1930.* Columbus: Ohio State University Press, 1999.
Bauerlein, Mark. *Negrophobia: A Race Riot in Atlanta, 1906.* San Francisco: Encounter Books, 2001.
Bauman, John F. *Public Housing, Race, and Renewal: Urban Planning in Philadelphia, 1920-1974.* Philadelphia: Temple University Press, 1987.
Bayor, Ronald H. *Race and the Shaping of Twentieth-Century Atlanta.* Chapel Hill: University of North Carolina Press, 1996.
Beard, Rick. "From Suburb to Defended Neighborhood: Change in Atlanta's Inman Park and Ansley Park." PhD diss., Emory University, 1981.
———. "From Suburb to Defended Neighborhood: The Evolution of Inman Park and Ansley Park, 1890-1980." *Atlanta Historical Society Journal* 26 (1982): 113-40.
———. "Hurt's Deserted Village: Atlanta's Inman Park, 1885-1911." In *Olmsted South: Old South Critic/New South Planner,* edited by Dana F. White and Victor A. Kramer, 195-221. Westport: Greenwood Press, 1979.
Belissary, Constantine G. "The Rise of Industry and the Industrial Spirit in Tennessee, 1865-1885." *Journal of Southern History* 19 (1953): 193-215.
Blomley, Nicholas. "Mud for the Land." *Public Culture* 14, no. 3 (2002): 557-82.
Blum, Sarah Hardin. "Race, Housing, and the Making of Twentieth-Century Louisville, Kentucky." PhD diss., University of Kentucky, 2006.

Board of Trade, UK. *Cost of Living in American Towns: Report of an Enquiry by the Board of Trade into Working Class Rents, Housing and Retail Prices*. London: UK Board of Trade, 1911.

Bodfish, Henry Morton. *History of Building and Loan in the United States*. Chicago: United States Building and Loan League, 1931.

Bodnar, John, Roger Simon, and Michael P. Weber. *Lives of Their Own: Blacks, Italians, and Poles in Pittsburgh, 1900–1960*. Chicago: University of Illinois Press, 1983.

Boger, Gretchen. "The Meaning of Neighborhood in the Modern City: Baltimore's Residential Segregation Ordinances, 1910–1913." *Journal of Urban History* 35 (January 2009): 236–58.

Bonilla-Silva, Eduardo. *Racism without Racists: Color-Blind Racism and the Persistence of Racial Inequality in the United States*. Lanham, Md.: Rowman and Littlefield, 2003.

Bonilla-Silva, Eduardo, and David G. Embrick. "'Every Place Has a Ghetto . . .': The Significance of Whites' Social and Residential Segregation." *Symbolic Interaction* 30, no. 3 (2007): 323–45.

Bonilla-Silva, Eduardo, Carla Goar, and David G. Embrick. "When Whites Flock Together: The Social Psychology of White Habitus." *Critical Sociology* 32, no. 2–3 (2006): 229–53.

Booza, Jason C., Jackie Cutsinger, and Georgia Galster. *Where Did They Go? The Decline of Middle-Income Neighborhoods in Metropolitan America*. Living Cities Census Series. Washington, D.C.: Brookings Institution, 2006.

Bourdieu, Pierre. *Practical Reason*. Stanford, Calif.: Stanford University Press, 1998.

Boyer, Christine. *Dreaming the Rational City: The Myth of American City Planning*. Cambridge, Mass.: MIT Press, 1983.

Brownell, Blaine A. *The Urban Ethos in the South, 1920–1930*. Baton Rouge: Louisiana State University Press, 1975.

Burgess, Patricia. *Planning for the Private Interest: Land Use Controls and Residential Patterns in Columbus, Ohio, 1900–1970*. Columbus: Ohio State University Press, 1994.

Burroughs, Nannie Helen, Charles Spurgeon Johnson, John M. Gries, and James Ford. *Negro Housing: Report of the Committee on Negro Housing*. Washington, D.C.: President's Conference on Home Building and Home Ownership, 1932.

Choco, Marc, and Richard Harris. "The Local Culture of Property: A Comparative History of Housing Tenure in Montreal and Toronto." *Annals of the American Association of Geographers* 80, no. 1:73–95.

Cocks, Catherine. *Doing the Town: The Rise of Urban Tourism in the United States, 1850–1915*. Berkeley: University of California Press, 2001.

Conley, Dalton. *Being Black, Living in the Red: Race, Wealth, and Social Policy in America*. Berkeley: University of California Press, 1999.

Conzen, Michael P., and Kathleen Neils Conzen. "Geographical Structure in Nineteenth-Century Urban Retailing." *Journal of Historical Geography* 5 (1979): 45–66.

Cooper, W. G. "Beautification of Cities." *South Atlantic Quarterly*, July 1908, 274–88.

Cosgrove, Denis E. *Social Formation and Symbolic Landscape*. Madison: University of Wisconsin Press, 1998.

Cronon, William. *Nature's Metropolis: Chicago and the Great West*. New York: W. W. Norton, 1992.

Crowe, Charles. "Racial Massacre in Atlanta, September 22, 1906." *Journal of Negro History* 54 (1969): 150–73.

———. "Racial Violence and Social Reform—Origins of the Atlanta Race Riot of 1906." *Journal of Negro History* 53 (1968): 234–56.

Cullen, Jim. *The American Dream: A Short History of an Idea That Shaped a Nation*. New York: Oxford University Press, 2003.

Daly, Janet R. "Early City Planning Efforts in Omaha, 1914–1920." *Nebraska History* 66 (1985): 48–73.

———. "Zoning: Its Historical Context and Importance in the Development of Pittsburgh, 1900–1923." *Western Pennsylvania Historical Magazine* 21, no. 2 (1988): 99–125.

Daunton, M. J. "Rows and Tenements: American Cities, 1880–1914." In *Housing the Workers: A Comparative History, 1850–1914*, edited by M. J. Daunton, 249–86. New York: Leicester University Press, 1990.

Davies, Pearl Janet. *Real Estate in American History*. Washington, D.C.: Public Affairs Press, 1958.

Davies, Richard O. *Housing Reform during the Truman Administration*. Columbia: University of Missouri Press, 1966.

D'Avino, Gail Anne. "Atlanta Municipal Parks, 1882–1917: Urban Boosterism, Urban Reform in a New South City." PhD diss., Emory University, 1988.

Dean, John P. "Only Caucasian: A Study of Race Covenants." *Journal of Land & Public Utility Economics* (1947): 428–32.

Deaton, Thomas M. "Atlanta during the Progressive Era." PhD diss., University of Georgia, 1969.

———. "James G. Woodward: The Working Man's Mayor." *Atlanta History* 31 (1987): 11–23.

Dittmer, John. *Black Georgia in the Progressive Era, 1900–1920*. Chicago: University of Illinois Press, 1980.

Dorsey, Allison. *To Build Our Lives Together: Community Formation in Black Atlanta, 1875–1906*. Athens: University of Georgia Press, 2004.

Downs, Anthony. "Policies in the New Millennium." Paper presented at the HUD Conference on Housing Policies for the Millennium, Washington, D.C., 2000. Available at http://www.brookings.edu/views/speeches/downs/20001003.htm.

Doyle, Don H. *New Men, New Cities, New South: Atlanta, Nashville, Charleston, Mobile, 1860–1910*. Chapel Hill: University of North Carolina Press, 1990.

Dreier, Peter. "Status of Tenants in the United States." *Social Problems* 30, no. 2 (1982): 179–98.

Duncan, James S. *The City as Text: The Politics of Landscape Interpretation in the Kandyan Kingdom*. New York: Cambridge University Press, 1990.

Duncan, James S., and Nancy G. Duncan. *Landscapes of Privilege: The Politics of the Aesthetic in an American Suburb*. New York: Routledge, 2004.

Dunn-Haley, Karen. "The House That Uncle Sam Built: The Political Culture of Federal Housing Policy, 1919–1932." PhD diss., Stanford University, 1995.

Feagin, Joe R. *Racist America: Roots, Current Realities, and Future Reparations*. New York: Routledge, 2000.

Federal Housing Administration. *Underwriting Manual*. Washington, D.C.: USGPO, 1936.

Ferguson, Karen. *Black Politics in New Deal Atlanta*. Chapel Hill: University of North Carolina Press, 2002.

Fishman, Robert. *Bourgeois Utopias: The Rise and Fall of Suburbia*. New York: Basic Books, 1987.

Flint, Barbara J. "Zoning and Residential Segregation: A Social and Physical History, 1910–40." PhD diss., University of Chicago, 1977.

Fogelson, Robert M. *Bourgeois Nightmares: Suburbia, 1870–1930*. New Haven, Conn.: Yale University Press, 2005.

Freund, David M. P. *Colored Property: State Policy and White Racial Politics in Suburban America*. Chicago: University of Chicago Press, 2007.

Frey, William H. *Diversity Spreads Out: Metro Shifts in Hispanic, Asian, and Black Populations since 2000*. Washington, D.C.: Brookings Institution, 2006.

Garb, Margaret. *City of American Dreams: A History of Homeownership and Housing Reform in Chicago, 1871–1919*. Chicago: University of Chicago Press, 2005.

———. "Drawing the 'Color Line': Race and Real Estate in Early Twentieth-Century Chicago." *Journal of Urban History* 32, no. 5 (2006): 773–87.

Garrett, Franklin M. *Atlanta and Environs: A Chronicle of Its People and Events*. Athens: University of Georgia Press, 1954.

———. *Atlanta and Environs: A Chronicle of Its People and Events*. 2 vols. Athens: University of Georgia Press, 1969.

Gelfand, Mark I. *A Nation of Cities: The Federal Government and Urban America, 1933–1965*. New York: Oxford University Press, 1975.

Godshalk, David Fort. *Veiled Visions: The 1906 Atlanta Race Riot and the Reshaping of American Race Relations*. Chapel Hill: University of North Carolina Press, 2006.

Goodson, Steve. *Highbrows, Hillbillies, and Hellfire: Public Entertainment in Atlanta, 1880–1930*. Athens: University of Georgia Press, 2002.

Gordon, David L. A. "Introducing a City Beautiful Plan for Canada's Capital: Edward Bennett's 1914 Speech to the Canadian Club." *Planning History Studies* 12 (1998): 13–50.

Gotham, Kevin Fox. *Race, Real Estate, and Uneven Development: The Kansas City Experience, 1900–2000*. Albany: State University of New York Press, 2002.

Grable, Stephen. "The Other Side of the Tracks: Cabbagetown—A Working-Class Neighborhood in Transition during the Early Twentieth Century." *Atlanta Historical Society Journal* 26 (1982): 51–66.

Grannis, Rick. "Importance of Trivial Streets: Pedestrian Street Networks and Geographic Patterns of Residential Segregation." *American Journal of Sociology* 103 (1998): 1530-64.

———. "T-Communities: Pedestrian Street Networks and Residential Segregation in Chicago, Los Angeles, and New York." *City & Community* 4, no. 3 (2005): 295-321.

Gries, John M., and James Ford, eds. *Housing Objectives and Programs.* Vol. 11, *President's Conference on Home Building and Home Ownership.* Washington, D.C.: National Capital Press, 1932.

———. *Planning for Residential Districts: Reports of the Committees on City Planning and Zoning.* Washington, D.C.: President's Conference on Home Building and Home Ownership, 1932.

Gries, John M., James Ford, and James Spear Taylor. *Home Ownership, Income and Types of Dwellings: Reports of the Committees on Home Ownership and Leasing.* Washington, D. C.: President's Conference on Home Building and Home Ownership, 1932.

Gries, John M., and James S. Taylor. *How to Own Your Own Home: A Handbook for Prospective Home Owners.* Edited by U.S. Department of Commerce. Washington, D.C.: USGPO, 1923.

Grossman, James R. *Land of Hope: Chicago, Black Southerners, and the Great Migration.* Chicago: University of Chicago Press, 1989.

Gunn, Simon. "From Hegemony to Governmentality: Changing Conceptions of Power in Social History." *Journal of Social History* 39, no. 3 (2006): 705-20.

Hale, Grace Elizabeth. *Making Whiteness: The Culture of Segregation in the South, 1890-1940.* 1st ed. New York: Pantheon Books, 1998.

Hanchett, Thomas W. "The Other 'Subsidized Housing': Federal Aid to Suburbanization, 1940s-1960s." In *From Tenements to the Taylor Homes: In Search of an Urban Housing Policy in Twentieth-Century America,* edited by John F. Bauman, Roger Biles, and Kristin M. Szylvian, 163-79. University Park: Pennsylvania State University Press, 2000.

———. *Sorting Out the New South City: Race, Class and Urban Development in Charlotte, 1875-1975.* Chapel Hill: University of North Carolina Press, 1998.

Handlin, David P. *The American Home: Architecture and Society, 1815-1915.* 1st ed. Boston: Little Brown, 1979.

Harlan, Louis R. "The Secret Life of Booker T. Washington." *Journal of Southern History* 37 (1971): 393-416.

Harley, Gertrude. "Multi-family Housing Units and Urban Tenancy." *Land Economics: A Journal of Planning, Housing, and Public Utilities* (1925): 371-72.

Harris, Richard. *Unplanned Suburbs: Toronto's American Tragedy, 1900 to 1950.* Baltimore: Johns Hopkins University Press, 1996.

Hayden, Dolores. *Building Suburbia: Green Fields and Urban Growth, 1820-2000.* New York: Pantheon Books, 2003.

Hays, R. Allen. *The Federal Government and Urban Housing: Ideology and Change in Public Policy.* 2nd ed. Albany: State University of New York Press, 1995.

Helper, Rose. *Racial Policies and Practices of Real Estate Brokers.* Minneapolis: University of Minnesota Press, 1969.

Hershberg, Theodore, and Robert Dockhorn. "Occupational Classification." *Historical Methods Newsletter* 9 (1976): 78–98.

Hickey, Georgina. *Hope and Danger in the New South City: Working-Class Women and Urban Development in Atlanta, 1890–1940.* Athens: University of Georgia Press, 2003.

Hillier, Amy E. "Redlining and the Home Owners' Loan Corporation." *Journal of Urban History* 29, no. 4 (2003): 394–420.

———. "Residential Security Maps and Neighborhood Appraisals in Philadelphia." *Social Science History* 29, no. 2 (2005): 207–33.

Hines, Thomas S. *Burnham of Chicago, Architect and Planner.* New York: Oxford University Press, 1974.

Hirsch, Arnold R. "Choosing Segregation: Federal Housing Policy between *Shelley* and *Brown*." In *From Tenements to the Taylor Homes: In Search of an Urban Housing Policy in Twentieth-Century America,* edited by John F. Bauman, Robert Biles, and Kristin M. Szylvian, 206–25. University Park: Pennsylvania State University Press, 2000.

———. "'Containment' on the Home Front: Race and Federal Housing Policy from the New Deal to the Cold War." *Journal of Urban History* 26, no. 2 (2000): 158–89.

———. "Less than *Plessy*: The Inner City, Suburbs, and State-Sanctioned Residential Segregation in the Age of Brown." In *New Suburban History,* edited by Kevin M Kruse and Thomas J. Sugrue, 33–56. Chicago: University of Chicago Press, 2006.

———. *Making the Second Ghetto: Race and Housing in Chicago, 1940–1960.* New York: Cambridge University Press, 1983.

Hopkins, Richard J. "Status, Mobility and the Dimensions of Change in a Southern City: Atlanta, 1870–1910." In *Cities in American History,* edited by Kenneth T. Jackson and Stanley K. Schultz, 216–31. New York: Knopf, 1972.

Hornstein, Jeffrey M. *A Nation of Realtors: A Cultural History of the Twentieth-Century American Middle Class.* Durham, N.C.: Duke University Press, 2005.

Hubner, Charles W. "Atlanta." *Appletons' Journal,* October 5, 1872.

Humphreys, Margaret. *Yellow Fever and the South.* New Brunswick, N.J.: Rutgers University Press, 1992.

Hunter, Tera W. *To 'Joy My Freedom: Southern Black Women's Lives and Labors after the Civil War.* Cambridge, Mass.: Harvard University Press, 1997.

Hutchison, Janet. "Building for Babbitt: The State and the Suburban Home Ideal." *Journal of Policy History* 9, no. 2 (1997): 184–210.

Ingersoll, Ernest. "City of Atlanta." *Harper's New Monthly Magazine* 60 (1879): 30–43.

Institute on Race and Poverty, University of Minneapolis. *Determining Equity in Access to Recent Dramatic Job Growth in the Atlanta Region.* Minneapolis: Institute on Race and Poverty, 2006.

———. *Minority Suburbanization, Stable Integration, and Economic Opportunity in Fifteen Metropolitan Regions.* Minneapolis: Institute on Race and Poverty, University of Minneapolis, 2006.

Jackson, Kenneth T. *Crabgrass Frontier: The Suburbanization of the United States.* New York: Oxford University Press, 1985.

Jenkins, Virginia Scott. *The Lawn: A History of an American Obsession.* Washington, D.C.: Smithsonian Institution Press, 1994.

Johnson, Harvey. "Atlanta, the Gate City of the South." *American City,* July–December 1911, 3–8.

Johnson, Mary Beth, and Thomas M. Shapiro. "Good Neighborhoods, Good Schools: Race and the 'Good Choices' of White Families." In *White Out: The Continuing Significance of Racism,* edited by Ashley W. Doane and Eduardo Bonilla-Silva, 173–87. New York: Routledge, 2003.

Joint Center for Housing Studies at Harvard University. *America's Rental Housing: Homes for a Diverse Nation.* Cambridge, Mass.: Joint Center for Housing Studies of Harvard University, 2006.

———. *State of the Nation's Housing 2006.* Cambridge, Mass.: Joint Center for Housing Studies at Harvard University, 2006.

Joint Committee on Housing. *Study and Investigation of Housing.* Atlanta: Joint Committee on Housing, 1947.

Kane, Margaret. "Opportunities in a Neglected Market." *Insured Mortgage Portfolio,* 4th qtr. (1948): 6–8, 32–33.

Karolak, Eric J. "'No Idea of Doing Anything Wonderful': The Labor-Crisis Origins of National Housing Policy and the Reconstruction of the Working-Class Community, 1917–1919." In *From Tenements to the Taylor Homes: In Search of an Urban Housing Policy in Twentieth-Century America,* edited by John F. Bauman, Roger Biles and Kristin M. Szylvian, 60–80. University Park: Pennsylvania State University Press, 2000.

Katzman, David. *Before the Ghetto: Black Detroit in the Nineteenth Century.* Urbana: University of Illinois Press, 1973.

Keating, Ann Durkin. *Building Chicago: Suburban Developers & the Creation of a Divided Metropolis.* Urban Life and Urban Landscape. Columbus: Ohio State University Press, 1988.

Keating, Larry. *Atlanta: Race, Class, and Urban Expansion.* Comparative American Cities. Philadelphia: Temple University Press, 2001.

Keating, Larry, and Carol A. Flores. "Sixty and Out: Techwood Homes Transformed by Enemies and Friends." *Journal of Urban History* 26, no. 3 (2000): 275–311.

Kelleher, Daniel T. "St. Louis' 1916 Residential Segregation Ordinance." *Bulletin of the Missouri Historical Society* 26 (1970): 239–48.

Kimble, John. "Insuring Inequality: The Role of the Federal Housing Administration in the Urban Ghettoization of African Americans." *Law & Social Inquiry* 32, no. 2 (2007): 399–434.

Kirby, Jack Temple. *Darkness at the Dawning: Race and Reform in the Progressive South.* New York: J. B. Lippincott, 1972.

Klima, Don L. "Breaking Out: Streetcars and Suburban Development, 1872–1900." *Atlanta Historical Society Journal* 26 (1982): 67–82.

Knights, Peter R. "City Directories as Aids to Ante-bellum Urban Studies: A Research Note." *Historical Methods Newsletter* 2 (1969): 1–10.
Knowles, Anne Kelly. "Emerging Trends in Historical GIS." *Historical Geography* 33 (2005): 7–13.
———. "Introduction to 'Historical GIS: The Spatial Turn in Social Science History.'" *Social Science History* 24 (2000): 451–70.
Krueckeberg, Donald A. "The Grapes of Rent: A History of Renting in a Country of Owners." *Housing Policy Debate* 10, no. 1 (1999): 9–30.
Kruse, Kevin M. *White Flight: Atlanta and the Making of Modern Conservatism*. Princeton, N.J.: Princeton University Press, 2005.
Kuhn, Clifford M. *Contesting the New South Order: The 1914–1915 Strike at Atlanta's Fulton Mills*. Chapel Hill: University of North Carolina Press, 2001.
Kusmer, Kenneth L. *A Ghetto Takes Shape: Black Cleveland, 1870–1930*, Urbana: University of Illinois Press, 1976.
Lasker, Bruno. "Atlanta Zoning Plan." *Survey* (April 22, 1922): 114–15.
Lassiter, Matthew D. *The Silent Majority: Suburban Politics in the Sunbelt South*. Princeton, N.J.: Princeton University Press, 2006.
Laurenti, Luigi. "Effects of Nonwhite Purchases on Market Prices of Residences." *Appraisal Journal* 20, no. 3 (1952): 314–29.
Lipsitz, George. *Possessive Investment in Whiteness: How White People Profit from Identity Politics*. Philadelphia: Temple University Press, 1998.
Litwack, Leon. *Trouble in Mind: Black Southerners in the Age of Jim Crow*. New York: Knopf, 1998.
Lloyd, Anne. "Pittsburgh's 1923 Zoning Ordinance." *Western Pennsylvania Historical Magazine* 57, no. 3 (1974): 289–305.
Logan, John. *Ethnic Diversity Grows, Neighborhood Integration Lags Behind*. Albany, N.Y.: Lewis Mumford Center for Comparative Urban and Regional Research, 2001.
Long, Herman H., and Charles S. Johnson. *People vs. Property: Race Restrictive Covenants in Housing*. Nashville: Fisk University Press, 1947.
Lyon, Elizabeth A. "Frederick Law Olmsted and Joel Hurt: Planning for Atlanta." In *Olmsted South, Old South Critic, New South Planner*, edited by Dana F. White and Victor A. Kramer, 165–93. Westport, Conn.: Greenwood Press, 1979.
Macieski, Robert. "The Home of the Workingman Is the Balance Wheel of Democracy: Housing Reform in Wartime Bridgeport." *Journal of Urban History* 26, no. 6 (2000): 715–39.
Mack, Curt C. "Covenants for New Subdivisions." *Insured Mortgage Portfolio*, 4th qtr. (1948): 9–11, 34–35.
Maclachlan, Gretchen Ehrmann. "Women's Work: Atlanta's Industrialization and Urbanization, 1879–1929." PhD diss., Emory University, 1992.
Marsh, Margaret. *Suburban Lives*. New Brunswick, N.J.: Rutgers University Press, 1990.
Massey, Douglas S., and Nancy A. Denton. *American Apartheid: Segregation and the Making of the Underclass*. Cambridge, Mass.: Harvard University Press, 1993.

Mayfield, Edward H. "Progress in Lynchburg, Virginia." *American City*, August 1911, 135.
Mayne, A. J. C. *The Imagined Slum: Newspaper Representation in Three Cities, 1870–1914*. New York: Leicester University Press, 1993.
McElreath, Walter. *Walter McElreath: An Autobiography*. Macon, Ga.: Mercer University Press, 1984.
McKinney, Karyn D. *Being White: Stories of Race and Racism*. New York: Routledge, 2005.
McLeod, Jonathan Woolard. "Black and White Workers: Atlanta during Reconstruction." PhD diss., University of California, Los Angeles, 1987.
———. *Workers and Workplace Dynamics in Reconstruction-Era Atlanta: A Case Study*. Los Angeles: UCLA Press, 1989.
Meck, Stuart. "Zoning and Anti-Semitism in the 1920s: The Case of Cleveland Heights Jewish Orphan Home v. Village of University Heights and Its Aftermath." *Journal of Planning History* 4, no. 2 (2005): 91–128.
Meier, August. "Negro Class Structure and Ideology in the Age of Booker T. Washington." *Phylon* 23, no. 3 (1962): 258–66.
Meier, August, and David Lewis. "History of the Negro Upper Class in Atlanta, Georgia, 1890–1958." *Journal of Negro Education* 28, no. 2 (1959): 128–139.
Mills, Charles W. "White Supremacy as Sociopolitical System: A Philosophical Perspective." In *White Out: The Continuing Significance of Racism*, edited by Ashley W. Doane and Eduardo Bonilla-Silva, 35–48. New York: Routledge, 2003.
Mitchell, J. Paul. "Historical Overview of Federal Policy: Encouraging Homeownership." In *Federal Housing Policy and Programs*, edited by J. Paul Mitchell, 39–46. New Brunswick, N.J.: Rutgers University Press, 1985.
Mixon, Gregory. *Atlanta Riot: Race, Class, And Violence in a New South City*. Gainesville: University Press of Florida, 2005.
Monchow, Helen C. "Review of John P. Dean, *Home Ownership: Is It Sound?*" *American Economic Review* 35 (1945): 734.
Nicolaides, Becky M. *My Blue Heaven: Life and Politics in the Working-Class Suburbs of Los Angeles, 1920–1965*. Chicago: University of Chicago Press, 2002.
Nightingale, Carl H. "Transnational Contexts of Early Twentieth-Century American Urban Segregation." *Journal of Social History* 39, no. 3 (2006): 667–702.
Oliver, Melvin L., and Thomas M. Shapiro. *Black Wealth/White Wealth: A New Perspective on Racial Inequality*. New York: Routledge, 1995.
Orfield, Gary. "Minorities and Suburbanization." In *Critical Perspectives on Housing*, edited by Rachel G. Bratt et al., 221–29. Philadelphia: Temple University Press, 1986.
Orfield, Gary, and Carole Ashkinaze. *The Closing Door: Conservative Policy and Black Opportunity*. Chicago: University of Chicago Press, 1991.
Orfield, Myron. *Metropolitics: A Regional Agenda for Community and Stability*. Washington, D.C.: Brookings Institution Press, 1997.
Osofsky, Gilbert. *Harlem: The Making of a Ghetto; Negro New York, 1890–1930*. New York: Harper and Row, 1966.

Otis, Robert R. "Atlanta's Plan, 1909–1932." MS. AHC.
Page, Max. *The Creative Destruction of Manhattan, 1900–1940*. Historical Studies of Urban America. Chicago: University of Chicago Press, 1999.
Palmer, Charles F. *Adventures of a Slum Fighter*. Atlanta: Tupper and Love, 1955.
Perin, Constance. *Everything in Its Place: Social Order and Land Use in America*. Princeton, N.J.: Princeton University Press, 1977.
Peterson, Jon A. *The Birth of City Planning in the United States, 1840–1917*. Baltimore: Johns Hopkins University Press, 2003.
———. "Frederick Law Olmsted Sr., and Frederick Law Olmsted Jr.: The Visionary and the Professional." In *Planning the Twentieth-Century American City*, edited by Mary Corbin Sies and Christopher Silver, 37–54. Baltimore: Johns Hopkins University Press, 1996.
Phillips, Meredith, and Tiffani Chin. "School Inequality: What Do We Know?" In *Social Inequality*, edited by Kathryn N. Neckerman, 467–519. Los Angeles: Russell Sage Foundation, 2004.
Porter, Michael L. "Black Atlanta: An Interdisciplinary Study of Blacks on the East Side of Atlanta, 1890–1930." PhD diss., Emory University, 1974.
Power, Garrett. "Advent of Zoning." *Planning Perspectives* 4, no. 1 (1989): 1–13.
———. "Apartheid Baltimore Style: The Residential Segregation Ordinances of 1910–1913." *Maryland Law Review* 42 (1983): 289–329.
Preston, Howard L. "Parkways, Parks, and the 'New South' Progressivism: Planning Practice in Atlanta, 1880–1917." In *Olmsted South, Old South Critic, New South Planner*, edited by Dana F. White and Victor A. Kramer, 223–38. Westport, Conn.: Greenwood Press, 1979.
Rabinowitz, Howard N. *Race Relations in the Urban South, 1865–1890*. New York: Oxford University Press, 1978.
Radford, Gail. *Modern Housing for America: Policy Struggles in the New Deal Era*. Chicago: University of Chicago Press, 1996.
Rafferty, Edward C. "Orderly City, Orderly Lives: The City Beautiful Movement in St. Louis." *Gateway Heritage* 11, no. 4 (1991): 40–62.
Rand Corporation. *A Million Random Digits with 100,000 Normal Deviates*. Glencoe, Ill.: Free Press, 1955.
Randle, William M. "Professors, Reformers, Bureaucrats, and Cronies: The Players in *Euclid v. Ambler*." In *Zoning and the American Dream: Promises Still to Keep*, edited by Charles M. Haar and Jerold S. Kayden, 31–69. Chicago: Planners Press, 1989.
Reid, Whitelaw. *After the War: A Southern Tour; May 1, 1865, to May 1, 1866*. Cincinnati: Moore et al., 1866.
Revell, Keith D. "Regulating the Landscape: Real Estate Values, City Planning, and the 1916 Zoning Ordinance." In *The Landscape of Modernity*, edited by David Ward and Olivier Zunz, 19–45. Baltimore: Johns Hopkins University Press, 1992.
Rice, Roger L. "Residential Segregation by Law, 1910–1917." *Journal of Southern History* 34 (1968): 179–99.

Richards, Franklin D. "How FHA Mortgage Insurance Operates." *Insured Mortgage Portfolio*, 1st qtr. (1952): 3–19.

Ritterhouse, Jennifer Lynn. *Growing Up Jim Crow: How Black and White Southern Children Learned Race*. Chapel Hill: University of North Carolina, 2006.

Roediger, David R. *The Wages of Whiteness: Race and the Making of the American Working Class*. Rev. ed. The Haymarket. New York: Verso, 1999.

Rothman, Norman C. "Curriculum Formation in a Black College: A Study of Morris Brown College, 1881–1980." PhD diss., Georgia State University, 1981.

Rusk, David. *Cities without Suburbs*. Washington, D.C.: Woodrow Wilson Center Press, 1993.

Russell, Horace. "Georgia." In Bodfish, *History of Building and Loan*, 353–57.

Russell, James Michael. *Atlanta, 1847–1890: City Building in the Old South and the New*. Baton Rouge: Louisiana State University Press, 1988.

Schuyler, David. *New Urban Landscape: The Redefinition of City Form in Nineteenth-Century America*. New Studies in American Intellectual and Cultural History. Baltimore: Johns Hopkins University Press, 1986.

Scott, Mel. *American City Planning*. Berkeley: University of California Press, 1969.

Seligman, Amanda I. *Block by Block: Neighborhoods and Public Policy on Chicago's West Side*. Historical Studies of Urban America. Chicago: University of Chicago Press, 2005.

Sewell, George. "Morris Brown College: Legacy of Wesley John Gaines." *Crisis* 88 (1981): 133–36.

Sewell, George A., and Cornelius V. Troup. *Morris Brown College, The First Hundred Years, 1881–1981*. Atlanta: Morris Brown College, 1981.

Shapiro, Thomas M. *The Hidden Cost of Being African American: How Wealth Perpetuates Inequality*. New York: Oxford University Press, 2004.

Sides, Josh. *L.A. City Limits : African American Los Angeles from the Great Depression to the Present*. Berkeley: University of California Press, 2003.

Sies, Mary Corbin. "The City Transformed: Nature, Technology, and the Suburban Ideal, 1877–1917." *Journal of Urban History* 14, no. 1 (1987): 81–111.

———. "'God's Very Kingdom on the Earth': The Design Program for the American Suburban Home, 1877–1917." In *Modern Architecture in America: Visions and Revisions*, edited by Richard Guy Wilson and Sidney K. Robinson, 3–31. Ames: Iowa State University Press, 1991.

———. "North American Suburbs, 1880–1950: Cultural and Social Reconsiderations." *Journal of Urban History* 27, no. 3 (2001): 313–46.

———. "Paradise Retained: An Analysis of Persistence in Planned, Exclusive Suburbs, 1880–1980." *Planning Perspectives* 12 (1997): 165–91.

———. "Toward a Performance Theory of the Suburban Ideal, 1877–1917." *Perspectives in Vernacular Architecture* 4 (1991): 197–207.

Silver, Christopher. "Racial Origins of Zoning: Southern Cities from 1910–40." *Planning Perspectives* 6 (1991): 189–205.

———. *Twentieth-Century Richmond: Planning, Politics, and Race*. Knoxville: University of Tennessee Press, 1984.

Silver, Christopher, and John V. Moeser. *The Separate City: Black Communities in the Urban South, 1940–1968*. Lexington: University Press of Kentucky, 1995.

Simon, Roger D. "City-Building Process: Housing and Services in New Milwaukee Neighborhoods, 1880–1910." *Transactions of the American Philosophical Society* 68 (1978): 3–64.

Sjoquist, David L., ed. *Atlanta Paradox*. New York: Russell Sage Foundation, 2000.

Smith, Carl S. *The Plan of Chicago: Daniel Burnham and the Remaking of the American City*. Chicago Visions and Revisions. Chicago: University of Chicago Press, 2006.

Smith, Mark M. *How Race Is Made: Slavery, Segregation, and the Senses*. Chapel Hill: University of North Carolina Press, 2006.

Sorensen, Annemette, Jr., Leslie Hollingsworth, and Karl Taeuber. "Indexes of Racial Residential Segregation for 109 Cities in the United States, 1940 to 1970." *Sociological Focus* 8 (1975): 125–42.

Spear, Allan H. *Black Chicago: The Making of a Negro Ghetto, 1890–1920*. Chicago: University of Chicago Press, 1967.

Stach, Patricia Burgess. "Deed Restrictions and Subdivision Development in Columbus, Ohio, 1900–1970." *Journal of Urban History* 15, no. 1 (1988): 42–68.

Stilgoe, John R. *Borderland: Origins of the American Suburb, 1820–1939*. New Haven, Conn.: Yale University Press, 1988.

Stone, Clarence Nelson. *Economic Growth and Neighborhood Discontent: System Bias in the Urban Renewal Program of Atlanta*. Chapel Hill: University of North Carolina Press, 1976.

Sugrue, Thomas J. *Origins of the Urban Crisis: Race and Inequality in Postwar Detroit*. Princeton, N.J.: Princeton University Press, 1996.

Sullivan, Patricia. *Days of Hope: Race and Democracy in the New Deal Era*. Chapel Hill: University of North Carolina Press, 1996.

Swartz, David. *Culture & Power: The Sociology of Pierre Bourdieu*. Chicago: University of Chicago Press, 1997.

Thernstrom, Stephan. *The Other Bostonians: Poverty and Progress in the American Metropolis, 1880–1970*. Harvard Studies in Urban History. Cambridge, Mass.: Harvard University Press, 1973.

Thompson, Robert A., Hylan Lewis, and Davis McEntire. "Atlanta and Birmingham: A Comparative Study in Negro Housing." In *Studies in Housing and Minority Groups*, edited by Nathan Glazer and Davis McEntire, 13–83. Berkeley: University of California Press, 1960.

Tobey, Ronald, Charles Wetherell, and Jay Brigham. "Moving Out and Settling In: Residential Mobility, Home Owning, and the Public Enframing of Citizenship, 1921–1950." *American Historical Review* 95, no. 5 (1990): 1395–1422.

Tough, Rosalind. "Life Cycle of the Home Owners' Loan Corporation." *Land Economics* 27, no. 4 (1951): 324–31.

Trowbridge, J. T. *The South: A Tour of Its Battle-fields and Ruined Cities*. Hartford, Conn.: L. Stebbins, 1866.

Tuttle, William M., Jr. *Race Riot: Chicago in the Red Summer of 1919*. Studies in American Negro Life. New York: Atheneum, 1970.

U.S. Bureau of the Census. *Housing: Analytical Maps: Atlanta, Georgia; Block Statistics (1940)*. Washington, D.C.: United States Bureau of the Census, 1940.

———. *Sixteenth Census of the United States: 1940; Housing*. Vol. 2, *General Characteristics*. Washington,: U.S. Govt. print. off., 1943.

———. *U.S. Census of Housing: 1940*. Vol. 2, *General Characteristics*. Washington: USGPO, 1943.

———. *U.S. Census of Housing: 1950*. Washington, D.C.: USGPO, 1950.

U.S. Commission on Civil Rights. "Housing: Hearings Held in New York, Atlanta, and Chicago." In *U.S. Commission on Civil Rights*. Washington, D.C.: USGPO, 1959.

Warner, Sam Bass, Jr. *Streetcar Suburbs: The Process of Growth in Boston (1870–1900)*. 2nd ed. Cambridge, Mass.: Harvard University Press, 1978.

Watts, Eugene John. "Characteristics of Candidates in City Politics: Atlanta, 1865–1903." PhD diss., Emory University, 1969.

Weiss, Marc. "Richard T. Ely and the Contribution of Economic Research to National Housing Policy, 1920–1940." *Urban Studies* 26, no. 1 (1989): 115–26.

———. *The Rise of the Community Builders: The American Real Estate Industry and Urban Land Planning*. New York: Columbia University Press, 1987.

White, Dana. "Black Sides of Atlanta: A Geography of Expansion and Containment." *Atlanta Historical Society Journal* 26 (1982): 199–225.

Whitten, Robert H. "City Zoning." *Journal of the Western Society of Engineers* 25 (1920): 1–6.

———. "Social Aspects of Zoning." *Survey* (June 15, 1922): 418–19.

Wiese, Andrew. "The Other Suburbanites: African American Suburbanization in the North before 1950." *Journal of American History* 85, no. 4 (1999): 1495–1524.

———. *Places of Their Own: African American Suburbanization in the Twentieth Century*. Chicago: University of Chicago Press, 2004.

———. "Stubborn Diversity: A Commentary on Middle-Class Influence in Working-Class Suburbs, 1900–1940." *Journal of Urban History* 27, no. 3 (2001): 347–54.

Williamson, Joel. *The Crucible of Race: Black/White Relations in the American South since Emancipation*. New York: Oxford University Press, 1984.

Wilson, William H. *The City Beautiful Movement*. Baltimore: Johns Hopkins University Press, 1994.

Woodward, C. Vann. *Origins of the New South, 1877–1913*. Baton Rouge: Louisiana State University Press, 1971.

Worley, William S. *J. C. Nichols and the Shaping of Kansas City: Innovation in Planned Residential Communities*. Columbia: University of Missouri Press, 1990.

Wotton, Grigsby Hart, Jr. "New City of the South: Atlanta, 1843–1873." PhD diss., Johns Hopkins University, 1973.

Wright, George C. "The NAACP and Residential Segregation in Louisville, Kentucky, 1913–1917." *Register of the Kentucky Historical Society* 78 (1980): 39–54.

Wright, Gwendolyn. *Building the Dream: A Social History of Housing in America.* Cambridge, Mass.: MIT Press, 1981.

———. *Moralism and the Model Home: Domestic Architecture and Cultural Conflict in Chicago, 1873–1913.* Chicago: University of Chicago Press, 1980.

Zunz, Olivier. *The Changing Face of Inequality: Urbanization, Industrial Development, and Immigrants in Detroit, 1880–1920.* Chicago: University of Chicago Press, 1982.

INDEX

Abram, Morris, 188
Abrams, Charles, 165, 181
academic community, homeownership promotion and, 130–31
Adair, Forrest, 110
Adair, George W., 19, 22, 24, 44–45, 88, 108, 110–11, 236n25, 238n48
Adair, R. B., 101–2
advertising: Buy a Home and Own Your Home campaigns, 111–12; homeownership promotion through, 113–18, 121–34; housing segregation and, 32–40; park-neighborhood development and, 45–46, 52–57; for rental housing, 23–24; restrictive covenants in, 138–40; urban development and, 15–17
African Americans: as construction contractors, 25, 187–90; Depression-era housing development for, 166–71; federal housing policies' exclusion of, 8–9; and head-of-household statistics, 34–37; and HOLC appraisal standards, 161–62; homeownership among, 168–71, 246n3, 257n40; housing development and construction by, 188–90, 206–11; housing segregation and, 2–3, 88–92, 101–4; impact of land-use zoning on, 153–57; in Jackson Hill, 77–81; migration to Atlanta by, 17–21; Morris Brown College relocation dispute and, 71, 81–92; neighborhood geographies and, 176–80; omitted from homeownership campaigns, 126; postwar advances of, 181–90, 260n83; public housing and, 171–74; race riots in Atlanta and, 75–76; and rental housing, 25–32, 98–99, 210–14; restrictive covenants for exclusion of, 54–56; "reverse" migration by, 209–11; subdivision development by, 140–41, 204–5; and washerwoman occupation, 32, 37–39, 234n65
Aiken, Walter, 9, 126, 167, 170, 184, 188, 191
Alexander, T. M., 187
Alexander Hamilton and Son, 25
Allen, Ivan, 101, 206
Alpharetta, Ga., 1
American Apartheid (Massey-Denton), 199–200
American City (Johnson), 41, 58
American Civic Association, 130
American Council of Human Relations, 183
Andrews, Sidney, 13
Andrews, Walter P., 53
Ansley, Edwin, 25, 33, 51–57, 71, 137, 238n48
Ansley, William, 151
Ansley Park (Atlanta), 5–6, 88; development of, 49, 51–56, 236n25, 237n35; exclusive image of, 138; expansion of, 135; homeownership rates in, 168; restrictive covenants in, 55–56, 98–99, 135, 260n72; security map of, 161
anti-Semitism: HOLC appraisal standards and, 162; restrictive covenants and, 138–40, 143
apartment housing: housing hierarchy and status of, 132–34, 146–48, 155–57, 253n39; immigrant population growth and development of, 211–14; suburban increase in, 208–11. *See also* rental housing
architectural design: FHA guidelines concerning, 163; rental housing production and, 25–32

281

Index

Architecture of Country Houses, The (Downing), 43
area descriptions, HOLC, 160–62
Arnall, Ellis, 187
Ashby Terrace (Atlanta), 168
Ashley, Claude, 89–91, 98, 106
Atlanta, a Twentieth Century City, 15
Atlanta, Ga.: city planning and urban aesthetics in, 4–5, 13; demographics of, 1; history of growth in, 12; homeownership campaign in, 12, 108–13, 120–26; immigrant population increase in, 209–11; land industry in, 21–22; land-use zoning restrictions in, 138–46; migration to, 17–21; park-neighborhood movement and, 41–70; population changes in (1870–1950), 18; post–Civil War rebuilding of, 14–17; postwar population changes in, 190–94; public housing in, 171–74; race and class divisions in, 1–2, 72–76; race riots in, 75–76, 99–100, 143, 152–53, 199, 229n7; racial heterogeneity in, 92–95; real estate trends in, 108–13, 246n3; "reverse" African American migration to, 209–11; segregation trends in, 32–40, 96–98; and South Atlanta subdivision, 234n61; subdivision building boom in, 135; suburban annexation by, 137–40; West End development initiatives in, 82–83
Atlanta and West Point Railroad, 16
Atlanta Board of Realtors, 23
Atlanta Chamber of Commerce, 15, 19, 41, 60, 63, 68, 84–85, 111, 142, 186, 205
Atlanta Constitution, 86; African American subdivisions and, 140–41, 251n22; Ansley Park development and, 51–52; City Beautiful movement and, 62–64, 66–67; class and political issues in, 19, 21, 23; FHA housing plans in, 166–67; homeownership promotion and, 121–26, 248n49; land-use planning and, 156–57; park-neighborhood promotion in, 128–29, 137–38; in Reconstruction era, 14; segregation issues and, 88, 90–91
Atlanta Cotton Factory, 18, 21
Atlanta Daily World, 181, 189
Atlanta Federal Savings and Loan, 188
Atlanta Federation of Trades, 20
Atlanta Housing Authority, 173–74, 186, 215
Atlanta Housing Council, 184
Atlanta Independent, 86, 90–91, 95–96, 102
Atlanta Journal, 33, 103; City Beautiful movement and, 65, 67–69; homeownership promotion in, 120; park-neighborhood movement and, 84, 143; segregation issues and, 74–75, 88, 100–101
Atlanta Journal-Constitution, 200; immigrant issues covered in, 210–14
Atlanta Life Insurance Company, 188
Atlanta National Bank, 121–22
Atlanta Neighborhood Development Partnership, 209, 217–18
Atlanta Normal and Industrial Institute, 243n37
Atlanta Paradox, The (Sjoquist), 199
Atlanta Park Commission, 61–65, 239n65
Atlanta Real Estate Board, 142
Atlanta Rolling Mill, 18
Atlanta Street Railway Company, 44
Atlanta University, 82
Atlanta Urban League, 9, 159, 184, 186–90, 194–98, 204, 206–8, 210
Atlanta Zone Plan (Whitten), 145–48, 151–57
"aversive" racism, homeownership and, 11

Baldwin, J. C., 85–86
Baldwin, Peter, 57
Baltimore, Md., 89–90, 92–93, 243n49, 245n78
Barfield, Carroll, 189

Bartholomew, Harland, 130
Beard, Rick, 46, 236n20, 237n35
Belissary, Constantine, 14
Bennett, Edward, 239n63
Bennett Heights (Atlanta), 189
Bilbo, Theodore, 116
Binford, W. D., 93
Black, Eugene R., 121, 123
Black, James R., 81
Black, W. A., 60
Bleckley, Haralson, 65–66, 68, 101
block sampling, 219–24, 266n12
Blomley, Nicholas, 4
Board of Trade, 15
Bodnar, John, 108
Bonilla-Silva, Eduardo, 3–4, 216–17
Bourdieu, Pierre, 10
Bowen, Annie, 154
Bowen, J. W. E., 190
Bowen v. Atlanta, 154
Brinkley, David, 183
Brookhaven Civic Association, 186
Brookwood Hills (Atlanta), 138–39, 168
Brownell, Blain, 58
Buchanan v. Warley, 92, 151–52
Buckhead (Atlanta), 170, 190
Buckhead Trade Association, 186
building-height restrictions, 41
Burdett Realty, 128
Burkheimer, William D., 165
Burnham, Daniel, 41, 45, 239n63
Burns, Harry, 167
business development, in post–Civil War Atlanta, 14–17
Buy a Home campaign, 111–12, 118–23

C. A. Dahl Floral Company, 128
Candler, Asa, 46, 63, 235n3
Candler, John S., 84
Carey, Dan, 63–65
Carey Shingles, 126–27
Carlisle, Mrs. J. E., 125

Carpenter, J. L., 151
Cascade Heights development (Atlanta), 166–67
Census, U.S. Bureau of the, 174–80
central business districts (CBDs), 208–11
Central of Georgia Railroad, 16
Chambless, Edgar, 102
Chamlee Lumber Company, 25
Chapman v. King, 187
Chattahoochee Brick Company, 21
Cheshire, T. J., 24
Chicago, Ill., 173–74
Chicago Defender, 89–90
Chidi, George, 211
children, homeownership promotion to, 125
Chin, Tiffani, 214
Chinese immigrants, 110, 144
citizenship, homeownership associated with, 10–11
Citizens Trust Company, 188
City Beautiful design aesthetic: in Atlanta, 5–6, 61–65, 69–70; national trends in, 239n63
city directories: block studies and, 220–24, 266n15; housing segregation reflected in, 96–98
City Planning and Zoning Committee, 131
City Planning Commission, 172
city services and infrastructure, elites' control of, 20–21
civic elites: Atlanta housing patterns and, 4–5; City Beautiful aesthetic and, 61–65; entrepreneurs as, 19–20; fire in Jackson Hill and, 101–6; HOLC appraisal standards and, 161–62; housing segregation and role of, 3–4, 92–95, 201–20; Jackson Hill segregation dispute and, 71–72, 77–81, 102–4; land-use zoning and, 141–57, 201–5, 251n27; Morris Brown College relocation effort and, 81–92; New Deal housing program

civic elites (*continued*)
and, 159–80; New South ideology and, 44–49; new urban aesthetic and, 42; park-neighborhood movement and, 42–44, 49–57, 237n35; postwar federal housing policies and, 182–90; power structure and role of, 20–21; public housing and, 171–74, 180; segregation ordinances and, 88–92; urban ethos and, 57–60; whiteness ideology and, 74–76, 211–14; zoning and planning initiatives and, 141–45

Civil Rights Commission, U.S.: housing segregation testimony before, 170; public housing testimony before, 173–74, 187

civil rights movement, public housing policies and, 181–90

Civil War, southern urban development in wake of, 13, 231n9

Clansman, The (Dixon), 75

class issues: City Beautiful movement and, 61–65, 239n68; and class categories in housing studies, 223–24; desegregation policies and role of, 3; economic inequality and, 200; in Jackson Hill development, 79–81; land-use zoning and, 150–57; neighborhood geographies and, 174–80; park-neighborhood movement and, 44–49, 49–56, 138–40, 237n35; politics and, 19–21; rental housing and, 24–32, 234nn61–62, 234n65; restrictive covenants and, 54–57; segregation in Atlanta and, 74–76, 243n42

Cleveland Heights, Ohio, 143

Cobb County, Ga.: immigrant population increase in, 209–11; whiteness ideology in, 214

Collier, C. A., 60

Collier Heights (Atlanta), 175

Collier Woods (Atlanta), 161

Collins Park (Atlanta), 151

"Colored Better Housing Campaign," 167

Commerce, U.S. Department of, 6, 112–13, 116, 126, 130–31, 249n74

"committee of ten" (in post-riot Atlanta), 241n10

Committee on Manufactures, Freight Rates and Statistics, 16

Committee on Manufacturing and Statistics, 15–16

Comprehensive Land-Use Plan, 136

Conference of Mayors, 130

conflict rhetoric, 245n78

construction industry, rental housing and, 25–26

conventions, development promotion and, 232n15

Conyers, B. J., 85

Cooper, Walter G., 41–42, 60, 63, 110

Cosgrove, W. L., 66, 68

Cotton States and International Exposition, 59

Country Club District (Kansas City), 150

Craighead, E. R., 168, 191

credit, social status conferred by, 231n24

Crisis, 89–90

Crittle, Luther J., 154

Cronon, William, 59

Crumbley, Wade, 200

culture: hegemonic power structure of, 218; housing policies and, 3–4, 12

curbstoners, 23, 233n38

Daily Intelligencer, 14

data acquisition and analysis, housing research and, 223–24

Davis, Alexander Jackson, 43, 46

Davis, Benjamin, 86, 90–91, 95–96, 102, 244n57

Dean, John, 107

deed covenants. *See* restrictive covenants

Denton, Nancy, 199
Department of Commerce, U.S., 6, 112–13, 116, 126, 130–31, 249n74
Department of Labor, U.S., 6, 113, 119, 125
Dillard, Douglas, 200
Dittmer, John, 75
Dixie Hills (Atlanta), 9
Dixon, Thomas, 75
Dodd, Philip, 19
Dodd, Thomas, 19
Dorsey, Allison, 241n6
Douglas, Lee, 53
Downing, Andrew Jackson, 43, 57
Doyle, Don, 231n9
Dreier, Peter, 107
Druid Hills (Atlanta), 5–7; anti-Semitism in, 162; deed restrictions in, 54–56, 237n47, 238n48; development of, 49–56, 236n24; exclusive image of, 138, 142–43
Du Bois, W. E. B., 73
Duncan, James, 3–4, 11
Duncan, Nancy, 3–4, 11
Du Vall, W. O., 170

Eagan, John Taylor, 261n93
East Atlanta Land Company, 45–46
electoral politics, racism and, 74–76
Elsas, Jacob, 19
Elsas, Oscar, 62
Ely, Richard, 130, 256n16
employment growth: land industry and, 21–22; urban migration and, 19
English, James, 52, 84, 241n10, 242n33
Euclid Heights (Cleveland), 52
Euclid v. Amber, 156–57, 203
exclusionary housing practices: economic inequality and, 199–200; land-use zoning and, 136; park-neighborhood construction and, 135–57; protection of privilege and, 215–17
Ezra Church Heights (Atlanta), 168, 191

Fairview Terrace (Atlanta), 167, 190–92
Farlinger, A. W., 90
Faulkner, Cindy, 212
Feagin, Joe, 4
Federal Home Loan Bank Board (FHLBB), 3
Federal Housing Administration (FHA), 3–4, 8; African American builders and, 188–90; black housing initiatives, 181, 260n83; housing segregation and, 167–71, 203–5; Mortgage Insurance Division, 257n30; neighborhood geographies and, 175–80; New Deal housing policies and, 158–60; postwar public housing policies and, 198; *Underwriting Manual*, 162–66, 256n17, 256n19, 256n21; during World War II and postwar era, 180–90
federal housing policy: homeownership promotion and, 107–8, 112–23, 130–34; neighborhood geographies and, 174–80; park-neighborhood movement and, 8, 12, 158–98; property value protection and, 213–14; public housing and, 171–74; segregation and role of, 3–4, 204–5; during World War II and postwar era, 180–90
Federal Reserve Act, 248n49
Felder-Williams bill of 1908, 241n6
Fifth Avenue Association (FAA; New York City), 144
Fishman, Robert, 235n11
Fogleson, Robert, 237n42, 237n47
Foley, Raymond, 181, 183
Frankston, Janet, 212
Freund, David, 3, 161, 255n6
Fulton Bag Factory, 18, 20
Fulton Cotton Mills, 19–20
Fulton County, Ga.: immigrant population in, 210–11; racial housing policies and, 8

Gaine, Marion, 19
Garb, Margaret, 3

Garden Hills (Atlanta), 151, 156, 191
Geographic Information Systems (GIS), 219–24
George, Walter, 182
Georgia Board of Realtors, 23
Georgia Federation of Women's Clubs, 64
Georgia Railroad, 16, 18–19
Georgia Railway and Power Company, 125
Georgia Supreme Court, 154
Gingrich, Newt, 214
Glenn, John Thomas, 15
Glenwood Park (Atlanta), 175–76
Goode, Samuel, 23–24
Goodrich, F. P., 116–17
Grady, Henry, 14, 19
Grannis, Rick, 219
Grant, John W., 84
Graves, Antoine, 77
Great Depression, housing development and, 158–59
Greater Georgia Association, 16
Green, L. C., 110
Green, Lorraine, 212
Greene, Ward, 100–101
Gregson, Wilfred, 186
Gries, John M., 131, 249n74
Grove Park Civic Association, 188
Grove Park (Atlanta), 168
Guide to Atlanta, 15–16
Guthright, W. E., 19
Gwinnett County, Ga., 210–12

habitus, homeownership culture and, 10–11, 231n23
Hallman, R., 182
Hamilton, Alexander, 77, 126
Hammer, Philip, 184
Hammond, Octavia, 14
Hanchett, Thomas, 157, 165
Hancock-Huddleston park system ordinance, 65
Handbook of the City of Atlanta, 15

Harden v. Atlanta, 244n65
Harlan, Louis, 243n53
Harley, Gertrude, 116
Harper's Weekly, 16
Harris, H. C., Jr., 183
Hartsfield, William, 189
Harvil, J. J., 25
Harvil, J. W., 25
Hathaway, Paul, 165
Hawkins, Frank, 64–66
Hay, T. P., 111, 119
Haynes, Eugene, 8
Haynes Manor (Atlanta), 8, 141, 170, 175
head-of-household data, 221–27, 266n10
Hege, S. E., 118–19
Heights Manor (Atlanta), 170
Henry County et al. v. Tim Jones Properties, Inc. et al., 199–200, 263n4
Herndon, Alonzo, 25, 73, 82
Hickey, Georgina, 18
Highland Park (Atlanta), 138
Highpoint Apartments (Atlanta), 188–91
highway development, housing segregation and, 206
Hill, DeLos, 104
Hillier, Amy, 3
Hines, Lizzie Wilson, 64
Hirsch, Arnold, 3, 181
Holyoke National Bank, 120
homeownership: advertising propaganda for, 113–18; by African Americans, 168–71, 246n3, 257n40; Atlanta's campaign for, 12, 108–13, 120–26; central business districts and, 208–11; credit as social status and, 11, 231n24; cultural ideology of, 9–10; Great Depression and, 158–59; housing segregation and, 93–95, 202–5; park-neighborhood movement and ideology of, 107–8, 126–34, 201–5; power negotiation and, 2; promotion of, 6–7, 12, 230n19; statistics on, 233n36
Homeownership: Is It Sound? (Dean), 107

Home Owners' Loan Corporation (HOLC), 3, 8, 158–60; housing segregation and policies of, 203–5; neighborhood geographies and, 174–80; security maps and area descriptions of, 160–62, 203–5, 219, 255nn4–5, 259n57
homeowner subsidies, 213–14
Hoover, Herbert, 112, 114, 130–31, 249n74
Hope, John, 73
Hosak, Rob, 210
Housing, Inc., 188
Housing Administration, U.S., 159, 172
Housing: Analytical Maps (U.S. Bureau of the Census), 168–71, 174–80, 219
housing construction, post–Civil War land industry and, 21–22
housing geography: *habitus* concept and, 10; history in Atlanta of, 12; neighborhoods and, 174–80; park-neighborhoods and federal policy and, 158–98; public housing and, 171–74; research on, 2–3; white control of, 170–71
housing-justice movement, 217–18
Housing Objectives and Programs (Gries and Ford), 131–32, 249n74
housing segregation: and African American economic and civil rights advances, 182–90; in Atlanta, 12, 32–40, 88–92, 243n53; conflict rhetoric on, 245n78; court challenges to, 98–100, 244nn65–66; FHA policies and, 167–71; in Jackson Hill, 92–95, 101–6; land-use zoning and, 136, 141–45, 151–57, 254n69; ordinances for, 89–92, 243n49, 243n52; park-neighborhood movement and, 141, 205–11; property values and, 214–15; protection of privilege and, 215–17; public housing and, 171–74; race and class factors in, 2–3; spatial organization and, 95–96; during World War II and postwar era, 180–90. *See also* segregation

Howell, Clark, 74–75, 143
Howell, Green, 25
Howell, Hugh, 188
"How to Own Your Home" (1918 U.S. Commerce Department pamphlet), 116
How to Own Your Home (Gries and Taylor), 109, 126, 131, 249n74
Hunter Hills (Atlanta), 167–70, 191
Hurt, Joel, 236n24, 236n29, 239n65; City Beautiful campaign and, 61–65; Morris Brown College dispute and, 71; park-neighborhood development and, 45–46, 49–56, 137, 142–43

Ickes, Howard, 171
immigrant population growth, 209–14
income inequality: historic trends in, 208–11; racial inequality and, 212–14, 265n30; urban development and, 199
indebtedness, as social good, 11, 231n24
index of dissimilarity, 219
industrialization, in post–Civil War Atlanta, 14–17
Inman, Samuel M., 84
Inman Park (Atlanta), 5–6; development of, 45–52, 138, 142, 237n35; restrictive covenants in, 54–56, 135
Insured Mortgage Portfolio (L. Elden Smith), 163, 260n83
International League of Press Clubs, 59
investment housing, 11, 25
Ives, L. M., 24

Jack, George, 15
Jackson, Kenneth, 3, 248n49
Jackson Hill (Atlanta), 6, 76–81; fire in, 100–104; integrated housing in, 183–84; Morris Brown College relocation dispute and, 71–72, 81–92, 218; racial heterogeneity in, 92–95; segregation in, 92–96, 100, 104–6, 152–56

Jamestown Exposition, 59
Jefferson, Thomas, 230n19
Jenkins, Virginia Scott, 43
jim crow laws, 72–76, 143
Johnson, Charles, 94
Johnson, Harvey, 41–42, 67
Johnson, Heath Beth, 216
Johnson, Joseph Forsyth, 45
Johnson, Reginald, 181
Johnson Estates (Atlanta), 138
Johnson Realty, 167–68
Johnston, Olin, 182
Johnston, S. R., 84
Joint Center for Housing Studies, 208
Jones, Tim, 199–200
Jordan, Millie, 77
Journal of the Western Society of Engineers, 146–48
Joyland Park (Atlanta), 140–41, 168
Joyner, Walthall, 63

Key, James L., 103, 123, 142, 152–53, 254n69
Kimball, Hannibal Ingalls, 19, 44, 236n25
Kimball House (Atlanta), 18
Kimble, John, 260n83
King, J. P., 135
Kirby, Jack Temple, 2–3
Kirkwood Land Company, 52–53, 143, 236n24, 242n33
Knights of Labor, 20
Kontz, Ernest C., 60, 151–53
Kozol, Jonathan, 216
Krueckeberg, Donald, 107
Kruse, Kevin, 2–3, 208, 214

Labor, U.S. Department of, 6, 113, 119, 125
labor issues, urban migration and, 19–21
Lakewood, Ohio, 143
Lakewood Heights (Atlanta), 168, 189
Land Economics, 116
land industry, 21–22

landscape aesthetics: City Beautiful movement and, 5–6; civic elites and, 49–50; culture of, 3–4; definition of, 230n18; exclusivity principles of, 56–57; homeownership promotion and, 128–34; housing segregation and, 93–95, 104; park-neighborhood movement and, 5–6, 12, 43, 49–56, 131–34, 137–38, 157, 235n7; parks development and, 61–65, 239n65; plaza design and, 65–69; as public policy, 61–65; safety issues linked to, 211–14
land-use zoning: in California, 144–45, 252n34; exclusionary results of, 136–57, 200–205; housing hierarchies and, 255n6; housing segregation through, 141–45, 202–5; low- and moderate-income housing and, 213–14; promotion of single-family housing with, 146–50
Lasker, Bruno, 150
Lassiter, Matthew, 2
lawns and gardens, park-neighborhood aesthetic and, 43, 235n7
League of American Municipalities, 60
Leavitt, Charles W., 101–2
LeBay, C. D., 259n57
Lee, D. J., 81
Lee, E. W., 83, 85
Lenox Park (Atlanta), 175
Lewis, Nelson P., 143
Life Insurance Company of Georgia, 188
Lipsitz, George, 4, 215–16
Little, A. A., 104
Llewellyn Park, N.J., 43, 46
"local control" ideology, 183–90
Long, Herman, 94
Los Angeles, Calif., 252n34
Louisiana Purchase Exposition, 59
Louisville Times, 93
low- and moderate-income housing: growth in Atlanta of, 208–11; suburban bias against, 212–14

Lowry, Robert J., 52
Lycott, Mrs. William, 125
Lynd, Robert, 130
Lyon, Elizabeth, 50

Mack, Curt, 164
Macon and Western Railroad, 16
manufacturing, Atlanta's promotion of, 16–17
map construction, housing research and, 222–24
Marencin, Jan, 210–11
Marietta, Ga., 212
Marlow, James, 182–83
Marsh, Margaret, 108
Martin, Thomas, 67
Martinez, Yolanda, 210
Massey, Douglas, 199
Mayson, James L., 91–92, 102–3
McBride, David, 19
McClure, C. W., 25
McDuffie, P. C., 156
McElreath, Walter, 77, 79, 85–86
McHenry, Jackson, 101
McKinney, Karyn, 216
Mertzke, Arthur, 130
migration patterns, urban development in Atlanta and, 17–21
Miller Lumber Company, 123
Milsaps, John, 167
Mims, Livingston, 58–60
Miramar (Atlanta), 138
Mitchell, Eugene, 86, 95–96, 101
Mitchell, F. M., 84
Mitchell, J. Paul, 107
Mitchell, Lane, 24–25
mixed-income housing development, 215, 217–18
mixed-race housing complexes, 177–80, 190–98, 258n46, 260n72
Mixon, Gregory, 20, 76
Modesto, Calif., 144

Monchow, Helen, 107
morality, homeownership linked to, 114–18
Morningside (Atlanta), 175
Morris Brown College, 6; attempted relocation of, 71–72, 77–92, 218, 241n21, 242n22, 242n36
mortgage industry: black mortgage companies and, 188; FHA policies and, 162–71, 259n57; homeownership promotion and, 112–13, 248n49; New Deal housing policies and, 159–80
Mount Laurel, N.J., 213
Mozley Park Home Owners Protective Association, 189
multifamily dwellings: housing hierarchy and status of, 132–34, 146–48; immigrant influx and growth of, 212–14. *See also* single-family homes
Municipal Housing Authority of Atlanta, 172–74
Murphy, Anthony, 19
Murphy, Paul, 111–12
Mutual Federal Savings and Loan, 188

National Anti-Tuberculosis Association, 60
National Association for the Advancement of Colored People (NAACP), 89–91, 180, 183
National Association of Real Estate Boards (NAREB), 6, 107–8, 205; Atlanta homeownership campaign and, 120–26; founding of, 110–11; homeownership promotion by, 111–18, 133–34, 248n49; park-neighborhood ideology and, 133–34, 150; sales force education by, 118–20
National Association of Real Estate Exchanges (NAREE), 108, 110
National Chamber of Commerce, 60, 205
National Conference on City Planning, 130, 150
National Council of Commerce, 60
National Hotel (Atlanta), 18

National Housing Act of 1937, 171
National Housing Association, 130, 167
National Industrial Recovery Act, 171
nationalist ideology, homeownership promotion and, 117–18
National Lumber Manufacturer's Association (NLMA), 114–16, 119–23, 125
National Municipal League, 60
National Real Estate Association, 22–23
National Real Estate Journal (*NREJ*), 110–11, 113–22
National Urban League, 180, 181, 183
neighborhoods: block-level organization in, 219–24; cultural ideology of, 9–10; geography of, 174–80; housing segregation and, 12, 93–95, 96–98; immigrant population growth and, 211–14; income inequality trends in, 208–11; racialization in Atlanta of, 32–40; rental housing production and changes in, 28–32; spatial organization in, 95–96. *See also* park-neighborhood movement
New Deal policies: homeownership growth and, 8, 158–59; park-neighborhood movement and, 159–80; racism and, 3
New South ideology: Atlanta urban development and, 14; homeownership promotion and, 110–13; Jackson Hill housing patterns and, 76–81; land-use zoning and, 142–45; park-neighborhood movement and, 44–49, 49–56
new urban aesthetic: park-neighborhood movement and, 41–70; as public policy, 61–65
Nichols, J. C., 50, 53–54, 150, 175
Nicolaides, Becky, 3
Nolen, John, 151
Norris, Claude, 32–33

Oak Knoll development (Atlanta), 167
Olmsted, Frederick Law, 235n11, 236n24, 236n29; City Beautiful movement and, 61–63, 132; deed restrictions and, 54–57; New South ideology and, 45–46; park-neighborhood movement and, 43, 49–51, 63, 143
Olmsted, John C., 49–51, 54, 61, 132, 236n24, 236n29
Osterman, Jim, 212
Otis, Robert, 142–43
"Own Your Home Campaign Handbook," 119
Own Your Own Home campaigns, 6–7, 110–12, 118–26, 128

Page, Max, 144
park-neighborhood movement: Atlanta's embrace of, 4–7, 12; in black subdivisions, 168–71; civic elites and, 42–44, 49–56; cultural ideology of, 9–10; exclusionary practices and, 135–57; federal housing policies and, 8, 12, 158–98; FHA guidelines concerning, 162–66; HOLC appraisal standards and, 160–62; homeownership ideology and, 107–8, 126–34, 201–2; housing segregation and, 95–96, 186–90, 205–11; land-use zoning and, 137–45; Morris Brown College relocation dispute and, 84, 88; neighborhood geographies and, 175–80; New Deal housing policies and, 159–80; New South ideology and, 44–49; new urban aesthetic and, 41–70; private interests and, 42–44; as public policy, 61–65; racial legacy of, 205–11; rental housing construction and, 25; restrictive covenants and, 53–57, 135, 138–40
parks development, 61–65, 239n65
Peachtree Heights Park (Atlanta), 138, 170, 175
Peachtree Hills (Atlanta), 138, 151
Perry, Heman E., 126
Peters, Richard, 19, 44–45, 236n25
Peterson, Jon, 235n11

Peters Park Improvement Company, 44
Peters Park (Atlanta), 5, 44, 47, 49
Philadelphia, Penn., 173
Philipp, E. L., 116
Phillips, Meredith, 214
Pine Acres (Atlanta), 167–68, 191
Pittman, Fred, 142
Pittsburgh, Penn., 147
Pittsburgh Courier, 89–90
Places of Their Own (Wiese), 3
planned communities, historical evolution of, 7
Planning for Residential Districts (Gries and Ford), 131
"Planning Project for Atlanta, A" (Whitten), 144–45
plaza design, landscape aesthetics and, 65–69
Pleasant Homesites (Atlanta), 166
politics, homeownership promotion and, 116–18
Pomeroy, Edgar, 84
Pool, R. P., 81
Pope, J. W., 60
popular literature, urban ethos in, 58–60
poverty rate, rental housing and, 214–15
Power, Garrett, 3
power structure: business elites and, 19–21; cultural creation of, 218; homeownership and, 2; housing segregation and, 37–40; immigrant influx and, 209–11; Morris Brown College relocation dispute and, 84–92; white civic elites and, 73–76, 241n6
President's Conference on Home Building and Home Ownership, 130–34
Proctor, Henry, 90
promotional activities and materials, urban development and, 15–17, 232n15
property, cultural constructions of, 3–4, 12
property values: desegregation and integration policies and, 206–11; government role in protection of, 213–14; housing segregation and, 93–95; immigrant population growth and, 212–14; map sources for, 244n66; mixed-race housing and, 177–80
"Proposed Expansion Areas for Negroes," 184–90
public health issues: City Beautiful aesthetic and, 64–65; immigrant housing patterns and, 209–11; mixed-race housing and, 177–80
public housing: federal policy and, 171–74; segregation of, 204–5, 258n46
Public Housing Administration (PHA), 159, 172
public policy: Morris Brown College dispute and, 85–92; new urban aesthetic as, 61–65; segregation and zoning and, 202–5
public-private partnerships: homeownership promotion and, 112; housing segregation and, 158–59; multiracial housing and, 190–98
Public Works Administration (PWA), 159, 171

race riots, Atlanta, 75–76, 99–100, 143, 152–53, 199
racism: in Atlanta, 72–76; Atlanta's housing practices and, 32–40; black subdivision construction and, 9; class issues and, 11–12; economic inequality and, 199; etiquette and social coding of, 79–81; FHA and, 166–71; federal housing policy and, 3–4, 8–9; historical evolution of, 2–3; in HOLC appraisal standards, 161–62; income inequality and, 212–14, 265n30; labor relations and, 20–21; land-use zoning and, 136, 150–57, 202–5; neighborhood geographies and, 174–80; park-neighborhood aesthetic and, 5–6; protection of white privilege

racism (*continued*)
and, 216–17; public housing and, 171–74; racial heterogeneity in Atlanta and, 92–95; in real-estate industry, 110–13; restrictive covenants and, 54–57, 238n48; spatial organization and, 95–96
Ragsdale, I. N., 155
railroads: development of, 16, 18–19; suburban development and, 44, 235n11
Randall Brothers lumber company, 21
Rankin, V. O., 67
Ransom, L. A., 60
real-estate industry: homeownership education and promotion and, 110–26; post–Civil War land speculation and, 21–22; rental housing production and, 22–32
Reed, David, 253n53
Reid, Whitelaw, 13, 21
rental housing: Atlanta land industry and growth of, 22–32; homeowners' distance from, 208–11; homeownership promotion and criticism of, 117–18, 123–26, 212–14; housing hierarchy and status of, 146–48, 253n39; minority share of, 210–14, 264n22; park-neighborhood ideology and exclusion of, 146–48; postwar trends in, 184–90; poverty rate in, 214–15; race and class issues in, 56–57, 238n48; segregation patterns and, 98–99; trends in Atlanta in, 108–13. *See also* apartment housing
Republican Party, 214
research methodology, Atlanta housing history and, 219–24
restrictive covenants: Atlanta's introduction of, 6, 50–58; FHA policies and, 170, 258n43; housing segregation and, 98, 203–5; neighborhood geographies and, 175–80; park-neighborhood development and, 53–57, 131–32, 135, 138–40, 237n37, 237n39, 237n42, 237n47, 254n73; property values and, 213–14; Supreme Court rulings against, 182–90
Rice, Frank P., 19
Richards, Franklin D., 183
Richland Park (Atlanta), 176
Richmond and Danville Railroad, 45
Riverside, Ill., 43, 46, 55
Robert, E. H., 32
R. O. Campbell Coal Company, 123, 126–27
Roediger, David, 3
Roosevelt, Franklin Delano, 159
Root, John Wellborn, 45
Roswell, Ga., 211
Roxboro Park (Atlanta), 135, 138
Rucker, J. T., 90
Ruff, Solon Z., 50–52, 236n24
Russell, James Michael, 20–21

safety issues, landscape aesthetics and, 211–14
Satterfield, M. B., 173–74
Saturday Evening Post, 16
Saunders and Johnson Company, 25
Savannah, Ga., 14
S. B. Turman and Company, 128–29
school demographics: apartheid in, 216–17; desegregation and integration policies and, 206–11; immigrant population growth and, 212–14; public school allocations and, 214–15; segregation policies and, 254n69
Schuyler, David, 57
Scott, H. M., 22
Scott, William A., Jr., 189
Section 8 housing vouchers, 215
security maps: neighborhood geographies and, 174–80, 259n60; park-neighborhood development and, 160–62, 203–5, 255nn4–5, 259n57, 259n59
segregation: Atlanta city ordinances for, 72, 88–92, 254n69; court challenges to,

98–100; economic inequality and, 199; historical trends in Atlanta of, 96–98; land-use zoning and, 146–57, 253n53; Morris Brown College relocation dispute and, 81–92, 243n53; park-neighborhood movement and ideology of, 57; population demographics and, 206–11; public policy and, 202–5; social rules of, 79–81; targeting of Jackson Hill for, 92–95. *See also* housing segregation
Service Company, 140–41, 191
Shadowlawn (Atlanta), 151
Shaker Heights, Ohio, 143
Shapiro, Thomas, 216, 265n30
sharecropping, urban migration and, 17–21
Shelley v. Kramer, 182–83, 258n43
Sherman, William Tecumseh, 13
Sies, Mary Corbin, 52
Silver, Christopher, 2–3
Simon, Roger, 108
Simpson Heights (Atlanta), 189
single-family homes: FHA policies and, 167–71; housing hierarchy and status of, 132–34, 146–48; immigrant extended families in, 210–14; New Deal ranking of, 161–62, 255n6
Sjoquist, David, 199
slum-clearance programs, 8–9
Smith, B. Lee, 86
Smith, Chauncey, 156
Smith, C. S., 83–84, 86, 242n31
Smith, Henry A., 102
Smith, Hoke, 52, 74–75, 143
Smith, John, 19
Smith, L. Elden, 163
Smith, Mark, 72–73
Smith v. Allright, 187
Smith v. Atlanta, 156
social improvement ideology: City Beautiful aesthetic and, 64–65, 240n79; park-neighborhood development and, 49–57

Socialist Labor Party, 20
South Atlantic Quarterly, 41
Southern Real Estate Improvement Company, 52–53
southern urban development: industrialization and, 14–17; in post–Civil War era, 13, 231n9
Souvenir Album, Atlanta, Georgia, 15–16
speculative real estate: Atlanta's land industry and, 21–22; in Jackson Hill, 79–81; rental housing and, 22–32
Spelman College, 82
Springvale Park (Atlanta), 45
Stach, Patricia, 237n47
Statesman, 182
states' rights ideology, 182–90
"status good set" cultural practices, 7
Steel Realty Development Corporation, 125
Stinson, Richard, 81, 83–84, 242n31, 243n37
streetcar development, 243n42
street-front sampling, 219–24
subdivision construction: by African Americans, 140–41, 167–71, 204–5; Atlanta boom in 1920s for, 135; deed covenants and, 53–56, 237n37, 237n39; neighborhood geographies and, 175–80; park-neighborhood development and, 50–56, 135, 138–39, 250n1; postwar racial tensions over, 190–98; post–World War I expansion of, 201
suburban development: Atlanta expansion and, 137–40; distance from central business districts and, 208–11; immigrant population growth and, 212–14; New South neighborhoods and, 44–49; park-neighborhood aesthetic and, 42–44; social value versus speculation in, 50–56; transportation networks and, 44, 235n11; whiteness ideology entrenched in, 210–11

Suggestions for Own-Your-Own-Home Campaigns (U.S. Department of Labor), 119
Summerhill (Atlanta), 37–39, 177
Supreme Court, U.S., 198
Survey, 151
Sylvan Hills (Atlanta), 135, 140

Talmadge, Herman, 182
taste culture: park-neighborhood aesthetic and, 42, 235n4; urban ethos and, 58–60
tax deduction for home mortgage debt, 248n49
Taylor, James S., 131, 249n74
Techwood Flats (Atlanta), 173–74
Temporary Coordinating Committee on Housing, 184
tenure status, trends in, 208–11
Terry, W. M., 85
Therrell, James, 186
Thompson, Robert, 181, 184–90, 260n83, 262n107
Thrower, M. L., 110, 151
Tishomingo Park (Atlanta), 140
Title II home mortgage program, 8
Torres, R. W., 254n73
"town beautiful" movement, 64–65
transportation networks, suburban development and, 44, 235n11
Trowbridge, J. T., 13, 21
Truman, Harry S., 183
Tuxedo Park (Atlanta), 138, 141, 170

Underwriting Manual (FHA), 4, 8, 162–66, 180–81, 204–5, 256n17, 256n19, 256n21, 256n28
Union Stock Yards, 17
urban development: in Atlanta, 4–5, 13–14; civic elites' ethos of, 57–60; economic inequality and, 199; inter-city cooperation concerning, 205; land-use zoning and, 141–45, 251n27; migration and, 17–21; in post–Civil War era, 13, 14–17, 231n9. *See also* new urban aesthetic
Urban League, Atlanta, 9, 159, 184, 186–90, 194–98, 204, 206–8, 210 260n83
Urban League, National, 180, 183
urban organizations, homeownership promotion and, 130
urban renewal projects, 209–11, 215
U.S. Bureau of the Census, 174–80
U.S. Civil Rights Commission, 170, 173–74, 187
U.S. Department of Commerce, 6, 112–13, 116, 126, 130–31, 249n74
U.S. Department of Labor, 6, 113, 119, 125
U.S. Housing Administration, 159, 172
U.S. Housing Corporation (USHC), 112

Vaughan, Charles J., 84–85
Vaux, Calvert, 57
Veiller, Lawrence, 60, 130
Veterans Administration, 8, 160, 166–71, 187–90, 204–5
Victory Heights (Atlanta), 176
violence: historical perspective on, 98–100; Jackson Hill neighborhood and, 183–84; and race riots in Atlanta, 75–76, 95–96, 99–100, 143, 152–53, 199, 229n7
voting rights: postwar African American gains in, 187; white power structure and, 73–76, 241n6

Walden, A. T., 190
Wallace, Joe, 183
Ware, Asa, 85
Warner, Sam Bass, Jr., 2
Warnock, Samuel D., 84–85
washerwomen, housing patterns for, 32, 37–39, 224, 234n65
Washington, Booker T., 82, 90, 243n53
Washington, Forrester, 184
Washington Heights (Atlanta), 169–70

Watson, Thomas E., 74–75
Watts, Eugene, 62
Wenz, Arthur, 116
Western and Atlantic Railroad, 16, 18–19
West Georgia Land Company, 125
West Side Mutual Development Committee, 189
W. E. Treadwell and Company, 25
White, John A., 154–55
White, Walter, 73, 77
White City (World's Columbian Exposition), 41
whiteness ideology: Atlanta segregation initiatives and, 72–76, 241n6; cultural constructions of, 3–4; elites' investment in, 215–17; HOLC appraisal standards and, 161–62; homeownership promotion and, 9–11, 126, 231n23; housing segregation and, 93–95; immigration issues and, 210–14; land-use zoning and, 136; park-neighborhood ideology and, 6–7, 133–34; restrictive covenants and, 138–40
white supremacists, segregation and, 73–76
Whitt, Richard, 211
Whitten, Robert, 52, 143–48, 150–52, 175, 253n39, 253n50
Wickersham, Charles, 142
Wiese, Andrew, 3, 187
Wilbur, Ray Lyman, 132–33
Wilentz, Robert N., 213
Williams, Rosa Mae, 183
Willis, George, 156

Wilson, George, 187
Wilson, Tom, 101
Winecoff, W. F., 53
Winn, Courtland S., 84–85
women: homeownership promotion and, 125–26; urban migration patterns of, 17–21; and washerwoman occupation, 32, 37, 234n65
Woodward, D., 60
Woodward, James, 61, 63, 75, 91–92, 239n68, 242n25
working-class housing: construction of, 24–32, 234nn61–62, 234n65; and head-of-household statistics, 225–26
World's Columbian Exposition (Chicago), 41, 59
W. R. Hanleiter Bookbindery, 19
Wright, George, 3
Wright, Gwendolyn, 43

Yarbrough, D. W., 103
Young, Leola, 17–18

Zone Plan (Atlanta Urban League), 206–8
zoning laws: economic inequality and, 199–200; housing-justice movement and, 217–18; housing segregation through, 8, 170, 202–5, 258n43; immigrant population growth and, 211–14; park-neighborhood movement and, 12; property values and, 213–14; restrictive covenants and, 138–45. *See also* land-use zoning
Zunz, Olivier, 2, 108, 219, 223

Politics and Culture in the Twentieth-Century South

A Common Thread: Labor, Politics, and Capital Mobility in the Textile Industry
by Beth English

"Everybody Was Black Down There": Race and Industrial Change in the Alabama Coalfields
by Robert H. Woodrum

Race, Reason, and Massive Resistance: The Diary of David J. Mays, 1954–1959
edited by James R. Sweeney

The Unemployed People's Movement: Leftists, Liberals, and Labor in Georgia, 1929–1941
by James J. Lorence

Liberalism, Black Power, and the Making of American Politics, 1965–1980
by Devin Fergus

Guten Tag, Y'all: Globalization and the South Carolina Piedmont, 1950–2000
by Marko Maunula

The Culture of Property: Race, Class, and Housing Landscapes in Atlanta, 1880–1950
by LeeAnn Lands

Marching in Step: Masculinity, Citizenship, and The Citadel in Post–World War II America
by Alexander Macaulay